JERUSALEM & THE HOLY LAND

GENEVIEVE BELMAKER

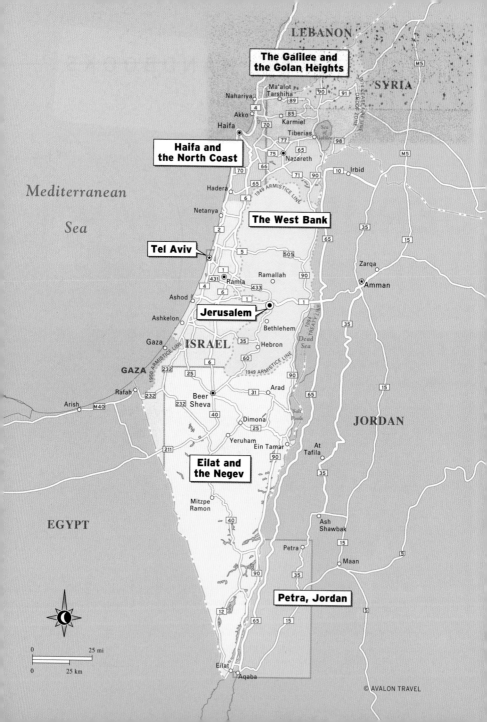

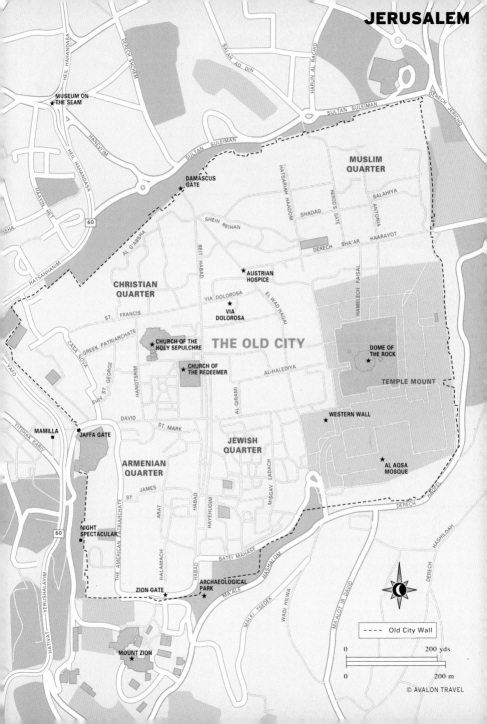

Contents

DISCOVER

Jerusalem & the Holy Land

Calls to prayer echo out over valleys and rooftops. The ringing of church bells and the wailing siren for Shabbat are omnipresent. This is a city of religious pilgrimages and a land of ancient stories, where even the bodies of water whisper of miracles.

Birthplace of the three largest monotheistic religions in the world—Judaism, Christianity, and Islam—the city of Jerusalem is filled with prayers and songs of different faiths. The time-worn, earthen-colored stones of the Old City have borne witness to thousands of years of history.

Pilgrims come here to walk in the footsteps that their religion took on its path to coming into the world: to touch the Western Wall, Judaism's holiest site; to stand where Jesus stood while crying over the coming destruction of Jerusalem; or to see the light gleaming off the golden Dome of the Rock, built over the stone where Muslims believe Muhammed ascended to heaven.

This diversity in beliefs and lifestyles can also make a trip to the Holy Land an ardent journey toward connection and understanding. As much as Jerusalem makes the past feel present, liberal, freewheeling

Tel Aviv is intently focused on the future. The fresh scent of sand and sea seems soaked into everything, and marketplaces smell of spices, falafel, and Turkish coffee. It's an assault on the senses, in the best possible way. North along the Mediterranean, in sparkling Haifa, Jews and Arabs coexist peacefully in the shadow of the world-famous Baha'i Golden Dome.

The West Bank, with its ancient cities of Bethlehem, Jericho, and Hebron, offers a journey into another world. On a hot summer day with the warm smell of olive trees set against a backdrop of rolling brown hills, you'll almost forget the political tensions that have troubled this area for centuries.

Many wait their entire lives to experience this timeless land. See it for yourself and you will begin to understand. Is it any wonder this region has inspired such passions, such devotion, such faith?

Planning Your Trip

Time can fly by when you are in this region as there is so much to see and do, and traveling about can be exhausting especially during the summer months. Plan your trip as carefully in advance as possible to make the most of your time.

Where to Go

Jerusalem

A city of 800,000 people and home to the three major religions of Judaism, Christianity, and Islam, Jerusalem seems older than time itself and is enthralling with its dozens of archaeological, religious, and historical sites and museums. When you tire of tours and history lessons, it is just as interesting to stroll through the unique districts of the city, such as the German Colony, with its interesting gardens, homes, shops, buildings, and people, and stop for a world-class meal in one of the city's many restaurants. A classic destination for religious pilgrimage, Jerusalem also has a lively arts scene and decent nightlife offerings. A claim to fame is that it is home to more museums than anywhere else in Israel.

Tel Aviv

Tel Aviv isn't called the "center" for nothing, with a dizzying offering of restaurants, clubs, museums, performing arts venues of all sizes, nightlife, music, beaches, surfing, and outdoor sports. The first modern Jewish city, Tel Aviv has earned its reputation as the center of Israeli life. It is a place known for its openly accepting atmosphere of all kinds of people, a high-powered technical and business sector, and the heart of the country's famed diamond industry. Tel Aviv's world-class parks

the *shuk* (outdoor market) in Nablus, the West Bank

IF YOU HAVE...

Knowing how to spend your time and where to go is crucial when traveling in Jerusalem and the Holy Land. There is so much to see and do that you could stay occupied for one week in just one region. Following are some recommendations for potential travel itineraries, by city and related region, depending on different amounts of time. No matter what other areas of the region you visit, old and new Jerusalem are musts.

- **ONE WEEK:** Jerusalem, Tel Aviv, and Caesarea
- **10 DAYS:** Add the Dead Sea, Tiberias, and Bethlehem
- **TWO WEEKS:** Add Beer Sheva, Haifa, Zichron Ya'akov, and Akko
- **ONE MONTH:** Add Nahariya, Ramallah, Eilat, and Petra

the Knesset Menorah, by sculptor Benno Elkan, Jerusalem

and recreation offerings are at the heart of its many summer festivals, events, and live concerts. It is, by far and away, the most popular place in Israel to party and just enjoy life.

Haifa and the North Coast

Once you're in Haifa, Israel's third-largest city and situated on the coast north of Tel Aviv, you can easily jump off to other charming coastal towns and nearby historical and religious sites, such as Akko, Caesarea, and Zichron Ya'akov, with minimal hassle. The life of Haifa, the only city in Israel with any public transportation on the weekend, revolves around the dominating Baha'i Gardens and Golden Dome. You can spend days just going between exploring Haifa's museums, restaurants, and beaches and then wandering through the serene and pristine grounds of the Baha'i Gardens.

The Galilee and the Golan Heights

The north of Israel encompasses the Upper Galilee, the Lower Galilee and the Golan Heights, home to some of the most gorgeous parks and nature reserves and best hiking and camping opportunities in the region. The area is known for its world-class wineries and numerous significant archaeological, religious, and historical sites. The Golan and the Galilee are also home to some fascinating people, like the Druze; important cities, like Nazareth; and spiritually moving locales, like the Sea of Galilee.

Eilat and the Negev

Home to the Negev Desert, which makes up more than half of Israel's land mass, the south is considered by many to be wild and untamed in many ways. A popular destination for desert ecotourism, the Negev is the perfect place to experience camping out under the stars and discovering the unique beauty of the desert on long hikes. Home to the Dead Sea, the lowest point on Earth, the south is sparsely populated, but boasts the thriving tourist hub of Eilat at its far south end. Eilat has some of the best coral diving in the world, tax-free shopping, and it is the gateway to Petra, Jordan.

The West Bank

Though not on every traveler's list, the West Bank is home to some important historic

Petra must be seen to be believed.

and religious sites, including the towns of Bethlehem, Jericho, and Hebron. The Arab city of Ramallah, just a short drive from Jerusalem, is the hub of Arab arts and culture in the West Bank, and is known for the important cultural festivals it puts on every year.

Petra, Jordan

No experience can compare to seeing the ancient Nabataean city of Petra with your own eyes. Once the capital city of powerful and wealthy spice route merchants, modern Petra is a massive archaeological site that takes several days to explore thoroughly. Replete with hikes of varying lengths that end at gorgeous archaeological sites, Petra can be experienced in tandem with the immediately-adjacent, charming Arab village Wadi Musa, with its many offerings of Bedouin food and hospitality.

When to Go

There are distinct high and low seasons in this region. The high season is in April-October (approximately from Passover through Sukkot on the Jewish calendar) and the low season is in November-March. Check the calendar carefully before planning your trip with an eye out for major Jewish, Christian, and Arab holidays. The airfare and cost of hotels will be much higher during those times, and many businesses and tourist sites will be closed or have shorter hours.

The three most challenging times to visit are during the Jewish holiday of Passover week (approximately the end of March), which ends in the Christian holiday of Easter Sunday, and during the week of the Jewish holiday of Sukkot (approximately the end of October). The month-long Muslim holiday of Ramadan, around July-August, depending on the year, puts a bit of a damper on any sightseeing related to Arab sites and in Arab regions.

A generally good period to visit, when it is not too hot and not too cold, and there are not too many holidays to affect the opening and closing of sites is any time in April-June.

Try to avoid visiting Jerusalem during

August, when the heat coupled with the chaos of annual vacations and events among local residents makes for an overwhelming (not in a good way) experience. Essentially, the city becomes extremely crowded everywhere, to the extent that you might see entire families of ultra-orthodox Jewish children on vacation swimming in public fountains.

Before You Go

Passports and Visas

Many countries have a visa waiver agreement with Israel, including the United States, Canada, and the United Kingdom, which means you only need to purchase a round-trip ticket or an exit ticket to show your impending departure. You will be issued a visa upon entering Israel. Your passport must be good for at least six months past the date of your departure from the country.

What to Take

Bringing the right clothing is incredibly important, particularly comfortable shoes, as there is a lot of rough terrain at various tourist sites and parks. In many places you will be required to dress conservatively, so bring a few long-sleeve shirts, pants, and long skirts.

Women should be aware of two things: It is windy and the streets are full of old cobblestones. That means that loose, flowing skirts above the knee and shoes with a heel higher than two inches will present challenges. Stick to skirts that are either below the knee or more fitted, so they won't blow up in Jerusalem's perpetual mountain breeze, and wear lower-heeled or flat shoes, preferably with more support so you won't twist your ankle while walking on the uneven stones.

No matter when you go, take some kind of a light jacket (heavier in the winter months), as it can get cool in many areas during the evening. Also bring a hat, sunglasses, and sunscreen if you have them, or be prepared to buy them once you are here.

Jerusalem apartments

Jerusalem has steep, cobblestoned lanes.

Best of Jerusalem and the Holy Land

If you travel to Jerusalem and the Holy Land with the intention of seeing a little bit of everything, having a general strategy is a must. This itinerary maps out how to get a taste of the best of the region in two weeks, and includes the major highlights and most popular sites of several cities and regions.

Jerusalem

DAY 1

Have breakfast at your hotel and get an early start on the Old City to beat the heat and crowds. Take the easiest entrance from Jaffa Gate, stopping by the information center for any current happenings and available tours. Next to Jaffa Gate, stop by either the Rockefeller Archaeological Museum or the Tower of David Museum.

Follow the main road downhill through the tightly packed shops selling all kinds of scarves, food, trinkets, jewelry, and souvenirs, and head for the Church of the Holy Sepulchre, built on the spot where it is believed that Jesus was crucified, buried, and resurrected. From here, head to the Austrian Hospice for an incredible view of the Old City and Jerusalem at large.

Have lunch in the soothing gardens of the Austrian Hospice and then spend some time wandering around the area, working your way toward the Western Wall and the Dome of the Rock. Pass the Western Wall and keep going toward the outer wall of the Old City, toward the City of David archaeological site. Here you can go on a guided tour and walk through the ancient Hezekiah's Tunnel, knee-high in water. Bring a flashlight or skip the tunnel if you are claustrophobic.

Go back toward the Old City gate you exited from and take one of the many waiting taxis to dinner in City Center, preferably somewhere off of King David Street or in Nachalat Shiva.

DAY 2

Take a taxi to Mamilla, where you can have

sunrise in Jerusalem

breakfast outdoors at one of the restaurants with a vista of the new city and the windmill. From Mamilla, it is a quick hop to the Old City, where you can check out anything you missed the previous day. If you have the time and energy, try the long walk up the belfry tower at the Church of the Redeemer for one of the most highly rated and under-visited 360° views of the Old City.

Before it gets too late, exit the Old City through Zion Gate and head up the hillside to Mount Zion, where some believe that Jesus had the last supper and King David's tomb can be found. Don't let anybody talk you into making a "donation" here; the site is free. At Mount Zion you will also find the lovely Dormition Abbey and a great view of the city from multiple vantage points.

Take a taxi to the top of the Mount of Olives, where you will see the view of the Old City of Jerusalem that Jesus is said to have shed tears over when telling of its coming destruction. Go by foot into the nearby Arab village Al-Suwaneh and have lunch at one of the many small restaurants serving Arab, food before heading back down the hillside by taxi. Ask to be dropped off at the Church of the Pater Noster, and then walk downhill to the nearby Dome and Chapel of the Ascension and the Garden of Gethsemane.

From the Garden of Gethsemane, it is a long walk or a quick taxi ride to a City Center restaurant; try something near Zion Square this time.

DAY 3

Enjoy breakfast at your hotel before heading out to see Jerusalem's museums. Go by bus or taxi to The Israel Museum, located on Museum Row. Allow at least half a day to explore the museum and its rich, famed exhibits specializing in Judaica and Jewish history as well as regional history. Take advantage of the museum's restaurant for lunch. Then take a taxi to the underrated Monastery of the Cross, located in the valley where the wood for Jesus' cross is said to have been taken. From here take another taxi to Yad Vashem Holocaust memorial, or walk to the light rail stop. Allow at least four hours at Yad Vashem, where you can also get something cold to drink or eat in the cafeteria and meditate on the view of the Jerusalem forest.

From Yad Vashem, take the light rail train to City Center and the famous Machane Yehuda Market (the *shuk*), where you can

locally made goods for sale in Jerusalem's Old City

wander around for an hour or so before having dinner in one of the *shuk's* many wonderful restaurants and cafés. In the evening, the *shuk's* nightlife cranks up and the quiet pubs turn into hopping parties, some with live music. Don't get back to your hotel too late, though; you have an early morning tomorrow.

Tel Aviv
DAY 4
BUS FROM JERUSALEM (1 HOUR)

Go by bus from Jerusalem to Tel Aviv in the morning after breakfast (and after rush hour). Drop your luggage off at your hotel before getting into the high-paced swing of the city. Start with a stroll around Dizengoff Center's great shopping district, and stop by the Bauhaus Center to pick up maps and information about Tel Aviv's famed White City and available tours. Stay near Dizengoff or a side street and enjoy one of the area's many outstanding restaurants and cafés for lunch.

After lunch, head back to your hotel and get ready for a late afternoon beach session, and remember to bring a change of clothes so you can go straight to dinner after. Try Aviv Beach, just north of Charles Clore Park, or any of the beaches that are north of Charles Clore Park but south of the Marina. From Aviv Beach, take a nice 25-minute stroll to the HaTachana Train Station Complex for some great shopping; make sure to check out the Made in TLV store. Five minutes away, wander through Tel Aviv's historic Neve Tzedek neighborhood, the oldest neighborhood in the city, for a European-style dinner, then stay out to party if you can wait until things get started at the clubs around midnight.

DAY 5

Before checking out of your Tel Aviv hotel, head to the north of the city and have a breakfast of *shakshuka* eggs at one of the Port of Tel Aviv's many seaside restaurants. If you time it right, you can catch the weekly outdoor market. Check out of your hotel but have them hold your luggage so that you can visit Old Jaffa for an afternoon of sightseeing at one of the oldest ports in the world.

Start just off Yefet Street and wander around the center of Jaffa's Old City and the nearby promenade for some great photographs. Look for the clock tower, surrounded by galleries and shops that you can browse through, as your most helpful anchoring landmark. Stay in Old Jaffa for lunch at one of their many

Jaffa is one of the world's oldest port cities.

the Roman ruins at Caesarea National Antiquities Park

world-class restaurants that serve up Arabic specialties, often with a European twist.

Pick up a rental car and go by your hotel for your luggage before you embark on the drive to Haifa, which is about an hour north of Tel Aviv. Once you've settled into one of Haifa's gorgeous boutique hotels in the historic German Colony, have dinner under the twinkling lights of the Baha'i Gardens and Golden Dome at one of the area's many excellent restaurants.

Caesarea and Zichron Ya'akov
DAY 6
DRIVE FROM HAIFA (30 MINUTES TO CAESAREA, THEN 20 MINUTES TO ZICHRON YA'AKOV)
Set out from Haifa in the morning for the Caesarea National Antiquities Park, where you can spend most of the day exploring the gorgeous Roman ruins by the sea that include the aqueduct, an amphitheater, mosaic floors, and bathhouses. There are many great options for lunch at the old Port, which also has some nice shops with the work of local artisans.

Just 20 minutes up the coast is the charming Mediterranean village of Zichron Ya'akov with a redesigned town center created to foster sidewalk café culture, with street musicians and all kinds of locally made arts. There are also several places to enjoy regionally produced wine. After dinner, head back to your hotel in Haifa.

Haifa
DAY 7
The drive along the coast south of Haifa is very beautiful and follows the shoreline of the Mediterranean closely. If you drive yourself, take a GPS because you'll need it to navigate Haifa's tricky streets.

At the top of the Baha'i Gardens and Golden Dome you'll have an incomparable view of the Mediterranean Sea and the Haifa Port. If you want to explore more of the gardens, you'll need to take the middle entrance. For more views and strolling, the nearby Louis Promenade off of Yefe Nof Street is fantastic and just next to it is the Mane Katz Museum and the Tikotin Museum of Japanese Arts.

DAY 8
At the top of Mount Carmel in Haifa is the Stella Maris Carmelite Monastery, with its small, but extensively painted, domed chapel and peaceful grounds with tropical plants

view of Baha'l Gardens, the Golden Dome, and Haifa

and flowers. Just across the street from Stella Maris is the San Francisco Observation Point with a multi-language and quite comprehensive audio history of the area. Steps away is Haifa's Cable Car, which will take you down the mountainside to Bat Galim Promenade. Next to the promenade are Elijah's Cave and the Israeli National Maritime Museum.

For dinner, some of the best options in the most idyllic setting are located in the German Colony, at the base of the Baha'i Gardens. The area is small, so it's easy to wander through and find a range of options.

Akko (Acre)
DAY 9
DRIVE FROM HAIFA (30 MINUTES TO AKKO, THEN 1 HOUR TO TIBERIAS)

Leave your hotel by car and take the short 30-minute drive to nearby Akko, where you can spend the day touring the Acre Old City and its network of Crusader walls, fortresses, knights' halls, and tunnels. Before lunch, take the long walk to the Templars' Tunnel, and stop near the *shuk* on the way back for some falafel and hummus. On your way out of Akko, you'll pass by the Baha'i Gardens, which are just as serene as their sister site in Haifa, but much smaller. Entrance is free and there is parking, so stop in for a look. Then make the one-hour drive from Akko to Tiberias, check into your hotel and have dinner at one of the many restaurants in the town center on the shore of the Sea of Galilee, where you can enjoy the sunset and the moonrise over the waters if you're lucky.

Tiberias
DAY 10

After breakfast in Tiberias, drive to the nearby grouping of historic and archaeological sites just 15 minutes away. Start at the Mount of Beatitudes, where the sermon on the mount was given by Jesus, with its serene gardens and wonderful vista of the Sea of Galilee. Then head to the incredible archaeological and religious site of Capernaum. From Capernaum, leave your car and follow the footpath that hugs the shore of the Sea of Galilee for about 30 minutes until you reach Tabgha and the Church of the Multiplication, where bread and fish were multiplied by Jesus to feed thousands. Have dinner in Tiberias or take a short drive to one of the regional, family-run restaurants in the area.

The Dead Sea
DAY 11
DRIVE FROM TIBERIAS (2.5 HOURS)

Drive from Tiberias straight south to the Dead Sea for some rest and relaxation. It's a 2.5-hour drive, so take a break along the way by stopping at the renowned archaeological site of Beit She'an. Once you're at the Dead Sea and have checked into your hotel, go to one of the many beaches to float on the salty waters and slather the therapeutic mud on your body. Take your time and enjoy a leisurely dinner before going back to your hotel.

DAY 12

Start out early before it gets too hot and stop by the Ein Gedi Nature Reserve and its 2,000-year-old natural spring that flows down the mountainside and forms multiple waterfalls and pools along the way. You can swim in many of the pools, the best of which is about a 15-minute walk from the park entrance. Drive from Ein Gedi to Eilat and stay overnight (2.5 hours).

Petra, Jordan
DAY 13
DRIVE FROM EILAT (2 HOURS)

Start out early and get to the Eilat-Aqaba border by taxi. After getting across the border, go by taxi to one of Aqaba's many car rental offices, and pick up a car for the two-hour drive to Petra. Once in Petra, take an afternoon hike, and a late afternoon lunch in one of the restaurants in the village adjacent to Petra, Wadi Musa. Spend the rest of the afternoon exploring Wadi Musa, and do a bit of shopping. After a rest at your hotel, head back by foot to get dinner in town, but this time make sure to try some Bedouin food.

DAY 14

Start off from your hotel early for a morning hike in Petra up one of the paths that leads to a high vantage point so you can see the area from a different perspective. Make sure to stop at the Petra Nabataean Museum and see the antiquities that have been found over the years. Go by foot back out to Wadi Musa for an early lunch and head out of town in your rental car for Aqaba and the Israel border.

Ride a camel in Petra.

Journey into Jerusalem

Though 10 days is just enough to scratch the surface of what Jerusalem has to offer, this section maps out a travel strategy that lays heavy emphasis on archaeological sites alongside new attractions and places to eat and play. Think ancient archaeological sites in and around the Old City by day, and rooftop drinks and food overlooking the city or live music by night. It also includes a few notable places in the vicinity of Jerusalem. The time frame is divided based on the days of the week, due to Jerusalem's limited access during Shabbat (Fri.-Sat. night).

Day 1, Sunday

After a good night's sleep at your hotel, put on your most comfortable shoes and get ready for some serious walking in the Old City. Start from the information center at Jaffa Gate, and pick a couple of key points in the Old City to explore, but allow for lots of wandering around time, as it is one of the best activities and you'll likely be on sensory overload.

From Jaffa Gate, you can easily explore the Armenian Quarter (mostly residential) and loop back up to the Jewish Quarter and the old Roman Cardo, which includes some high-end shopping. Keep going north to the Christian Quarter and you can see a number of churches, including the Church of the Holy Sepulchre.

Head back out toward Jaffa Gate and stop at one of the pizza shops or cafés for lunch that are just next to the information center. If your hotel is close by, go back and rest up from the noonday sun, or take in the air-conditioned shops and bookstores at modern and upscale Mamilla, at the foot of Jaffa Gate.

In the afternoon, walk from Mamilla to Nachalat Shiva, where you can spend a couple of leisurely hours exploring the shops, full of handmade crafts, before you walk to the Jerusalem Time Elevator exhibit for a 2D and sensory-enhanced trip through Jerusalem history. Stay in Nachalat Shiva for dinner to experience one of Jerusalem's most famous and authentically Middle Eastern restaurants, Tmol Shilshom.

the symbol of Jerusalem, a lion, on a fountain in the Old City

A MIDDLE EAST FEAST

Particular towns in Israel and the West Bank are known for certain types of cuisine. While in some cases there are longstanding debates over who has the best of a certain food, other towns are the undisputed reigning champions.

For **hummus,** everyone knows to go to Ein Kerem, a suburb village of Jerusalem. There you will see signs claiming to be the home of the best hummus ever. If you find yourself farther up the coast, Akko's Hummus Said is known far and wide.

Ruin yourself on the popular Arab sweet treat **_knafe_** by trying it first in the West Bank Arab village of Nablus. Instead of buying it already packaged, go to the Old City where you can see vendors making it fresh.

Good **falafel** can be found almost everywhere, but if you really want to experience it hot and fresh, go to the _shuk_ in almost any town, particularly Jerusalem.

Also one of the reigning champions of the popular and ubiquitous spread and dip **tahini** is Nablus. If you ask around at some of the local vegetable grocers in Jerusalem, you'll find it by the container.

In south Tel Aviv's Jaffa neighborhood, their claim to fame is Abulafia Bakery, which sells renowned **pita** and Arab sweet treats.

Many try to claim the title of the best **_shakshuka_** ever created, but if you're new to the dish, Jerusalem's Tmol Shilshom has mastered this regional staple dish of eggs, tomatoes, and other vegetables.

Day 2, Monday

After a leisurely breakfast, get a picnic lunch and work your way over to The Israel Museum by taxi or bus for a late morning museum session of antiquities and Jewish and regional history and art, including the Shrine of the Book, which houses the Dead Sea Scrolls. Directly across the way is the Bible Lands Museum, with its gorgeous ancient jewelry displays and emphasis on biblical history.

When you've had enough air-conditioning, take a quick taxi ride or a 25-minute walk to a free tour of the Supreme Court of Israel; tour starts at noon and then just hop over to the Knesset (Israeli Parliament) for another free tour, starting at 8:30am, noon, and 2pm,

the Dome of the Rock

if you have time. After your tours, stop by the Wohl Rose Garden overlooking Jerusalem to eat your picnic lunch. The roses will stay in full bloom late into the year, and after lunch you can spend some time exploring the grounds and its approximately 400 varieties of roses.

Head back to your hotel by taxi and rest up before dinner at any one of the City Center restaurants near Zion Square. After dinner, take a stroll through Zion Square with its lively evening atmosphere, and get dessert from one of the ice cream shops or the local favorite hole-in-the-wall dessert waffle shop.

Day 3, Tuesday

Make sure you are conservatively dressed or have something to cover your shoulders and legs, but with pants that can be rolled up, and head back to the Old City in the morning (bring a flashlight). This time take a taxi to Damascus Gate in East Jerusalem, and enter the Old City through the gate where you can explore the Muslim Quarter and see some of the stations along the Via Dolorosa, where it is believed Jesus carried his cross on his way to

be crucified. Continue along the Via Dolorosa to the northern side of the Dome of the Rock, Al Aqsa Mosque, and the Western Wall, holy sites to Christians, Muslims, and Jews. Just before the entrance to the Western Wall there are a number of restaurants where you can get lunch and rest before continuing.

Exit the Old City just past the Western Wall and you'll be in the east Jerusalem neighborhood of Silwan, where the City of David is located. Make sure you buy a ticket that includes a trip through Hezekiah's Tunnel (a good activity when the midday sun is out). After traipsing through the 2,700-year-old tunnel for 580 yards to the Pool of Siloam and touring the City of David, take a rest back at your hotel and freshen up for the evening.

Before dinner, take in the sunset at the swanky Mamilla Hotel's rooftop terrace bar and restaurant (make reservations in advance). You can stay for dinner after enjoying the view of the old and new cities, or head downstairs to try one of Mamilla's restaurants.

Day 4, Wednesday

Start your day with breakfast at the hotel and

the Fifth Station of the Cross on the Via Dolorosa

get out early to the Mount of Olives for the awe-inspiring sunrise. Get a taxi to take you to the top of the Mount of Olives' highest vista point, above the old Jewish cemetery, right next to the Seven Arches Hotel. From here, enjoy the incredible view of old and new Jerusalem. Take a leisurely walk down the hill and go through the Jewish cemetery, or just continue downhill to various vista points for photos. Continue downhill toward the Old City, stopping to see the inside along the way. It's a long walk, but taxis will pass you the whole way, so you won't be at risk of getting stuck.

When you've had enough churches, take a taxi to the Mount Scopus campus of Hebrew University, where you can explore the campus, see the adjacent Jerusalem Botanical Garden, and have a late lunch.

After lunch, take a bus from campus back to City Center that is bound for the Machane Yehuda market (the *shuk*). Ask anyone how to get to the *shuk;* most people will know. Once you get there, take your time and enjoy exploring the massive market with its fresh produce and delicious snacks. Make sure to stop off at one of the *shuk's* many restaurants for

a late afternoon coffee and then head back to your hotel with some *shuk* food for dinner and rest up for tomorrow.

Day 5, Thursday

Use Thursday to do some more low-key sightseeing. Start in the beautiful residential area of Talbiyeh, home to the Israeli presidential residence. Stop in the L.A. Mayer Museum for Islamic Art and check out their exhibits, then take a short walk to the Jerusalem Theatre to see if an art exhibit is up and what upcoming performances they might have during your visit. From there, take a 15-minute walk downhill toward the historic German Colony neighborhood and note the exquisite parks you pass by that are full of shady, peaceful corners.

Once in the German Colony (Emek Refaim St.), enjoy the architecture of the many beautiful, Templar-style buildings and homes. Stay in the German Colony for lunch, and hop one street over to the Railway Park and follow it in the direction of city center. Along the way you will find the newly created HaTachana train station culinary and shopping complex,

at the *shuk* (outdoor market) in Jerusalem

built from the foundation of Jerusalem's former main train station, which is more than 120 years old. After you've shopped a bit here and enjoyed the atmosphere with a post-lunch latte, continue on the railroad track park to the end and the hilly Lion Park with its beautiful fountain and pathways. Walk through the park until you reach the Montefiore windmill and the sweeping vista of east Jerusalem and the separation barrier in the distance. Continue on to the King David Hotel and the YMCA, both of which have historic architecture and idyllic outdoor seating and serve dinner. After dinner walk over to the Old City for the Night Spectacular light show near the Tower of David Museum citadel at Jaffa Gate.

Day 6, Friday

Take a taxi to Mount Zion just outside Zion Gate at the Old City, and explore Dormition Abbey and the area near King David's tomb. If you have time, stop at the small Holocaust museum. Then go by foot or bus to City Center just uphill from Zion Square off of King David Street for the Friday Shabbat festivities, including a street fair with local arts,

crafts, and food. Make sure to also explore the shops at the top of King David Street and the Bezalel Arts Academy, where the Bezalel Art Fair takes place every Friday. They sell Israeli-designed and made fashions including shoes, dresses and other clothing, and accessories. Find a spot at one of the busy restaurants in the area for lunch before things start to shut down around 3pm. If you're interested, Friday is also the day for Jewish and Muslim religious services, which you can find at the nearby Jerusalem Great Synagogue or Al Aqsa Mosque. You must be Muslim to enter Al Aqsa Mosque during prayer time.

Otherwise, take the opportunity on Friday night to relax at your hotel as most of the city shuts down. If you're near City Center and hear an alarm around sunset, don't be worried: It is the Shabbat alarm telling religious Jews that the Sabbath has started. If you plan to go out to dinner on Friday night to one of the restaurants that is not kosher and remains open after sunset, make reservations in advance.

Day 7, Saturday

Saturday in Jerusalem is like being in a ghost

one of the stained glass windows at the Jerusalem Great Synagogue

town. Very few things are open and there is no public transportation. If your hotel is near the Old City (which is open and less crowded than usual), go to the Rockefeller Archaeological Museum to see antiquities and then spend some time hanging around the Old City. This is a good day to hire a professional tour guide.

In the afternoon, you can take a rental car and drive through the alpine Jerusalem Forest to the nearby idyllic village of Ein Kerem for some short hikes and lunch at one of the village's many excellent restaurants. The restaurants are all within easy walking distance of each other, but make reservations in advance.

Then take your pick of a variety of tourist activities in the town where John the Baptist was born and the Virgin Mary visited while pregnant with Jesus (note Mary's Well). It is a small town and the signage is well arranged, so you don't need to plan in advance what you'll do. However, if you plan to take one of the small area hikes in the surrounding forest to the Shrine of the Visitation or the golden-domed Gorny Monastery, wear comfortable clothing and bring water.

Ein Kerem has a surprisingly active nightlife scene (though relatively low-key), so you can also plan to stick around for drinks on the terrace of one of the restaurants later in the evening and watch the sunset and possibly enjoy some live music.

Day 8, Sunday
Take a bus to City Center and Zion Square, with its mixture of tourist shops, street musicians, and cafés, the best of which are just off of the main artery of the square. After a bit of shopping, go to the bottom of Zion Square toward City Hall and catch the light rail train to Yad Vashem and Mount Herzl. Start with Yad Vashem, which can take several hours (children under the age of 10 are not allowed in the main hall). On your way back to the light rail stop by Yad Vashem shuttle bus, visit Mount Herzl, where you can get an audio-visual history of Zionist leader Theodor Herzl.

Day 9, Monday
Take an urban walking tour around Jerusalem with the Society for the Protection of Nature in Israel, a half-day archaeological tour, or a

shops on King David Street

double-decker Egged bus tour. Whichever you choose, you'll get a more in-depth perspective on the city and its treasure trove or historical, religious, and archaeological gems.

Then stop by east Jerusalem's Temple Mount Sifting Project near the Old City, where you can play archaeologist alongside experts by sifting through dirt for ancient remnants and objects. After you're done making important historical discoveries, head to the Museum on the Seam by foot or taxi for a detailed and clear-eyed look at the juxtaposition of east and west Jerusalem from the political to the historical and religious. If you have the time and energy, get tickets near the Jaffa Gate for the Ramparts Walk along the top of the wall surrounding the Old City.

You'll be exhausted from a day of walking, so have dinner either in or nearby your hotel.

Day 10, Tuesday

Use Tuesday to do anything you just didn't have time for in the previous nine days. If you don't have a leftover agenda, head to the edge of east and west Jerusalem and the Sherover-Haas Promenade. Take a bus along Hebron Road to Yehuda Street and hop down to the charming neighborhood of Bak'a for breakfast at the Grand Café, which opens very early and makes their own croissants and other pastry treats, and is one of the most popular restaurants in the area. Have a cappuccino with the locals at the restaurant's wraparound outdoor patio and revel in the Jerusalem morning sun.

When you're done, take a short taxi ride or long walk to the promenade, where you'll get a unique vista of Jerusalem, including the Dome of the Rock. If the weather is clear, you can also see Jordan in the distance. The lengthy promenade makes for the perfect leisurely walk along a gently inclined pathway that extends all the way down the hillside. If you are there during the right time of day, you will hear the distant sounds of the Muslim call to prayer sounding out across the hills and valley. It is the perfect place for quiet reflection and introspection after days of intense touring.

For a quiet dinner and wine with a rooftop view of the city, go by taxi to the imposing Pontifical Institute Notre Dame's four-star Roof Top Wine and Cheese Restaurant.

Ancient Terrain: Desert Hikes and Coastal Waters

To reach Petra, start in Jerusalem, head south and just keep going.

The Dead Sea
DAY 1
DRIVE TO EIN GEDI (1.5 HOURS)
Leave Jerusalem in the morning and go by rental car south to the Dead Sea, the lowest point on Earth. Stay in either Ein Gedi, exploring the ancient spring in Ein Gedi Nature Reserve and hiking and swimming, or go to one of the Dead Sea's many beaches along its western shore. Spend the night in one of the Dead Sea hotels and luxuriate in the area's many offerings.

Beer Sheva
DAY 2
DRIVE TO BEER SHEVA (1.5 HOURS); BEER SHEVA TO MITZPE RAMON CRATER (1 HOUR); MITZPE RAMON TO EILAT (1.5 HOURS)
Continue southwest toward Beer Sheva, the largest city in the south of Israel. Start just north of Beer Sheva in the Lahav Forest, where you'll find the one-of-a-kind Museum of Bedouin Culture at the Joe Alon Center. After experiencing some Bedouin culture and history, drive south to the ancient archaeological site of Tel Beer Sheba. From here it is just a short drive to the city of Beer Sheva, where you can have lunch at one of the many restaurants in City Center, near the municipal buildings. Also near city center is the Negev Museum of Art, which you can take in after lunch. From Beer Sheva, take the one-hour drive to the enormous Mitzpe Ramon Crater, for a short desert hike and a look at the ancient crater before it starts to get dark. After your tour, drive the remaining approximately 90 minutes to Eilat, check into your hotel, and call it a night.

Eilat
DAY 3
Start off your morning in Eilat by taking breakfast at your hotel if you can, and then go by taxi to the Dolphin Reef Diving Center for a guided swim with the dolphins. Take a bus back to Eilat's City Center for lunch and then head to one of the many beaches to swim, or take a dive if you have the time and the desire. If you have no experience diving, allow an entire day for it.

After freshening up at your hotel, go by foot or taxi to the Royal Garden Hotel shops avenue for upscale shopping. One of the numerous nearby restaurants will be perfect for dinner.

DAY 4
Make an early start and go again by taxi to the Coral World Underwater Observatory to see the many varieties of bright, rare fish. Then head out by taxi to the slightly over

the Dead Sea

casual dining beside the Red Sea in Eilat

the top, but fun, biblical theme park, King's City, where you can also have lunch inside the park, though it won't be gourmet. Have an early dinner in City Center at one of the many beachfront restaurants and then take in an evening performance of The WOW Show.

Petra

DAY 5

GO BY TAXI FROM EILAT HOTEL TO THE EILAT-AQABA BORDER (ABOUT 10 MINUTES)

Go early and meet a pre-arranged tour group guide at the Eilat-Aqaba border or get picked up at your hotel if possible. Pay attention during the two-hour ride to Petra to all the unusual rock formations with ribbons of mineral deposits in the hills along the way. Watch out for Wadi Musa on the right. Get a look at Petra for a few hours after arriving, and have lunch in Petra's modern neighboring village, Wadi Musa. Though it is small, Wadi Musa is geared heavily toward tourists and you can find some interesting shopping in the town's center, especially if you gravitate around

Al-Shaheed Roundabout. Take a break from the heat and rehydrate with water before going out for dinner in town, preferably at one of the home-style Bedouin restaurants.

DAY 6

Get an early start to Petra and take a hike up one of the paths that leads to a higher vantage point so that you can see the area from a different perspective. Make sure to stop at the Petra Nabataean Museum to see many of the antiquities that have been found over the years.

Go by foot back out to Wadi Musa by late afternoon and rest up at your hotel before dinner. Later in the evening, go back to Petra's Treasury for the idyllic Petra by Night show with stories and music.

DAY 7

DRIVE TO JERUSALEM (7 HOURS)

Get as early a start as possible in the morning in your rental car and head out to Jerusalem. It's a very long drive, about 7 hours with a few stops along the way.

Outward Bound: Excursions from Jerusalem

Using Jerusalem as your base, venture out to explore nearby areas including Tel Aviv, the West Bank, Beer Sheva, and the Dead Sea.

The West Bank (1-2 days)

GO TO THE WEST BANK BY BUS, SHARE TAXI, TAXI, OR WITH A TOUR GROUP (MAXIMUM OF 1 HOUR TO EACH LOCATION)

Go with a tour guide to Bethlehem for the day, where you can explore the various religious and cultural sites, focusing on the area near Manger Square in the town center. Make sure you bring your passport, as you'll have to cross through a checkpoint both exiting and entering the town.

Stay overnight in either Bethlehem or Ramallah, and spend the next day exploring Ramallah's shopping and dining offerings. Get oriented at the Al Manara roundabout, which is a central point of town. Look for the Stars & Bucks Café if you feel lost or want a specific destination to start from.

There aren't many sights here, but it's a great place for window-shopping and dining at one of the city's many great restaurants, known for their ability to fuse east and west.

Since Ramallah is only a short drive by taxi or bus to Jerusalem, dinner at Rooftop is a good choice to round out the day. It has a impressive view of Jerusalem and the Old City in a setting that feels more like Tel Aviv.

Tel Aviv (3 days)

DRIVE (1 HOUR) OR TRAIN (1.5 HOURS) FROM JERUSALEM

A good start in Tel Aviv is always one of the city's many beaches for some afternoon fun in the sun and water. The proximity of restaurants and cafés to the beachfront makes it easy to go straight from the Mediterranean to get a drink or something to eat. Tel Aviv's active and famously-late nightlife (especially in the summer) means you won't miss much if you take your time at your hotel before going

Wadi Musa at night

PILGRIMAGE SITES

Church of the Nativity

Religious and spiritual sites are the reason to visit this region, which isn't known as the Holy Land for nothing. Here is a list of the most important sites.

- **Basilica of the Annunciation** is believed to be built over the site of the Virgin Mary's original home (Nazareth).
- **Capernaum** is believed to be the location of a village where Jesus and some of his disciples lived for a time on the shore of the Sea of Galilee (near Tiberias).
- **Cave of the Patriarchs** is widely recognized as the burial place of the patriarchs and matriarchs of the Jewish people, including Abraham, revered by all three monotheistic religions (Hebron).
- **Church of the Holy Sepulchre** is widely recognized as the site of the crucifixion and resurrection of Jesus (Jerusalem, Old City).
- **Church of the Multiplication** is believed to be the location where Jesus turned a few fish and a couple loaves of bread into enough food for thousands (Tiberias).
- **Church of the Nativity** is widely believed to be the location where Jesus was born (Bethlehem).
- **Dome of the Rock and Al Aqsa Mosque** is the second holiest site in all of the Muslim world (Jerusalem, Old City).
- **Mount of Olives** is the site of many miraculous occurrences and is an extremely significant location in Judaism, Christianity, and Islam (Jerusalem, near the Old City).
- **Mount Zion** is the possible site of the Last Supper and is the locale of King David's Tomb (Jerusalem).
- **Tomb of Rabbi Meir** is significant to Jews all over the world as the tomb of the rabbi who was nicknamed the miracle worker and in whose name charity is often given (near Tiberias).

out to dinner at one of the city's many fine restaurants. In fact, the later, the better.

If it's your first time in town, try one of Neve Tzedek's many European-style restaurants for your first evening meal. From here you can easily walk to the lively nightlife and shopping scene at the HaTachana Train Station Complex, and you're also not far from Dizengoff's numerous bars, pubs, and clubs. For some of the most exciting nightlife in town, the north of the city at the Port of Tel Aviv has tons of seaside clubs, pubs, restaurants, and bars, as well as an enormous promenade right on the water with street performers, huge outdoor bars and restaurants, great stops for dessert, and plenty of strolling space.

Children play on the beach in Tel Aviv.

Mornings in Tel Aviv are lovely for a stroll and a leisurely breakfast on the waterfront, exploring Old Jaffa in the south, or getting out to HaYarkon Park in the north for a stroll before the heat becomes unbearable. The park has bicycle and boat rentals, and plenty of space for a picnic lunch or you can dine in a restaurant by the lake, on the eastern side under the massive trees.

If you're looking for some city tours, you can arrange to see Tel Aviv's famed White City with an English-speaking guide at the Bauhaus Center, or get a map for a self-guided experience through the area. There are always good shopping, dining, and entertainment options around Dizengoff Street, and on certain days of the week the Port of Tel Aviv has an outdoor farmer's market.

Also worth exploring is the largest non-profit art gallery in Israel in the Shalom Mayer Tower and its Discover Tel Aviv Center, with its general history of Tel Aviv. From the Shalom Mayer Tower, it's a short walk to Neve Tzedek, where you'll find the Rokach House Museum and the Nachum Gutman Museum of Art, with a bit about the history of Neve Tzedek and how Tel Aviv's first neighborhood started.

Hebron (1 day)
DRIVE FROM JERUSALEM WITH TOUR GUIDE OR GROUP (1 HOUR)

With a pre-hired tour guide, take the one-hour drive to Hebron to see some of the ancient city's sights, including the Cave of the Patriarchs and Ibrahimi Mosque.

One of Hebron's highlights is their Arabic-style food, but since it's a bit impractical to go there without a tour guide or group, you'll likely do whatever the tour group does, which will include a restaurant and shopping. You can also request to see one of Hebron's famed ceramic or glass shops.

The Dead Sea (2 days)
DRIVE OR TAKE THE BUS FROM JERUSALEM (1-2 HOURS)

Drive from Jerusalem about an hour south to the Dead Sea, where you'll find a number of great beaches that offer different Dead Sea experiences. About midway down the western shore of the Dead Sea just 15 minutes past Ein

Tourists take out boats in Jaffa.

Gedi, you'll find the mountaintop fortress of Masada.

Masada is a good stop before hitting the beaches (there won't be much shade and it will be unbearable in the afternoon), where you can take in the vista of the Dead Sea from the

Ein Gedi Nature Reserve

vantage point of a high peak. The Yigal Yadin Masada Museum, which has a very interesting and easy to digest walk-through exhibit with an audio guide, is included with a full ticket and is a must-see.

Near most of the Dead Sea beaches you can have a light lunch or drink. In the area where hotels are concentrated, there are numerous restaurants to choose from, some of which are on the water.

Once you're in the sea, you can float on the salty waters and rub therapeutic mud onto your body. All of the beaches have outdoor showers where you can rinse off most of the salty water.

Just at the edge of where the Dead Sea meets the border of the West Bank is Ein Gedi Nature Reserve, with its 2,000-year-old spring and relatively steep hike up the mountainside. You can see ibexes and hyrax on the way into the park, and take a 30-minute hike before reaching one of many freshwater pools and waterfalls where you can swim. It's always best to go as early in the day as possible, as the park attracts crowds of people and it gets punishingly hot in the summer after about noon.

JERUSALEM

It's impossible to imagine the Holy Land without thinking of Jerusalem, the region's religious, historical, and political center. Jerusalem is known to locals as the spiritual and intellectual core of Israel.

Most people start their visit in the Old City, the original city of Jerusalem that is contained within Ottoman-era walls and

HIGHLIGHTS

LOOK FOR ◖ TO FIND RECOMMENDED SIGHTS, ACTIVITIES, DINING, AND LODGING.

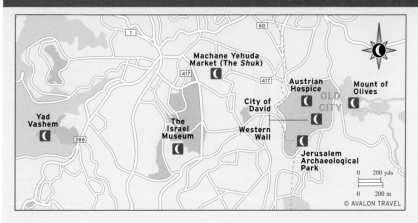

◖ **Machane Yehuda Market (The *Shuk*):** The outdoor market near City Center is frequented by locals of all ages and is practically a required experience for visitors (page 45).

◖ **Western Wall:** The most important site in Judaism, the Western Wall, also known as the Kotel, is situated in the southeastern corner of the Old City (page 50).

◖ **City of David:** Play archaeologist by wading through an ancient aqueduct or sifting through ancient dirt (page 50).

◖ **Austrian Hospice:** Hidden from most tourists by a non-descript outer wall, this oasis in the Old City offers respite and an amazing vista (page 56).

◖ **Mount of Olives:** One of the most dramatic views of Jerusalem exists alongside numerous important religious and historic sites (page 57).

◖ **Jerusalem Archaeological Park:** Five thousand years of remains from the Bronze Age onward are on display (page 60).

◖ **The Israel Museum:** The museum's rich, detailed exhibits on Jewish history, archaeology, and regional treasures are a must-see (page 62).

◖ **Yad Vashem:** The largest Holocaust museum in the world is a solemn pilgrimage (page 63).

divided into four distinct, but overlapping quarters: Muslim, Jewish, Christian, and Armenian. Thousands of years of history are contained within the walls of the Old City.

The historical and biblical stories of Jerusalem come to life in the Old City: the city's destruction; the tragedies and triumphs on Temple Mount for Jews, Christians, and Arabs; and the final moments of the life of

Jesus. It all happened here and is still happening. Events that take place in the Old City today are often significant and newsworthy. It is much more than a tourist attraction; it is a part of Jerusalem's modern life.

Outside of the Old City walls, the culture of Jerusalem embodied in the new part of the city is generally laid back, with an emphasis on spiritual, social, and family life.

© GIDON BELMAKER

The Old City surrounds the Dome of the Rock and Al Aqsa mosque in the distance.

Jerusalem has a long and complicated history that is told and retold in different versions based on who is doing the telling. Differences in opinion over which version of history is accurate has an impact on present relations. These differences are the root of underlying tension among ethnic, religious, and political groups over issues ranging from land ownership to conduct and customs. There are multiple readings of Jerusalem's history, and nowhere is this more evident than in the Old City at the point where the Western Wall and Al Aqsa Mosque converge. It is the ethnic, political, and historical epicenter of Jerusalem, whose story encapsulates the complex and tragic history of the city that is still evolving to this day.

ORIENTATION

Jerusalem is a very ancient and complex city that has more than 2,000 major and minor archaeological sites. Most visitors explore the city by starting with major tourist spots that include the **Old City, the Mount of Olives, the Western Wall,** and **City Center.**

City Center

Jerusalem's City Center is vibrant and often a bit touristy, boasting excellent restaurants and cafés. Just west of City Center proper is the world renowned **Machane Yehuda Market** (the *shuk*). City Center is bordered on the west by King George Street until it turns into Agripas Street in the north and meets with Agron Street on the south. It is bordered on the east by Shivtet Israel Street and on the north by Hanevi'im Street.

The highlights of Jerusalem **nightlife** are found in City Center, including live music venues, street music, pubs, wine bars, clubs, restaurants, and cafés that stay open into the wee hours. There are also a couple of good **museums,** numerous **hotels,** and some of the best **shopping** in town. It's the most convenient place to go for anything you need during your travels, from electric converters to toiletries to money changing.

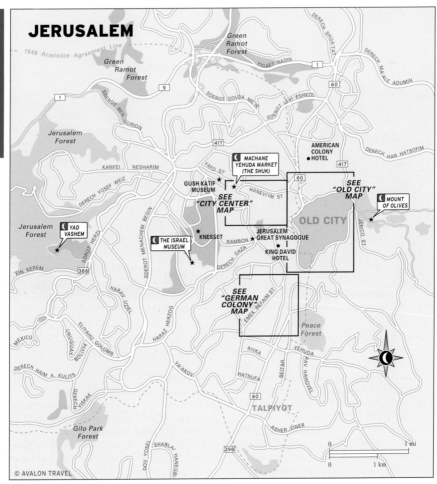

JERUSALEM

1949 Armisitce Agreement Line

Green Ramot Forest

Green Ramot Forest

Jerusalem Forest

Jerusalem Forest

Jerusalem Forest

KANFEI NESHARIM

DERECH YOSEF WEIZ

SDEROT BEN GURION

SDEROT HERZL

EIN KEREM

MEXICO

ELIYAHU GOLUMB

URUGUAY

BOLIVIA

DERECH HAIM A. KULITS

YISKAK

Gilo Park Forest

DOV YOSEF

SHABLAI

HANEGBI

HARAV UZIEL

HARAZ HERZOG

HARAZ

YA'AKOV

YAFO ST

GUSH KATIF MUSEUM

MACHANE YEHUDA MARKET (THE SHUK)

HANEVI'IM ST

SEE "CITY CENTER" MAP

YAD VASHEM

THE ISRAEL MUSEUM

KNESSET

RAMBON

DERECH GAZA

JERUSALEM GREAT SYNAGOGUE

KING DAVID HOTEL

SEE "GERMAN COLONY" MAP

EMEK REFAIM ST

RIVKA

HATNUFA

BEITAR

YEHUDA

RAV HAHOVEL

YA'AKOV

TALPIYOT

ASHER VINER

AMERICAN COLONY HOTEL

SEE "OLD CITY" MAP

OLD CITY

MOUNT OF OLIVES

JERICO ST

DERECH HAR HATSOFIM

DERECH SHUTAT

DERECH MA'ALE ADUMIN

YIGAET YADIN

SDEROT GOLDA MEIR

SDEROT LEVI ESHKOL

SDEROT MENACHEM BEGIN

Peace Forest

1

60

417

60

60

9

1

417

386

398

60

Talpiyot

0 ____ 1 mi

0 ____ 1 km

© AVALON TRAVEL

The Old City

The Old City is an unforgettable experience that is quintessential Jerusalem. You could come to Jerusalem and easily spend several days exploring the layers of history from thousands of years.

The Old City is divided into four main quarters dating back Roman times: **the Muslim Quarter, the Christian Quarter, the Armenian Quarter, and the Jewish Quarter.** Each quarter has many **free sights** that you

will want to visit, and there are seemingly endless rows of **ancient shops,** selling everything from scarves to antiquities.

Many people follow the **Via Dolorosa,** believed to be the last steps of Jesus on his way to be crucified. The route has 14 stations of historical significance and is rich with history that came well after Jesus's time. Following the Via Dolorosa is a good way to learn some of the Old City's story.

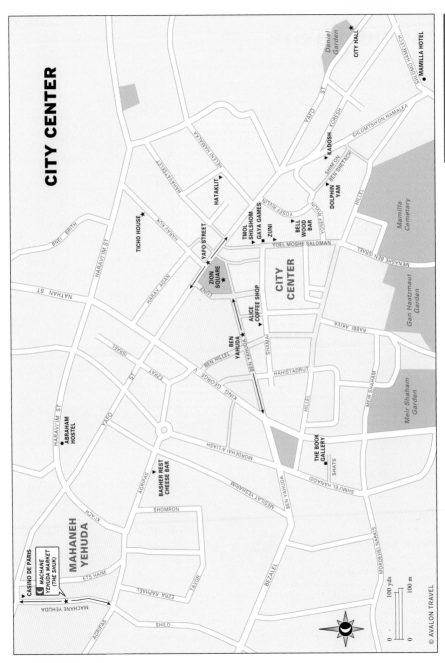

CITY CENTER

CITY HALL

Daniel Garden

MAMILLA HOTEL

SHLOMO HAMELECH

YAFO ST

KOResh

SHLOMTSIYON HAMALKA

KADOSH

SHMON

BEN SHETACH

DOLPHIN YAM

YOSEF RIVLIN

Mamilla Cemetery

HELENI HAMALKA

HARAV KUK

HATAKLIT

TICHO HOUSE

YAFO STREET

TMOL SHILSHOM

GAYA GAMES

ZUNI

BELL WOOD BAR

YOEL MOSHE SALOMAN

HILLEL

MENASHE BEN ISRAEL

BNEI BRITH

HARAVIM ST

NATHAN ST

HARAV AGAN

ZION SQUARE

LUNZ

CITY CENTER

Gan Haatzmaut Garden

ALICE COFFEE SHOP

RABBI AKIVA

ISRAEL

BEN HILLEL

BEN YAHUDA

SHAMAI

HAHISTADRUT

HILLEL

MEIR SHAHAM

Meir Shaham Garden

HARAVIM ST

EZRAT

KING GEORGE V

ABRAHAM HOSTEL

YAFO

MORDEHAI ELIASH

THE BOOK GALLERY

BEN YAHUDA

SHMU'EL HANAGID

SHATS

AGRIPAS

BASHER REST CHEESE BAR

MESILAT YESHARIM

BEZALEL

MORDEHEI NARKIS

KI'ACH

SHOMRON

MAHANEH YEHUDA

CASINO DE PARIS

MACHANE YEHUDA MARKET (THE SHUK)

ETS HAIM

EZRA RAPHAEL

TAYOR

SHILO

MACHANE YEHUDA

AGRIPAS

100 yds

100 m

© AVALON TRAVEL

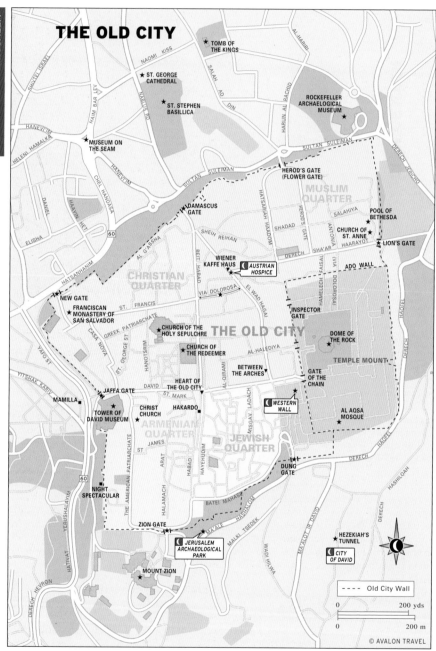

THE OLD CITY

TOMB OF THE KINGS

ST. GEORGE CATHEDRAL

ST. STEPHEN BASILLICA

ROCKEFELLER ARCHAEOLOGICAL MUSEUM

MUSEUM ON THE SEAM

SULTAN SULEIMAN

HEROD'S GATE (FLOWER GATE)

MUSLIM QUARTER

DAMASCUS GATE

POOL OF BETHESDA

CHURCH OF ST. ANNE

LION'S GATE

WIENER KAFFE HAUS

AUSTRIAN HOSPICE

CHRISTIAN QUARTER

ADO WALL

VIA DOLOROSA

NEW GATE

FRANCISCAN MONASTERY OF SAN SALVADOR

INSPECTOR GATE

CHURCH OF THE HOLY SEPULCHRE

THE OLD CITY

DOME OF THE ROCK

CHURCH OF THE REDEEMER

BETWEEN THE ARCHES

GATE OF THE CHAIN

TEMPLE MOUNT

JAFFA GATE

HEART OF THE OLD CITY

WESTERN WALL

MAMILLA

TOWER OF DAVID MUSEUM

CHRIST CHURCH

HAKARDO

AL AQSA MOSQUE

ARMENIAN QUARTER

JEWISH QUARTER

DUNG GATE

NIGHT SPECTACULAR

ZION GATE

JERUSALEM ARCHAEOLOGICAL PARK

HEZEKIAH'S TUNNEL

CITY OF DAVID

MOUNT ZION

- - - - Old City Wall

0   200 yds

0   200 m

© AVALON TRAVEL

© GENEVIEVE BELMAKER

A vendor carries trays of cups for Arabic coffee in the Old City.

East Jerusalem

Once you cross the (now invisible) line between east and west Jerusalem, there is a palpable sense of stepping into a different culture. East Jerusalem's mostly Arab population offers a glimpse into one of the many worlds inside Jerusalem.

East Jerusalem has a good selection of **hotels** at affordable rates, **shopping** options on Salah al-Din Street, and a wide variety of **Arab and Persian food** from Lebanon, Syria, Iraq, Iran, and Turkey.

Because of the Arab cultural and religious stigma against drinking, east Jerusalem is not necessarily the best place to have a night out with a few beers and music. Many restaurants do offer the traditional *nargila* (water pipe) that can be smoked with a menu of flavored tobacco after a meal.

German Colony and Bak'a

The German Colony and Bak'a are two neighborhoods immediately adjacent to each other that are decidedly under the influence of Americans (particularly New Yorkers). The area is somewhat of a triangle shape, with Emek Refaim Street as its southwest-northwest border, Yehuda Street on the south, and Derech Hevron on the east. The area just north of the northern tip of the triangle, known as **Yemin Moshe-Mishkenot Sha'ananim,** is a contained area surrounded by **parks** and frequented by residents of the German Colony and Bak'a.

Originally settled by German Templars, the German Colony is where you'll find **Emek Refaim Street,** popular with tourists and locals for its hip combination of **restaurants,** set against a very Israeli backdrop of old homes. Bak'a's inhabitants were once mostly Arab, which can be seen in the style of many buildings. It is largely residential and part of a larger enclave of Americans.

Givat Ram and Rehavya

Givat Ram and Rehavya offer many interesting and important sights slightly off the beaten path. These neighborhoods are west of City Center and feature a group of museums that

THE FIRST AND SECOND TEMPLES

No visitor to Jerusalem can escape hearing references to the First Temple and the Second Temple, which refer to historical time periods when two different massive Jewish temples stood approximately where Al Aqsa Mosque is now located. Both temples were destroyed, and the main remnant is the outer western wall of the Second Temple courtyard, where people flock from all over the world to pray (known as the Wailing Wall, the Kotel, or the Western Wall).

According to Jewish traditions, both temples were destroyed on the 9th of Av on the Jewish calendar. Every year, those destructions are marked by the day of mourning called Tisha B'av. There are several other tragic dates in Jewish history associated with Tisha B'av. But, because of its relation to the destruction of the temples, the plaza of the Western Wall is filled with throngs of Jewish mourners every Tisha B'av (in August).

During the First Temple period (1200-586 BC), the First Temple was built in 1000 BC by King Solomon after King David conquered Jerusalem and made it his capital. The Temple was destroyed in 586 BC by Nebuchadnezzar, the King of Babylon, when he conquered Jerusalem. There are scant remains of the temple on the south hill of the City of David. Evidence of the conquering and destruction of the city can be found in the Burnt House and the House of the Bullae.

From the First Temple period, in 701 BC, there are significant remains of preparations made by King Hezekiah when a siege on the city by Sennacherib King of Assyria was imminent. Those remains include Hezekiah's Tunnel and the Broad Wall in the Jewish Quarter.

The beginning of the Second Temple period (586 BC-AD 70) is marked by the return of Jews to Jerusalem from their exile in Babylon in 538 BC. They were allowed to return under an edict issued by Cyrus King of Persia. By 515 BC the reinstated Jewish residents had completed building the Second Temple.

The time of the Second Temple is divided into different periods: the Persian period (586-332 BC); the Hellenistic period (332-63 BC); and the Roman period (63 BC-AD 324). In 37 BC, King Herod enlarged the Temple Mount and rebuilt the temple with the consent of the public. During the Roman period, in AD 70, the Second Temple was destroyed, along with Jerusalem, by Titus' army. It was also during this period that Jesus was in Jerusalem. He was crucified about 40 years before the destruction of the city.

There are significant archaeological remains from the Second Temple period, including the Kidron Valley tombs, the Western Wall, Robinson's Arch, the Herodian residential quarter, numerous other tombs, and walls.

BCE (Before Common Era) and CE (Common Era) are used throughout Israel and are numerically equivalent to BC and AD, respectively.

are within walking distance or a short cab ride of each other. They range from Islamic art to contemporary exhibits and everything in between.

Rehavya is one of the planned garden neighborhoods that were established to introduce and preserve a healthy amount of greenery in the city's landscape. Architecture fans will find many of its buildings interesting.

Givat Ram is home to the **Israel Museum, the Bible Lands Museum,** the future site of the **Israel Antiquities Authority Museum,** and several others. There is little else to do in this area besides exploring the museums and taking nice, long walks.

PLANNING YOUR TIME
Jerusalem is layered in complexity both in the terrain and the sights within it. It would be difficult to see the major highlights of the city in fewer than three full days. Seven days allows you to comfortably visit all of the best sights as well as enjoy some of the local culture, cuisine, and make a few day trips to nearby spots.

GERMAN COLONY

CHOPIN
DAVID MARCUS
DUBNOW
DAVID REMEZ

JERUSALEM THEATRE

EMEK REFAIM STREET
LEV SMADAR

RACHEL IMEINU
LUCIANA
Smuts Garden

EMEK REFAIM ST
HARACKEVAT ST
BEIT LEHEM ST
HEVRON ST

Peace Forest

250 yds
250 m

TAMAR RESIDENCE

© AVALON TRAVEL

When to Go

There are two major considerations when planning the time of year to visit Jerusalem: the weather and the holiday schedule. The climate is inviting—the average temperature in summer months can typically go above 80-90°F, but when the sun goes down, pleasant, cool, breezy evenings in the mid-70s are the norm.

The best time of year to visit is May-July. August-September is very hot but bearable weather-wise, but could prove very tricky logistically. For three weeks in August, the Jewish orthodox community has a major vacation season and they flood nearly every corner of the city's museums and parks. At the end of August, the Muslim community of the city finishes their holy month of fasting for Ramadan and come out to enjoy the end of summer in the parks. During August, it is not uncommon to see popular gathering places like Gan Sacher Park overflowing with large families cooking out and playing in fountains. The major Jewish holidays of Yom Kippur and Sukkot usually fall in September (check the Jewish calendar, which changes by the year).

Getting Around

Jerusalem is an ancient city that can be tricky to maneuver if you take a wrong turn, especially when traveling by car. It's highly recommended to go by foot or take advantage of Jerusalem's efficient bus system, many taxis, and the new light rail train to get where you're going.

Getting around Jerusalem is fairly easy if you have a clear idea of how much time and money you want to spend. Taxi cabs are everywhere but cost 25 percent more on weekends and 9pm-5am. There is a discounted public transportation ticket for tourists for access to both the light rail and the public buses. However, the light rail does not have an extensive network of stops throughout the city and the bus system, while convenient once you get the hang of it, can be tricky at first. There is also a double-decker city tour bus that you can hop on and off all day long at major sights after buying a 24- or 48-hour ticket.

HISTORY

Jerusalem's history, like the city itself, is winding, confusing, and full of unexpected twists and turns. For millennia, it has been a religious center for peoples of three major faiths: Jewish, Christian, and Muslim. In modern times, it is still a flashpoint of religious, ethnic, and geopolitical tension.

In ancient times, Jerusalem was the area now known as the Old City, contained within the walls that offered protection from attackers, invaders, and other more wild elements. The city has been conquered, destroyed, and rebuilt more than once. In fact, it has long been an object of pursuit for ambitious rulers and empires. The first evidence of human life in Jerusalem is around 4500 BC. The first reference to the name Jerusalem (Urushalimum) was in 1500 BC.

In modern times, largely since the return of the Jewish diaspora to Israel, there have been raging battles and political debates over who controls and has a claim on Jerusalem.

In 1948, soldiers from the Transjordan's Arab Legion (which became the Hashemite Kingdom of Jordan in 1949) tried to capture the entire city during the War of Independence. But Israeli fighters were able to defend significant portions of the western part of the city. After the Arab Legion destroyed the Jewish Quarter of the Old City and expelled the

© GENEVIEVE BELMAKER

Yemin Moshe-Mishkenot Sha'ananim

residents, a cease-fire agreement was signed. Outside of the walls was known as the New City and was mostly Israeli-controlled.

In April 1949, an armistice agreement was signed along the 1948 ceasefire line between Israel and Transjordan forces. The line between east and west was divided by barbed wire, concrete walls, minefields, and bunkers. East Jerusalem, including holy sites, was occupied by Transjordan and west Jerusalem became the capital of Israel.

In 1967, the Israeli Defense Force (IDF) battled again with Jordan and took control of east Jerusalem. The city was reunified and came under Israeli control, with a promise that religious sites for all faiths would be protected. For Jews this meant that they gained access to Temple Mount and the Western Wall and could freely visit and pray at these sites.

Today you can still see the dividing line between east and west Jerusalem. You can stand along the route taken by the light rail train near the Old City, and you'll see a now-invisible line that used to be walls and barbed wire. The east side of Jerusalem is a bit more ramshackle, the roads aren't well maintained in many places, and the architecture is more distinctly Arab. The west side of Jerusalem is more upscale and most residents are distinguishable as Jews by their dress.

Tensions between east and west Jerusalem are ongoing but take on more subtle and political forms. The Arab neighborhood of Silwan is one of the starkest examples. Under court order, a series of Arab residents have been told that their homes do not legally belong to them. Violence between Arabs and Israelis sometimes erupts in the area with Israelis firing rubber bullets and Arabs throwing stones and burning large trash cans.

Sights

You could spend every day for weeks sightseeing in Jerusalem and never run out of interesting things to see, experience, and learn about. This is especially true for those with a love of history, archaeology, and spirituality. It is one of the most overwhelming cities in the world; for all the mysteries you discover, there are always a dozen more you have yet to learn.

Many of Jerusalem's major sights are centered on the Old City and the nearby Mount of Olives and Mount Zion. The Old City is the heart of Jerusalem, and includes major sights such as the Western Wall, the Dome of the Rock, the Church of the Holy Sepulchre, the Via Dolorosa, and many, many more. The Mount of Olives is also layered with sights significant to Christians, Muslims, and Jews. Not far from the Old City, the city becomes more residential and moves to the rhythm of its residents, who live in and around important museums, well-known parks, the world famous Machane Yehuda market, and the compound of the national government of Israel.

The trick to sightseeing in Jerusalem is to know what interests you and how much energy and money you are willing to expend. There are no special combination tourism tickets and the sights that have an entrance fee range from an average of NIS20-50 per person, sometimes more. Some sights that seem fascinating and worth paying the entrance fee are run by organizations that have a political or religious agenda and you might be held captive to a monologue about it during your tour.

Some museums are open late one day of the week and have days or times during the year when there is limited free admission. Many of the best things to do and see in Jerusalem are free or cost very little.

CITY CENTER
Jerusalem Time Elevator

This unique trip through Jerusalem's history (37 Hillel St., Agron House, 02/624-8381, www.time-elevator-jerusalem.co.il, 10am-5pm Sun.-Thurs., 10am-2pm Fri., noon-6pm Sat., adult NIS54, senior NIS46, Internet booking NIS46, reservation recommended) gives visitors a sensory overload. Using crashing ceilings, splashing water, and other special effects, it takes you through 3,000 years of history in 2D and surround sound.

The Ticho House (Israel Museum)

Built by an Arab dignitary in the latter half of the 19th century, it was one of the first houses constructed outside of the Old City walls. The **Ticho House** (9 Harav Kook St., 02/624-5068, www.go-out.com/ticho, 10am-5pm Sun.-Mon. and Wed.-Thurs., 10am-10pm

---

JERUSALEM'S CONQUERORS

The list of those who have conquered, occupied, and destroyed Jerusalem is lengthy:

- King David conquers Jerusalem in 1000 BC.
- Nebuchadnezzar, King of Babylon, conquers Jerusalem and destroys the First Temple in 586 BC.
- Alexander the Great conquers Jerusalem in 332 BC.
- Antiochus III conquers Jerusalem in 200 BC.
- Pompeius conquers Jerusalem in 63 BC and Roman rule begins.
- Herod occupies Jerusalem and fortifies significant public buildings.
- Titus' army destroys Jerusalem and the Second Temple in 70 AD.
- Transjordan captures east Jerusalem in 1948.
- Israel reunifies east and west Jerusalem in 1967.

© GIDON BELMAKER

the walls of the Old City from the outside

Tues., 10am-2pm Fri., free) was home to well-known painter Anna Ticho and her husband Dr. Avraham Albert Ticho, who bought the house in 1924. The house includes cozy galleries and a massive, enchanting garden restaurant (10am-11pm Sun.-Thurs., 10:30am-2pm Fri.) that hosts live musical performances on Tuesday, Wednesday, and Saturday nights. The reference library of books about art, literature, and Jerusalem (11am-6pm Sun.-Mon. and Thurs., 2pm-6pm Tues., 10am-noon Fri., free) is a unique place to sit and have a quiet moment.

Yafo Street (Jaffa Street)

Busy **Yafo Street** (also known as Jaffa) is flourishing after being the victim of a years-long construction project for the now-functioning light rail train. Only pedestrian and train traffic are allowed to pass through the length of the street that runs through the heart of town, passing always-happening **Zion Square,** near where Yafo intersects with Shamai Street, which is full of tourists, souvenir shops, ice cream shops open late, juice bars, and several overpriced cafés and restaurants.

Just a five-minute walk off of Yafo Street to the east is **City Hall** (Jerusalem Municipality Complex at Safra Square, 02/624-1379, www.jerusalem.muni.il, tours 10am Mon., free) and several restaurants and coffee shops.

Ben Yehuda Street (Pedestrian Mall)

One of the main pedestrian arteries that leads to Zion Square, **Ben Yehuda Street** is full of shops that tend to cater to tourists and sell items such as souvenirs and Judaica. In the past, the highly trafficked area made it a target for terrorist bombings—look for silver plaques on the ground and sides of buildings marking spots where bombings took place. The triangle formed by Ben Yehuda, King George, and Yafo Streets is partially inhabited by shops founded after attacks on the Mamilla commercial center just days after the UN vote on the partition of Palestine in 1947.

Proceed farther down Yafo (it's a long walk) in the direction of the central bus station, and you'll come upon the small, but unique, **Gush Katif Museum** (5 Sha'arei Tsedek,

02/625-5456, www.gushkatifmuseum.org, 10am-6pm Sun.-Thurs., 9am-1pm Fri., NIS15), the only museum in the world that tells the story of the Jewish settlement Gush Katif in the Gaza Strip before it was broken apart in the 2005 disengagement and Israel's unilateral pullout from the Gaza Strip.

Machane Yehuda Market (The *Shuk*)

Also accessible by Yafo Street is the open-air market world-famous for its colorful produce stands, restaurants, and characters, and known to locals as the *shuk*. **Machane Yehuda market** (between Yafo St. and Agripas St. at Beit Ya'acov and Eitz HaChaim, www.machne. co.il/en, 8am-7pm Sun.-Thurs., 8am-3pm Fri., free) is overwhelming in its sights, sounds, and tastes. No matter which entrance you take (and there are about a half a dozen ways to enter), you will find yourself in a seemingly endless maze

Spices are typically sold in open bins by bulk at the *shuk*.

© GIDON BELMAKER

of bins overflowing with fruits and vegetables, sweets and olives, and all kinds of spices and teas. You can enjoy one of the market's many restaurants, shop for produce, spices, or sweets, or just browse the ordered chaos of the place.

One of the most interesting things about the *shuk* in Jerusalem is the mixture of people, ranging from the locals who eagerly elbow their way to the vendors and the tourists who wander around taking photographs.

The secret to enjoying the *shuk* as a visitor is deciding what type of experience you want. The most intense time and day of the week is 11am-3pm on Friday. The level of activity reaches a fever pitch as closing time gets closer and vendors want to sell more goods and shoppers want to buy their last items before Shabbat.

The most low-key time to visit is generally any weekday before about 10:30am. You will have plenty of space to move about and enjoy the market without worrying about battling the crowds. You won't get many deals, though. The best deals are cut closest to closing time.

Later in the day, especially on Thursdays and Fridays, you can find all kinds of interesting characters in the main alley that runs through the market and is outdoors. You will likely see some characters here that are fixtures, including the man who takes photographs and sells them, and college kids or tourists who sit down in the middle of the pathway to drink beer and hang out. There is also often live music. It's just lovely, colorful chaos.

King George Street

A main street leading into Jerusalem's heart is **King George Street.** As with many streets in Jerusalem, the street name changes from Keren HaYesod as you leave the German Colony-Bak'a area at the intersection of Ramban. The intersection is significant for orienting yourself toward the Old City, City Center, Givat Ram, and the German Colony-Bak'a area.

Go north on King George Street toward City Center and you will pass the **Jerusalem Great Synagogue** (56 King George St., 02/623-0628, www.jerusalemgreatsynagogue.com, group tours by appointment only by emailing rabbigeorge@gmail.com), an imposing structure that was opened in 1982 and dedicated to the memory of the six million Jewish victims of the Holocaust. The synagogue's internationally-acclaimed choir is one of the world's chief repositories for Jewish Ashkenazic liturgical music, and stained glass windows adorn the main building. The synagogue's annual operating budget of US$1 million comes entirely from donations.

Next door to the synagogue is **Hechal Shlomo The Jewish Heritage Center** (58 King George St., 02/588-9010, http://eng.hechalshlomo.org.il, 9am-3pm Sun.-Thurs., lobby gallery 9am-8pm Sun.-Thurs. and 9am-noon Fri., adult NIS20, senior and child NIS15), which houses the **Wolfson Museum of Jewish Art** and serves as a Jewish spiritual and cultural center. Aside from Hechal Shlomo's cultural events that include live music and its several permanent exhibits, it also houses the 300-year-old Renanim Synagogue, which was transported from Italy. The active synagogue is decorated lavishly in 18th century Italian style.

Just up the road from the Great Synagogue is the somewhat worn looking **Old Knesset** building that housed the Israeli parliament from 1950 to 1966. The building is currently being used by other branches of the Israeli government. Note the plaque near the building that commemorates a terrorist bombing in that spot.

Museum on the Seam

On the old border between east and west Jerusalem is the **Museum on the Seam** (4 Chel Handasa St., 02/628-1278, www.mots.org.il, 10am-5pm Sun.-Thurs., 10am-2pm Fri., adult NIS30, senior and student NIS25), a socio-political contemporary art museum that focuses on the social situation created by regional conflict. Established in 1999, the museum is not well known among locals, but comes highly recommended by visitors to Jerusalem who are interested in learning more about the regional conflict and artistic interpretations of their affect on the residents of the city.

THE OLD CITY
The Muslim Quarter

One of the **Muslim Quarter**'s most famous sites, and one of the most-experienced in all of Jerusalem, is the **Via Dolorosa,** the path that Jesus is said to have walked on his way to his crucifixion more than 2,000 years ago. The path, marked by 14 "stations" where something significant is said to have happened while Jesus walked through the Old City, starts just inside the **Lion's Gate.** It is possible to visit Via Dolorosa without a guide as the stations are literally along the streets of the Old City, but there are a number of guided tours available. Check with the tourist information center when you enter the Old City, just inside Jaffa Gate. As with many other sights, maps, audio tours, and video are available on the Old City's official website (www.jerusalem.old-city.org.il).

Near the beginning of the path is the **Church of St. Anne** (near the Lion's Gate in the Old City off Sha'ar HaArayot St., 8am-noon and 2pm-5pm Mon.-Sat., NIS10), which Catholic tradition says is the birthplace of the Virgin Mary. Nearby accessible with entry to the church is the **Pool of Bethesda** (paid entry), mentioned in the New Testament of the Bible as the place where Jesus cured a crippled man. The area is an archaeological site that includes five pools and ruins of Byzantine, Crusader, and medieval churches.

Exit out of **Herod's Gate** (also known as Flower Gate because of the floral designs on its facade) and go right, following the Old City wall, until you reach the **Rockefeller Archaeological Museum** (27 Sultan Suleiman St., 02/670-8074, www.imjnet.org.il follow link to Wings, 10am-3pm Sun.-Mon. and Wed.-Thurs., 10am-2pm Sat., free). Recommended by most locals, the museum is home to thousands of artifacts displayed in chronological order from prehistoric times to the Ottoman period. Among the treasures are a 9,000-year-old statue from Jericho and pieces of gold jewelry from the Bronze Age.

Re-enter the Old City through **Damascus Gate,** an ornamented gate built in the

on the Via Dolorosa

the Damascus Gate entrance to the Old City

VIA DOLOROSA: THE LAST STEPS OF JESUS

a station along the Via Dolorosa

Via Dolorosa is a numbered trail that winds through the Old City, marking locations of significant moments during Jesus' journey bearing the cross he was crucified on. It begins in the Muslim Quarter and ends in the Christian Quarter, and pilgrims frequently kneel in prayer at different stations.

A free MP3 audio file and map of the trail from the Jerusalem Development Authority can be downloaded from www.jerusalem-old-city.org.il. You can also join the Via Dolorosa procession led by the Franciscans on Fridays at 3pm from Station 1.

· **Station 1:** Just inside the Lion's Gate and marked with a round, black seal imprinted with the Roman numeral I on the wall of the street is the former seat of Pontius Pilate, who condemned Jesus to death. The station is located at the northwest corner of Temple Mount.

· **Station 2:** Across the street is the Roman numeral II. Here Jesus was given his cross, whipped, and mockingly dressed in a robe

Ottoman period (according to a dedication on the wall) under the auspices of Sultan Suleiman the Magnificent, who restored the Old City walls. Follow El Wad Street past the Austrian Hospice until you reach **Lady Tunshuq Palace,** a 14th-century structure, built by Muslim Sufi mystics under the direction of Lady Tunshuq, which today is a working school.

Continue east toward **Temple Mount–Al Haram al-Sharif** (main access for non-Muslims is between the Western Wall and Dung Gate, 02/622-6250, www.noblesanctuary.com, 7:30am-11am and 1:30pm-2:30pm Sun.-Thurs. Apr.-Sept.; 7:30am-10am and 12:30pm-1:30pm Sun.-Thurs. Oct.-Mar., dress modestly, bring passport, entrance subject to change, free). Here you will find and given a crown of thorns by Roman soldiers. The compound includes the Roman Catholic Church of the Condemnation and the Convent of the Flagellation.

- **Station 3:** The corner of Via Dolorosa and El Wad (Hagai) Street is station 3 and marks where Jesus fell under the weight of the cross for the first time. The route then traces the western side of Temple Mount. The Polish Catholic church, the Austro-Hungarian Hospice (a hospital), and a 15th-century chapel are nearby.

- **Station 4:** On El Wad Street is the Roman numeral IV, where Jesus met his mother, Mary. Between stations 3 and 4 is a short section of the Roman-Byzantine street, which was paved over the same street that Jesus walked on.

- **Station 5:** At the corner where El Wad Street meets up again with Via Dolorosa is the Roman numeral V. A small Franciscan church built in 1229 marks the location where Simon bore the cross for Jesus. An old square stone to the right of the door of the church is said to bear the handprint of Jesus.

- **Station 6:** Uphill is the Roman numeral VI and the station where a woman named Veronica wiped the face of Jesus. A small Greek chapel at the site is called The Holy Face.

- **Station 7:** The Roman numeral VII marks where Jesus fell for the second time. Behind the black doors is a small chapel. Just beyond a massive Roman column is the Chapel of the Seventh Station.

- **Station 8:** Close to the Church of the Holy Sepulchre, marked with the Roman numeral VIII, this station is also marked by a stone embedded in the wall with the engraving IC-XC NI-KA, which means "Jesus Christ conquers." The Greek Orthodox Church dedicated the station to Saint Charalampos and built a monastery behind the wall. This is where Jesus spoke to the women of Jerusalem and told them not to weep for him, but for themselves and their children.

- **Station 9:** A cross painted on a stone pillar next to stairs and an archway is where Jesus fell for the third time. Adjacent to the Church of the Holy Sepulchre, the route here winds around the building of the Coptic Patriarchate. Nearby is the Ethiopian Church of St. Michael and a Coptic church with paintings depicting Biblical scenes.

- **Station 10:** At the entrance of the Holy Sepulchre is the Chapel of the Franks, where Jesus was stripped of his clothes.

- **Station 11:** The interior of the Church of the Holy Sepulchre where Jesus was nailed to the cross is station 11.

- **Station 12:** A Greek Orthodox crucifixion altar inside the church marks where Jesus was crucified and died on the cross. A silver disk with a central hole under the altar marks where the cross stood, and pilgrims can be seen kneeling and kissing it.

- **Station 13:** A large stone where the body of Jesus is said to have been laid and prepared for burial after he died is encased with the top open for pilgrims to touch.

- **Station 14:** The tomb of Jesus and the final station of the Via Dolorosa is in the rotunda inside a small inner chamber past the Chapel of the Angel. A marble lid covers the tomb.

a complex of about 100 buildings known as the Noble Sanctuary by Muslims, which includes the Dome of the Rock, Mount Moriah, Al Aqsa Mosque, and many other sites. It is recommended to exercise caution doing anything resembling praying in the area because of serious tensions over religious and territorial claims. If you do enter the mosque, be very conservatively dressed.

The Islamic Museum of Temple Mount (southwest corner of the compound grounds, near the Western Wall, 02/628-3313, 8am-11:30am and 2pm-4pm Mon.-Sat., NIS38 at stone kiosk between Al Aqsa Mosque and the Dome of the Rock) is one of the oldest museums in the country and has a large collection of Korans, coins, glassware, guns, swords, daggers, and Islamic ceramics.

© AVNER RICHARD/123RF.COM

the golden Dome of the Rock in the Old City

The Jewish Quarter
WESTERN WALL

Just down from Temple Mount is the most famed religious site in all of Judaism. Named for its position as the outer western wall of the destroyed Second Temple's courtyard, the **Western Wall** (Jewish Quarter of the Old City, 02/627-1333, http://english.thekotel.org, www. jewish-quarter.org.il, 24 hours daily, free, extremely crowded on certain holidays, modest dress required) is also called the Wailing Wall or the Kotel. The Western Wall is visited by hundreds of thousands of people from countries all over the world every year.

It is considered particularly significant to Jews because it is the last remaining piece of the great temple, the most significant site in all of Judaism. The imposing wall is the destination for the faithful who come to pray before it. An upper plaza in the southeastern corner offers an excellent view of the Wall and the Dome of the Rock behind it.

On the northern end of the Kotel is the **Chain of Generations Center** (near the Western Wall, 02/627-1333, visits by reservation in advance

Sun.-Thurs. and Fri. morning, NIS20, children NIS10), which tells the story of the Jewish people over 3,500 years and spans history from exile to statehood. The Center uses a combination of music, sculpture, archaeology, and light effects and is divided into several rooms. Each room covers a different period and has works of art made from layers of glass lit up by rays of light that shine from dark rooms. There is also a view of the Western Wall from one of portion of the Center.

Go south from the Western Wall toward **Dung Gate** and you will come upon the **Western Wall Excavations** (Western Wall, Jewish Quarter, 02/627-1333, http://english. thekotel.org follow link to Tunnels, www.jewish-quarter.org.il, 7am-11pm Sun.-Thurs., depending on reservations, 7am-noon Fri. and holiday eves, adult NIS25, child NIS15). This 75-minute tour explores hidden layers of the Western Wall and is given only by schedule in advance and with a guide. The underground excavations tell the story of ancient Jerusalem.

CITY OF DAVID
Just a few steps from the archaeological park, you will find the **City of David** (off Ophel St. in Silwan, 02/626-8700, www.cityofdavid.org. il, 8am-5pm Sun.-Thurs., 8am-2pm Fri. Nov.-Mar., 8am-7pm Sun.-Thurs., 8am-4pm Fri. Apr.-Oct., closed for Shabbat and holidays, adult NIS27, senior and child NIS14, 3-D film add NIS13, guided tour adult NIS60, guided tour senior and child NIS45), controversial for its location in the Arab neighborhood of Silwan but fascinating for the many historical and archaeological treasures that it encompasses. Part of the controversy over the City of David is the claim that its very existence is a surreptitious attempt to circumvent the law and establish an Israeli presence in east Jerusalem.

Turn left out of Dung Gate and after about 150 feet make a right. The City of David will be on the left-hand side.

Among the highlights in the City of David is the incredible **Hezekiah's Tunnel,** which is a wonder of ancient engineering. The tunnel starts at Gihon Spring, a major source of water

© GENEVIEVE BELMAKER

prayers at the Western Wall

for ancient Jerusalem for 1,000 years. If you are adventurous (and not claustrophobic) you can wade through the 2,700-year-old tunnel for 580 yards to the Pool of Siloam, the source for drawing water during biblical times. Make sure to bring a flashlight with you. The tunnel was built by King Hezekiah in preparation for the Syrian siege, and was painstakingly chipped away by hand by two groups of workers. One group started from the top and the other from the bottom, and they met in the middle to join the tunnel and ensure the safety of the city's water supply from impending invaders.

Also in the City of David, the **Temple Mount Sifting Project** (entrance to Emek Tzurim National Park on the ascent to the Mt. of Olives, 02/628-0342, templemount. wordpress.com, 8am-4pm Sun.-Thurs., 8am-1pm Fri. Nov.-Mar., 9am-5pm Sun.-Thurs., 8am-1pm Fri. Apr.-Oct., closed for Shabbat and holidays, adult NIS20, senior and child NIS16, reservation required, free parking) affords a rare experience for the most curious of visitors. The project offers visitors a two-hour participatory archaeological experience. You can sift through rubble that was dug up and dumped during construction and then reclaimed for the purpose of checking for ancient treasures. Any findings during the sifting tour are explained by archaeologists and expert guides at the site.

Go back into the Old City through the Dung Gate, noting the grouping of stones protruding off the outer wall. The stones are known as **Robinson's Arch** for the American who discovered them, Edward Robinson, and are believed to date back to the Second Temple period.

Continuing north, follow the main street as it curves around, and go west at the first possible turn until you get to HaKarim Street and the **Herodian Quarter and Wohl Archaeological Museum** (1 Ha-Karaim St., 02/626-5922, www.jewish-quarter.org.il, 9am-5pm Sun.-Thurs., 9am-1pm Fri. and on eve of Jewish holidays, NIS18, combined ticket with the Burnt House NIS35). Here you'll find a six-house compound on the slope of the hill

© GENEVIEVE BELMAKER

the East Jerusalem Arab neighborhood of Silwan, which abuts the City of David

facing the Temple Mount that highlights three main points: The Western House, the Middle Complex, and the Palatial Mansion. All thought to be homes of aristocrats and priests during the Herodian period, they are designed in the Hellenistic/Roman style. The 600-square-meter Palatial Mansion is the largest, and gives clues to the lifestyle of the wealthy of that time. It includes rich floor mosaics and remarkably preserved wall frescoes. Also unearthed here were utensils, artifacts, decorated plates, and imported wine jugs.

Continue west and you will pass by the **Ha-Tkuma Garden,** also known as Resurrection Park. You will also see the large white roof of the **Hurva Synagogue** looming in the distance. The synagogue has an interesting history. Construction began on it in 1700, but in 20 years it was still not complete, and the unfinished building was torched (giving it the name Hurva, which means ruin). It was rebuilt in the mid-1800s, only to be destroyed by the Transjordan Legion Army in the War of Independence in 1948. When the

Old City was recaptured by Israel in 1967, the site of the ruins was commemorated but nothing was rebuilt there until 40 years later. In 2005, construction on the current Hurva Synagogue began, and it was finished in early 2010.

Continue north and just around the corner you will find the **Burnt House** (Tiferet Israel St., 02/626-5921, www.jewish-quarter.org.il, 9am-5pm Sun.-Thurs., 9am-1pm Fri. and on eve of Jewish holidays, NIS25, combined ticket with Herodian Quarter NIS35), the remains of a house that burned during the destruction of the Second Temple. Archaeological artifacts and a multi-media presentation describe the daily life of the people who lived in the house. The movie is screened every 40 minutes starting at 9am.

Practically next door to the Burnt House is **The Temple Institute** (19 Misgav Ladach St., 02/626-4545, www.templeinstitute.org, adult NIS25, child NIS20), a non-profit religious organization that works to educate people about the Jewish Temple and advocates for

© VITALII MYKHAILOV/123RF.COM

Hurva Synagogue

building the Temple again. Their Treasures of the Temple Exhibition includes examples of priestly garments worn when the Temple existed, paintings, and models of the Temple.

In a similar vein, just north at the next corner is the **Rachel Ben Zvi Center** (7 Bonei ha-Khoma, 02/628-6288, www.ybz.org.il, 9am-4pm Sun.-Thurs., NIS10), home to a model of the First Temple and more.

Nearby you will find the remnants of an impressive seven-meter-wide wall that extends westward toward HaYehudim Street, known as the **Broad Wall (Wide Wall)** (Plugot HaKotel St., 02/626-5900 ext. 102, www.jerusalem-old-city.org.il, 24 hours daily, free). When it was in use, the wall encircled the current site of the City of David and protected Jerusalem on its north side, forming a single large city.

The exposure of the Wide Wall ends near the **Ramban Synagogue** (enter via Jewish Quarter St. next to Hurva Synagogue, 02/627-1422, call in advance to visit, modest dress required), the oldest synagogue in the Old City. It is believed to have been built on Mount Zion and then

moved to the Old City in the 14th century. Closed by the Ottomans in 1589, it was only reopened in 1967.

Walk away from the white dome of Hurva Synagogue going south, and take your first right to find the **Cardo** (HaKardo St., 02/626-5900 ext. 102, www.jewish-quarter.org.il, 8am-6pm Sun.-Thurs., 8am-4pm Fri., closed for Shabbat, free), the remnants of an ancient Roman double-columned main street (always called a *cardo maximus*) and its shops that were a fixture in many Roman cities. The Old City's Cardo stretched from the Damascus Gate to the Zion Gate.

The southern section of the Cardo was excavated and buildings from later periods were removed to reveal the Byzantine Cardo. Some of the columns from that period were reconstructed and restored, allowing visitors to experience a taste of the 6th century Cardo.

Just ahead is the covered section of the Cardo, which dates back to the Crusader period; shops from that time were located in the same place as the shops today. Most of the

JERUSALEM

© GENEVIEVE BELMAKER

the remains of the Roman Cardo in the Old City

Cardo shops sell higher-end items like jewelry and Judaica.

Going north along the Cardo toward David Street you will come upon the ruins of five Roman columns, where you'll find the original paving stones of the street, dating to the Byzantine period. Farther on is a reproduction of a section of the Madaba Map, the oldest known map that depicts Jerusalem in the 6th century.

The Armenian Quarter

This section of the Old City is largely residential and makes for a lovely and interesting place to take a quiet stroll that is very different from most other areas in the Old City.

Just inside Zion Gate and then as far west as you can go until you reach the city wall is the **Armenian Patriarchate of St. James** (02/628-2331, www.armenian-patriarchate.org, nourhan@netvision.net.il, 6:30am-7:30am and 3pm-3:30pm Mon.-Fri., 8:30am-10:30am and 3pm-3:30pm Sat., free), or St. James Cathedral, with its magnificent cathedral built on the

tombs of St. James the Apostle and St. James the brother of Jesus. The interior of the cathedral is decorated with ancient hanging oil lamps, and has three chapels. There are also two thrones at the front of the church. The church served as a bomb shelter for residents of the Armenian Quarter during the War of Independence in 1948.

Continue north along Armenian Patriarchate Road, turn right before you reach David Street and you will see **Christ Church** (Omar Ibn Al Hatab St. just inside Jaffa Gate, 02/628-7487, www.jerusalem-oldcity.org.il, www.cmj-israel. org, call in advance before visiting, NIS10) compound on the right of the street. This is the oldest Protestant church in the Middle East, and it houses a hostel, a heritage center, and a coffee shop. There is a tunnel beneath it dating to the Second Temple period.

A unique aspect of Christ Church is that it was completed in 1849 in preparation of the return of the Jews to Israel. The believers of the church wanted to establish themselves in Jerusalem in order to be in a position to help

© GIDON BELMAKER

the Tower of David

the Jews when they returned. Due to its history, there are Hebrew inscriptions inside the church, and modern services have incorporated some Hebrew.

For a different and extremely interesting view of the Old City, climb up onto the 16th century wall surrounding the city and try the **Ramparts Walk.** The southern route starts at the Tower of David and ends at the Dung Gate, the northern route starts at Jaffa Gate and ends at the Lion's Gate. You can also walk around the entire rampart in 3-4 hours.

Just south of **Jaffa Gate** is the **Tower of David Museum** (02/626-5333, www.towerof-david.org.il, 10am-4pm Sun.-Thurs., 10am-2pm Sat. and holidays Sept.-June, 10am-5pm Sat.-Wed., 10am-7pm Thurs., 10am-2pm Fri. July-Aug., adult NIS30, senior and child NIS15), located in a medieval citadel. The museum tells the story of Jerusalem and includes the archaeological site of the citadel. It is also home to a unique sound and light show, the **Night Spectacular** (9pm and 10:30pm, adult NIS55, senior and child NIS45; museum admission plus show adult NIS70, senior and child NIS55).

The Christian Quarter

Return inside the Old City by following the outer wall northwest from Jaffa Gate along the broad plaza and turning to the right where you will see the **New Gate.** Just inside the gate you will find the **Franciscan Monastery of San Salvador,** also known as St. Savior Church, (1 St. Francis St., 02/626-6595, catholicchurch-holyland.com, 8am-5pm daily, free). The visit of St. Francis of Assisi to the Holy Land in 1219 marked the beginning of the Franciscan monks following in his footsteps, and to this day the St. Salvador Monastery in the Old City is the center of the Franciscan Order in the Holy Land and the Middle East.

The monastery, which visitors cannot enter, does have a church that is free to enter with a magnificent vaulted ceiling and pipe organ. Construction on the church was completed in the 19th century.

You might see members of the Franciscan Order while walking about the Old City. They are distinguishable by their simple, brown robes with a rope belt knotted three times in honor of the vows of their order: obedience, poverty, and chastity.

Continue south and you will find yourself on the **Greek Orthodox Patriarchate.** Follow the road east until you reach a large courtyard (usually filled with pilgrims and tourists) that leads to the **Church of the Holy Sepulchre** (Suq Khan e-Zeit and Christian Quarter Rd., 02/627-3314, www.holysepulchre.com, 5am-8pm daily Apr.-Sept., 5am-7pm daily Oct.-Mar., free), one of the most popular tourist destinations in Jerusalem. The Church is an important site for Christians for several reasons.

The massive courtyard leads to the interior of the church, which is also the end of the Via Dolorosa. At the entrance is the Chapel of the Franks and the looming and gloomy interior includes a Greek Orthodox crucifixion altar where Jesus is said to have been crucified. A large stone to the left is the place where, according to tradition, the body of Jesus was prepared

the bell tower of the Church of the Redeemer

for burial. In the rotunda inside a small inner chamber, past the Chapel of the Angel, is a marble encased tomb said to be the place where Jesus was buried.

Encircling the area where the church is located are several other religious sites, including the **Coptic Orthodox Patriarchate,** Mosque Sheikh Lulu, Dir A-Sultan, Muristan, and Omar Mosque. Just east of the Omar Mosque and south of the Church of the Holy Sepulchre is the Lutheran **Church of the Redeemer** (24 Muristan Rd., 02/627-1111, www.elcjhl.org, 9am-1pm and 1:30pm-5pm Mon.-Sat., NIS10). The church includes a vista from its bell tower that can be reached by trekking up almost 200 steps. The church itself was built by Kaiser Wilhelm in the late 1800s, and he later brought his wife with him and personally dedicated it in 1898. He was the first Western ruler to visit Jerusalem and infamously ordered Jaffa Gate to be destroyed so he could enter the Old City unimpeded. The gate was never repaired and is the only point in the Old City that doesn't have a full gate.

The Lutheran church is home to other Lutheran congregations that speak Arabic, German, English, and Danish. The interior of the church is simple and unadorned white stone with massive arches. It is the site of frequent musical performances.

◖ AUSTRIAN HOSPICE

Follow the Via Dolorosa station numbers backwards until you reach a courtyard-like intersection where security and police are often stationed to find the **Austrian Hospice** (near Damascus Gate, 37 Via Dolorosa, 02/626-5800, www.austrianhospice.com, 24 hours daily, free) of the Holy Family.

You could easily pass by this gem in the Old City without knowing it is here. The location was chosen by Austria's first consul general as a place to build (and establish a local presence) in Jerusalem and was opened as a pilgrims' house in 1856. There are numerous rooms that visitors use for accommodations, and the hallways are filled with photographs of the Holy Land.

There are two points here not to miss: the garden café with its famed apple strudel and the spectacular view of the Old City and the Dome of the Rock from the top of the building. You can reach the roof by taking the elevator or the stairs, but the final leg of the journey is stairs only. Once on the roof you can enjoy the view from a bench, and take your time to absorb the awesome sight of the Old City from above. You can also take as long as you like at one of the many outdoor tables in the garden (which is elevated two stories above street level) to have a very quiet coffee or beer or snack. It is one of the most serene spots in the Old City and missed by most people because of the nondescript outer appearance. Buzz the outer door to gain access, and buzz again if the inner gate is locked.

Mount Zion

From the far southern end of the Armenian Quarter, you can exit through **Zion Gate** and take a short walk up the hillside to **Mount Zion,** which is actually a series of sites which include **Dormition Abbey** (Mount Zion, 02/565-5330,

© GIDON BELMAKER

The unassuming door of the Austrian Hospice hides some of the best garden dining and apple strudel in town.

www.dormitio.net, 8am-noon and 2pm-6pm daily, free); **King David's Tomb** (next to Dormition Abbey, 8am-6pm and until 2pm on Fri., free); and **St. Mark's Church** (Ararat St., 02/628-3304, 8am-6pm daily, free) or Monastery of St. Mark—the possible site of last supper. You can enter Dormition Abbey, built near the place where Catholic tradition says the Virgin Mary ascended to heaven, and tour the German Benedictine basilica that was finished in 1910.

Several mosaics can be seen inside the abbey, including some from a former Byzantine church that was previously at the same location. King David's Tomb and the Room of the Last Supper can be visited with a short walk from the basement level (the tomb) to a nearby room of stone with enclaves and support pillars. Be wary if you are invited to make a donation to see either site, as there is no fee to enter. There is some dispute about the veracity of claims made about both the tomb and the

supposed room of the last supper due to centuries of war and subsequent destruction and rebuilding in the area. Docents will openly tell you that some theorize that the actual sites are nearby, but a bit farther downhill.

EAST JERUSALEM
◖ Mount of Olives

Exit from the eastern Lion's Gate of the Old City and you will find yourself heading toward the **Mount of Olives** (www.mountofolives.co.il/eng). At the foot of the Mount of Olives is the **Kidron Valley** (24 hours daily, free), home to the tombs of Zechariah, Bnei-Hezir, and Absalom, which are actually rather massive ancient structures and not simple gravestones.

The tombs are the oldest graves of the ancient **Jewish Cemetery** (02/627-5050 for help locating a grave or to arrange a memorial service), which is considered by Jews to be sacred and the future sight of the resurrection. The oldest Jewish cemetery in the world, it covers

Dormition Abbey on Mount Zion

© GENEVIEVE BELMAKER

the entire western and much of the southern slope of the Mount of Olives and is not technically open for public access, although there are no gates to keep people out.

Start or end your journey at the **Rehav'am Lookout** (turn off from Jericho Rd. and go uphill until the road runs out, follow the signs, free parking), one of the highest points in Jerusalem. From April-September, try to get here before 10am or after 4pm to enjoy the unbelievable view without the heat.

Due to the sacredness of the Mount of Olives to Christianity, Judaism, and Islam, there are several holy sites in the area.

If you start from the base of the Mount of Olives, go north along Al-Mansuriya Road and then west along El Monsuriyya toward the **Church of the Assumption** or the **Tomb of the Virgin Mary** (intersection of Jericho Rd. and Al-Mansuria Rd., 6am-noon and 2:30pm-5pm Mon.-Sat., free), an underground tomb thought to be the resting place of the Virgin Mary. The site also includes a place for Muslims to pray, as St. Mary is

highly regarded in Muslim tradition. Above the tomb is the 12th-century church. You can enter the tomb area via a set of wide steps that go underground.

Just south of Mary's Tomb on Jericho Road is the **Basilica of the Agony** or the **Church of All Nations** (Jericho Rd., 02/628-4371, 8am-noon and 2pm-4:30pm Mon.-Sat., free), with a magnificent mosaic on the front and a row of pillars directly facing the road. The church was completed in 1924 with donations from a dozen different countries.

The impressive interior of the church includes massive frescoes painted on vaulted walls and a large rock believed to be the place where Jesus prayed the night he was betrayed. The symbols of the 12 countries that contributed to the building of the church are woven into the 12 inlaid gold cupola ceilings.

Accessible from an alley toward the north side of the church is the **Garden of Gethsemane** (8am-noon and 2pm-6pm Mon.-Sat., free), where Jesus is said to have been betrayed by Judas. The garden is a grove of ancient olive

© GIDON BELMAKER

the ancient Jewish cemetery on the Mount of Olives

trees, some of which are over 2,000 years old. It is completely surrounded by a wrought-iron fence, making it impossible to touch the trees or sit or walk among them.

Farther up the hill is the Catholic Franciscan **Dominus Flevit Church** (accessible by a footpath from the base of the Basilica of Agony or from the top of the Mount of Olives, 02/627-4931, 8am-noon and 2pm-5pm Mon.-Sat., free), a church dating back to the Bronze age. The current structure was built in 1954 over the ruins of other buildings that have stood at the location, including a Byzantine period monastery and church whose mosaic floor can still be seen to the left of the entrance. The building has a tear-shaped dome on top that is on the grounds of the Mount of Olives cemetery. This is the site where Jesus is said to have looked over Jerusalem and wept at its future destruction.

Farther up the road is the **Church of the Pater Noster** (E-Sheikh St., 02/626-4904, 8:30am-noon and 2:30pm-4:30pm Mon.-Sat., NIS7), the traditional place where Jesus taught his disciples the Lord's Prayer. It is famed for the 140 inscriptions of the Lord's Prayer throughout the church in different languages.

Near the Garden of Gethsemane are the golden domes of the **Russian Orthodox Church of St. Mary Magdalene** (Al-Mansuriya Rd., 02/628-4371, www.jerusalem-mission. org, 10am-11:30am Tues. and Thurs., free), impossible to miss with its Russian architecture built in the Muscovite style with golden onion domes or cupolas.

Finally, grouped near one another are the **Dome and Chapel of the Ascension** (al-Tur Village on Rub'a el-Adawiya St., 02/628-4373, www.jerusalem-mission.org, 8am-6pm daily, NIS5), where Jesus is said to have risen to heaven 40 days after his resurrection, and the **Greek Orthodox Church of Viri Galilaei** (just north of the Chapel of the Ascension, left off Rub'a el-Adawiya St., free), a small Greek Orthodox church that is one of three places on the Mount of Olives marking Jesus' ascension to heaven. The church is surrounded by an olive grove.

Orson Hyde Memorial Park

Heading back toward the Old City from the Mount of Olives, you will come upon the two-acre wooded **Orson Hyde Memorial Park** (next to Brigham Young University Mormonic Jerusalem Campus on Hadassa Lampel Rd., free) known for its views of the Kidron Valley and the Old City. The park is named in honor of Orson Hyde, a prominent member of the Mormon Church who traveled in the Holy Land in the late 19th century.

◖ Jerusalem Archaeological Park

The **Jerusalem Archaeological Park** (Temple Mount Excavations, near the Old City's Dung Gate, 02/627-7550, www.archpark.org.il, 8am-5pm Sun.-Thurs., 8am-2pm Fri., NIS30 adult, NIS16 senior, student, and child) covers a vast area near the Old City. The park extends from the north at the Temple Mount to the slope of the Mount of Olives and the Kidron Valley on the east, and on the west and south to the Valley of Hinnom.

Considered Israel's most significant antiquities site, it includes 5,000 years of history from the Canaanite (Bronze) age and through the days of the Israelite monarchy in the First Temple period. At the entrance to the park is the **Davidson Center,** a virtual reconstruction and exhibition center that uses state-of-the-art computer technology to give visitors an historical and archaeological orientation.

The Sherover-Haas Promenade

A paved walking trail slightly off the beaten path, the **Sherover-Haas Promenade** (enter off of Daniel Yanovski St. at Olei HaGardom St., 02/626-5900 ext. 102, www.s-aronson. co.il, 24 hours daily, free, limited parking) has an excellent view of east Jerusalem, the Old City walls, and the Judean Desert. The winding walk down the promenade is nearly one mile (there are stairs at different points) and is full of native plant and flower gardens, quiet places to sit, and viewing pergolas along the way. The bottom of the promenade is the edge of the Judean Desert. Parking is limited, so take bus 71, 72, 74, or 75 along Derech Hevron and

get off at Yehuda Street, then walk 15 minutes east to the promenade, or take a taxi here.

The Separation Barrier

At several points near the Old City and at the border of east and west Jerusalem, you will be able to clearly see the **Separation Barrier,** also known as the Security Barrier, that separates Israel from the West Bank. The barrier directly abuts neighborhoods and villages along its route, and is not complete. If completed, it would span a distance of about 708 miles from north to south. It is currently about 440 miles long, and the structure varies from fence with barbed wire to concrete walls. Throughout Jerusalem it is mostly concrete.

The politics behind the Separation Barrier are significant, as some neighborhoods were divided when it was built, and many people who live on the east side of the wall are actually Israeli citizens. Their daily life involves driving around the wall and passing through one of the checkpoints to get between work and home.

Nablus Road (Shekhem Road)

If you exit from the Damascus Gate of the Old City and cross the street, go up Nablus Road; you will quickly come up Conrad Schick Street on the right, where the **Garden Tomb** (Conrad Schick St., 02/627-2745, www.gardentomb. com, 8:30am-noon and 2pm-5:30pm Mon.-Sat., free) is located. It is the only other place in Jerusalem other than the Church of the Holy Sepulchre that claims to be the site of the resurrection of Jesus.

Just next to it is the **St. Stephen Basilica** (6 Nablus Rd., 02/626-4468, www.ebaf.edu, call in advance to visit as there is locked gate, free), home of the world famous Ecole Biblique (French Biblical and Archaeological School). The original church at this location was built at the end of the 5th century as a resting place for the relics of St. Stephen, the first Christian martyr. The massive adjacent monastery was home to an unbelievable 10,000 monks by the end of the 6th century. Destroyed in the 12th century by Crusaders, it was not until 1900 that a new church was rededicated at the site

© GENEVIEVE BELMAKER

The separation barrier that divides the West Bank from Israel can be seen from many points in Jerusalem.

on the base of the ruins. Founded in 1890, the Ecole is the oldest research institute in the Holy Land and has an extensive collection of 20,000 glass photo plates dating from 1890 that are partially on exhibit.

Continue along Nablus Road until you reach **St. George's Cathedral** (20 Nablus Rd., near the intersection with Salah al-Din St., 02/628-9386, 8am-7pm daily, call in advance as hours change, free), the Episcopal Diocese's center in Jerusalem, established in 1899. The Cathedral includes a guesthouse and St. George's College for theology studies. The guesthouse is centered around an English garden and includes a basement bar and a restaurant.

From the Cathedral, follow Nablus Road to Salah al-Din Street until you find the **Tomb of the Kings,** also known as Tomb of Queen Helene of Adiabene (at the corner of Abu Ubaida just north of the Old City, always open, free); you will see a sign that says "Tombeau des Rois" on the left. Go down the stairs and you'll find a courtyard that is the family tomb of Queen Helena of the Mesopotamian province of Adiabene.

GERMAN COLONY AND BAK'A
Talbiyeh

The neighborhood of **Talbiyeh** abuts the German Colony and is home to several buildings that were constructed by the Israeli government in the 1970s after they acquired a plot of land from the Greek Orthodox Church. The buildings are all on Hanasi Street and include the Academy of Science, the Van Leer Institute, and the official residence of the President of Israel.

The neighborhood is also home to the **L.A. Mayer Museum for Islamic Art** (2 HaPalmach St., 02/566-1291, www.islamicart.co.il, 10am-3pm Sun.-Thurs., until 7pm Tues. and Thurs., 10am-2pm Fri. and eves of holidays, 10am-4pm Sat. and holidays, NIS40), where you can find a small but exquisite collection of Islamic art and antique watches and clocks. It also has rotating exhibitions.

© DOMINIQUE LANDAU/ISTOCK.COM

The Israel Museum

GIVAT RAM AND REHAVYA
◖ The Israel Museum

From Talbiyeh, you can make your way to the unofficial museum district (called Museum Row) of Jerusalem, a bit off the main concentration of the city. The area is home to **The Israel Museum** (11 Ruppin St., near the intersection with Kaplan St., 02/670-8811, www.imj.org.il, 10am-5pm Sun.-Mon. and Wed.-Thurs., 4pm-9pm Tues., 10am-2pm Fri. and holiday eves, adult NIS50, student NIS37, senior, child, and disabled NIS25, NIS25 on repeat visit within 3 months, paid parking). Even among locals, the Israel Museum is lauded as one of the must-see spots in the city. Home to the Shrine of the Book and the Dead Sea Scrolls, the museum finished a major renovation in 2010 throughout its 20-acre campus to increase exhibition space, expand structures, and add exhibits.

The museum was founded in 1965 and is Israel's largest cultural institution. It also enjoys the renown of being one of the best art and archaeology museums in the world. It is home

to artifacts from prehistory to the present time, and has the most extensive biblical and Holy Land archaeology in the world.

Among the museum's most spectacular collections are the Dead Sea Scrolls, housed in the unusual-looking building on the museum campus called the Shrine of the Book. You will also want to see the outdoor model of the Second Temple, which covers almost one acre.

Bible Lands Museum

Just across the road is the **Bible Lands Museum** (25 Avraham Granot St., across from the Israel Museum, 02/561-1066, www.blmj.org, 9:30am-5:30pm Sun.-Thurs., closes at 9:30pm Wed., 9:30am-2pm Fri. and holiday eves, 10am-2pm Sat., NIS40). The Bible Lands Museum is the only museum in the world dedicated to the history of the Bible and the ancient Near East. The permanent exhibition, which is made up almost entirely of the former private collection of Dr. Elie Borowski, art collector and academic, spans from earliest civilization to the early Christian era in the lands of the Bible.

Bloomfield Museum of Science

Continue on toward the Hebrew University's Givat Ram campus and you will find the small, but extremely ambitious, **Bloomfield Museum of Science** (Hebrew University on Museum Blvd., 02/654-4888, www.mada.org.il, 10am-6pm Sun.-Thurs. and until 8pm in Aug., 10am-2pm Fri., 10am-3pm Sat., NIS40, senior NIS20), a very hands-on, interactive museum designed for children from a very young age to about age 12. Consisting of three above-ground levels and two below-ground levels and indoor and outdoor exhibits, the museum is full of science lessons that are built to be played and experimented with. Some of them are a bit worn from excessive play, but it's easy to move on to something else. The museum also hosts rotating exhibits, special events, and has an underground auditorium for shows.

There is a small cafeteria on premises, but limited seating. Visitors are allowed to bring in their own food and eat in a designated area with tables and chairs.

National Government Compound

East of the museum district is the **National Government Compound** and its grouping of significant government buildings, some of which are open for tourists to visit.

A visit to **The Knesset** (parliament) (intersection of Kaplan St. and Rothschild St. in Givat Ram, 02/675-3337, www.knesset.gov.il, tours@knesset.gov.il, tours 8:30am-2pm Sun.-Thurs., English tours 8:30am, noon, and 2pm Sun.-Thurs., reservations not needed for individuals, just show up 30 minutes before tour starts, free) should include one of the free, guided tours that are available, as you will be unable to enter the building unaccompanied. The tours include a general tour, the workings of the Knesset, art work in the Knesset, architecture, and a combined tour with the Supreme Court. The only independent tour is the Knesset Archaeology Park tour, which includes findings from the Second Temple period through the Ottoman period.

In walking distance is the **Supreme Court of Israel** (intersection of Yitzhak Rabin St. and Rothschild St. in Givat Ram, 02/675-9612, www.court.gov.il, English tours noon Sun.-Thurs., free), known for its grand architectural design created by the brother-sister team of Ram Karmi and Ada Karmi Melamede from Tel Aviv. Opened in 1992, the building includes several noteworthy points of interest, including a massive restored mosaic, the panoramic window, and the unique library that is an architectural representation of the Second Temple. The overall structure was created to integrate post-modern architectural elements and reflect Jerusalem's rich architectural history. It was also designed to express the values of justice, law, and righteousness.

Monastery of the Cross

Just south of the government complex is the **Monastery of the Cross** (enter on Shota Rustaveli St. in Rehavya Valley, 02/679-0961, 10am-4:30pm Mon.-Sat., NIS10), rebuilt most recently in the 11th century. Resembling a fort, the Greek Orthodox monastery is on the site where Christian tradition says the tree that made the cross Jesus was crucified on grew.

It was originally built in the 6th century, destroyed in the Persian invasion in 614, and rebuilt again in 1038. An important Christian theological seminary through the 20th century, it has 16th- and 17th-century frescoes and mosaics and includes a courtyard café for visitors.

◖ Yad Vashem

Nothing can prepare you for the enormous psychological and emotional impact of visiting this spot. More of an institution than a museum, **Yad Vashem** (enter the Yad Vashem campus via the Holland Junction, on the Herzl Route opposite the entrance to Mount Herzl and the descent to Ein Kerem, 02/644-3802, www.yadvashem.org, 9am-5pm Sun.-Wed., 9am-8pm Thurs., 9am-2pm Fri. and holiday eves, closed Sat. and all Jewish holidays, free, no children under 10 years old in Holocaust History Museum and main exhibits, last visitor one hour before closing, paid parking, free shuttle from Mount Herzl stop on the light rail) is an astounding window on Jewish history and culture.

Because of the size of Yad Vashem and the amount of information, it is advisable to plan to spend at least half a day here. Start with the Holocaust History Museum, the building behind the main entrance to Yad Vashem. You can rent an audio guide (NIS20) and buy a guide map (NIS10).

When you are ready to take a break, go downstairs to the kosher cafeteria for a coffee or ice cream and take in the panoramic view of the Jerusalem Forest. Hold off on buying a meal, though, as you might be disappointed in what you get for the price.

Also make sure to take in the Holocaust Art Museum, Hall of Remembrance, and Hall of Names.

Unless you are near a light rail station, getting to Yad Vashem without a vehicle can be a little tricky. From Yad Vashem it is simple to take the light rail back to City Center. From the Valley of the Cross, it is about a 15-minute drive (insist your taxi driver use the meter, as they will assume you are a tourist because of the destination, and try to negotiate a predetermined rate).

Herzl Museum

At the entrance to the Yad Vashem campus, is Mount Herzl's **Herzl Museum** (Herzl Blvd., Mt. Herzl, 02/632-1515, www.herzl.org, 8:30am-6pm Sun.-Wed. with last tour at 5pm, 8:30am-7pm Thurs., 8:30am-1pm Fri. with last tour at 12:15pm, tours must be arranged in advance or on a first-come first-served basis, NIS25, child NIS20). The museum gives visitors an audio-visual history of Zionist leader Theodor Herzl through a one-hour program.

SPECIAL TOURS
Tour Guides

As with any major tourist destination, there are a number of fly-by-night tour guides and companies in Jerusalem selling their services. A good rule of thumb is to work with someone who is a licensed tour guide.

The official travel website of Israel (http://goisrael.com) has a complete listing of tour guides authorized by the Ministry of Tourism who offer services in a wide range of languages. You can also choose a guide who has a car as part of their services. Check under the "Before You Go" tab on the website, and choose "Tour Guide Search" from the left tab.

Asher Altshul (052/232-3219, www.asheraltshul.com) is a private licensed tour guide based in Jerusalem who is fluent in English and Hebrew.

Sandeman's New Europe (www.newjerusalemtours.com) is a large, international company with a good reputation that offers a variety of tours in Jerusalem, including free daily tours of the Old City. They can be contacted online in advance of any special tour you'd like to arrange.

Nature Tours

The **Society for the Protection of Nature in Israel** (02/625-2357 or 03/638-8688, www.teva.org.il) gives urban walking tours in English, but not on a fixed schedule. You must call to see if an English tour is available, as they typically only take groups of 10 or more. Their website has a green map that contains useful information about green spaces within the city. They also give ecotours throughout Israel, including relatively cheap places to stay called field schools in more remote regions of the country. They can also be contacted in their U.S. offices.

Archaeological Tours

For tours with an archaeological twist, try **Archaeological Seminars Institute Ltd.** (02/586-2011, www.archesem.com, US$200 and up pp, plus VAT and entrance fees) for one of their varied half- and full-day private walking tours for up to 10 people. Some of the tour types include archaeology as it relates to religion, and retracing the footsteps of ancient Jewish residents of the city.

Bus Tours

For those who would rather ride, Egged bus line's **Double-Decker Bus Tour** (www.egged.

FREE SATURDAY TOURS

© GENEVIEVE BELMAKER

Sunlight streams over a stone wall in Jerusalem's German Colony.

Saturday is one of the best days of the week to go on a free tour in Jerusalem. Most of the city shuts down and doesn't start opening again until late Saturday evening so there is very little foot and vehicular traffic. It's also a good chance to explore some of Jerusalem's neighborhoods (for detailed tour listings by type, go to www.itraveljerusalem.com).

Several types of three-hour-long Saturday tours depart at 10am from Safra Square (24-26 Yafo St., 02/531-4600, free).

· **The Explore Ethiopia Tour** explores Eliezer Ben Yehuda's old neighborhood (he was instrumental in reviving the Hebrew language) and also goes through the Russian Compound, Beit Anna Ticho, Ethiopia Street, Bnei Brit Library, and Beit Tavor Street.

· **The German Colony Tour** takes you through the neighborhood built by German Templars at the end of the 19th century and includes a route from King David Street down through Emek Refaim Valley.

· **The Hanevi'im Tour** takes visitors through the history of Hanevi'im Street and its ties to the British, Germans, Italians, and Ethiopians. Some of the buildings on the tour help tell the stories of famous leaders, ambassadors, doctors, poets, artists, and hermits.

· **The Kidron Valley Tour** explores the burial grounds of the Second Temple period, the Kidron River and its streams, and the story behind four rock-hewn graves here. The route goes through Jaffa Gate, the Jewish Quarter, Dung Gate, Kidron Valley viewpoint, and Kidron Valley proper.

· **The Muslim Quarter Tour** takes you from Damascus Gate in the Old City to the Western Wall.

· **The Rehavya Walking Tour** includes national institutions in the Rehavya neighborhood, including a monastery and the President of Israel's home.

· **Sandeman's New Europe Free Jerusalem Tour** meets just inside the Old City's Jaffa Gate by the tourism information stand (8:45am and 11am Fri., 8:45am, 11am, and 2pm Sat.-Thurs.). Look for the guides in the red Sandeman's T-shirts; guides might encourage you to tip them.

co.il, from 9am Sun.-Thurs., NIS60-130), which is Route 99, could be a great way to see the city if you're independent enough to hop on and off the big red bus at some of the 24 stops that it makes. One- and two-day passes are available, and stops include several major tourist spots in Jerusalem, including Yad Vashem, the Botanical Garden, several stops around the Old City, the National Government Compound, and the Israel Museum. It also includes local spots, like Malha Mall. Each seat is equipped with headphone guides in several languages. If you are organized enough and like to stay on a schedule, this could be an efficient way to hit several major sites with less transportation hassle and cost.

UNDERGROUND ARCHAEOLOGICAL TOURS

Above the ground, Jerusalem is rich and fascinating. Underground lies another layer of the city that will convince even the most frugal traveler of the value of paying for a tour. These are some of the best underground tours in Jerusalem:

- **Burnt House:** Part of a larger complex under the Old City's Jewish Quarter, the remarkable charred remains date back to AD 70 (www.jewish-quarter.org.il).

- **Herodian Quarter and Wohl Archaeological Museum:** The basement of a Jewish seminary covers the remains of a mansion

from the Second Temple period (www.jewish-quarter.org.il).

- **Hezekiah's Tunnel:** You can wade through the water in this 2,700-year-old tunnel, part of the City of David, for 580 yards (www.cityofdavid.org.il).

- **Warren's Shaft:** An underground waterworks system that dates back to the age of the kings of Judea was discovered in 1867 by British engineer Sir Charles Warren (www.cityofdavid.org.il).

- **The Western Wall Tunnels:** This 75-minute tour explores hidden layers of the Western Wall (http://english.thekotel.org).

Entertainment and Events

Jerusalem, with its emphasis on spiritual and family life, has not typically been known for its thriving nightlife scene. But new initiatives by the city municipality and new ventures by industrious business owners are changing that. If you are looking for nightlife, you can find a nice variety of bars, pubs, and live music clubs as well as performing arts venues, although they are a bit off the beaten path or concentrated in City Center. If you are looking for nightlife, be prepared to go to a bit more effort to find something worthwhile.

LIVE MUSIC BARS
City Center

Surprisingly, Machane Yehuda (the *shuk*) has varied nightlife tucked into its nooks and crannies and can be a good place to start an evening of bar hopping. After the market closes for shopping, it keeps going for dining, drinks, and music.

Start with **Casino de Paris** (Machane Yehuda 3, Machane Yehuda market, 02/650-4235, noon-2am, Sun.-Thurs., closed for Shabbat and opens again after 9pm on Sat., no cover), which was once the gathering place

for British officers during the British mandate period. Now revived to cater to the bar scene, it features a unique menu of cocktails and a limited fish and vegetable menu.

Not far from the *shuk,* toward Ben Yehuda Street, is **Avram Bar** (97 Yafo St., 07/445-0701, 11am till last customer daily, closed for Shabbat, no cover), offering business lunch deals at affordable prices. It is best to reserve a table in advance for the evening. It features an incredible 1,500 different musicians and artists a year from all musical genres including rock, blues, jazz, indie, electronic music, flamenco, Andalusian, and Indian music. Established by music lover Yossi Vazana, it has a varied kosher meat menu by chef Itamar Halawa.

Near Ben Yehuda Street is **Birman Musical Bistro** (8 Dorot Rishonim St., 02/623-6115, 2pm-3am Sun.-Thurs., no cover), a restaurant-bar with a nightly offering of jazz music by local musicians and a cozy atmosphere with a loft and couches. The menu features a selection of non-kosher Middle Eastern meat dishes.

Blaze Sport 'N' Rock Bar (23 Hillel St., 054/816-5488, http://blazebar.co.il, 4pm-2am daily, no cover), just south of Ben Yehuda

Street, is considered to be the closest thing to a biker bar in the city and is owned by one of Jerusalem's leading thrash-metal musicians, Shworchtse Chaye's lead vocalist. Every night of the week the bar features live rock music and alternative bands, and the menu includes over 30 draught and bottled beers. They have live big screen sports broadcasts.

The trendy **HaTaklit** (7 Heleni HaMalka St. 02/624-4073, 8pm-last customer, no cover) was founded by three music industry Jerusalemites who adorned the walls with vinyl record sleeves. The full bar serves cocktails, and there is beer on tap, English football screenings, live music, DJs, and independent performers. The happy hour (4:30pm-9pm daily) includes buy one tap beer, get one free.

German Colony and Bak'a

Just off one of Jerusalem's main streets is the stylish and upscale **Zappa** (28 Derech Hevron, 03/762-6666, www.jvpvc.com and go to JVP Community, price varies by show but generally NIS50 and up). This is the Jerusalem branch of a set of live music venues with locations in Tel Aviv, Herzliya, and Binyamina. It features high-quality local and international music, light food and drinks, and a sizable stage for performers situated within a close distance to the audience, as well as some major names in jazz, rock, and reggae.

CLUBS
Talpiyot

An adventurous spirit is required to trek out to Talpiyot at night if you are a visitor to Jerusalem. Off the typical tourist's radar, Talpiyot offers some interesting choices for music.

17 (17 Haoman St., 02/678-1658, 9pm-3am Tues., 9:30pm-5am Thurs., 9:30pm-3am Sat.) is a warehouse-size club featuring Israeli music on Tuesdays, house music on Thursdays, and funky music on Saturdays.

Pierre 28 (28 Pierre Koenig St., 050/244-4204, 8pm-last customer, no cover) is a salsa club, and oddly also a venue for Bar Mitzvah parties and other events.

The **Yellow Submarine** (13 Herkevim St., 02/679-4040, http://yellowsubmarine.org.il, shows daily from around 8pm or later, entrance NIS30 and up depending on show) bills itself as a multidisciplinary music center and has a varied offering of live musical performances. It also houses rehearsal rooms, recording studios, and an annual international music showcase.

City Center

The **Bass Club** (1 Hahistadrut St., 050/477-7791, http://bassclub.wordpress.com, daily 8pm until last customer, cover varies from about NIS30, call in advance) is known for its variety of music, featuring bass music as well as reggae and dancehall music nights.

BARS, PUBS, AND WINE BARS
City Center

Tucked inside the Mamilla Hotel is the posh **Mirror Bar** (11 King Solomon St., 2nd Fl., 02/548-2230, www.mamillahotel.com, 8pm-last customer Sun.-Thurs., 9:30pm-last customer Sat., no cover), which caters to the slick set in town with its stylish interior and a selection of cigars that can be enjoyed in a glassed-in smoking room.

Dublin Irish Pub (4 Shamai St., 02/622-3612, http://dub.rest-e.co.il, 5pm-3am Sat.-Thurs., 5pm-5am Fri., no cover) is part of a chain in Israel. The Jerusalem pub features Gothic and Irish design elements with heavy wooden furniture from Ireland and serves 300 drinks and 70 different beers (18 on tap) and has several flat screen TVs for sports. There is a happy hour (5pm-8pm daily) and a menu of non-kosher food.

Heder Vehetsi (31 Yafo St., 054/642-4242, 6pm until late daily, no cover), in the Feingold Courtyard off Jaffa Road, is a popular hangout for university students.

Mike's Place (33 Yafo St., 054/5313255, www.mikesplacebars.com, 11am-last customer Sun.-Thurs. and until 2pm on Fri. and opens after 8pm on Sat., no cover) is very well known and caters to an international crowd. It features booths and wood paneling, big screen TVs, and there is a kosher food menu, a global selection of beers, and a daily happy hour.

Bellwood Bar (Yosef Rivlin and Hasorag St. 5, 050/486-3333, http://eng.bellwood.co.il, 5pm-midnight daily, no cover) gets its inspiration from traditional English pubs and is decorated all in wood. It features over 100 varieties of whiskey and 15 international beers on tap, as well as a food menu of classic pub items like fish and chips and hamburgers.

PERFORMING ARTS
Cultural Centers

If you're in the mood for something with an ethnic cultural flavor, **Beit Avi Chai** (44 King George St., 02/621-5300, www.bac.org.il, 1pm-9:30pm Sun.-Thurs., 9:30am-noon Fri.) features speakers and artists, including Israeli musicians every Monday, a summer music concert series of Israeli musicians in the courtyard, weekly Saturday night concerts by Jerusalem and Israeli musical favorites, and more.

The **Gerard Behar Center** (11 Bezalel St., 02/625-1139, http://gerard-behar.jerusalem.muni.il) is home to two acclaimed dance troupes, Kolben Dance Co. and Vertigo, and also plays host to independent productions and collaborations including their hot jazz series.

You can also find very well done performances in English hosted by the World Union for Progressive Judaism at **Beit Shmuel** (6 Shama St. off King David, 02/620-3427, www.beitshmuel.com). They play host to a wide variety of staged performances including plays, musicals, ethnic music, and educational and cultural activities.

One of Jerusalem's finest centers for cultural activities is **Mishkenot Sha'ananim** (9 Yemin Moshe St., 02/629-2220, www.mishkenot.org.il), which hosts a wide variety of festivals, screenings, and lectures, and is home to the INFO Press Club for foreign journalists.

Theaters and Cinemas

The **Jerusalem International Convention Center** (1 Shazar Blvd., 02/655-8537, www.iccjer.co.il/en) has the largest auditorium in Israel

with 3,000 seats and is the home of the Israel Philharmonic Orchestra while in Jerusalem. It is part of a larger complex called Binyanei Ha'uma that also houses the **Globus Movie Theater** (02/622-3685).

The **Jerusalem Theatre** (20 David Marcus, 02/560-5757, www.jerusalem-theatre.co.il), with its five halls, hosts everything from musical performances to dance, festivals, plays, and films, and is home to the Jerusalem Symphony Orchestra.

For mostly stage performances of plays and musicals, the **The Khan Theatre** (2 David Remez Sq., 02/671-8281 www.khan.co.il) offers a variety of performances in a quaint and intimate setting, including special children's performances.

A nearby venue, the **Old Train Theater** (Liberty Bell Park, 02/561-8514, www.traintheater.co.il) is home to the annual International Festival of Puppet Theater and a variety of other shows geared toward children.

VISUAL ARTS
Movie Theaters

Several venues in Jerusalem are dedicated to movies, although their presentation has a decidedly European twist. Take note that some theaters will give you an assigned seat, which is generally okay to move from once you can see where empty seats are. Also be warned that food and drinks are not always allowed inside the theater.

Lev Smadar (4 Lloyd George St., 02/560-6039, www.lev.co.il, daily, NIS38) is situated in the upper-class area of the German Colony among houses and shows American and European films with English subtitles (usually). It is fronted by a wonderful café that offers everything from pizza to popcorn and drinks that you can take into the movie.

The **Jerusalem Cinematheque** (11 Derech Hevron, 02/565-4356, www.jer-cin.org.il, NIS38) is an upper-crust movie theater that shows films both old and new from Europe and America, as well as some television episodes, independent films, and live in HD performances.

There is a concessions area, but no food is allowed in the theaters. Many movie-goers tend to eat at the Cinematheque's adjacent Lavan restaurant before or after a film.

The **Globus Movie Theater** (1 Shazar Blvd., 02/622-3685) and **Rav Hen** (19 Haoman, 02/679-2799) offer more standard-style theaters with multiplex settings and more mainstream American movies.

Light Show

The Tower of David Museum hosts a **Night Spectacular** (south of the Old City's Jaffa Gate, 02/626-5333, www.towerofdavid.org. il, 9pm and 10:30pm, adult NIS55, senior and child NIS45, or museum admission plus show adult NIS70, senior and child NIS55), where the walls of the Old City are used for a show of lights and images, accompanied by music.

FESTIVALS AND EVENTS

In the past few years, the number and types of festivals and music events taking place in the city have increased dramatically.

Spring

The annual **International Writer's Festival** (writersfestival.mouse.co.il/en) is relatively new to Jerusalem, but its scope and scale are huge. The festival, which is held at Mishkenot Sha'ananim features a huge number of events, including talks with famous authors, film screenings, and events for kids. Many of the events are in English.

Check out the **Jerusalem Season of Culture** (www.jerusalemseason.com/en) for a wide listing of major events taking place starting in May with the mostly English-language International Writer's Festival and ending in September. It also includes Contact Point All Night Art Festival, Balabasta festival in the *shuk,* and many more.

Summer

The **Jerusalem International Film Festival** (various locations, 02/565-4350, www.jff.org.

il, July, NIS42) has been running for almost 30 years and is primarily focused on Israeli film.

Just as charming as it sounds, the **Jerusalem Beer Festival** (Old Train Station, 050/594-8844, www.jerusalembeer.com/en) has been in action for almost eight years and is staged on the grounds of the Old Train Station. Featuring about 30 different types of beers, both international and local, the festival lasts two days and includes live music.

The **Jerusalem Woodstock Revival** (Kraft Stadium, 02/623-6443, www.woodstockrevival.com, Aug., NIS85-140) features musical acts performing covers from Pink Floyd, Neil Young, Bob Dylan, and others.

The **Zion Reggae Festival** (Gan Sacher, 03/602-3619, Aug. annually) features major reggae performers including Ziggy Marley, Alpha Blondy, and Barrington Levy.

A bit more refined crowd can be found at the **Jerusalem Wine Festival** (Billy Rose Garden of the Israel Museum, 02/625-9703, 8:30pm-11pm, NIS80/evening pp, includes a wine glass, unlimited tasting, and admission to the museum galleries until 9pm on Tues.), which takes place over three days at the end of July. The festival brings together some of the best wines from Israel's varied collection of local wineries.

The **End of the Summer Festival** (20 David Marcus, 02/560-5755, www.jerusalem-theatre.co.il) is three days at the end of August of Israeli and foreign artists and performers. The festival consists of some of the latest work in performance art and film. It's hugely popular amongst locals.

Fall

The **Jerusalem International Chamber Music Festival** (YMCA Mary Nathaniel Hall, 02/625-0444, www.jcmf.org.il/en, Sept., NIS80-150) is a several days-long concert series that highlights a different area of classical music every year.

For a close encounter with an Israeli VIP, go to the **President's Open House** (President's residence, Hanasi St. in Talbiyeh, Sukkot week) and be received by the President of Israel in his traditional Sukkah. It's an old tradition that is not known to many tourists.

A series of other events take place during Sukkot week, check with the Jerusalem Municipality (www.jerusalem.muni.il) for details and listings of events, as the exact dates change every year.

The **Abu Ghosh Vocal Music Festival** (www.agfestival.co.il/en) takes place every year in the Arab village of Abu Ghosh. Concerts are performed in the 12th-century Crusader-Benedictine Church in the heart of the village, and at the Kiryat Ye'arim Church.

Winter

Taking place for almost 30 years, **The Jerusalem International Book Fair** brings together agents and exhibitors. The festival's Jerusalem Prize is awarded to a writer who exhibits the principles of individual freedom in society.

Shopping

Jerusalem has a wide variety of shops, with an emphasis on religious ornaments and objects, clothing, and locally handmade ceramics. Types of shopping can be divided mainly into Judaica, antiques, jewelry, gifts and souvenirs, regionally designed and manufactured clothing, and outdoor markets. Home decor and houseware shops, shopping malls, and furniture stores are largely concentrated in the neighborhood of Talpiyot, which is difficult to reach without a car, confusing to navigate, and frequented mostly by locals. When buying anything of value, do not leave the shop without the proper paperwork for customs, and also

© GIDON BELMAKER

Trinkets and souvenirs are easy to find in the Old City.

make sure to ask for the **tax rebate** calculation on your receipt.

THE OLD CITY
Jaffa Gate

If you enter through Jaffa Gate, follow the flow of foot traffic as it goes past the **Ministry of Tourism Information Center** (1 Jaffa St., 02/627-1422, 8:30am-5pm Sun.-Thurs., 8:30am-noon Fri., closed Sat.) to HaNotsrim Street, a narrow pedestrian street in the Christian Quarter where you can find **religious items, souvenirs, clothing, and jewelry** that should satisfy any urge you have for doing a minor shopping and bargaining. If you stay on the main road from Jaffa Gate (David St.) until you reach the second to last right turn, you'll get to *HaKardo* or the **Cardo** (02/626-5900 ext. 102, business area and shops 8am-6pm Sun.-Thurs., 8am-4pm Fri.) with its numerous high-end gift shops and galleries for Judaica. This is the border between the Jewish and Armenian Quarters, the latter of which has some interesting shops that sell jewelry, antiques, and textiles.

Damascus Gate

For a vibrant shopping experience (as in, loud and extremely physical), just inside of Damascus Gate at the intersection of Beit Habad Street and El Wad Hagai Street, is the gateway to the **Arab Souk,** where you can find trinkets, clothes, spices, sweets, jewelry, raw meat, and other food. Watch out for people running through with carts!

Mamilla

Though not technically connected, the Old City and Mamilla definitely feed off of each other. Go down the stairs from the Old City's Jaffa Gate plaza and you'll reach the soothing commercial calm atmosphere of **Mamilla** (street entrance is at the intersection of Shlomtsiyon HaMalka and Shlomo HaMelech, just across the street from the David Citadel Hotel, www.mamillaavenue.com, shop hours are generally 9am-10pm Sun.-Thurs., 9am-3pm Fri.).

Mamilla shopping center offers high-end stores, air conditioning, restaurants, and restrooms just steps from the Old City.

SHOPPING IN THE OLD CITY

© GIDON BELMAKER

Tourists wander through the Old City, which is full of places to shop.

Shopping in the Old City can be a fun or intimidating experience. In many cases, aggressive shop owners won't allow you more than two seconds to glance at their products before pushing you to buy. It is also a notoriously expensive place for English-speaking customers, particularly Americans.

Be prepared in advance to do the dance of bargaining if you plan to buy something, which might include literally walking away to get the best price. You can bargain if you are confident, but the best bet for avoiding some serious unplanned spending is to decide in advance on your limit.

There are seemingly endless streets of shops and cavernous stalls that are open seven days a week, mostly selling very similar items. They fall mainly into the categories of jewelry, religious items, souvenirs, clothing, antiques, and food. Most visitors enter the Old City area from Jaffa Gate and turn down HaNotsrim Street, a narrow pedestrian street in the Christian Quarter.

A good approach to shopping in this area is to walk past vendors and stores, and only slow down if you are seriously interested in buying something. Otherwise you will spend a great deal of time extricating yourself from aggressive negotiations with shop owners.

Shops selling antiques and artifacts, including Roman-glass inlaid jewelry and other locally handmade items, can be found mainly in the Christian and Jewish Quarters, although such stores are scattered throughout all four quarters. Be very cautious when purchasing antiques. You will need the appropriate legal certificate to take the item out of the country, largely due to problems with grave robbers and antique theft from archaeological sites. Check with the information center about the proper documentation necessary or visit the Israeli Antiquities Authority website.

Most vendors are more than willing to take American dollars, and you can find nice scarves, sweets, and cute trinkets. One of the great advantages to shopping in this area is that almost everything is open on the weekend.

MAMILLA'S NUMBERED STONES

Throughout Jerusalem you will see stone buildings with the curious characteristic of sequential numbers scrolled by hand on each stone. These are historically significant buildings that have been disassembled, preserved, and put back together. The numbers have been left to indicate the act of preservation and to distinguish the building among its neighbors as having special historic value. It is also a way to honor the authenticity of Jerusalem as an ancient city.

Stroll through Mamilla Alrov Quarter, and you will see five such examples of buildings preserved in this way, either in their entirety or by being incorporated into new buildings. The preservation was done under the guidance of the Israel Antiquities Authority.

Two particular buildings in Mamilla have been left in place. The Stern House, situated at about the center of Mamilla's pedestrian promenade, was built in 1877 and hosted Zionist Theodore Herzl on his only trip to Israel. The Clark House was constructed by American evangelicals in the late 19th century.

Many shops here are Israeli or international chain stores for clothing, jewelry, and makeup, which makes it a convenient place to go if you find yourself in need of some clothes while in Jerusalem. There is also a chain pharmacy for SuperPharm. Brands represented include Rolex, MAC, H. Stern, Nike, Polo Ralph Lauren, Gap, Nautica, bebe, and Tommy Hilfiger, as well as local brands like Fox, Castro, Ronen Chen, and Steimatzky Books. You can also come across musical street performers here, which makes it a fun place to wander and windowshop, and it stays active late into the evening.

Take a look inside the **Eden Fine Art** store (Alrov Mamilla Ave., 02/624-2506, www.edengallery.com) for a glimpse at this international art representative. The shop sponsors artwork, sculptures, and photographs from select leading Israeli and international artists. The bright, small shop caters to upper-crust clients and art collectors, and has some interesting pieces from Israeli artists.

The **Stern House** is a charming and interesting preserved and reconstructed building that played host to Theodor Herzl during his visit to Jerusalem in 1898, and now houses one of the **Steimatzky Books** chain stores (02/625-7268), which has a good selection of English books and magazines, and a **Café Café** (02/624-4773) chain coffee shop, a place to get a bite to eat or coffee.

One of the leading jewelry chains in Israel,

Miller Jewelry (02/622-3414) has a store on the smaller end in Mamilla with a highly selective number of their finest pieces.

CITY CENTER
Zion Square

Shopping in City Center rotates on the axis of **Zion Square,** which runs between **King George Street** and **Yafo Street** and is at the foot of both **Ben Yehuda Street** and **Yoel Moshe Salomon** pedestrian malls. All of these shopping areas are mostly shut down for Shabbat and Jewish holidays, with the exception of a couple of 24-hour markets and a handful of coffee shops and restaurants. Much of the shopping in the area is limited to a few types of stores that sell souvenirs and Judaica, embroidered *kippas* and souvenir T-shirts, camera equipment, electronics and housewares, and local brands of clothing and shoes.

At the top of Zion Square, check out **The Book Gallery** (6 Schatz St. at corner of 26 King George St., 02/623-1087, www.bookgallery.co.il, 9am-7pm Sun.-Thurs., 9am-2pm Fri.), the largest second-hand bookstore in Israel. It includes two floors with a separate section for old and rare books and a large basement.

Southeast of Zion Square

Small and mostly housed with books and materials in French, **Vice-Versa** (1 Shim'on Ben Shetach St., 02/624-4412, www.viceversalib.

Yafo Street is pedestrian and light rail traffic only and serves as an artery between several major shopping points in City Center.

com, 9am-6pm Sun.-Thurs., 9am-1:30pm Fri.) is a sweet shop with a warm atmosphere that highlights the fact that Jerusalem has a subculture of French residents. Mostly fun for browsing, the shop does sell some gift-related items like wrapping paper and cards and also has some interesting items for children.

Adjacent to the base of Zion Square, where it abuts Yafo Street and then around to the right, is **Nachalat Shiva** (Yoel Moshe Solomon St. and Ma'alot Nachalat Shiva St. between Yafo St. and the southern and eastern border of Rivlin St.), full of numerous art galleries, Judaica and jewelry stores, locally handmade ceramics, and unique souvenirs. This pedestrian mall is something in between Mamilla and Zion Square, catering to upper middle-class tourists. It has a surprisingly wide array of restaurants that range from fine dining to common fare.

For a unique experience, **Gaya Games** (7 Yoel Moshe Solomon St. at the end of Shamai St., 054/392-0115, www.gaya-game.com, 10am-10pm Sun.-Thurs., 9am-3pm Fri., 7pm-11pm Sat.) has a cozy atmosphere of unique

wooden games and brain teasers that surround you when you descend their entrance steps. The cavernous feel of their Jerusalem store, one of four locations in Israel, caters to adult customers who are interested in challenging play. Their **Creative Thinking Seminars** (contact Galit, 03/903-3122, galit@gaya-game.com) allow you to play with some of their games and engage in challenging your brain.

The Cadim Ceramics Gallery (4 Yoel Moshe Solomon St., 02/623-4869, www.cadim-gallery.co.il/Eng, 10am-10pm Sun.-Thurs., 9am-3pm Fri.) is a small, charming gallery and shop that serves as the storefront for a cooperative of 15 Israeli ceramists, who also run and staff it. Objects are displayed in groups by artist and every purchase includes the story of the artist. Prices start on the affordable end and go up, and objects include functional pottery, decorative objects, sculptural pieces, Judaica, and jewelry.

Just around the corner, **The Eighth Note** (12 Ze'ev Raban St.) is located by the small, black-and-white sign on its storefront. This side-street basement store has a nice collection of Arabic, Greek, Turkish, and other Middle Eastern CDs

© GENEVIEVE BELMAKER

Zion Square is a popular tourist destination in City Center with a variety of shops, bookstores, and restaurants.

and DVDs. The friendly and knowledgeable sales staff allow you to listen to selections that you're interested in buying and will do their best to make sure you don't leave empty-handed.

South of Zion Square

For Jewish jewelry and Judaica, **Baltinester Bros.** (31 Yafo St., 02/625-2967, www.baltinesterjewelry.com, 10am-7:30pm Sun.-Thurs., 10am-2:30pm Fri.) is a family owned and operated business that opened in 1949 and is currently run by two brothers. The store's unassuming storefront belies the high-quality jewelry and Judaica contained inside. The small store is packed with all types of jewelry inspired by Israel and Jerusalem. Baltinester specializes in custom-made pieces and has a wide range of prices for its varied customer base, including an extensive online storefront.

OUTDOOR MARKETS

Every Friday you can find vendors at the outdoor **Bezalel Art Fair** (Schatz St. and Bor Shiber Garden by the Mashbir, www.bezalelfair.co.il, 10am-4pm Fri.) selling paintings,

wood crafts, textiles, jewelry, glass works, special and unique handicrafts, and food. The lively fair consists of carefully chosen vendors to maintain an overall atmosphere and a varied selection of art and artistic displays. Staged next door to the historic campus of the Bezalal Art Academy, the outdoor fair also includes a tour at noon from Bezalel to City Center.

Also on Fridays you can find **Emek Refaim's Friday Outdoor Street Market** (across the street from the Coffee Mill at 23 Emek Refaim St., 10am-2pm Fri.) that includes vendors selling jewelry, ceramics, toys, food, and a wide variety of other items for very affordable prices.

SHOPPING MALLS
Jerusalem (Malha) Mall

Farther away from the center of town, the massive **Jerusalem (Malha) Mall** (Agudat Sport Beitar 1 across from Teddy Stadium, 02/679-1333, www.jerusalem.azrieli.com, 9am-10pm Sun.-Thurs. and until 3pm Fri.) is reminiscent of a southern California shopping mall in its size, parking, range of stores, and dining options. With 215 stores, it is Jerusalem's largest and nicest mall.

Sports and Recreation

Jerusalem's location in the mountains at about 2,500 feet means that even in the hot summer months it boasts a cool, soothing breeze in the mornings and evenings. This makes outdoor activities a common pastime, including visiting natural springs, hiking, biking, swimming, camping, and cooking out (which is practically a national sport). Many Jerusalemites enjoy taking long walks through the city's scenic (and often hilly) terrain. Playing soccer, having a picnic, or simply sitting and relaxing are common.

PARKS AND GARDENS
Gan Sacher
At little over half a mile long, **Gan Sacher** (between Ben Zvi Blvd. and the Knesset, 24 hours daily, free) is easily the park with the largest expanse of open green space in Jerusalem. As a result, it is a staging ground for major outdoor concerts during the summer, and on major national holidays it is covered with a haze of smoke and full of families cooking out. It is home to two play areas for children, basketball and tennis courts, soccer fields, a skateboarding park, a jogging path, and a set of tunnels that run under Ben Zvi Boulevard and have been used in recent years for graffiti by local artists.

Follow the woodland paths up the hill toward the Knesset near the center of the park and you'll come upon the **Bird Observatory** (02/653-7374, www.jbo.org.il, 24 hours daily, free), run by the Society for the Protection of Nature in Israel. The observatory is home to the Israel national bird-ringing center (schedule online) and features a window with an opening for viewing the myriad wild animals that spend time in this richly preserved and fortified natural habitat. Try going at night to watch the nocturnal animals by moonlight.

Liberty Bell Park
Just at the edge of the German Colony is **Liberty Bell Park** (crossroads of Keren HaYesod and King David St. down to the beginning of Emek Refaim St., 24 hours daily, free). It is not the most stunning park unless you happen to visit in the spring while the purple wisteria flowers at the eastern end are in full bloom. The western end of the park is home to a very accurate reproduction of the Liberty Bell, but it has been vandalized in recent years. The park includes several different playgrounds, walking paths, basketball courts, and picnic areas. A fairly unique feature of the park is that both Arab and Jewish residents regularly come here to relax and play. It also hosts festivals, performances, and fairs, and is home to the Train Theater.

Railway Park
Parallel to Emek Refaim Street is the **Railway Park** (Chan Station, through Bethlehem Rd. and up to the Oranim Junction, 24 hours daily, free entry, paid neighborhood parking), which gives visitors to Jerusalem a glimpse into local life and architecture. At just over one mile long, the Railway Park is a natural favorite spot for Jerusalemites to walk, jog, bike, and get from place to place. The park, which is in its third phase of construction, was built around a blighted area that was home to old railroad tracks leading to the now defunct Jerusalem Railway Station. Consisting of a two-way bicycle path and a boarded walkway covering the old railroad tracks, the park has lovely plants, flowers, and grass along its entire route. It is an important shortcut through the residential areas of the Germany Colony and Bak'a, and has easy side street access to tourist hotspot Emek Refaim Street. The park is best enjoyed in the mornings before 10am or in the evenings after the sun starts to go down.

Bloomfield Garden
Literally across the street from Independence Park is **Bloomfield Garden** (runs along King David St. from the base of Keren HaYesod St. to Elimelech Admoni St. and west to Mishkenot

© GENEVIEVE BELMAKER

Independence Park in City Center

Sha'ananim St., 24 hours daily, free). The park features a unique landmark on its southern end of a fountain with distinct bronze lions encircling it (the symbol of Jerusalem). If you walk north through the park, which has a good amount of shaded areas, but is very hilly, you will come upon the venerable artist colony and center Mishkenot Sha'ananim and the little-known **Gozlan Garden,** a beautiful, small park with fountains behind the King David Hotel.

Wohl Rose Garden

This spot would be easy to miss if you weren't looking for it. The **Wohl Rose Garden** (Government Center opposite the Knesset, 02/563-7233, www.jerusalem.muni.il, 24 hours daily, free, paid parking) covers an area of almost 20 acres and is home to about 400 varieties of roses on 15,000 bushes. The park also has a variety of charming nooks and crannies, including an observation point and an ornamental pool. The park can be reached by foot from Gan Sacher park through a footpath in the woods, or by car at the intersections of

Kaplan Street and Rothschild Street. It is also adjacent to other major tourist spots, including the Supreme Court and the Israeli Parliament.

Independence Park

Just on the edge of City Center, you will find the massive, sprawling expanse of **Independence Park** (bordered by Gershon Agron St. and King George St., 24 hours daily, free), which has several good places to sit and enjoy the shade. Its terraced landscaping is dotted with a waterway system of an artificial creek and pools and is frequented by families and children, but is rarely crowded except for the rare outdoor concert or event. The American Consulate is just across Gershon Agron Street. The park makes for a nice shortcut if you are trying to get to the action in City Center.

Talbiyeh Rose Garden

Talbiyeh has a few interesting museums, gardens, and buildings. If you are on foot, you can pass through **Gan HaShoshanim** (Rose Garden Park) (intersection of Tsvi Graetz St.

and Dubnov St. in Talbiyeh, walking distance from Emek Refaim St. 24 hours daily, free), which was built in the 1930s during the British mandate and was used for official state ceremonies for a time after the founding of the state of Israel. The park has classic landscaping and a fountain, with benches and cool, shaded corners to rest on a hot day.

Jerusalem Botanical Garden

Many visitors to Jerusalem enjoy a trip to the **Jerusalem Botanical Garden** (1 Yehuda Burla St., 073/243-8914, http://en.botanic.co.il, 9am-7pm Sun.-Thurs., 9am-5pm Fri. and holiday eves, 9am-6pm Sat. and holidays, hours and price subject to change for special events, adult NIS30, senior and child NIS20). With its 30 acres of landscaped grounds that include a renowned bonsai collection, a small, charming pond greets visitors at the entrance, where they can also sit out and enjoy a cup of coffee. The garden has about 10,000 varieties of plants from Europe and North America. Inside the grounds of the garden you can ride the Flower Train or walk along leafy paths. It also includes an indoor tropical conservatory, plants of the Bible trail, an herb and medicinal plant garden, and an African savannah grass maze.

BICYCLING AND SEGWAY RIDING

A tour on wheels is a unique way to see and experience Jerusalem, especially at night without the hot Middle Eastern sun beating down on you. Biking and segway tours also allow you to cover more ground in a shorter time by taking you places that would be impossible to reach by car, but a bit far to reach by foot.

There are several different tours to choose from, including the **Jerusalem Midnight Biking** tour (departs from Sherover-Haas Promenade, 054/636-2884, http://jerusalem-biking.com, 9:30pm Wed., NIS110, NIS220 with bike and helmet). The tour is approximately a five-mile circular route and includes hills, so you should be comfortable on a bicycle. It passes through Abu-Tor, Yemin Moshe, and parts of the Old City.

Gordon Active provides a variety of bicycle tours, including **Bike and Eat Jerusalem** (departs from Abraham Hostel at 67 Nevi'im St., 03/765-9018, www.gordonactive.com, 10am Tues. and Sat., NIS220). The seven-hour tour goes on a fairly exhaustive route and includes passing through the historic center of the city, the Calatrava Bridge, the Knesset and Supreme Court, Valley of the Cross, Rehavya, Talbiyeh, the German Colony, the Sherover-Haas Promenade, Mishkenot Sha'ananim, Jaffa Gate, and the Russian Compound.

Quickly becoming a popular way to experience Jerusalem, **Segwayz** (052/811-9996, www.segwayz.co.il, tours daily, NIS180-330 pp) offers a variety of tours that allow you to see more of the (very hilly) city without getting worn out or stuck in traffic.

HIKING AND WALKING

For very serious walkers, the **Jerusalem Trail** (www.jerusalemtrail.com) forms a circular route about 26 miles long. It is part of the larger **Israel National Trail** that runs from the north to the south of the country. The trail is supposed to be marked with blue and white or blue and gold signs along the route, but it is highly recommended to download a GPS map from the trail's website. Between Mount Scopus and Yad Vashem it has occasional markings.

Rehavya Park (the forest next to Gan Sacher off of Ben Tsvi St., enter anywhere from the park, 24 hours daily, free) has extensive trails that are easy to navigate if you have good shoes, and can be reached through the adjacent neighborhood. The trails are a bit rocky, but the views of the Valley of the Cross and its monastery below are magnificent. Walking in this area is better suited for cloudy days or in the evening.

The **Jerusalem Forest** (just past Yad Vashem or on the way to Ein Kerem and Abu Ghosh along Highway 1, 24 hours daily, free) also affords several good places to take relatively easy hikes if you have a reliable, sturdy car that can handle the sometimes extremely rough and rocky roads that lead to the hiking trails in the forest. If you are persistent, you can even find a spring to swim in along the way.

TENNIS

The **Hebrew University** maintains 10 out-door, flood-lit tennis courts and two multi-purpose courts (1 Churchill St., Mt. Scopus, 02/588-2796, http://overseas.huji.ac.il, www.cosell.co.il, 3pm-10pm Sun., 8am-10pm Mon.-Thurs., 7am-5pm Fri., 8am-4pm Sat., daytime court rental NIS20/hour, evening court rental NIS25/hour, racket rental NIS20, purchase three balls NIS30) as part of its Lerner Center at its Mount Scopus campus.

The **Jerusalem Tennis Center** (1 Elmali'akh St. near Teddy Stadium and Malha Mall, 02/679-1439, http://israeltenniscenters.com) boasts 19 courts, a practice wall, dressing rooms, a sporting goods store, and a snack bar. Part of the Israel Tennis Center network, the center has a special purpose and mission to help underprivileged and disadvantaged youth.

SWIMMING

There are several public and private pools in the city that can be accessed, but some of them for a rather high fee. Check the hours beforehand because there are separate hours for men and women as well as coed hours. The **Jerusalem Pool** (43 Emek Refaim St., 02/563-2092, www.jerusalempool.co.il, 5:30am-8:45pm Sun.-Thurs. with varying hours depending on the day, weekdays adult NIS55, child NIS45, weekends adult NIS60, child NIS50) is an Olympic-size covered pool with five lanes, a large outdoor kiddie pool, and one water slide. The grassy area near the outdoor pool and the locker room are both a bit run down, but the location is extremely convenient.

The half-Olympic-size pool at **Beit Yehudah Guest House** (Haim Kulitz Rd. 1, Givat Massuah, 02/632-2777, www.byh.co.il, 10am-6pm summer Sun.-Thurs., NIS70) is in the hills of Jerusalem right near the Biblical Zoo.

The **Leonardo Plaza Hotel** (47 King George St., 02/629-8666, www.leonardo-hotels.com, 10am-7pm daily, weekdays adult NIS55, child NIS40, Sat. adult NIS70, child NIS60) doesn't include a kids' pool but there are lounge chairs and the pool is situated in a calming garden.

GYMS, SPAS, AND MORE

The **Dan Jerusalem Hotel** (32 Lehi St., Mt. Scopus, 02/533-1234, 6:15am-9pm Sun.-Fri. and 8:45am-9pm on Sat., NIS80) has a range of facilities including a gym, Turkish bath, whirlpool bath, saunas, and indoor and outdoor pools (in season).

Accommodations

Most hotels, motels, and hostels will accept payment in U.S. dollars, and they will often list their rates in dollars, rather than shekels for tourists.

Jerusalem has two main types of accommodations: those that are situated conveniently based on overall general location (such as City Center) and those that are situated as close to major tourist sites as possible (such as the Seven Arches Hotel at the top of the Mt. of Olives). Beyond that, there are a wide variety of types of accommodations, including hostels, hospices, guest houses, *zimmers* (bed-and-breakfasts), and kibbutz hotels.

CITY CENTER
Under US$100

Recommended by locals, **❰ Abraham Hostel** (67 Hanevi'im St., 02/650-2200, www.abraham-hostel-jerusalem.com, US$83 d) is a medium-size hostel in the heart of Jerusalem that offers a range of rooms from single private rooms to a 10-bed dorm room. The hostel was founded by backpackers and caters to independent travelers by aiming to be a one-stop location. The rooms are austere and sparsely furnished, but the hostel, which is the first in what is now a national chain, includes a Wi-Fi lounge, common lounge area, dining hall, kitchen, laundry facilities, rooftop terrace, and a TV lecture room. All common areas are open 24 hours a day. The hostel also offers tours and activities.

US$100-150

If you're looking for luxury at an amazing price, check the **City Center Suites** (2 Hahistadrut St. on the corner of 13 King George St., 02/650-9494, www.citycentervacation.com, US$136 d). It has elegant and modern apartments for short stays and long-term visits. Just at the base of Ben Yehuda Street, City Center Suites' rooms include studio, deluxe studio, and suite, and feature kitchenettes or kitchens, balconies, closet space, toiletries, and housekeeping service. The apartments have clean, modern lines and enough space for a comfortable stay.

The **Caesar Premier Jerusalem** (208 Yafo St., 02/500-5656, www.caesarhotels.co.il, US$139 d) is a three-star hotel with 150 rooms and an intimate atmosphere. A standard room includes a mini-refrigerator, cable TV, breakfast, and wireless Internet.

© GENEVIEVE BELMAKER

the YMCA Three Arches Hotel

US$150-200

The **Notre Dame Center** hotel (3 Paratroopers Rd., 02/627-9111, www.notredamecenter.org, US$200 d) is part of the massive, towering Pontifical Institute Notre Dame of Jerusalem that is situated just behind a hill from the Damascus Gate entrance to the Old City. There are 150 rooms, and the hotel caters to Christian guests making a pilgrimage to the Holy Land, though it welcomes guests of any faith. Amenities and facilities include a cafeteria, fine dining on the rooftop terrace, a chapel, and Wi-Fi for an extra fee. The rooms are decorated in a somewhat plain manner, but are spacious and full of light and the room price includes breakfast.

The **Jerusalem Tower Hotel** (23 Hillel St., 02/620-9209, www.jerusalemtowerhotel.com, US$155 d) is right in the middle of the center of the city, making it an ideal place to stay if you want easy access to the nightlife and a wide array of restaurants. The rooms are decorated with a very stark, modern feel with large, bright paintings on very white walls. Of the 120 rooms in the hotel, the rooms on the higher floors have views of the Old City. Amenities are very basic.

Over US$200

The **YMCA Three Arches Hotel** (26 King David St., 02/569-2692, www.ymca3arch. co.il, US$229 d) is one of the more interesting hotels in Jerusalem. A broad and picturesque veranda wraps around the building and the lobby is massive, with an arched and tiled ceiling that exudes Middle East charm. The hotel is part of a larger complex that includes a pool and gym that are used by members who live in the area. The rooms are not fancy, but you can't beat the location on King George Street just a few blocks from both City Center and the Old City.

Popular, trendy, and smack in the middle of the city's action in Nachalat Shiva is **Harmony Hotel** (6 Yoel Moshe Solomon St., 03/542-5555, www.atlas.co.il, US$338 d). One of the more popular downtown hotels for its blend of modern urban in an ancient location, Harmony offers a happy hour in the hotel's English club business lounge with a billiards table, free computer for Internet use, free Wi-Fi, rooftop lounge area, and rooms with a mini-fridge, safe, and multi-channel LCD TV. Part of the Israeli Atlas boutique hotel group, Harmony's 50 rooms are decked out with bright, modern bedding, rugs, and furniture.

Without a doubt, the **(King David Hotel** (23 King David St., 02/620-8888, www.danhotels.com, US$600 d, includes large breakfast) is one of the most beautiful and elegant places in Jerusalem's City Center. Look for the massive table in the rich, lavish lobby where Israeli Prime Minister Yitzhak Rabin and Jordan's King Hussein signed their historic peace agreement in 1994. The patio and pool area behind the hotel make for a charming (and surprisingly affordable) place to have an elegant outdoor lunch. If you wander far enough behind the hotel, you will find the hidden gem, Gozlan Garden. The staff is exceptionally classy and accustomed to dealing with high-profile guests such as heads of state, but is equally gracious to the common visitor.

The **Jerusalem Gold Hotel** (234 Yafo St., 02/501-3333, www.jerusalemgold.com, US$240 d) is a classy, medium-size hotel with a little bit of European sass. The rooms are decorated with heavy drapes and rich tapestries, and have extra-long beds, black-out curtains, and double glazed windows for extra quiet. Guests can select their pillow from a menu, and video games and a laptop-size safe are available. The hotel is also close to several restaurants, shops, and entertainment venues.

The **Waldorf Astoria Jerusalem** (www.waldorfastoriajerusalem.com), scheduled to open in late 2013 or early 2014, promises to be the height of luxury. It is competing with some giants, though, with the Mamilla Hotel directly across the street and the incomparable King David just around the corner. The hotel, which will have 223 rooms for guests, also has thirty luxury private homes built to specific tastes and needs of customers.

© GIDON BELMAKER

Waldorf Astoria Jerusalem

THE OLD CITY
Under US$100

The **Hashimi Hotel** (73 Khan El Zeit St., 054/547-4189, www.hashimihotel.com, US$90 d) is situated in a building that is over 400 years old and is at the center of the Old City. The interior is modern, though, with marble throughout and a rooftop terrace. The rooms in this medium-size hotel are quite bare, including bed frames made of wrought iron and rather thin mattresses. Wi-Fi, cable TV, and air-conditioning are included.

Just inside Jaffa Gate is **New Petra Hostel** (1 David St., 02/628-6618, www.newpetrahostel.com, US$80 d), which offers free parking, a communal kitchen, and a rooftop terrace with panoramic views across Jerusalem. This small hostel has 42 private and dormitory rooms, a TV lounge, Internet, and free safety deposit boxes, as well as laundry service.

Jaffa Gate Hostel (Jaffa Gate in front of David's Tower, 02/627-6402, www.jaffa-gate.hostel.com, US$78 d) includes linens in the price, towels and hairdryers for rent, a place to park bicycles, a tour desk, luggage storage, currency exchange, and a postal and fax service. Dormitories and private rooms are available, and there are evening movie screenings, free Wi-Fi, *nargilot* (hookahs), a terrace area, and space for barbeques.

Although the accommodations are a bit sparse, the **Austrian Hospice** (37 Via Dolorosa, near Damascus Gate, 02/626-5800, www.austrianhospice.com, US$75 d) is sitting on one of the best locations in the Old City. It offers somewhat plain rooms and dormitories with bunk beds and only the bare minimum of amenities. The small lobby is abutted by one of the most redeeming factors of the entire place: the private, outdoor garden seating for guests and customers of the Austrian Hospice café. Some of the staff are Austrian and have a bit of a reputation for being rather unfriendly, although they are efficient and helpful. The rooftop view is one of the best in the area and a secret favorite spot among locals.

Over US$200

Easy to miss in the hustle and bustle immediately after exiting the Old City by Jaffa Gate and continuing to the end the Mamilla shopping center, **◖ Mamilla Hotel** (11 King Solomon St., 02/548-2222, www.mamilla-hotel.com, US$370 d) affords an incredible number of subtle charms for hotel guests and passersby alike. From its rooftop bar and restaurant to its wine bar, Saturday disco, live weekly jazz music in the lobby, and other varied offerings, the Mamilla is a bit like a world unto itself. The rooms are designed with sleek, efficient lines and are accented with international touches such as Asian-influenced bathrooms and showers, and movable walls. Subtle touches of art throughout the hotel invite you to interact with your surroundings.

Connected to the Mamilla shopping center physically and historically, the Mamilla Hotel's owner had a direct hand in helping to revitalize the once-blighted area. There are some spots within the hotel that offer quiet places to sit and have a coffee, which could be a welcome respite after the crowds and chaos of the Old City and shopping in Mamilla. Try the outdoor patio adjacent to the massive dining room for a swing in a hammock seat and a view of the stars. The Espresso Bar, with a very calm, European vibe, is a lovely place to sit and work.

EAST JERUSALEM
Under US$100

Opposite the Old City's Damascus Gate, **New Palm Guesthouse** (4 Hanevi'im St., 02/627-3189, www.newpalmguesthouse.hostel.com, US$70 d) offers package deals that include airport transportation. Private rooms are available, and there is free Wi-Fi. Breakfast is available for an additional cost. The very simple accommodations at this small hostel also include free luggage storage, a common area TV, and a fully equipped kitchen. They also offer tours of Masada and the Dead Sea.

Near Herod and Damascus Gates in the Old City, **Victoria Hotel** (8 Al Masoudi St., 02/627-4466, http://4victoria-hotel.com, US$90 d) is also close to numerous convenient amenities, including the central bus station, shops, and banks. The hotel has 49 rooms, was recently renovated, and most rooms include a balcony. Breakfast is included with the room, and there is free Wi-Fi, 24-hour room service, cable TV, and hairdryers in the rooms.

Capitol Hotel (17 Salah al-Din St., 02/628-2561, www.jrscapitol.com, US$99 d), located on famous Salah al-Din Street, has 54 rooms that include 24-hour room service, satellite TV, air-conditioning, a mini bar, and laundry service. The interior of the hotel is very simple, but nice enough for the rate. The ground floor of the hotel has a garden area with a fountain that is used for special events. The hotel's dining room can also seat up to 120.

US$100-150

Close to both the Old City and City Center, **Legacy Hotel** (29 Nablus Rd. (Derech Shekhem), 02/627-0800, www.jerusalemlegacy.com, US$150 d) has 49 rooms with sitting areas and hairdryers, a fitness center, and a restaurant with Middle Eastern food and an outdoor panoramic view of the city. There is also a bar, buffet, sushi bar, coffee shop, and garden restaurant.

US$150-200

Near the British consulate, the family-run boutique **Addar Hotel** (53 Nablus Rd., 02/626-3111, www.addar-hotel.com, US$167 d) was rebuilt from a 19th-century building. VIPs have been known to stay in this medium-size hotel that features a marble lobby. Many of the rooms are equipped with marble whirlpool tubs, a balcony, French windows, and a sitting area. The hotel restaurant has outdoor garden seating, and it is five minutes by foot to the Old City.

A boutique hotel near the Old City, the **National Hotel** (4 Al Zahra St., 02/627-8880, www.nationalhotel-jerusalem.com, US$199 d) is also close to east Jerusalem's shopping district of Salah al-Din Street. Amenities include newspapers, hotel shops, a gym, and free parking for guests.

The **Ritz Hotel** (8 Ibn Khaldoun St.,

02/626-9900, www.jerusalemritz.com, US$175 d) is a 104-room hotel that was recently renovated and boasts a lovely rooftop terrace dining area, a bar, 24-hour reception service, and satellite TV. Each room has a personal safe, and the hotel is within easy walking distance to the Old City.

Over US$200

Right on the doorstep of the Old City, the **St. George Landmark** (Omar Ibn Al Ass St., 02/627-7232, http://stgeorgelandmark.com, US$270 d) has 130 rooms, a Lebanese restaurant, and a rooftop pool with a panoramic view. Every room features free Wi-Fi, an espresso machine, and tea and coffee machines. Many rooms also include balconies and views of the city.

Located within walking distance to the Old City, the **Grand Court Hotel** (15 St. George St., 02/591-7777, www.grandhotels-israel.com, US$216 d) has 446 rooms, including family rooms and rooms that are equipped for people with physicial disabilities. There is free Wi-Fi and a pool and sundeck that overlook the Old City. There is also a dining room, garden terrace, and lounge bar in the hotel.

Just 10 minutes from the Old City, the **Olive Tree Hotel** (23 St. George St., 02/541-0410, www.olivetreehotel.com, US$300 d) is built around an ancient olive tree, which, according to legend, shaded pilgrims on their way to Jerusalem in ancient times. This large hotel has 304 rooms throughout eight floors and is newly renovated. Rooms have over 50 international channels on the televisions and capability to dock laptops using the TV screen. There is also a business center and large, inviting lobby with accents of Jerusalem stone.

Once known as the gathering place for Jerusalem's foreign press, **The American Colony** (1 Louis Vincent St., 02/627-9777, www.americancolony.com, US$400 d) is still a posh meeting place and a world unto itself in the somewhat desolate surroundings of its east Jerusalem neighborhood. Full of quiet corners and beautifully landscaped grounds, it is the perfect place for escaping from the heat and chaos of Jerusalem. Boasting three gardens, this five-star hotel includes a pool and sauna, fitness and business centers, and a shop with antiques. The 93 rooms in four buildings offer a variety of luxurious accommodations, and the hotel has a decidedly Middle Eastern feel throughout the premises, from the beautiful tile flooring to the stone walls and general decor. All of the staff are highly professional and speak excellent English, and the clientele tends to be seriously upper-crust (dignitaries and famous individuals have been known to stay here).

GERMAN COLONY AND BAK'A
Under US$100

Behind a stone wall in the heart of the German Colony is **St. Charles Hospice** (12 Lloyd George St., 02/563-7737, pilgerhaus@yahoo.com, US$90 d). Catering to Christian pilgrims and with limited amenities, this small guesthouse offers rooms at a very low rate. It is just around the corner from some of the best restaurants in town on Emek Refaim Street. Also nearby is the Railway Park that stretches about one mile, running a good length of the way to the Old City.

US$100-150

Tucked away in the heavily American-occupied neighborhood of Bak'a is the ⟨ **Tamar Residence** (70 Beit Lechem Rd., 077/270-5555, www.tamarsuites.com, US$134 d). Just far enough off the beaten path to be more affordable, but not too far to be inconvenient, part of Tamar is situated above the popular Grand Café. Long-term stays are also available, but book as far in advance as possible, especially for stays during the Jewish holidays. Each room comes equipped with a kitchenette, and several have an outdoor terrace. Most rooms also have a separate living room area. Compared to other places to stay in the immediate area, this is by far the best option for the price range. Inquire in advance about rates for a long stay.

Keeping with the overall trend of guesthouses in the German Colony, **Darna Guest House** (12 Hanania St., 054/565-7001

or 054/227-2370, http://bnb.co.il/darna, US$105 d) offers three locations of different furnished apartments in central locations around the German Colony. A member of the Home Accommodation Association of Jerusalem, Darna offers flexible rates for long stays.

US$150-200

Avissar House in Yemin Moshe (12 Hamevasser St., Yemin Moshe, near the Windmill and the Sultan's Pool, 02/625-5447, www.jeru-avisar-house.co.il, US$180 d) has a small, but very nice selection of four do-it-yourself vacation suites. Though this type of suite is a specialty of the Jerusalem hospitality industry, Avissar House has something truly unique to offer: its location. Situated in the Yemin Moshe Artists' Quarter, Avissar is perfect for writers and artists, or those with artistic souls who like to be surrounded by beautiful flowers and the city's ancient stone. You can see the walls of the Old City, the Valley of Hinnom, and surrounding villages from the suites. It's also a short, easy walk to City Center and within walking distance to entertainment.

Part of the Little Houses in Jerusalem group, the **Little House in the Colony** (4a Lloyd George St., 02/566-2424, www.jerusalemhotel.co.il, US$179) offers just 22 rooms, but includes full amenities such as Wi-Fi, shuttle service to and from the airport, 24-hour concierge service, and breakfast.

Over US$200

If you're looking for a more customized experience, **Jerusalem Harmony** (various locations throughout the German Colony, 054/420-2198, http://jerusalemharmonystudio.com, Skype revamann, reva_l@inter.net.il, rates vary) presents some interesting options. Accommodations include a wide variety of guesthouses and vacation apartments in prime spots throughout the German Colony; sizes vary from small to very large, accommodating up to eight people. With writer Reva Mann as the property owner, the emphasis is on spaces that are conducive to fostering creativity.

GIVAT RAM AND REHAVYA
Under US$100

The **Agron Youth Hostel and Guest House** (6 Agron St., 02/594-5522 ext. 3, agron@iyha.org.il, US$98 d) is a 55-room hostel with air-conditioning, showers and bathrooms, TV and Internet, and a mini-bar in some rooms. It caters to students and younger travelers and features basic, but clean, accommodations and the price of the room includes breakfast. The reception desk is closed for Shabbat, and cultural activities are offered on Sundays and Thursdays. The front desk sells discount tickets to some of the major sites in the city.

US$150-200

The **Leonardo Inn Hotel Jerusalem** (4 Vilnay St., 02/655-8811, www.leonardo-hotels.com, US$156 d) is a 200-room hotel situated at the entrance to Jerusalem near the Knesset. Some of the amenities include a spa and health club with sauna, whirlpool tub, and outdoor and indoor swimming pools. The light rail has a stop in front of the hotel, which seriously ups its level of convenience even though it is not situated in the heart of town. The decor of the rooms is plain and simple, and the hotel caters to practical guests who are also looking for a certain level of comfort, but nothing ostentatious.

Over US$200

Right at the nexus between the German Colony, the Old City, and City Center, **Prima Kings** (60 King George St., 02/620-1201, www.prima-hotels-israel.com, US$217 d) is in an ideal location for visitors who plan on extensive sightseeing. The lobby feels a bit dark and small, but the 217 units in the hotel range in size from rooms to suites, some with balconies. There is a large and very useful information rack near the front door with a variety of tourist booklets and restaurant coupons for free. The hotel caters to observant Jewish guests with a synagogue on the premises and a Shabbat elevator. There is also a dining room, coffee shop, and business center, all of which are kosher.

Leonardo Plaza Hotel Jerusalem (47 King George St., 02/629-8666, www.leonardo-hotels.com, US$450 d) is one of the easiest hotels to spot if you are in the middle of City Center. The hotel's tower overlooks the rolling green lawns of Independence Park. The 270 rooms are decorated in rich, bright colors and there is an Italian restaurant on the premises. Guests have access to the new spa, seasonal pool, fitness room, and whirlpool tub.

Just off King David Street is **Beit Shmuel Hotel and Hostel** (6 Shamai St., at the corner of 13 King David St., 02/620-3455, www.bshmuel-hotel.com/en, US$205 d), designed by renowned architect Moshe Safdie. The distinctive glass dome covering the building's main dining area can be seen from Jaffa Gate and Mamilla. The modern, clean, bright interior of Beit Shmuel makes for a welcoming atmosphere, and the location is central to sights, food, and entertainment in both the Old City and new city. Small overall, but with a variety of accommodations, the guesthouse has 28 rooms for up to six people each, there are 12 hotel rooms for up to four guests each, and one apartment for a family or group visiting for a long-term stay.

Food

Restaurants, coffee shops, and other places to eat and drink in Jerusalem tend to be grouped together. In some cases, the distance between these groupings is significant, so it's best to always carry some water and a snack to tide you over if you're out sightseeing. In places like City Center and Emek Refaim, there are food-related establishments every five feet.

Although it seems as though the city completely shuts down from late Friday afternoon to late Saturday evening for Shabbat, there is still a good selection of places to eat and drink if you know where to look.

CITY CENTER
American
Meatburger Iwo (28 Hillel St., 02/622-2513, http://iwos.co.il, 10am-3am Sun.-Thurs., 10am-7pm Fri., 10am-4pm Sat., NIS40) makes decent hamburgers, wraps, and grilled chicken sandwiches that are larger than you'd expect. They are also English-speaking and deliver to your door, and they have a convenient online ordering system. It's better for takeout or delivery, as atmosphere is not a strong point.

Bakeries
Along the main street of the covered area of the *shuk,* about halfway in and on the left, you will find **Teller Bakery** (Machane Yehuda, NIS20), considered to be one of, if not the, best bakery in Jerusalem. Teller's breads can be found in many grocery stores around town, but nowhere is it as fresh as at their stand in the *shuk.* You can buy something small for a snack or a larger loaf for a picnic.

Coffee Shops and Cafés
Nestled discreetly behind a row of buildings and up several staircases in the

Try freshly baked bread in Jerusalem.

© LOUIS CAPELOTO/123RF.COM

popular tourist neighborhood of Nachalat Shiva, **Tmol Shilshom** (5 Solomon St. through the back alley, 02/623-2758, www. tmol-shilshom.co.il, 9am-1am Sun.-Thurs., 9am-3pm Fri., NIS55) is one of the best ways for visitors to Jerusalem to experience local culture. Housed in a 130-year-old building and famous as a gathering place for well-known authors to read their works in English and Hebrew, Tmol Shilshom has hosted writers

RESTAURANTS AND CAFÉS OPEN ON SHABBAT

From late Friday afternoon to late Saturday evening, if you don't have some insider information, you'll find it difficult to go out for a meal because most places are closed for Shabbat. Scattered throughout the city are some outstanding non-kosher establishments that do stay open. You just have to know where to look.

CITY CENTER AND NEAR THE OLD CITY

This is where most of the open places are concentrated.

- **Adom** (31 Yafo St. at Feingold Courtyard, 02/624-6242)
- **Austrian Hospice Café** (Old City near Damascus Gate, 37 Via Dolorosa, 02/626-5800, www.austrianhospice.com)
- **Blue Dolphin** (7 Shim'on Ha'tsadik St., 02/532-2001)
- **Dublin Irish Pub** (4 Shamai St., 02/622-3612, http://dub.rest-e.co.il)
- **Focaccetta** (Shlomtzion Hamalkah St. 4, 02/624-3222, www.restaurant.mouse.co.il, 8am-2pm Sun.-Thurs. and 11am-2pm, NIS80)
- **Focaccia Bar** (4 Rabi Akiva St., 057/944-3123, http://fucaccia-bar.rest-e.co.il)
- **Gabriel's Chef Restaurant** (7 Shim'on Ben Shetach St., 02/624-6456, www.gabriel-jerusalem.co.il)
- **Lavan at the Cinematheque** (11 Hebron Rd. near the Old City, 02/673-7393, www.jer-cin.org.il)
- **Link** (3 Hama'alot St., 053/809-4510, www.2eat.co.il/eng/link)
- **Meatburger Iwo** (28 Hillel St., 02/622-2513, http://iwos.co.il)
- **Notre Dame Roof Top Wine and Cheese Restaurant** (3 Paratroopers Rd., 02/627-9111, www.notredamecenter.org)

- **YMCA Three Arches** (26 King David St., 02/569-2692, www.ymca3arch.co.il)
- **Zuni** (15 Yoel Moshe Solomon, 2nd Fl., 057/934-5582, http://zuni.rest-e.co.il)

EAST JERUSALEM

Most places in east Jerusalem are open, but it can be a bit trickier to navigate than west Jerusalem. The following are a couple of recommendations on the seam.

- **Askadinya Restaurant Bar** (11 Shim'on Ha'tsadik St., 02/532-4590)
- **Pasha's Restaurant** (13 Shimon Siddiq in Sheikh Jarrah, 02/582-5162, www.pashasofjerusalem.com)

GERMAN COLONY AND BAK'A

This area has slim, but quality, pickings.

- **Colony** (7 Beit Lechem Rd., 02/672-9955, www.2eat.co.il/colony)
- **The Culinary Workshop** (28 Hevron Rd. in the JVP Media Quarter, 057/934-4990, http://hasadna.rest-e.co.il)
- **Scottish Guesthouse Restaurant** (1 David Remez St., uphill from the intersection of Emek Refaim and Keren Hayessod, 02/673-2401, www.scotsguesthouse.com)
- **Smadar Café** (4 Lloyd George St., 02/560-6039 or 02/560-6039)

GIVAT RAM AND REHAVYA

This area is popular with locals.

- **Café Paradiso** (36 Keren HaYesod St., 02/563-4805, http://cafparadiso.rest-e.co.il)
- **P2** (36 Keren HaYesod St., 02/563-5555)
- **Restobar** (corner of Ben Maimon and Azza Sts., 02/566-5126, www.restobar.co.il)

including Amos Oz, Yehuda Amichai, David Grossman, and others. An interesting and unique feature is the café's completely separate rooms for smoking and non-smoking customers. Among favorite menu items is their Amanda salad, salmon filet in fig sauce, and cheesecake. Their coffee is also excellent, and the cool, cavelike atmosphere makes it the perfect place for a late-night powwow with friends or as a temporary escape from the midday sun.

A nice alternative to some of the crowded coffee shop chains is **Alice Coffee Shop** (17 Shamai St., 02/624-6663, 8am-last customer Sun.-Thurs., 8am-3pm Fri., NIS50), about midway up Shamai Street and just a hop from Zion Square. Aside from excellent coffee and pastries, it serves lunch and dinner and has an unusually spacious and calm atmosphere compared to other similar places in the area, Wi-Fi, and very accommodating waitstaff. Outdoor tables are situated in a charming side alley where you can absorb the bustle of Jerusalem life in a cool and shady spot. It's a great place for some peace and quiet if you need a couple of hours to yourself to sip a big cappuccino.

Babis (16 Yoel Moshe Solomon St., 077/527-2538, 10am-11pm daily, NIS45) is a small coffee shop with a very limited menu, which includes some nice dessert items such as its chocolate cake. They often play loud music here and the outdoor seating is a haven for smokers. Among their other qualities, they serve hard liquor and beer, are open for Shabbat, and the staff is friendly and cheerful.

Not far off of Yafo Street is a charming Jerusalem institution called **Kadosh** (6 Shlomtsiyon HaMalka, 02/625-4210, http:// thefoodblog.co.il, 7am-midnight Sun.-Thurs., 7am-4pm Fri., NIS50). Known among many locals as a good first-date restaurant, Kadosh's floor plan is smallish, but its atmosphere exudes the charm of Jerusalem. Kadosh serves an excellent, hearty, Mediterranean, prix-fixe breakfast that includes a variety of salads, omelets and eggs, fresh bread, juice, and coffee. They also have a good selection of tasty patisserie and *burekasim*. They can get very crowded, so

service is sometimes slow, but the food and coffee are consistently delicious.

Dessert

Babette (16 Shamai St. at Yoel Moshe Solomon St., 02/567-1047, 4pm-2:30am Sun.-Thurs., 11am-3pm Fri., NIS30) is one of the coolest little hangouts in City Center; little being the operative word. It's easy to overlook their cramped seating arrangements when you get your hands on one of their delicious waffle dessert combinations with chocolate and whipped cream. You'll want to head straight for the nearest coffee shop after indulging at this favorite haunt of college students.

Zion Square is full of a variety of different ice cream and yogurt stores, but **Max Brenner/ Aldo** (21 Ben Yehuda St., 02/656-5656, akodan@gmail.com, 8am-2am Sun.-Thurs., 8am-5pm Fri., NIS20) is one of the best and safest bets out of all of them. The nice variety of rich ice creams and gelatos is made even better by the fact that the small shop is open extremely late, so it's perfect for a midnight stroll if you have a sweet tooth and your hotel is in the area.

French

At the foot of Nachalat Shiva on Yosef Rivlin Street, standing with Zion Square ahead of you, to your right and uphill you will find Shim'on Ben Shetach Street, a quiet oasis of upper-crust bistros, with sidewalk dining in warm weather, stacked in a row for half the cobblestone sidewalk. You might not see a street sign, so look for the ◖ **Dolphin Yam** (9 Shim'on Ben Shetach St., 02/623-2272, 11am-midnight daily, NIS60-100) sign on the corner and a row of sidewalk dining. Dolphin Yam is one of the best known seafood restaurants in the city, and emphasizes serving moderately priced non-kosher seafood ranging from Israeli favorites to more commonly known items like bass. The menu also includes meat and pasta dishes. The atmosphere caters to more refined diners, but as with most restaurants in Israel, it is also kid-friendly. From late afternoon, the bars and pubs in the area start to set up for the evening crowd and the area gets progressively rowdier.

Next door to Dolphin Yam is **Gabriel's Chef Restaurant** (7 Shim'on Ben Shetach St., 02/624-6456, www.gabriel-jerusalem.co.il, noon-5pm and 7pm-midnight Sun.-Thurs., noon-3pm Fri., NIS130) with its refined atmosphere of indoor and roped-off outdoor seating and delicate, artistic dishes of meat and fish. Some more unique menu items include the seafood ceviche appetizer and the lamb asado cooked in Guinness beer.

Next door is Gabriel's sister restaurant, **Gabriela Cucina** (5 Shim'on Ben Shetach St., 02/624-6261, www.gabriela-jerusalem.co.il, 8am-11:30pm Sun.-Thurs., 8am-5pm Fri., NIS80). This venue is a bit more affordable, with mid-range prices and a nice breakfast menu that includes items like sheep yogurt, smoked salmon accents, herb pancakes with spinach, and a coffee and pastry combo for NIS20.

From Yosef Rivlin Street at the base of Yoel Moshe Solomon Street, follow Yosef Rivlin to your first left and enter the heart of Nachalat Shiva, where you'll come upon the **Feingold Courtyard,** distinguishable by the restaurant signs above the entrance to the courtyard. Chief among the favorites here is **Adom** (31 Yafo St. at Feingold Courtyard, 02/624-6242, 6:30pm-3am Sun.-Fri., 1pm-3am Sat., NIS80), a great spot for the late risers and night owls. The bar-restaurant is built into a stone building with attractive arches and an outdoor courtyard dining area. Adom's specialty is wine and international cuisine with French and Italian influences, and there are different menus for evening and late at night. Adom's owners, Assaf and Noam Rizzi, are regionally known for what locals call their "restaurant empire," which includes one kosher and three non-kosher establishments, all close to City Center (Lavan, Adom, Colony, and Grand Café).

Italian

The area in and around Machane Yehuda (the *shuk*) has some very good options for eating. For some nice Italian fare, try **Topolino** (62 Agripas St., 02/622-3466, www.topolino. biz, 8am-11pm Sun.-Thurs., 8am-2:30pm Fri., NIS60), a favorite Italian restaurant among locals, replete with red and white checkered tablecloths. Known for its superior service (waitstaff will bend over backward to accommodate you) and its variety of world-class pasta dishes, Topolino, with its immediate proximity to the *shuk*, is worth trying.

Café Mizrahi (12 Hashezif St. in Machane Yehuda, 02/624-2105, 7am-10pm Sun.-Thurs., 7am-2pm Fri., NIS40), whose full name in Hebrew translates to "everything for the baker and coffee too," is a small café tucked into the *shuk*. The inviting shop has indoor and outdoor (under cover) seating, and in addition to food and coffee, it sells items for the home baker. The dairy menu includes sandwiches, salads, soup, and baked goods. It is popular with locals and is usually crowded.

Middle Eastern and European Fusion

One of the few restaurants in the city that is open 24 hours a day and serves bacon, (**Zuni** (15 Yoel Moshe Solomon St., 2nd Fl., 057/934-5582, http://zuni.rest-e.co.il, 24 hours daily, NIS60) is centrally located, has incredibly friendly waitstaff, and has an excellent breakfast menu. Housed on the second floor, Zuni is decorated in rich, dark wood with an enclosed bar and several tables as its smoking area when you enter. The restaurant has breakfast, evening, and late-night menus that offer fare to accommodate the mood of the time of day. The late-night menu features several desserts familiar to a North American palate, as well as a good selection of seafood and pasta. The morning menu offers various combination breakfasts with coffee and juice included in the price. The evening menu features items like mussels, grilled eggplant, risotto, and quiche. Every menu has the option to add—yes, you guessed it—bacon.

YMCA Three Arches (26 King David St., 02/569-2692, www.ymca3arch.co.il, 7am-11pm daily, NIS50) is the perfect place to enjoy a peaceful, shaded afternoon coffee alone or

Zuni is open 24 hours a day, seven days a week.

© GENEVIEVE BELMAKER

with a friend on the YMCA building's massive veranda. The large front lawn and trees face the splendid King David Hotel across the street, and you're far away enough from traffic that it is no bother. The service can be slow and the menu is limited to a few pasta and egg items. There is a daily breakfast buffet (7am-10am).

If you know in advance that you are going to eat out while in Jerusalem and want to experience something that is seriously hyped by Jerusalemites, call in advance for a reservation at **Machane Yehuda Restaurant** (Beit Yaakov 10, 02/533-3442, 12:30pm-4:30pm and 6:30pm-midnight Sun.-Thurs., noon-4pm Fri., 8:30pm-midnight Sat., NIS100). Run by three Jerusalem chefs, Assaf Granit, Yossi Elad, and Uri Avon, the food is prepared with ingredients brought in fresh daily from the *shuk*, and the dishes are designed to reflect the character of each chef. The menu changes on a daily basis and the kitchen is open for viewing. The general atmosphere of the place is rustic nouveau, which means your food might be served in a jar or on a cutting board, but the dishes are seriously delicious. In the evening, the small place is packed with tables and gets progressively louder and rowdier until you feel like you're in a club. It's not the place to go for a quiet, intimate dinner.

Pub Fare

Mike's Place (33 Yafo St., 054/531-3255, www.mikesplacebars.com, 11am-last customer Sun.-Thurs., 11am-3pm Fri., NIS55) is part of a chain of pubs across Israel and has a sports bar atmosphere. Unique on the menu is the offering of a variety of Mexican food favorites, which is next to impossible to find in Jerusalem. They also serve a wide variety of hamburgers, sandwiches, barbecue, pizza, and salad.

O'Connell's Irish Pub and Restaurant (3 Shim'on Ben Shetach St., 02/623-2232, 6pm-last customer Sun.-Thurs., NIS50) has a huge beer selection and is more on the refined end for a pub. Some of the menu selections include hamburger sliders, fish and chips, wraps, and a lamb burger.

Dublin Irish Pub (4 Shamai St.,

JERUSALEM'S RESTAURANT CULTURE

Dining out in Jerusalem is a fun diversion and there are some genuinely wonderful gastronomic experiences to be had, but deciphering the unique rules of Jerusalem restaurants is a challenge. The following is a basic primer.

- **Closed for Shabbat:** This means several things, chief among them that they are probably kosher (but not always) and close sometime on Friday afternoon anywhere between 3pm-5pm and usually reopen on Saturday evening around 8:30pm. The times vary a bit by season, but Shabbat is generally from sundown on Friday evening until three stars are out on Saturday evening.

- **Check:** You will never, ever get your bill in a restaurant in Jerusalem, or Israel for that matter, until you ask for it.

- **Coffee Shops:** Due to the strength of several national chain cafés that also serve as coffee shops, the presence of simple coffee shops or espresso stands is non-existent. You can get a good latte (or cappuccino as locals call them) almost anywhere, though. Ironically, the best coffee is not served in the chain cafés.

- **Kosher:** The kosher system dictates keeping dairy and meat separate, and kosher restaurants serve either milk or meat (which includes fish). Kosher certification is officially issued and has degrees of strictness.

This means you cannot get a cappuccino in a kosher meat restaurant.

- **Restrooms:** A cup with handles next to the restaurant's bathroom sink is for religious hand washing (not drinking) and means you are in a kosher establishment. Some places will have a special sink with a cup in the restaurant itself.

- **Security:** Watch out for the security fee that some places tack onto your bill. It is only a few shekels, but you can ask to have it removed if you spot the number of diners times a small shekel amount equals the fee. It is easy to spot even if you can't read Hebrew.

- **Service:** It is not unusual to have no specified waiter or waitress, especially if you are in a busy place. Feel free call on any staff member you see.

- **Tipping:** The tip is almost never included in the bill, and there will be a large note in English on the bottom of your bill indicating that. 10-15 percent is a standard tip.

- **Water:** There is a major shortage of water in this part of the world, so you have to request tap water and usually you have to request refills as well. Try asking for a bottle of tap water.

- **Wi-Fi:** Almost every single restaurant and coffee shop in Jerusalem has free wireless Internet, just ask.

057/944-3740, http://dub.rest-e.co.il, 5pm-3am Sat.-Thurs., 5pm-5am Fri., NIS50) is impossible to miss if you find yourself wandering in the vicinity of Zion Square. With its huge trademark painting of a toucan drinking a Guinness beer on a black background, Dublin is very bold about its presence. Inside there is a similar vibe, with a spacious floor plan that features solid wooden chairs and booths, a huge bar, and TVs for sports games. The menu features stock pub items like hamburgers, pizza, sandwiches, desserts, and a large snack menu to go with their huge bottled and draft beer list. Cocktails and every kind of hard liquor you could want are also available.

South American

El Gaucho (22 Yosef Rivlin St., down the alley, 02/624-2227, www.elgaucho.co.il, noon-midnight Sun.-Thurs., 12:30pm-3:30pm Fri., NIS110) is an upscale restaurant hidden in one of Nachalat Shiva's back alleys that serves an array of cuts of South American beef and a variety of wines. One of seven other El Gaucho restaurants throughout Israel, the interior of the Jerusalem location feels like a cave and is calm and inviting. The menu features items like asado (grilled steak), prime rib, baked potatoes, and meat skewers. They also have a dessert of the day and a children's menu.

Wine, Cheese, and Rooftop Dining

Also near the *shuk* is the **Basher Resto Cheese Bar** (21 Agripas St., 02/534-0400, noon-last customer Sun.-Thurs., 10am-4pm Fri., NIS80), which the owners of one of the finest cheese shops in town opened in mid-2012. Although still not well known, it is earning a reputation for a good place to try local and international wines while nibbling on one of the various plates of the most select, finest cheeses from around the world.

Even though the Pontifical Institute Notre Dame of Jerusalem Center is a massive building in the center of the city, you could easily pass by without noticing it. Set back from the road behind stone walls and a security gate, the institute is home to the **Roof Top Wine and Cheese Restaurant** (3 Paratroopers Rd., 02/627-9111, www.notredamecenter.org, 5pm-midnight Mon.-Thurs., noon-midnight Fri.-Sun., reservations recommended, NIS70), which offers outdoor dining on a beautiful rooftop terrace overlooking the city. The menu ranges from wine and cheese selections to full dinners. Although the general atmosphere of the institute is not posh or luxurious, there is a certain spare and relaxing charm to the restaurant, particularly with its view overlooking the city.

The Mamilla Hotel has two nice spots for drinks and mingling. **Winery** (11 King Solomon St., 2nd Fl., 02/548-2222, 3pm-8pm Sun.-Thurs., 2pm-6pm Fri., NIS40) has a selection of 300 Israeli wines that gives a nice introduction to the region's vines and it sells kosher wines. The **Rooftop** (11 King Solomon St., 8th Fl., 02/548-2222, 6pm-midnight Sun.-Thurs., noon-11pm Fri.-Sat. with a cold Shabbat menu, NIS85) has a commanding view of Jerusalem and the Old City in a setting that feels more like Tel Aviv. The Rooftop caters to the wealthy and elite set, with a wide variety of beautiful people among its customers. A long bar is complemented by a wooden deck and a row of small bar tables and stools near the front, while the back area (with the better view) has a larger area with seating for dinner.

THE OLD CITY
Near Zion Gate

At the juncture of the old Roman city's center and the current end of the partially renovated Cardo is a cavernous Arab restaurant with multiple names, but most easily located by its large sign outside the southern entrance that says **Heart of the Old City** (end of Cardo, 02/627-3408, 8am-8pm daily, NIS35). The restaurant staff is friendly and serves up basic dishes of falafel, hummus, shwarma, and the like. It is also known as Afandi Restaurant.

Near Jaffa Gate

Inside Jaffa Gate's David Street, just east of the Church of St. John the Baptist, is Muristan Street, which has a row of several cafés and small eateries, many of which specialize in freshly squeezed juice drinks. Their hours vary depending on how many customers they have, but the general hours of these eateries are 9am-8pm daily. **Geo's Espresso Bar** (Muristan St. row of sidewalk cafés near the Church of the Holy Sepulchre, NIS20-75) serves chicken dishes, hummus plates, sandwiches, salads, falafel, and kebabs.

Jerusalem Pizza (end of Muristan St., 8am-8pm daily, NIS30) serves pizza at a storefront reminiscent of New York City, with a few guys behind a counter dishing up slices.

Na'aman Old City Coffee Shop (Muristan St., NIS55) looks pleasant as you pass by, and the menu includes *labaneh* (strained yogurt) plates, hot and cold drinks, sandwiches, and salads, but they encourage customers to pay rather high prices in U.S. dollars and the quality of the food leaves quite a lot to be desired.

The Armenian Tavern (79 Armenian Orthodox Patriarchate Rd., turn right at the Tower of David and restaurant is downstairs, Armenian Quarter, 02/627-3854, 11am-10:30pm Tues.-Sun., NIS50) serves meat dishes with special touches like mint and grape leaves. The interior is what charms most customers the most, though, with its arched ceilings dating to the crusader period and an indoor fountain.

Near Damascus Gate

The **Wiener Kaffe Haus** (37 Via Dolorosa, 02/626-5800, www.austrianhospice.com, 10am-10pm daily, NIS40) is a well-kept secret passed around only among those who know Jerusalem the best. Housed on the ground floor of the Austrian Hospice, which is actually one story above the Old City streets, this café has ample indoor seating and an expansive outdoor terrace with a canopy of trees. Wrapped around the building is a veranda with more seating, and there are several additional tables and chairs on more secluded vestibules raised above the patio. The menu is small, but has a selection of items for a light meal including soups, salads, and toast. Tea in a pot, wine, and beer are also available, but it's the Viennese apple strudel that is the main attraction.

Near the Western Wall

Just before the security gate to enter the plaza for the Western Wall is a relatively good find for dining inside the Old City. **Between the Arches** (174 HaGay St., HaKotel HaMaaravi St., 02/628-8680, www.2eat.co.il/eng/bta, 9am-6pm Sun.-Tues., NIS65) serves a fairly standard fare of sandwiches, salads, fish, and pasta dishes. The restaurant is located in an area that is part of a system of 13th-century tunnels, and you go rather deep underground to reach the restaurant. The restaurant is easy to find, and an array of fish tanks and nice touches of decoration contribute to a relaxed atmosphere for a leisurely lunch.

Just Outside the Old City Walls

Nestled inside of the Jerusalem Cinematheque is **Lavan at the Cinematheque** (11 Hevron Rd., 02/673-7393, 10am-midnight daily, NIS60), an ideal place for a quiet meal with a scenic view of the Valley of Hinnom and the walls of the Old City. Lavan is heavy on atmosphere and light on the substance of the food. The menu is a fairly generic version of what you can find all over Jerusalem, including pasta, egg breakfasts with cheeses, bread, and salad, and fairly good cappuccino. The restaurant's main advantages are its close proximity to the Old City, its quiet atmosphere, its home inside the Cinematheque complex, and the fact that it is open on Saturday.

If you exit from Jaffa Gate and take the stairs down to Mamilla, you will find a variety of places to eat, most of which are domestic chains and are often extremely crowded, particularly on Fridays. But **Roladin** (Mamilla Ave., 02/623-1553, www.roladin.co.il, 7:30am-11pm Sun.-Thurs., 7:30am-3pm Fri., NIS40) bakery and café is always hopping, and for good reason. Its selection of sweet treats are pre-packaged to be easily taken out and they are the main draw for customers, even though a typical selection of egg dishes, sandwiches, and pasta can also be had. During Hanukkah, Roladin customers flock to buy their donuts (a traditional Hanukkah treat), which have earned a reputation for being the best in the city.

Montefiore (Yemin Moshe St., below the windmill, 02/623-2928 or 057/943-8439, http://montefiore.rest-e.co.il, 7am-2am Sun.-Thurs., 8am-3pm Fri., NIS90) is a fine dining Italian restaurant with a menu that includes seafood such as salmon, and also offers pasta and pizza. The establishment's main draw is its proximity to both the Old City and to the Jerusalem Cinematheque in the adjacent Mishkenot Sha'ananim complex. Outdoor balcony seating overlooks the Valley of Hinnom and has a nice view of the Old City. It is open into the wee hours.

EAST JERUSALEM
Arab

For a taste of home-cooked Arab food, **Pasha's Restaurant** (13 Shimon Siddiq in Sheikh Jarrah, 02/582-5162, www.pashasofjerusalem.com, noon-11pm daily, NIS70) will pick you up from any Jerusalem hotel within 15 minutes of you calling them. Their sister establishment, **Borderline** stays open until about 1:30am and offers a menu of water pipes to smoke from for after-dinner relaxation. Pasha's menu includes traditional Arab fare of lentil and other soups, hot and cold appetizers, lamb dishes with mint, and a variety of international dishes such as beef stroganoff.

Continental

The American Colony (1 Louis Vincent St., 02/627-9777, www.americancolony.com, call for hours, open daily, NIS80) has several dining options for every day of the week in a beautiful five-star setting. Even if you're not a guest at the hotel, it's worth enjoying if you're willing to spend a bit more. Their Saturday brunch is extensive, delicious, and includes rare items like bacon. Options for dining include the Arabesque Restaurant, The Courtyard, Val's Brasserie, The Cellar Bar, The Summer Bar, and The Terrace Café.

More bar and courtyard dining can be found at **Askadinya Restaurant Bar** (11 Shim'on Ha'tsadik St., 02/532-4590, noon-midnight Wed.-Mon., 7pm-midnight Tues., NIS80), where they have created a blend of east meets west with meat dishes served with an Asian flair in addition to more common pasta and salad dishes. Try the steak with raisin and caramel sauce.

Lebanese

Blue Dolphin (7 Shim'on Ha'tsadik St., 02/532-2001, noon-11pm daily, NIS80) has a variety of seafood dishes that include some local favorites like St. Peter's fish, baby sea bass, and others. You can call in advance to order for the freshest possible fish. Adjoining the restaurant is its sister establishment, **Al Wad,** which offers Lebanese favorites. There is a separate dining area for those who want alcohol with their meal. Situated just on the seam of the old division between east and west Jerusalem, you should avoid arriving by cutting through the west Jerusalem orthodox neighborhoods of Meah Shearim and Ma'alot Dafna if you are going during Shabbat.

GERMAN COLONY AND BAK'A
Asian

Sushi Rechavia (29 Emek Refaim St., 02/563-7777, noon-midnight Sun.-Thurs., noon-4pm Fri., NIS50) is the Emek Refaim branch of a popular sushi bar in Rehavya. In addition to sushi, the restaurant also has noodle dishes, Japanese-style grilled chicken, gyoza, and stir fried dishes, and caters to the trendy set of Jerusalem that likes to try restaurants. The atmosphere is very modern with a large enclosed patio for outdoor seating.

Ryu (25 Emek Refaim St., 02/561-1344, www.ryu.co.il, noon-midnight Sun.-Thurs., noon-4pm Fri., NIS80) is a cavernous Asian restaurant near the beginning of Emek Refaim that caters to the upper crust lovers of Asian food. The large dining room includes a bar and gives way to a back dining area of windows that extend from the floor to the ceiling. The Asian fusion menu includes Peking duck, a variety of noodle dishes, and sushi. The distinguishing factor of Ryu is how it blends Asian concepts of food with local flavors, including specialties like salmon in a kefir-lime soy syrup.

Coffee Shops and Cafés

There is a lot of hype surrounding **The Coffee Mill** (23 Emek Refaim St., 02/566-1665, 7am-midnight Sun.-Thurs., 7am-3pm Fri., NIS30) and some of it is deserved. The very small shop's walls are plastered with old covers of New Yorker magazines, and the menu is bright and creative with pictures of most of the drinks and food. Its late hours during the week make it a great place to stop in for a coffee after dinner somewhere nearby.

If you happen to find yourself in Bak'a, **Grand Café** (70 Beit Lechem Rd., 02/570-2702, 7am-midnight Mon.-Thurs., 7am-3pm Fri. Nov.-Mar., 7am-midnight Mon.-Thurs., 7am-4pm Fri. Apr.-Oct., NIS55) is a newer restaurant that is a good place to stop for a nice salad or toast. They also make excellent coffee. The restaurant is the latest installment in a small empire of restaurants that includes other places around the city, and has tons of outdoor seating in the summer. The waitstaff can be a bit frazzled and hard to catch at times because they are often packed with customers, but overall it's a nice place for a leisurely breakfast or lunch.

It's not much to look at, but **Smadar Café** (4 Lloyd George St., 02/566-0954 or 02/560-6039, 8am-midnight daily, NIS50) has some of the best pizza and friendliest waitstaff in town.

They also offer a decent brunch, tapas, and vegetarian food. Catering to the middle-class, English-speaking crowd in the neighborhood, Smadar is part of Lev Smadar movie theater, making it the perfect spot to grab a bite and see a film. It gets very crowded right before the start of a movie, so it's a good idea to check the Lev Smadar website beforehand.

Contemporary

The Culinary Workshop (28 Hevron Rd. in the JVP Media Quarter, 057/934-4990, http://hasadna.rest-e.co.il, 6pm-1am Sun.-Fri., noon-1am Sat., NIS80) is very easy to miss during a trip to Jerusalem, which would be a shame. This relatively new establishment is tucked into the JVP Media Quarter next door to Zappa, a live music bar that has performances almost nightly. The Culinary Workshop has an enormous open kitchen, a multi-layered floor plan with soft lighting and outdoor deck seating, and a small, but inventive menu. Dishes are prepared to give just the right balance of flavors, as with the artichoke à la Romana salad, which will win over anyone who isn't already a fan of artichoke. There is also a nice selection of steak cuts at not outrageous prices, a rare find in Jerusalem.

Around the corner is **Colony** (7 Beit Lechem Rd., 02/672-9955, www.2eat.co.il/colony, noon-last customer daily, NIS70), known for its massive selection of wine, beer, and alcohol, and its status as one of the few restaurants in the neighborhood open during Shabbat. The Colony is a favorite gathering place for foreign journalists and offers some fairly standard menu items, including schnitzel and hamburgers, but it also has outstanding crème brule and excellent cappuccino. Housed in an old warehouse, Colony has tons of outdoor patio seating and the atmosphere ranges from plush living room to tropical cabana. The waitstaff tends to be a bit rushed and hard to flag down, but they are always accommodating and friendly.

Italian

Strolling down busy and somewhat touristy Emek Refaim Street, there is one standout among the numerous restaurants along the roadside. ❰ **Luciana** (27 Emek Refaim St.,

Italian favorite Luciana restaurant, in the German Colony

057/934-4979, http://luciana.rest-e.co.il, 8am-midnight Sun.-Thurs., 8am-3pm Fri., about 9pm-midnight or last customer Sat., NIS50) is a kosher Italian restaurant in a 19th-century building with both indoor and outdoor seating. Luciana is the perfect place to have a leisurely dinner on a hot summer evening, and it has a warm, inviting atmosphere and friendly wait-staff. The clientele are locals from the neigh-borhood. The vegetarian cheese lasagna is sumptuous, especially if you are a fan of cheese. They also have a fine selection of other varied Italian fare, excellent coffee, and a wide variety of desserts. The VIP room on the second floor accommodates up to 45 people.

For some of the best Italian food in the German Colony, **Masaryk** (31 Emek Refaim St., 02/563-6418, 7:30am-midnight Sun.-Thurs., 7:30am-4pm Fri., NIS60) is a good bet. Situated on the corner of Emek Refaim and Masryk Streets, it takes advantage of its po-sition and puts the customers right up against the colorful flow of sidewalk traffic. The pasta and fish menu includes some nice choices,

including red tuna schnitzel and goat cheese gnocchi. A great place for an early morning breakfast or a late-night dinner, the restaurant has staff that is extremely relaxed and the gen-eral atmosphere is not rushed.

Middle Eastern

HaMoshava54 (54 Emek Refaim St., 02/563-5454, www.hamoshava54.co.il, noon-last cus-tomer Sun.-Thurs., noon-3pm Fri., NIS50) is at the end of Emek Refaim Street and has a large wraparound bar and a bright, modern interior. The meat menu features a variety of chicken and beef dishes, including fried chicken, steak, sandwiches, fries, and salad, prepared in a somewhat uninventive manner that is good for patrons who favor simplicity and large portions.

Marvad Haksamim (Magic Carpet) (42 Emek Refaim St., 02/567-0007, http://marvad. mapme.co.il or http://marvadhaksamim.rest-e. co.il, noon-11:30pm Sun.-Thurs., 9am-3:30pm Fri., NIS55), considered a Jerusalem institu-tion, has been in business since 1948, on the eve of the founding of the country. Originally

the popular Marvad Haksamim restaurant on Emek Refaim

© GENEVIEVE BELMAKER

located on King George Street, the restaurant is known for its Yemenite food and convenient catering services. The interior has the look of a diner with Middle Eastern touches, and they emphasize their takeout service. The menu includes a variety of hummus dishes, Middle Eastern soups and salads (try the Moroccan carrot salad), as well as meat skewers and stuffed grape leaves.

Scottish

If you're in the mood to step back and get some perspective, the **Scottish Guesthouse Restaurant** (1 David Remez St., uphill from the intersection of Emek Refaim and Keren HaYesod, 02/673-2401, www.scotsguesthouse. com, 11am-3pm Fri.-Sat., NIS80 pp) is a good pick. Its large outdoor veranda overlooks the Old City and west Jerusalem, and it is one of the quietest places in the city. They only serve a Scottish style brunch, and only on the weekend for one price. The food is average, but it's a nice change of pace.

South American

For South American fare, try **La Boca** (46 Emek Refaim St., 02/563-5577, http://laboca.rest-e.co.il, noon-11:30pm Sun.-Thurs., noon-4pm Fri., NIS90), which is in a restored Templar building and features a different wine every month. Their menu is heavy on anything to do with meat, including rump steak, chili con carne, as well as some chicken and liver dishes. The atmosphere is upscale and slightly trendy, and it is one of the more well-known restaurants on Emek Refaim Street.

GIVAT RAM AND REHAVYA
Coffee Shops and Cafés

Cup O' Joe (38 Keren HaYesod St., 02/561-0555, www.joe.co.il, 8am-1am Sun.-Thurs., 8am-4pm Fri., NIS40) is a chain café and coffee shop that serves fairly run of the mill food and drinks, but has a nice selection of deserts. As far as this type of coffee chain, Cup O' Joe is the closest thing to an American coffee shop that you can find in Jerusalem. It's less of a restaurant than Café Café, Hillel, and Greg, and

The Aroma icon of a large coffee cup on Emek Refaim Street is easy to recognize.

© GENEVIEVE BELMAKER

has more of a nice coffee shop atmosphere than **Aroma,** the other major coffee shop chains in town. Not far down the street closer to City Center, there is another Cup O' Joe (41 King George St.). That location is a bit more conveniently situated, but on a hot day the glass-dome front of the building makes the whole place heat up like a greenhouse.

Contemporary

If you happen to be visiting the Israel Museum and just can't wait for dinner at a different location, there is always **Modern** (Ruppin through 11 of the Israel Museum, 02/648-0862, www.modern.co.il, noon-midnight Sun.-Mon. noon-4pm Fri., NIS65). The restaurant includes a huge patio area that is mostly used for private events, and a rather small but elegant interior. Known as a spot for frequent VIP sightings, including the President of Israel, Modern has a menu with a fairly standard selection of fish and pasta dishes. Their claim to fame is their Thursday night live jazz music and wine tasting.

Halvrit Café at Cossell Jerusalem Sports Center (The Hebrew University at Givat Ram, across from the Bloomfield Science Museum, 8am-11pm Sun.-Thurs., 8am-2:30pm Fri., NIS45) is one of, if not the only, place to have a light lunch if you are in the vicinity of Museum Row. Directly across the street from the Bloomfield Science Museum, Halvrit offers health conscious food to complement the large number of customers coming and going from its sports center. Many of the choices on the menu are light salads and the like. There is nice, shady outdoor seating with a grassy area where kids can run around, but the indoor café is slightly crowded.

Restobar (corner of Ben Maimon and Azza Sts., 02/566-5126, www.restobar.co.il, 7:30am-last customer daily, NIS70) is right at the beginning of the upscale and hip Rehavya neighborhood, just after you leave City Center. The only word for Restobar is cool. Whether it is the clientele, the atmosphere created by the restaurant's unusual rectangle shape with outdoor seating in the front and a smoking room in the back, or the fact that it's open every day, Restobar feels more like Tel Aviv than Jerusalem. The crowd is distinctly late 20s to early 40s and there is a huge bar in the middle of the main dining room where wine, beer, and cocktails are served. The menu varies widely but emphasizes Middle Eastern-influenced dishes. The menu also changes according to the time of day, but try the cauliflower in tahini on the dinner menu or the croquet madame with smoked goose breast on the breakfast menu.

Italian
P2 (36 Keren HaYesod St., 02/563-5555, noon-midnight daily, NIS40) is a small, mostly pizza and some pasta restaurant that is open daily. The pasta is made on the premises in a large pasta machine at the front of the restaurant. The thin crust pizza is served up with high-quality ingredients and expert care. There's limited seating, including barstools and outdoor chairs.

Middle Eastern
Café Paradiso (36 Keren HaYesod St., 02/563-4805, http://cafparadiso.rest-e.co.il, noon-1am Mon.-Thurs., 10am-1am Fri., 11am-1am Sat., NIS80) is an understated restaurant serving up creative Mediterranean and Middle Eastern dishes, including grilled baby octopus, Thai lamb patties, and chicken livers on lentils. There's plenty of indoor and outdoor seating, although the interior feels a bit like it was arranged for a cafeteria setting rather than a restaurant.

Seafood
Olive and Fish (2 Jabotinsky St., 02/566-5020, noon-11pm Sun.-Thurs., NIS80) is conveniently located next to Liberty Bell Park and in walking distance from the Mamilla shopping district. The restaurant features special seafood dishes as well as salads, chicken, and kabobs. Try the hot salmon salad or the St. Peter's fish filet. The interior of the restaurant is decorated with antique photographs of Jerusalemites through the generations, and is spacious and classy, with an indoor veranda.

Information and Services

INFORMATION
Tourist and Travel Information
The hotline of the Jerusalem municipality is **106** (from out of the city call 02/531-4600). It covers advisories and basic information for tourists. There are several places throughout Jerusalem that act as information centers. Some are better than others. In the Old City, the **Jaffa Gate Tourist Information Center** (1 Jaffa Gate, 02/627-1422, 8:30am-5pm Sun.-Thurs., 8:30am-noon Fri.) is in a convenient location but has limited information and resources. The **Christian Information Center** (Jaffa Gate, 02/627-2692, hours vary) is nearby and can also offer some help.

Outside of the Old City, near the City Center, the **Abraham Hostel Information Center** (67 Hanevi'im St., 02/650-2200, www.abraham-hostel-jerusalem.com) has a 24-hour front desk and an information center that caters to independent travelers and its guests. The **Prima Royale Hotel** (3 Mendele Mocher Sforim, at the corner of Keren HaYesod St.) has an extensive and very helpful tourist information rack just inside its front doors. Many of the tourism booklets include coupons for discounts on food and drinks.

Tourist Visas
Tourists automatically get a three-month tourist visa at Passport Control, which can be renewed at the **Jerusalem Ministry of Interior** (1 Shlomtsiyon HaMalka St., 02/629-0231). A tourist visa can usually be extended for up to 24-27 months, but only in increments of 3-6 months and there is a fee of about NIS400 every time you extend your visa.

Media and Internet Resources
The **Jerusalem Development Authority** (www.jda.gov.il) recently partnered with the **City of Jerusalem** (www.jerusalem.muni.il) to create the **Official Tourism Website of Jerusalem** (www.itraveljerusalem.com). All three websites have useful information for tourism in the city, but the City of Jerusalem site has very relevant information on basics under its "visitors" section.

A website that is full of very useful information on food, accommodations, and entertainment written from the perspective of locals is **www.GoJerusalem.com.**

There are several locally broadcast radio stations, including 101.3FM and 88.2FM (not 88.0FM, which is a different Kol Israel network). 88.2FM has an additional 10pm broadcast that is a relay of the international broadcast Reshet Hey to shortwave overseas listeners. **IBA World Service Israel International Radio and TV** (www.iba.org.il/world/#) has an English-news radio broadcast online and a TV broadcast at 5pm Sunday-Thursday on Israel Channel 3 (33 on cable) and 6pm Friday-Saturday. On Israel Channel 1, a 9-minute version broadcasts at 4:50pm Sunday-Thursday.

The official tourism website of Israel is **www.goisrael.com.**

Maps
The best place to find tourist maps in Jerusalem is through information centers or from the information racks that some hotels have in their lobbies. No matter which map you use, you will find many differences in street names and the names of sights. These are not errors of the map makers, but are due to the city's long history of places and streets being named by different groups, inconsistencies in translating words and names from Arabic and Hebrew to English, and sometimes there are political factors at play.

Holidays
There are several major holidays during the calendar year that draw visitors to Jerusalem from all over the world or greatly impact services and access if you are already in the city. The most impactful are Jewish holidays, and their dates vary slightly from year to year because they are

based on the Jewish calendar. It's necessary to check a calendar to see when the holidays will occur.

The most major holidays are **Sukkot** (Oct.), **Yom Kippur** (Sept.), and **Passover** (late Mar. or early Apr.).

Hospitals

There are several hospitals in Jerusalem: **Bikur Holim Hospital** (02/646-4111, www.bikurholim.org.il); **Hadassah Hospital** (02/584-4111, www.hadassah.org.il/Hadassa) at Mount Scopus; and **Herzog Hospital** (02/531-6875, www.herzoghospital.org).

Emergency Services

You can dial for emergency services from any phone by calling **Police,** 100; **First-Aid,** 101; **Fire Department,** 102; **Electric Company Hotline,** 103; and **Municipal Emergency Situation Room,** 02/625-6202 (for information during emergencies).

SERVICES
Currency Exchange and Money

There are several "Change" stands located throughout the city that will change foreign currency into New Israel Shekels (shekels for short) and vice versa. Change offices are concentrated in and around Zion Square and in the German Colony and Bak'a.

Post offices (www.israelpost.co.il) cash foreign currency checks and traveler's checks. The official symbol of the post office is a red sign with white writing and an ibex leaping with its horns above the title of the post office. A complete listing of the post office branches in Jerusalem can be found on the post office website.

Banks are open 8:30am-12:30pm Sunday-Friday (closed for Shabbat and holidays) and some also open in the afternoons. There are several bank branches in Jerusalem that change money, including the **Jerusalem Center Branch** (33 Jaffa St.), the **City Center Shamai Branch** (6 Shamai St.), and the **Old City Jewish Quarter Branch** (69 Hayehudy St.). Near Nachalat Shiva and directly next door

to the Ministry of Interior is **Hillel Change** (1 Shlomtsiyon HaMalka St., 02/623-0656), which operates under the supervision of the Bank of Israel.

ATMs

There are ATMs outside of most banks and they take foreign bank cards. There is a fee of US$3-9 charged by most banks for using their card at a foreign ATM.

Zion Square has two conveniently located banks with outdoor ATMs that take foreign cards. **Bank Hapoalim** (www.bankhapoalim.co.il) has red, blue, and white colors on its sign and other branches can be found throughout Jerusalem, including in Emek Refaim across the street from Masaryk restaurant, in Bak'a downhill from the Sherover-Haas Promenade, and at the base of Zion Square where it meets with Yafo Street. The **Israel Discount Bank** (www.discountbank.co.il) has green and white colors and has branches throughout Jerusalem, including on King George Street, in Zion Square going downhill on the right side just before Steimatzky bookstore, and in the German Colony just before the Coffee Mill.

Internet

There are a few Internet cafés around Jerusalem, but they are few and far between. The next closest thing if you don't have a laptop with you is the business center in your hotel lobby. Free wireless Internet (often without a password) is available almost everywhere in the city, particularly in restaurants and cafés.

There are about 100 Wi-Fi hotspots in convenience stores adjacent to gas stations, and other spots are available at universities, colleges, museums, visitors' centers, convention halls, marinas, tourism sites, and shopping malls.

There is free Internet service in the German Colony, the downtown pedestrian shopping center, and at Safra Square next to Jerusalem City Hall.

Postal Service

There are more than 20 branch **Post Offices** (main branch at 23 Yafo Street opposite Safra

Square, 02/629-0676, www.israelpost.co.il, most operate 9am-3pm Sun.-Thurs., 9am-2pm

Fri.) throughout Jerusalem. Check the branch for hours.

Getting There and Around

GETTING THERE
By Air

The airport closest to Jerusalem is the **Ben Gurion International Airport** (03/975-2386, www.iaa.gov.il) located outside Tel Aviv. There are several ways to reach Jerusalem from the airport if you are not staying at a hotel with a shuttle service.

The national airline, **El Al Airlines** (www.elal.co.il) has frequent flights to Tel Aviv from all over the world, and provides kosher meals for passengers. Most major international airlines offer at least one flight a day to Tel Aviv.

Jerusalem is about one hour by car from the airport, about two hours by train, and a little over one hour on the many frequent, convenient, and comfortable buses. Public transportation does not run during Shabbat (from Fri. afternoon through 8pm or 9pm Sat.), but it is possible to get a service taxi from certain locations during that time.

SHABBAT AND HOLIDAYS

Be careful to plan your flight around Shabbat or major Jewish holidays. The airport will shut down from Friday late afternoon to Saturday late evening, with no flights going in or out. You will also have a more difficult time reaching your final destination if you arrive later in the day on Friday and don't have a ride from the airport.

SECURITY CHECKPOINTS
AND VEHICLE SEARCHES

Israel is a country that is under constant threat from terrorists, and is sometimes attacked domestically or overseas. It is not unusual to be stopped and questioned coming and going from the airport. If you are in a car, the trunk might be searched, you might be asked for your ID, and you might be questioned. Try to refrain

from making any jokes with security personnel or telling them that you have any gifts in your bag. They might search your luggage and test it for bomb-making materials.

By Train

Israel Railways (Route 90, www.rail.co.il/EN, NIS22.5) has a train that takes two hours from the airport to Jerusalem, and stops for 29 minutes between the second and third stops. Once you get to Jerusalem, you will be a good 15 minutes from the City Center and will need to go by car or bus to your final destination.

By Share Taxi

Just north of Zion Square on Harav Kook Street is an unofficial way station for share taxis going to and from Tel Aviv and other locations. The cost is about NIS25, and the vans will not leave until they are full, so you might have to wait for a while. Check with the driver before getting in that they are going to your destination.

GETTING AROUND
Driving

Visitors to Israel are allowed to drive with their foreign license for up to one year from arrival in the country. As most street signs are in English, it is relatively easy for someone who doesn't speak Hebrew to drive in Jerusalem.

With three locations in Jerusalem, **Hertz** offices can be found in Givat Shaul, King David, and Romema. The King David branch (19 King David St., 02/623-1351, www.hertz.co.il) is centrally located in the city and you can get compact Suzukis and Hyundais starting at US$37 a day.

Budget (23 King David St., 03/935-0015) has a wide variety of car models, from compact cars to SUVs and two locations in

Jerusalem. Their main Jerusalem office is just a few doors down from the Hertz office on King David Street.

The parking system in Jerusalem has some strict rules, and some that you can break. For instance, you might see cars parked on the sidewalk, or facing the wrong direction. One rule you break at your peril, though, is not feeding the meter. Red and white stripes means no parking, blue and white stripes is paid parking by a street meter, and gray is free parking. Other paid parking in certain neighborhoods or small lots will have a yellow and black sign with hours of paid parking; for these, you must buy a ticket and leave it in your car dash with the date stamp showing. These machines often only take coins and nothing else, so keep coins handy.

If you are going to be in Jerusalem and driving on a daily basis, Yellow gas stations sell an automatic pay-in-advance meter that you leave on the side of your vehicle. The meter costs NIS100 and you can pay for time on it as you go.

Taxis

Taxis in Jerusalem are white cars with a yellow light on the roof and are often BMWs. You can get almost anywhere in the city (without heavy traffic) for NIS50 or less. Drivers might offer you a fixed rate or simply not turn their meter on, but you can rarely beat the meter with a set rate. There is a NIS10 (about US$1.25) drop charge at the start of every ride, and an additional NIS5 charge for summoning a taxi to a hotel. There can be an additional charge for luggage, and some drivers might try to charge more for two or more passengers.

The legal fare system is 25 percent higher during Shabbat and holidays (sundown on Fri. until it is dark on Sat. night, usually about 8pm). Fares are also 25 percent higher at night, 9:01pm-5:29am.

Tips are not generally expected, unless your driver does something extra helpful. If you need a taxi for a long distance, it is better to call and order a cab.

Two reputable taxi companies in Jerusalem are **Rehavya Taxi** (3 Agron St., 02/625-4444 or 02/622-2444) and **HaPisga Taxi** (2 HaPisga St., 02/642-1111).

Public Transportation

Jerusalem's city bus line, **Egged** (03/694-8888 or *2800 from any local phone, www.egged. co.il), provides service throughout the country. Within the city, it costs about NIS7 for a one-way ticket that can be used for a return or transfer within 90 minutes of purchase. Egged's bus 99 offers a panoramic tour of Jerusalem aboard a red double-decker tour bus with stops that you can hop on and off with a one- or two-day pass (NIS39).

The **Central Bus Station** (218 Yafo St., 054/797-1147) is a somewhat grimy transportation hub with several levels that also has shops and places to eat or get a snack. Bus tickets can be purchased at the information window on the second level, or directly from your driver if you are paying cash. Bus seats are on a first come, first served basis and people stand and sit in the aisles if the bus is crowded.

Overseas visitors can buy Israbus tickets, valid on all Egged bus lines and on the Light Rail Train. They are available at all branches of Egged Tours.

The **Light Rail Train** (073/210-0601 or *3686 from any local phone, www.citypass. co.il, NIS6.60) is a fast and convenient way to get around in certain parts of the city. It is the most convenient way, for example, to get from City Center to Yad Vashem. But its route is rather limited and does not include most major tourist sites. As it runs roughly along the old border between east and west Jerusalem, it is very convenient if you want to get somewhere in east Jerusalem. All tickets are valid for continued use for 90 minutes from the time they are purchased.

Vicinity of Jerusalem

Not far from Jerusalem there are several enchanting and interesting places for a different perspective on the region. Visitors with an interest in history, archaeology, spirituality, and nature will find something to pique their interest. It is particularly recommended to visit areas outside of Jerusalem during Shabbat, as the majority of restaurants and sights remain open.

SIGHTS

Marc Chagall Stained Glass Windows at Hadassah Hospital

If you're a serious art lover, it might be worth your while to take a major detour to Hadassah Hospital, where you'll find **Marc Chagall Stained Glass Windows** (off of Route 396 near Ein Kerem, 02/677-7111, www.hadassah.org.il), a series of 12 arched, stained glass windows surrounding the hospital's synagogue. Chagall

called them his "modest gift to the Jewish people." They were renovated in fall 2012. The drive to Hadassah through the Jerusalem forest is very scenic, and there are numerous other works of art throughout the hospital donated by the artists themselves or supporters. Nearby Ein Kerem offers several interesting sights as well as a variety of good dining and drinking options.

Ein Kerem

About 30 minutes outside of Jerusalem lies the scenic valley village of **Ein Kerem,** believed to be the birthplace of John the Baptist, whose mother was the Virgin Mary's cousin. One of the sites often visited here is **Mary's Well** (southern end of HaMa'ayan St., near the music center), which Christian tradition says was a site visited by the Virgin Mary when she

© GIDON BELMAKER

Gorny Monastery, in the village of Ein Kerem

stopped here to drink from the spring. A 19th-century mosque can be seen above the spring.

Following a path near Mary's Well, you will come to a southern hill facing Ein Kerem and the **Shrine of the Visitation** (southern hill facing the village at the top of the pedestrian extension of HaMa'ayan St., 02/641-7291, www.custodia.org, 8am-noon and 2:30pm-6pm Mon.-Sat., NIS5). The church has a facade on the front with a series of arches, a bell tower, and a painting of the Virgin Mary riding a donkey and accompanied by angels on the front outer wall. The two-story church has large color paintings throughout depicting biblical scenes. It is also home to a guesthouse run by nuns.

Not far away is the Russian **Gorny Monastery**, also known as Moscavia for its distinctive gold onion domes that are clearly visible from the village. You can reach the church by walking up a steep, winding footpath. The 19th-century Russian Orthodox church is also home to a convent. The compound's buildings are closed to the public, but you can get an excellent view from the parking lot on HaOren Street next to Shibboleth Lane.

The **Sisters of Zion Convent** (1/2 HaOren St., 02/641-5738, 9am-noon and 2pm-5pm Mon.-Fri., 9am-5pm Sat., ring for entrance, NIS2) is home to an archaeological garden and chapel.

The **Church of St. John** (Mevo Hasha'ar, 02/632-3000, 6am-noon and 2pm-5pm daily, free) is built at the location where John the Baptist was believed to have been born. The church has a grotto beneath it with the remains of a Byzantine mosaic.

Herodium (King Herod's Palace-Fortress)

About eight miles south of Jerusalem is King Herod's Palace-Fortress, **Herodium** (south of Jerusalem and east of Bethlehem on edge of Judean Desert, 050/623-5821, www.parks.org.il, 8am-5pm Apr.-Sept., 8am-4pm Oct.-Mar. daily, NIS27). According to one historical account, he built it after winning a victory over the Hasmoneans and Parthians. The palace is

758 meters above sea level. The site contains extensive palatial ruins, including a living quarter complex, an ancient synagogue, and underground tunnels, and it can be accessed by foot.

Mini-Israel Model

One way to cover a lot of ground in a short time is to see **Mini-Israel** (0.25 mile from Kahativa 7 Junction, 700/559-559, dalia@minisrael.co.il, www.minisrael.co.il, 10am-6pm Sept.-June, 5pm-10pm July-Aug. Sun.-Thurs. except 10am-2pm Fri., adult NIS79, child NIS59). The miniature theme park has 385 exact replica models on a 1:25 scale of Israel. The models are positioned among bonsai trees and miniature figurines of Israelis. There is also a 3D movie of Israeli landscapes, a restaurant and cafeteria, multi-media and play area for kids, and a new MiniMax aerial movie of Israeli sites.

Ein Hemed (Aqua Bella)

Just outside of Jerusalem near the villages of Bet Nekofa and Abu Gosh is **Ein Hemed (Aqua Bella)** national park (off the main Hwy. 1 from the Hemed off-ramp, opposite Kibbutz Kiryat Anavim and the town of Abu Gosh, 02/534-2741, 9am-6pm daily, NIS20), which was once used as a way station for Crusaders. You can still find the remains of a ruined Crusader farmhouse and a park with an olive press.

Latrun Monastery

Just off of Highway 1 between Jerusalem and Tel Aviv is the **Latrun Monastery** (08/922-0065, 9am-1pm and 2pm-5pm Mon.-Sat., free), founded in 1890 and home to an order of silent monks up until the 1960s. The site consists of a large church and living quarters on the monastery grounds, garden, vineyard, and orchards. In late 2012, the monastery was vandalized by Jewish settlers angry over being removed by the government from their settlement. As you enter the site, you will find a shop selling Domain de Latroun wines, liqueurs, spirits, and olive oil and honey that was made at the monastery.

Jerusalem Biblical Zoo

A short drive from the center of town is the

Jerusalem Biblical Zoo (1 Aharon Sholov Rd., 02/675-0111, www.jerusalemzoo.org. il, 9am-6pm Sun.-Thurs., 9am-4:30pm Fri. and holiday eves, 10am-6pm Sat. and holidays, adult NIS50, child, senior, and student NIS40), a remarkably diverse zoo that is also a non-profit organization owned equally by the Municipality of Jerusalem, the Jerusalem Foundation, and the Jerusalem Development Authority. Opened in 1993, it is home to an incredibly wide array of animals, including monkeys, elephants, lions, lemurs, snakes, flamingos, and more.

ACCOMMODATIONS
Under US$100
The **Rosary Sisters Ein Kerem Guest House** (3 HaMa'ayan HaBikur St., 02/641-3755, www.rosary-einkarem.com, US$90 d) is a small guesthouse run by nuns in the hills of Ein Kerem at the site of Sisters of Zion Convent. The rooms are small and simply furnished, and facilities include a reception area and a small dining room.

The **Sister of Sion Guest House** (23 HaOren St., Ein-Kerem D, 02/641-5738, http://sion-ein-karem.org, US$80 d) offers a small selection of simple rooms with free Wi-Fi for singles, couples, and families. All rooms have heating, but only some have air-conditioning.

US$100-150
Just at the entrance to the city is the **Jerusalem Gate Hotel** (43 Yirmiyahu, 02/500-8500, www.jerusalemgatehotel.com, US$150 d), in close proximity to the convention center and the central bus station, from which you can travel cheaply all over Israel. This large hotel has 298 rooms and caters to business travelers with its understated interior and proximity to the convention center. The rooms are a good size and simply decorated. Every room has Wi-Fi, a safe, and hair dryers.

US$150-200
Beit Yehudah Guest House (Haim Kulitz Rd. 1, Givat Massuah, 02/632-2777, www.

byh.co.il, US$200 d) is in the hills of Jerusalem, close to the zoo, Yad Vashem, and Malha shopping mall. The 129 rooms offered by the hotel include satellite TV, mini-bars, and many have a view of the gardens and the Jerusalem hills. A swimming pool and café are also on site. It is the perfect setting if you want to visit Jerusalem in style, but prefer to be a bit removed from the hustle and bustle of the city.

The **Rimonim Shalom Jerusalem** (24 Shachrai St., Bait Va'gan, 02/675-2222, www. rimonim.com, US$198 d) is a luxury hotel on the outskirts of Jerusalem with 287 rooms, room service, panoramic views from floor-to-ceiling windows in every room, Wi-Fi, a restaurant, and 24-hour concierge service. The rooms are decorated in a standard style, although they are a bit on the drab side.

Over US$200
The lovely **Ramat Rachel Kibbutz Hotel** (Kibbutz Ramat Rachel, Tzfon Yehuda, 02/670-2555, www.ramatrachel.co.il, US$220 d) is just the right distance from Jerusalem (it's a 15-minute drive) to make it feel like a getaway in the city. The 165-room, four-star hotel is situated on the grounds of one of the oldest settlements outside the Old City walls in Jerusalem. Hotel amenities include an outdoor swimming pool, variety of room types, country club, kosher restaurant, money changing services, and an active synagogue.

FOOD
Abu Ghosh
There are several good options in Abu Ghosh for Arab cuisine, including hummus, falafel, and shwarma. Try **The Original Abu Shukri** (15 Hashalom Way, 02/652-6088, 8am-8pm daily, NIS45), which gets its name from a dispute with another restaurant. The dispute is that one (nobody is sure which anymore) is regarded as having the best hummus in all of Israel. The interior of the restaurant is very simple and homey and the dining experience is, like most hummus dining, without much fanfare. But the food is delicious and comes

to your table quickly, the service is good, and there is free parking.

If you're tired of Middle Eastern food, you can find the **Elvis American Diner** (near the Neve Ilan gas station, 02/534-1275, 7am-midnight daily, NIS80) in Abu Ghosh, serving up what are widely reputed to be some of the best hamburgers in the area. A large statue of Elvis is outside the building, and Elvis pictures cover the walls inside.

Ein Kerem

Ein Kerem is a fun place to go during the weekend when not much is happening in Jerusalem. You can do a little sightseeing, take a stroll, get a drink, or have dinner and enjoy a leisurely coffee and dessert. The main concentration of places to get food and drinks are on two roads: to the end of HaMa'ayan Street and along the part of Ein Kerem Road 74 where it passes through the village.

Try **Charlotte** (25 Ein Kerem Rd., 02/643-4545, noon-11pm Sun.-Thurs., NIS70) if you're in the mood for something grilled. Though they are one of the few places not open on the weekend, Charlotte offers a nice array of chicken and beef dishes, and has the unusual offering of goose breast skewers. All of their entrées are served with salad, and their interior is large and spacious with wood paneling and huge windows that give it the feeling of a cabin.

Brasserie (15 HaMa'ayan St., 02/566-5000, 10am-last customer daily, NIS60) has a large patio on its second level for outdoor seating in good weather. The patio affords a nice view of the scenic setting. Serving seafood, including mussels and shrimp, the restaurant also has a good selection of steak, chicken, and French-inspired dishes (try the camembert croissant). Brasserie also has a nice liquor and wine selection, and customers can arrange a menu for wine tasting. Four beers on tap are served, as well as an array of signature cocktails.

Karma (74 Ein Kerem Rd., 02/643-6643, 10am-last customer daily, NIS70) has a nice layout and very accommodating waitstaff. The

Karma offers outdoor seating on the veranda.

© GENEVIEVE BELMAKER

menu is a fairly typical blend of pasta, salad, and meat selections, but there are a few surprises. Try the taboon-baked flatbread covered with vegetables and eggs or the Druze-inspired appetizer platter, which consists of a thin pita overstuffed with lamb cuts, pine nuts, red sauce, tahini, and roasted eggplant. Karma also has enclosed veranda seating on the first floor and tons of balcony seating on the second floor.

GETTING THERE AND AROUND
By Bus
To get to Ein Kerem, take Egged bus 17 from City Center; it takes about 25 minutes. To Abu Ghosh, take bus 185 or 186, and to Hadassah Hospital (where you can see the famed Chagall windows), take bus 19. If you are venturing out to Herodium, go and return by tour bus. A trip to Mini-Israel is best achieved by taking an Egged Tour Bus on Tuesday and Thursday (call 700/707-577) or the Egged public bus to "Kahativa 7 Junction" and walk about 15 minutes to the site.

For the gorgeous parklands of Ein Hemed (Aqua Bella), the Superbus 185 leaves from Jerusalem every hour. Just get off at Beit Nekufa and walk for 10 minutes over the bridge that goes over Road 1.

On the outskirts of the city, the Jerusalem Zoo can be reached by Egged Tour Bus 99.

By Car and Taxi
You can take a taxi to any of the locations outside of Jerusalem, but the fare will be very costly. A 20-minute ride will cost about NIS120 or more. A rental car is a good option, as all of the signs are posted in English.

By Train
The Jerusalem Zoo can be reached by the Israel Railway train (www.rail.co.il/en), which also stops at Malha mall.

TEL AVIV

The city of Tel Aviv is the first modern Jewish city, functioning as a beacon of progress and modernity for Israel. It is the ulti-mate combination of the old customs and traditions blended with the newness of the still relatively young country of Israel. Called "the center" by Israelis, Tel Aviv, like many major cities, is a melting pot of the best and worst from the entire country.

© VADIM BERESTETSKY

HIGHLIGHTS

LOOK FOR ◖ TO FIND RECOMMENDED SIGHTS, ACTIVITIES, DINING, AND LODGING.

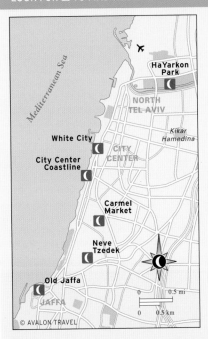

© AVALON TRAVEL

◖ **City Center Coastline:** This coastline has the best collection of beaches that are clean, easy to find, and well-equipped with changing facilities, lockers, and restrooms. And you get to take a swim in the Mediterranean (page 114).

◖ **White City:** One of the best examples of Bauhaus architecture in the world, Tel Aviv's White City is a UNESCO World Heritage Site. It's interesting to architecture, design, and urban enthusiasts alike (page 118).

◖ **Neve Tzedek:** Nowhere in Tel Aviv does old-world European charm meet modern city life as it does in Neve Tzedek. The charming neighborhood is full of interesting shops, museums, and restaurants (page 119).

◖ **Old Jaffa:** One of the oldest port cities in the entire world, Old Jaffa is also one of the best places in Tel Aviv to experience authentic Arab culture (page 122).

◖ **Carmel Market:** Tel Aviv's answer to Jerusalem's famed *shuk*, the Carmel Market is a delight for the senses—filled with exotic spices, fruits, smells, and sounds (page 132).

◖ **HaYarkon Park:** Along the northern border of Tel Aviv, the massive HaYarkon Park is a playground for all kinds of outdoor sports and recreation. When the sun goes down, it's a great place to take an evening stroll (page 137).

The low-key and peaceful village life that defines Jerusalem is almost nowhere to be found here unless you're deep inside the massive HaYarkon Park in the north of the city. Tel Aviv is a bustling, incredibly humid (in the summer) mixture of commerce, people walking the streets in beachwear, and great wealth with harsh pockets of poverty. The immigrant community from Ethiopia is much larger and more obvious here than in other parts of the country, and it is one of the few places where you can sense the tension of race issues.

Tel Aviv, for all intents and purposes, acts as a magnet for talent and ambition from all over Israel. Its beaches, nightlife, business and commercial sectors, fashion and modeling industries, media and arts industries, and impressive array of high-tech companies, massive, gorgeous parks, and secular lifestyle make for a dizzying, attractive blend. Often described by Israelis as the place where everything happens and by visitors as just pure fun, Tel Aviv, on any given day of the week, has offerings for every taste and budget. Its nightlife scene is legendary and infamous for not even really starting until after midnight—at the earliest.

Adjoining Tel Aviv and under the same municipality jurisdiction is Jaffa, one of the oldest cities in the world. Jaffa is predominately Arab and Christian and is home to some of the best fine dining in town. Just after Israel became a state in 1948, the southern neighborhood of Jaffa was joined with Tel Aviv to form Tel Aviv-Yafo.

Known as Israel's new city, Tel Aviv was founded before Israel was a state. Tel Aviv's name is, in a way, its defining characteristic. The word *tel* is the ancient word for "city," and the word *aviv* means "new." That very deliberate blend of old and new is what makes Tel Aviv so unique. It's a place where you can find the entire range of ancient Jewish traditions and customs alongside the new ways of doing things, the most advanced modern technology, and a hub of progressive thinking about the world. The metropolis is the center of arts, culture, and technology for the entire country.

ORIENTATION

It takes about one hour from Jerusalem by car, *sherut* (share taxi), bus, or train to reach Tel Aviv's city center and beaches for a day of fun. The city is laid out in the shape of a rectangle with nothing but beach along the western border.

North Tel Aviv is generally made up of neighborhoods with small areas that are great for shopping, entertainment, and food. The unofficial dividing line between North Tel Aviv and Tel Aviv's City Center is the Tel Aviv Marina. The north section of the city is home to the massive HaYarkon Park, with all of its outdoor diversions as well as the Marina, with its shopping, sightseeing, dining, and nightlife options. At the edge of North Tel Aviv are also some nice museums.

Tel Aviv's City Center is roughly south of the Marina and north of Charles Clore Park. A large majority of action happens in this part of the city, and it is where most of the designated beaches with lifeguards and major (as well as minor) hotels are located. Every kind of shopping, dining, and entertainment can be found in the center. If you are visiting the city for a

Tel Aviv translates to "new city."

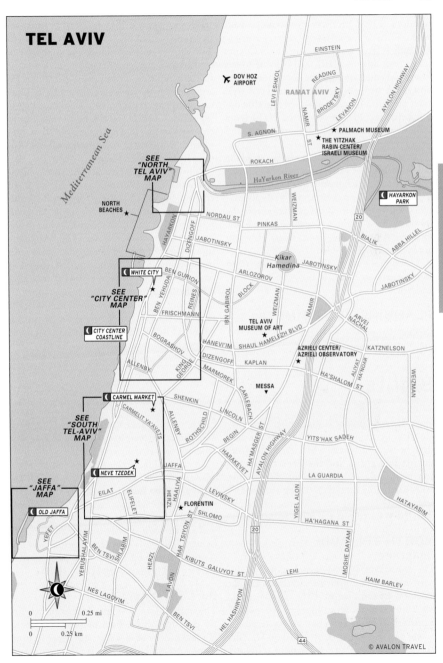

TEL AVIV

✈ DOV HOZ AIRPORT

EINSTEIN

READING

RAMAT AVIV

LEVI ESHKOL

NAMIR

BRODETSKY

LEVANON

AVALON HIGHWAY

S. AGNON

ST.

★ PALMACH MUSEUM

★ THE YITZHAK RABIN CENTER/ ISRAELI MUSEUM

ROKACH

Mediterranean Sea

HaYarkon River

☾ HAYARKON PARK

SEE "NORTH TEL AVIV" MAP

NORTH BEACHES ★

NORDAU ST

PINKAS

WEIZMAN

20

BIALIK

ABBA HILLEL

HAYARKON

DIZENGOFF

JABOTINSKY

Kikar Hamedina

JABOTINSKY

JABOTINSKY

☾ WHITE CITY

BEN GURION

ARLOZOROV

SEE "CITY CENTER" MAP

BEN YEHUDA

REINES

FRISCHMANN

IBN GABIROL

BLOCK

WEIZMAN

NAMIR

ARVEI NACHAL

☾ CITY CENTER COASTLINE

BOGRASHOV

HANEVI'IM

TEL AVIV MUSEUM OF ART ★

SHAUL HAMELEZH BLVD

KATZNELSON

ALLENBY

KING GEORGE

DIZENGOFF

MARMOREK

KAPLAN

AZRIELI CENTER/ AZRIELI OBSERVATORY ★

HA'SHALOM ST

ALIYAT HANOAR

WEIZMAN

☾ CARMEL MARKET ★

SHENKIN

CARLEBACH

▼ MESSA

CARMELIT YA'AVETS

ALLENBY

ROTHSCHILD

LINCOLN

BEGIN

HA'MASGER ST

AVALON HIGHWAY

YITS'HAK SADEH

SEE "SOUTH TEL-AVIV" MAP

HARAKEVET

JAFFA

LA GUARDIA

HATAYASIM

☾ NEVE TZEDEK ★

HAALIYA

LEVINSKY

YIGEL ALON

SEE "JAFFA" MAP

EILAT

ELIFELET

HERZL

★ FLORENTIN

SHLOMO

20

HA'HAGANA ST

MOSHE DAYAM

☾ OLD JAFFA

YEFET

YERUSHALAYIM

BEN TSVI

SHABIM

HAR TSIYON ST.

KIBUTS GALUYOT ST

LEHI

HAIM BARLEV

☾

NES LAGOYIM

LAVON

BEN TSVI

HEL HASHIRYON

44

0   0.25 mi

0   0.25 km

© AVALON TRAVEL

few days, it is an excellent area to use as your base.

South Tel Aviv is approximately from Charles Clore Park down to Jaffa, and is home to the lovely and entertaining Neve Tzedek neighborhood with its high-end shops, European-style cafés and restaurants, and varied nightlife options that include the converted HaTachana train station compound with shops, coffee, and live entertainment.

At the farthest south point is Jaffa, one of the oldest cities in the world. It is today part of Tel Aviv and very much intertwined with the city's daily life. Jaffa's predominately Arab population gives it a completely unique flavor from the rest of the city, and it is famed for being home to some of Israel's best chefs, many of whom are internationally known.

Throughout all of Tel Aviv from north to south, there are miles of boardwalks, parks, and beaches.

PLANNING YOUR TIME

Particularly in the sweltering summer months, Tel Aviv really only comes alive when the sun starts to go down. Plan to spend at least two days and nights in the city to get the right amount of sand, sun, food, and nightlife. In the summer, plan on air-conditioned downtime in the afternoon to keep your energy up for any late nights. The summer heat in Tel Aviv can be brutal, so pace yourself and keep drinking water. The city is active year-round, but as temperatures go down a bit during the winter months from November through March, people naturally move indoors.

Most of the sights and activities are concentrated in and near City Center, but it is a small city, so you don't have to go far to find a museum, a tour group, outdoor sports, or good restaurants. If you stick somewhat close to the beach and promenade between Old Jaffa in the south and the port in the north, you won't run out of things to do or find yourself easily lost or stranded. The city doesn't get particularly crowded or congested, unless you happen to be driving a car on the Ayalon Highway that runs through the city. The best bet for getting around efficiently is to use the convenient train. Buses are also frequent and convenient.

Sights

Since Tel Aviv proper is shaped like a rectangle with a curving eastern border and a pin-straight western border where the land meets the Mediterranean Sea, the city's 13 beaches and boardwalk that stretch for almost nine miles are highly accessible. Using the sea as a reference point, you can enjoy nearby restaurants, bars, museums, and other attractions.

NORTH TEL AVIV
Coastline
The crowds on Tel Aviv beaches differ. The northern locations inside the city limits include **Mezizim Beach,** just near the old city port. Mezizim is known for its hip, trendy crowd of beautiful people and can be a bit boisterous.

Nordau Beach (off of Nordau St. and HaYarkon Rd.) is the city's only religious beach, with separate swimming areas for men and women. It's best to visit only if you are also religious or extremely conservative.

In the middle of the service road between Mezizim Beach and the marina is the highly popular **Hilton Beach,** favored by surfers (it is equipped with lights for night surfing), hippies, and dog-owners and their pooches. It is most well known for being gay-friendly and is popular with Tel Aviv's gay community. It also has excellent access for people with physical disabilities and is next to the Hilton Hotel.

Port of Tel Aviv
The object of a major transformation within the past decade, the **Port of Tel Aviv** (where HaYarkon Road's most northern point turns east and becomes HaTa'arucha St.,

NORTH TEL AVIV

Mediterranean Sea

SHABLUL JAZZ CLUB
PORT MARKET
PORT OF TEL AVIV ★
NAMAL TEL AVIV
HATA'ARUCHA ST
NORTH BEACHES ★
MUL YAM ▼
HOSHEA
NAMAL TEL AVIV
HAYARKON ST
BEN YAHUDA
DIZENGOF
Mezizim Beach
0   200 yds
WHITE PERGOLA ▼
ARMON HAYARKON ▼
HAVAKUK
NAHUM
MICHA
0   200 m
© AVALON TRAVEL
Atzmant Garden

During the hot summer months, the boardwalk is crowded late into the night with everyone—even children. Most of the restaurants don't serve remarkable food and are mainly valuable for their location.

Ramat Aviv

The area of **Ramat Aviv,** just north of the tip of Tel Aviv, is home to some worthwhile museums. Start with **The Yitzhak Rabin Center** (8 Chaim Levanon St., 03/745-3322, www.rabincenter. org.il, 9am-5pm Sun.-Mon. and Wed., 9am-7pm Tues. and Thurs., 9am-2pm Fri., adult NIS50, senior and child NIS25), which includes the **Israeli Museum** (03/745-3345), the first and only museum in Israel that deals with the development of the State of Israel as a young democracy. Built in a downward spiral, smart audio guides (NIS10) recognize where you are as you move through the 1,500 striking photographs, extensive memorabilia, and documentary films on assassinated Prime Minister Yitzhak Rabin and the history of the State of Israel. The building is adjacent to the Eretz Israel Museum, and you should allow 2-3 hours for a visit.

03/544-1505, www.namal.co.il) was once desolate, but now with its marina and boardwalk is one of the most happening places in the city. There is no swimming (legally) in the area, but Tel Avivians come out in droves in the evening to enjoy the seaside; the massive, sloping boardwalk; street performers; and the many restaurants and sweet shops.

TEL AVIV

The Port of Tel Aviv affords great views of the Mediterranean.

© YAIRA YASMIN

The **Eretz Israel Museum** (2 Chaim Levanon St., 03/641-5244, www.eretzmuseum.org.il, 10am-4pm Sun.-Wed., 10am-8pm Thurs., 10am-2pm Fri.-Sat., NIS42, under 18 free) is an eclectic structure built partly on top of an archaeological site. It bills itself as a spiritual and cultural center of Tel Aviv and Israel. The museum includes several exhibition pavilions, each dedicated to a different cultural field and subject in Israel, including archaeology, Judaica, ethnography, as well as more modern art and cultural pieces. Some key permanent exhibitions are the ceramics exhibit and the ethnography and folklore pavilion. The museum's running theme is to highlight life in Israel from ancient times up through modern day. It is easy to walk through the various exhibits. The outdoor archaeological exhibit is accessible even after closing hours. The gift shop's unique items and the building's open-air pavilions are popular draws that make an excellent spot for a leisurely visit.

The extremely popular **Palmach Museum** (10 Chaim Levanon St., 03/643-6393, http://info.palmach.org.il, 9am-4:30pm Sun.-Mon., 9am-8pm Tues., 9am-1:30pm Wed., 9am-4pm Thurs., 9am-11:30am Fri., NIS25) is an experiential museum documenting the history of the elite underground Jewish fighting forces in pre-state Israel. Instead of displays or documents, a 90-minute group tour includes fascinating personal accounts of historical characters alongside three-dimensional decor, films, and special effects that incorporate documentary materials. Visits must be arranged in advance, especially for English-speaking visitors.

A good way to combine a museum visit with a visit to the campus of Tel Aviv University is a stop at **Beit Hatfutsot, The Museum of the Jewish People** (Tel Aviv University campus, Klausner St., in Ramat Aviv, entrance through Matatia Gate 2, www.bh.org.il, 10am-4pm Sun.-Tues., 10am-7pm Wed.-Thurs., 9am-1pm Fri., adult NIS70, child NIS55, senior NIS30). The permanent and rotating exhibits that trace the story of the Jewish people over the last 2,500 years include models, short films, and texts on the history and ongoing stories of the Jewish Diaspora. A lack of upgrades in years past have now led the museum to initiate renovations, but it is still possible to spend hours exploring. Don't miss the miniature synagogue exhibit with models of famous synagogues from all over the world including Europe, Asia, and the Middle East. Also of interest is the genealogy section where you can research on computers and add information to the database.

CITY CENTER
◀ City Center Coastline
A good place to start when visiting the beaches of Tel Aviv are the beaches along the **City Center coastline** (03/724-0340), which runs roughly between Charles Clore Park and the Tel Aviv Marina. Along this stretch of coastline, there are about half a dozen beaches that are easy to access, free, quite clean, and safe.

At the northern tip of City Center's beaches, which includes a good number of designated beaches that have a lifeguard, start with **Gordon Beach.** Also known as Gordon-Frishman, it is extremely popular for its beach volleyball (even at night), hip beach bars, DJs, central location, and proximity to the Tel Aviv Marina. There are a large number of hotels nearby, shaded covers, public toilets and dressing rooms, sports facilities, cafés and restaurants, and a playground. You can rent lounge chairs and sunbathing beds, and there is a water sports area north of the sunbathing area for surfing, windsurfing, and kayaking.

Just south are **Frishman Beach** and **Bugrashov Beach** (both undesignated beaches with no lifeguard), which have nearby public restrooms and are close to public transportation.

Farther south is **Jerusalem Beach** (just across from the Opera Tower at 1 Allenby St.), a designated beach with a lifeguard. The geometric-shaped shopping center used to be home to the Israel Opera and is built on the site of the first Israeli parliament. It's a great place to get some air-conditioning during a day at the beach. The beach is close to places to eat and paid parking, and you can rent sunbathing and lounge chairs.

On the southern end is **Aviv Beach,** another

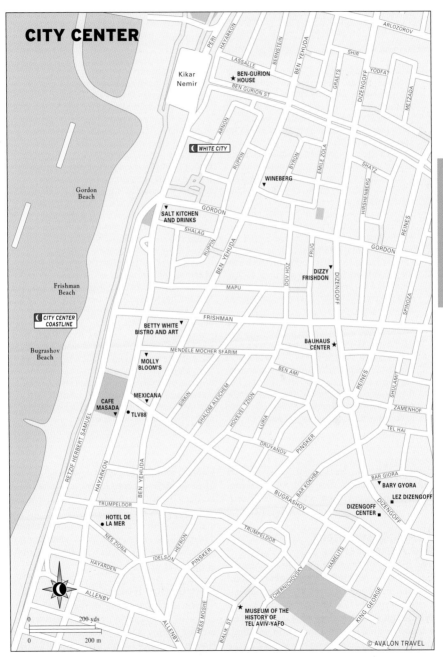

CITY CENTER

TEL AVIV

Kikar
Nemir

★ BEN-GURION
HOUSE

BEN GURION ST

◖ WHITE CITY

▼ WINEBERG

Gordon
Beach

▼ SALT KITCHEN
AND DRINKS

GORDON

SHALAG

DIZZY
FRISHDON

Frishman
Beach

MAPU

◖ CITY CENTER
COASTLINE

FRISHMAN

Bugrashov
Beach

▼ BETTY WHITE
BISTRO AND ART

MENDELE MOCHER SFARIM

BAUHAUS
CENTER ★

▼ MOLLY
BLOOM'S

BEN AMI

MEXICANA ▼

CAFE
MASADA

● TLV88

ZAMENHOF

TEL HAI

DRUYANOV

BAR GIORA

▼ BARY GYORA

LEZ DIZENGOFF

BUGRASHOV

DIZENGOFF
CENTER ■

TRUMPELDOR

HOTEL DE
● LA MER

NES ZIONA

IDELSON

TRUMPELDOR

HAYARDEN

ALLENBY

★ MUSEUM OF THE
HISTORY OF
TEL AVIV-YAFO

0   200 yds

0   200 m

© AVALON TRAVEL

Street labels: ARLOZOROV, PERI, HAYARKON, LASSALLE, BERNSTEIN, BEN YEHUDA, SHIR, GRAETS, DIZENGOFF, YODFAT, METZADA, ARNON, RUPIN, BYRON, EMILE ZOLA, SHATZ, HIRSHENBERG, REINES, GORDON, BEN YEHUDA, RUPIN, DOV HOZ, FRUG, DIZENGOFF, SPINOZA, SHULAMIT, REINES, SHALOM ALEICHEM, SIRKIN, HOVEVEI TZION, LURIA, PINSKER, BAR KOKHBA, DIZENGOFF, HAMELITS, KING GEORGE, TCHERNICHOVSKY, HESS MOSHE, BIALIK ST, ALLENBY, PINSKER, HERON, HAYARKON, BEN YEHUDA, RETZIF HERBERT SAMUEL

TEL AVIV'S COASTAL CULTURE

Israelis love to say that Tel Aviv is their "version of New York City" because of its bustling pace. In fact, it more closely resembles a beach town that just loves to party. Tel Aviv's surf-loving partying atmosphere is apparent everywhere, from the scantily clad to those crossing the street with a surfboard.

It is a city that has good reason to be so obsessed with the sea. Tel Aviv's entire western border is the Mediterranean, and it has a tremendous influence on the city's lifestyle, leisure activities, and atmosphere.

There are two types of Tel Aviv beaches: official and unofficial. Official beaches are designated as safe areas for swimming and have lifeguards. Unofficial beaches have no lifeguards and are often blocked off (such as at the Old Tel Aviv Port). Some beaches, such as Hilton, are gay-friendly, while others are brimming with surfers, and others are jam-packed with tourists.

Four major points of reference on the Tel Aviv coast are the Jaffa Port, the Dolphinarium, the Tel Aviv Marina, and the Tel Aviv Port.

The **Jaffa Port** is on the southern end of the city and near the Old City of Jaffa and the southern end of Tel Aviv. Here you can find restaurants, ancient architecture, and general sightseeing in a scenic setting at what is believed to be one of the oldest ports in the entire world.

The **Dolphinarium** is just north of the oldest part of the *tayalet* (promenade) and the spacious Charles Clore Park, with gorgeous views of both Jaffa and Tel Aviv. The Dolphinarium was the site of a horrific terrorist bombing in 2001 during the second Intifada. The burned-out building is easily visible from HaYarkon Street and Herbert Samuel Street, though the City of Tel Aviv has long been discussing plans to raze the building completely. Regardless of whether the building is there or not, the location is a major landmark. Nearby is the Israel Surf Club, where you can rent equipment and take lessons. Just southeast are the hip and happening adjacent districts of Shabazi Street, Neve Tzedek, and HaTachana.

Due north up the coast is the **Tel Aviv Marina,** another hub of activity and central launching point for activities. Here you will find the heated saltwater Gordon Swimming Pool, Atarim Square, and more excellent surfing spots and beaches.

Continue north to the **Tel Aviv Port** to find a tremendous center of activity, including a scenic boardwalk, restaurants, shops, a farmer's market, and a couple of beaches. The area has been revitalized in recent years and is a beehive of activity, especially in the late summer evenings when locals looking to escape the stifling heat get out and about.

designated beach. Near major transportation hub Carmelit bus station and paid parking, Aviv Beach is also known as Drummers' Beach for its popularity among drumming circles.

Azrieli Observatory and Azrieli Center

The highest observation point in the Middle East is the **Azrieli Observatory** (132 Menachem Begin Rd., 3rd Fl. designated elevator, 03/608-1179, http://mitzpe49.co.il, NIS22) on the 49th floor of **Azrieli Center,** a multi-level mall with a train stop and multiplex cinema. The observatory, located in the

Center's round tower, has a commanding view of the coastline from Gedera in the south to Hadera in the north and of Tel Aviv. Some vantage points are only accessible from the bar and restaurant, often closed for private events. There is little explanation of the view, but it is good for a combined visit with the mall and a gorgeous at sunset.

Ben-Gurion House

The former home of one of the fathers of the nation of Israel, David Ben-Gurion, is still intact for visitors. The very modest **Ben-Gurion House** (17 Ben-Gurion Blvd., 03/522-1010,

TEL AVIV

© GENEVIEVE BELMAKER

the Mediterranean Sea just off the Charles Clore Park promenade

© YAIRA YASMIN

the tower of Azrieli Center in downtown Tel Aviv

www.ben-gurion-house.org.il, 8am-3pm Sun. and Tues.-Thurs., 8am-5pm Mon., 8am-noon Fri., 11am-2pm first Sat. each month, free) includes Ben-Gurion's library of approximately 20,000 books and is an example of the Bauhaus/International design so well-preserved in Tel Aviv. The museum's signage is mostly in Hebrew, but it is still worth a visit to explore the residence and some of the photos, letters, and gifts from world leaders. Call in advance to ask for a possible English-speaking guide.

Tel Aviv Museum of Art

Opened in 1932 in the home of Tel Aviv's first mayor, Meir Dizengoff, and since moved to a distinctive, futuristic-looking building, the **Tel Aviv Museum of Art** (27 Shaul HaMelech Blvd., 03/607-7020, www.tamuseum.com, 10am-4pm Mon. and Wed., 10am-10pm Tues. and Thurs., 10am-2pm Fri., 10am-4pm Sat., adult NIS48, senior NIS24, under 18 free) hosts a vast collection of art from the 16th century through modern times, including

A BRIEF HISTORY OF ISRAEL'S "NEW CITY"

Tel Aviv draws at least some of its inspiration for being vibrant and exciting from its status as Israel's "new city." The name Tel Aviv literally translates as "spring mound" but the more intuitive meaning is "old new city," as its name was inspired by founding father Theodore Herzl's book bearing that title. The founding and creation of Tel Aviv was, and is, seen as the center of the revival of the new Jewish state in the ancient homeland.

Tel Aviv's official name, Tel Aviv-Yafo, stems from its connection to the ancient port city of Jaffa (Yafo) that is at the southern end of the city. Jaffa, which is predominately Arab, is estimated to be about 4,000 years old.

The first modern Hebrew city, Tel Aviv was established in 1909 by a group of 60 families who self-assigned plots of land. But as the population of Tel Aviv grew, so did tensions with Arab neighbors in Jaffa who had been living there for years.

Suffering from a long history of instability and insecurity, on the eve of the establishment of an independent Jewish state in 1948, Jewish and Arab forces battled for control of Tel Aviv, and Arab forces and residents were violently pushed into Jaffa. In 1949, Tel Aviv's second mayor, Israel Rokach, united Tel Aviv and Jaffa under the auspices of the Tel Aviv-Yafo municipality.

Today, Jaffa accounts for about 12 percent of Tel Aviv's total area and is home to about 45,000 Arab, Christian, and Jewish residents. It is famed for having some of the best fine dining in the country.

contemporary Israeli art. Made up of a main building, a new wing opened in 2011, an art education center, and a sculpture garden, this vast art museum hosts at least half a million visitors a year. The old masters collection is on par with European museums, and in general there is a surprising array of pieces in both the permanent and changing exhibits.

Israel Defense Forces History Museum

Situated near the HaTachana train station compound, the **Israel Defense Forces History Museum** (Shimtat Shlush St. at the corner of Ashkelon St., 03/517-2913, toldot_zahal_museum@mailto.mod.gov.il, 8:30am-3:30pm Sun.-Thurs., NIS20) depicts the history of the Israeli army from 1948 through today. With a bunker-like exterior, the museum is spread out through five buildings and includes extensive outdoor pavilions with exhibits that include films, photographs, maps, historic documents, and authentic tanks, cars, and weapons.

Old City Hall

The beautiful, grand Bauhaus building that served as Tel Aviv's **Old City Hall** with

colonnades and facing entrance staircases is now home to the **Museum of the History of Tel Aviv-Yafo** (27 Bialik St., 03/517-3052, 9am-2pm Mon.-Thurs., free). The collection of photos and old video clips from Tel Aviv residents chronicles the history of the city over the past 100 years. The office of Tel Aviv's first mayor, Meir Dizengoff, has been restored with a view of Bialik Square and Bialik Street's Bauhaus architecture. Rotating exhibitions of local and international artists and designers are also on display. The museum is a pleasant, easy to reach stop on the way to see the White City.

◖ White City

Tel Aviv's **White City** (between Allenby St. in the south, Begin Rd. and Ibn Gabirol St. in the east, the Yarkon River in the north, and the Mediterranean Sea in the west, www.whitecity.co.il) is a UNESCO World Heritage Site and considered an outstanding example of new town planning and architecture in the early 20th century, adapted to the cultural and geographic context of Tel Aviv. Based on a design by Scottish Sir Patrick Geddes, the 4,000 buildings of the White City were built between the early 1930s through the 1950s. They are a definitive part of Tel Aviv's character and what UNESCO calls an "outstanding architectural ensemble of the Modern Movement in a new cultural context."

The buildings in the White City were designed by European-trained architects who practiced their profession abroad before immigrating to Israel. Most of the buildings are 3-4 stories high and have flat roofs, plaster rendering, some decorative features, and a monochromatic color scheme of cream to white. The buildings are located mainly along Rothschild Boulevard, around Dizengoff Circle and on Bialik Street.

On Fridays, the one-room **Bauhaus Foundation Museum** (21 Bialik St., 03/620-4664, 11am-5pm Wed., 10am-2pm Fri., free) offers free tours that last two hours. Call in advance for specific times.

The **Bauhaus Center** (99 Dizengoff St., 03/522-0249, www.bauhaus-center.com, 10am-7:30pm Sun.-Thurs., 10am-2:30pm Fri., noon-7:30pm Sat., free) is dedicated to the public recognition of the White City as a unique architectural and cultural site. The center is rather small but has an interesting array of Bauhaus memorabilia and a second-floor gallery with permanent and changing art exhibitions. The ground floor gift shop sells books in English on the subject of the White City

and Bauhaus. Guided tours in English (10am Fri., NIS60) are available here either with a tour guide or by renting audio headphones (anytime, NIS60). Both types of tours take about two hours.

The City of Tel Aviv also offers **Walk this Way** (White City tour: meet at 46 Rothschild Blvd. on the corner of Shadal St., www.visit-tlv.com, 11am Sat., free), a variety of free walking tours that include a route of the White City. Other tours include Tel Aviv University, Tel Aviv by Night, Tel Aviv Art and Graffiti, and Old Jaffa.

SOUTH TEL AVIV
Coastline
Relatively isolated on the southern end of the city is peaceful **Charles Clore Beach** (at HaMered St. and Kaufman St., 03/724-0340), tucked into gorgeous, sprawling Charles Clore Park on the border of Jaffa. Popular with dog owners, the beach is near paid parking; a designated area for surfing, windsurfing, and kayaking; and a boardwalk with hotels, restaurants, and clubs. There is no lifeguard.

(Neve Tzedek
Decades before Tel Aviv was even formally established as a city, **Neve Tzedek** (which means oasis of justice) had already sprung up

THE WHITE CITY

In 1925, as Tel Aviv grew and developed, Scottish urban planner Sir Patrick Geddes was brought in to help plan a modern urban city in response to the sprawling expansion with no overall cohesion. Geddes's vision for a Tel Aviv master plan was a garden city with clear separations between main streets, residential streets, and vegetation-filled pedestrian boulevards. One of the plan's key elements was creating shared public spaces in parks, squares, and in residential blocks. It was a significant part of the Bauhaus movement, a highly influential, modernist approach to art and design that manifested in architecture, as buildings (indi-

vidually and as groups) centered on purpose, and integration with the needs of modern city life and its surroundings.

Using Geddes's urban plan, from the early 1930s until the 1950s, the White City came into being. Designed by architects who had trained and practiced in Europe, the design of the White City reflects modern organic planning principles, and ultimately became what UNESCO calls "an outstanding architectural ensemble of the Modern Movement in a new cultural context."

Declared a UNESCO World Heritage Site, the White City can be toured today and its buildings are protected structures.

TEL AVIV

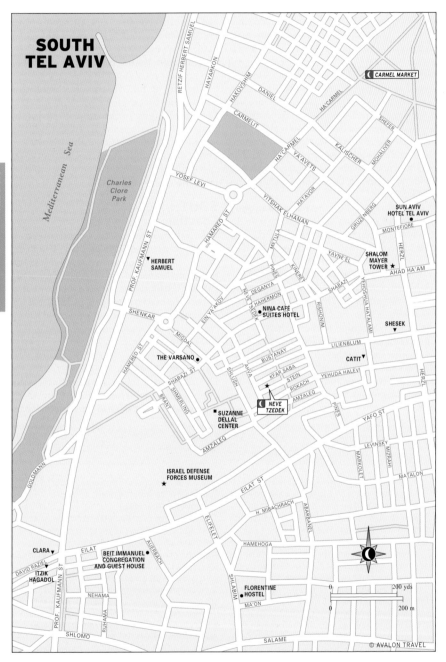

SOUTH TEL AVIV

Mediterranean Sea

Charles Clore Park

CARMEL MARKET

RETZIF HERBERT SAMUEL
HAYARKON
HAKOVSHIM
DANIEL
CARMELIT
HA'CARMEL
SHEFER
HA'CARMEL
KALISCHER
YA'AVETS
MOHALIVER
HERZL
HATAVOR
YOSEF LEVI
YITSHAK ELHANAN
GRUZENBERG
SUN AVIV HOTEL TEL AVIV
MONTEFIORE
METULA
PINES
YAVNE EL
SHALOM MAYER TOWER ★
AHAD HA'AM
PROF. KAUFMANN ST
HAMARED ST
▼ HERBERT SAMUEL
KINERET
SHABAZI
YEHOSHUA HA'ALAMI
DEGANYA
NEVE TSEDEK
HAHERMON
RISHONIM
▼ SHESEK
SHENKAR
● NINA CAFÉ SUITES HOTEL
HAMARED ST
MIGDAL
EIN YA'AKOV
LILIENBLUM
CATIT ▼
● THE VARSANO
BUSTANAY
KFAR SABA
YEHUDA HALEVI
SHABAZI ST
SLUSH
AVIA
STEIN
SIMMERING
BOKACH
AMZALEG
HERZL
BRANT
★ NEVE TZEDEK
YAFO ST
■ SUZANNE DELLAL CENTER
PINES
AMZALEG
LEVINSKY
MARKOLE
MIZRAHI
GOLDMANN
★ ISRAEL DEFENSE FORCES MUSEUM
EILAT ST
MATALON
H. MIBACHRACH
ELIFELET
ABARBANEL
HAMEHOGA
CLARA ▼
EILAT
AUERBACH
DAVID RAZIEL
● BEIT IMMANUEL CONGREGATION AND GUEST HOUSE
ITZIK HAGADOL
SHLABIM
PROF. KAUFMANN ST
NEHAMA
● FLORENTINE HOSTEL
0   200 yds
RUHAMA
MA'ON
0   200 m
SHLOMO
SALAME

© AVALON TRAVEL

© YAIRA YASMIN

a house in the old Neve Tzedek neighborhood

in 1887. It is Tel Aviv's oldest neighborhood, and the first one inhabited by Jewish residents. Prominent artists and writers like S. Y. Agnon and Nachum Gutman called Neve Tzedek home during the early 20th century, and it still has a bohemian, European vibe. It is by far one of the coolest places in the city to stroll around and take in the atmosphere; browse designer boutique stores, crafts shops, and bookstores; and enjoy one of the area's fine cafés or restaurants. The main (very narrow) throughway in Neve Tzedek is Shabazi Street, an excellent place to see historic Tel Aviv architecture.

Start at the **Nachum Gutman Museum of Art** (21 Shim'on Rokach St., 03/516-1970, www.gutmanmuseum.co.il, 10am-4pm Sun.-Thurs., 10am-2pm Fri., 10am-3pm Sat., entrance fee, free on Fri., NIS24, free on Fri.) with its distinctive bright yellow colonnade fence around an historic house dating to the founding of the neighborhood. The charming, small museum showcases works by Nachum Gutman, a beloved Israeli artist and children's author. You can see hundreds of his illustrations

and drawings as well as oil, watercolor, and gouache paintings.

The **Rokach House Museum** (36 Shim'on Rokach St., 03/516-8042, www.rokach-house. co.il, 10am-4pm Sun.-Thurs., 10am-2pm Fri.-Sat., schedule English tours in advance, NIS10) was also built in 1887 and is famous for its domed roof. Now a museum named for Shim'on Rokach, a prominent Jewish public servant and co-founder of Neve Tzedek, the museum focuses on Rokach's notable artist and sculptor granddaughter, Lea Majaro-Mintz. There's also an English video and photographs depicting Neve Tzedek's history.

Shalom Mayer Tower

Just east of Neve Tzedek is the **Shalom Mayer Tower** (9 Ahad Ha'am St., 03/510-0337, www. migdalshalom.co.il/eng, 8am-7pm Sun.-Thurs., 8am-2pm Fri. and holidays, free), an interesting stop for art enthusiasts. The spacious, modern layout includes exhibits in the lobby and a first floor **art gallery** (10am-5pm Sun.-Thurs., 10am-1pm Fri. and holidays, free), one of the largest non-profit art galleries in Israel. Works include pieces from contemporary Israeli painters, sculptors, and photographers and a dozen permanent and alternating exhibits from Israel's best museums.

The Tower also houses the **Discover Tel Aviv Center** (9 Ahad Ha'am St., for tours email tiki@discover-telaviv.co.il, 10am-5pm Sun.-Thurs., free) on the ground floor with an interactive multimedia display about Tel Aviv's development, history, and famous residents. It depicts the history of the city through paintings and photographs and offers professionally guided tours in Tel Aviv and throughout Israel.

JAFFA (YAFO)

The port city of Jaffa (Yafo) is believed to be one of the most ancient cities in the world. An area with a strong Arab flavor, Jaffa is an important part of a visit to Tel Aviv. It is directly adjacent to the rest of the city and is easy to reach by bus or car. It is full of charming, interesting sights, restaurants, and shopping. For a scenic route to reach Jaffa, walk on the paved beachfront boardwalk at Charles Clore Park

and cross the pedestrian bridge that is the unofficial boundary between Tel Aviv (the new city) and Jaffa (the old city).

◖ Old Jaffa

Old Jaffa (access through the promenade or off of Yefet St.) is contained largely near the port on a hill overlooking the Mediterranean and

Old Jaffa is full of ancient stone.

© VADIM BERESTETSKY

has many corners to explore. You'll find archaeological sites here, but also upscale shops, some of the best fine dining in Tel Aviv, an artists' quarter, renovated Ottoman-era houses, and several important landmarks.

Start on the east side of Old Jaffa at **Clock Tower Square,** which is a popular meeting place and home to the **clock tower,** built in 1901 by Turkish Sultan Abed-el-Hamid II and one of Jaffa's most easily recognizable sites. Here you will also find the **former governor's house** and a jailhouse used by the Turks and British known as the **Kishle.** On Yefet Street in the immediate vicinity is the famous **Abulafia Bakery** (7 Yefet St., 03/681-2340, NIS20), which also has a 24-hour street bakery nearby. The plaza area is encircled by several galleries, restaurants, and souvenir shops, and you can hear free concerts here during the summer.

In the Clock Tower Square is the **Visitor's Center** (Clock Tower Square, 03/603-7686, www.oldjaffa.co.il, 10am-5pm Sun.-Thurs., 10am-3pm Fri., 10am-5pm Sat. Nov.-Mar.; 9am-7pm Sun.-Thurs., 9am-4pm Fri., 9am-7pm Sat. Apr.-Oct.), a good place to get started. It is also an archaeological site and a museum about the area's history. The Visitor's Center is located in an underground building that includes exhibits of archaeological ruins from the Hellenistic and Roman eras and three-dimensional illustrations of Jaffa's legends and historical events of the past 2,000 years. There are also eight paintings done over the past 300 years of Jaffa from the perspective of the sea. The Visitor's Center's light and sound show tells the story of the past and present of the Old City.

Along **Mifrats Shlomo Promenade** you will find a large structure that is historically and architecturally unique and made up of several historical buildings, built over Crusader-era remnants. Dating to the 18th century, it has served as the seat of the Ottoman governor, a post office, and a guard house. A well-known Christian family by the name of Demiani bought part of the building in 1733 and converted it into a successful soap factory. Abandoned during Israel's War of Independence, it now houses the **Jaffa**

TEL AVIV

© VADIM BERESTETSKY

St. Peter's Monastery

Museum of Antiquities (10 Mifrats Shlomo St., 03/682-5375, www.oldjaffa.co.il, 4pm-8pm Mon.-Wed., 4pm-9pm Thurs., 10am-4pm Fri.-Sat., NIS30) with permanent exhibits on archaeology and changing exhibits on modern art. It is small and comprehensive enough to be informative but not exhausting.

Built over medieval fortress remains and the ruins of a Byzantine church, **St. Peter's Monastery** (1 Mifrats Shlomo St. next to Clock Tower Square, 03/682-2871, 8am-noon and 3pm-6pm Apr.-Oct., 8am-noon and 3pm-5pm Nov.-Mar. daily, free) is a Franciscan church built at the beginning of the 20th century. It features a unique brick facade and towering belfry that overlooks the sea from where it sits at the top of Jaffa mound. The iconic building's silhouette is visible from the southern end of Tel Aviv and the picturesque view is frequently photographed. The location has been a center for Christianity for thousands of years, and it is believed that Napoleon once stayed here. The church has a spectacular interior with a vaulted ceiling, stained glass windows, and marble walls.

Old Port

From the old city's Clock Tower Square, you can find small winding streets leading down to the **Old Port** area, one of the most ancient ports in the world. The Bible's Book of Jonah mentions Jaffa's port; Napoleon's army destroyed it in 1799, and it was later rebuilt by the Ottomans. The port has served as the main point of entry for thousands of Jewish immigrants, and it has boating excursions and good seafood restaurants. The main hangars were restored to house art galleries, cafés, restaurants, and shops.

A highly popular draw is the startling and unusual **The Nalagaat Center** (Retsif Haaliya Hashniya at Jaffa Port, 03/633-0808, www.nalagaat.org.il, call for reservations). It is an artistic complex operated by the deaf and blind community, complete with a unique restaurant and café.

Entertainment and Events

As soon as the sun goes down in Tel Aviv, residents come out in droves to party, eat, drink, and enjoy the beautiful evenings and wide array of entertainment. No matter what kind of entertainment you are looking for, you will find it. Always carry some kind of ID and check the age range of the venue beforehand, as some places draw very young crowds or change the minimum age by the night. Have a backup plan, too, in case your destination has closed (as some venues in Tel Aviv do).

BARS, CLUBS, PUBS, AND LIVE MUSIC

Tel Aviv nightlife can be broken down into a few categories. Bars, clubs, pubs, and live music venues offer everything from beers and billiards to small venue rock concerts and are great for hanging out and having a few drinks.

North Tel Aviv

The seaside to the west of HaYarkon Park right where the Yarkon River empties into the Mediterranean has a nice variety of places for evening fun, many at or nearby the **Old Port of Tel Aviv.**

For a classy beachside experience, check out **Galina** (19 Hangar at the Port of Tel Aviv, 03/544-5533 or 052/245-8600, www.galina-bar.co.il, 7pm-last customer daily, minimum age varies, no cover), a huge dance club and bar with a very mainstream and upscale interior. The club has a dress code and pretty steep prices such as NIS20 for a beer or NIS50 for a shot of vodka, but it also boasts a large deck with views of the Mediterranean. It's a good place to see and be seen.

Along Ben Yehuda Street, local institution **Eliezer** (186 Ben Yehuda St., 057/943-9156, 8pm-last customer daily, drinks NIS20 and up) is considered the grandfather of the Tel Aviv bar and club scene. Some of Israel's popular DJs spin rock and current pop music here, there's a modest food menu to choose from, and the space is classy but not huge. Though not impressive on the surface, Eliezer is a bar scene standard and consistently ranked as a local favorite.

One of Tel Aviv's longest streets, Dizengoff Street runs from the north through the center of town, and is full of interesting spots all along the way. One of them, **Rosa Parks** (265 Dizengoff St., 054/643-9958, 8pm-last customer daily, no cover), is a laid-back bar that caters to a 25-plus, sophisticated, and upwardly mobile crowd. It has two levels with a pool table and a small upstairs bar with a view of the street.

One of the oldest clubs in the city, the **TLV Club** (Old Port, 03/544-4194, midnight-6am Mon. and Fri.-Sat., cover varies depending on who is performing) is a large discotheque and live music venue that features Israeli rock and pop stars. The age of the crowd varies widely, and the line to get in is usually fairly long. TLV Club's atmosphere is all about partying hard.

For a relatively low-key evening and change of pace in an intimate, high-end setting, the **Shablul Jazz Club** (Hangar 13 at the Port of Tel Aviv on Nemal St., 03/546-1891, www. shabluljazz.com, doors open 8pm, concerts start 9pm Sun.-Thurs., jam sessions 10:30pm, matinee shows 4pm Fri. and Sat., closed for Shabbat, cover NIS50-150, NIS60 for food menu) features live music nightly, including famous domestic acts and international acts including the group Harp Concert Jazz. On Friday afternoons they offer a bistro menu with their matinee show and always serve top-shelf alcohol.

City Center

The area around **Allenby Street** has some popular local spots and highly posh and trendy clubs (think dress code and VIP rooms). You can also get extra dressed-up if you want to try your luck at getting admission to some of the more exclusive spots that aren't afraid to turn customers away.

Referred to by the popular Tel Aviv moniker of "sleazy" (which might be an odd translation from Hebrew), **Allenby 40** (40 Allenby St., 052/892-9218, hours vary widely, generally open from about midnight at earliest until 9am at the latest daily, no cover) is a dimly-lit and fairly basic bar frequented by locals. It does have a dance floor and a wide variety of beer, and is oddly popular because of its somewhat gritty, no frills atmosphere that is favored among Tel Aviv's strippers and other local night owls.

Off of Allenby Street, **Beit Ha'amudim** (14 Rambam St., 03/510-9228, 10am-1am Sun.-Thurs., 10am-sunset Fri., from 7pm Sat., NIS45), which means "house of columns," is a bar with jazz concerts, an intimate neighborhood crowd, and art exhibits. They are also popular for their jazz brunches, and the food menu is all vegetarian.

One of the more artsy areas in town is near **King George Street** in close proximity to **Dizengoff Center.** On the upper side of King George you can find some alternative cafés and bars that make for a nice spot to start the evening before the clubs get going around 11pm or later.

At **Sonia Getzel Shapira** (1 Simta Almonit St., 057/944-2801, http://soniagetzelshapira. rest-e.co.il, 9am-midnight daily, NIS50) the atmosphere is simple and calm and there are nooks and crannies where you can gear up for a night of fun. The secluded outdoor garden is a popular place to have a drink and something light to eat, particularly among the local clientele. The later it gets, the busier it gets as it is a favorite spot to start a typically late Tel Aviv night on the town.

The **Little Prince** (18 Nahalat Binyamin St., 03/528-2404, 10am-2am Sun.-Thurs., NIS30) is an artsy bar, bookstore, and coffee shop, with tons of books and wood paneling lining the walls. It plays host to a hipster crowd and stays open late. It is known for its central role in the young poetry revival movement and hosts writing salon groups and story slams (like poetry slams but with stories).

North from Dizengoff Center on Dizengoff Street there are a nice variety of nightlife spots. On the northern end of Dizengoff, bar-lounge **Dizzy Frishdon** (121 Dizengoff St., 03/523-4111, 8:30pm-3am Mon.-Thurs., 9pm-3am Fri., 8:30pm-3am Sat.-Sun.) is a popular hangout with a fun-loving crowd. It's an easy place to get into if you're willing to wait in line and make new friends. The interior is dimly lit and they serve decent food.

Just off of Dizengoff is the **Seret Club** (30 Ibn Gabirol St., inside the London Ministore mall, 054/740-6024, www.telavivme.com, eitan@seretbar.co.il, 9pm-3pm daily, no cover). To get inside, go into the mall, go to floor minus 1 (one below ground floor) and find the entrance to the club off the parking lot. Once inside, you'll be in a movie-themed wonderland (*seret* means "movie" in Hebrew) that includes movie-theater chairs and marquee lights. It is crucial that you call or email in advance to book a table for your group, and they don't take traveler's checks.

A popular Irish pub is **Molly Bloom's** (2 Mendele St., at the corner of HaYarkon St., 03/522-1558, www.molly-blooms.com, 4pm-last customer Sat.-Thurs., 2pm-last customer Fri., NIS55), whose claim to fame is that they were the first Irish pub in Tel Aviv when they opened in 2000. Still a neighborhood favorite, it has a standard pub and sports bar interior of wood, bar stools, and TVs. There's live Irish music every Monday starting around 9:30pm and open-microphone sessions on Fridays starting at 5pm.

If you're in the mood for a place with a smoking room, a pool table, and more of a neighborhood vibe, go to **Bar Giora** (4 Bar Giora St., at the corner of Dizengoff St., 03/620-4880, http://bargiyora.co.il, 9am-2am daily, NIS45) with its café, bar, and live music, including a nightly "BBQ live music" from 9:30pm. There are multiple levels and it is an old standard bar-coffee shop-restaurant that has survived the frequent changes of the Tel Aviv nightlife scene. There is a two-for-one

happy hour (5pm-9pm daily), a food menu with Middle Eastern and Persian dishes, and comfortable booths to sit in. The pool tables are not always open to the public, so call ahead if you want to play.

In front of Rabin Square, look for the neighborhood **Otto Bar** (76 Ibn Gabirol St., 077/414-5043, 9pm-5am daily, NIS45), known as a place that Israeli celebrities like to hang out. It is well lit with a pool table but definitely has the feel of a bar with a nicely decorated interior and tons of bar stools. It's not huge, but is one of three locations that Otto has in Tel Aviv (the other two are at 48 Ahad Ha'Am St. and 302 Dizengoff St.). The bar is restricted to ages 25 and older.

UNDERGROUND NIGHTLIFE AND AFTER PARTIES

Underground nightlife and after parties are venues that are harder to find, more exclusive, and have bizarre hours such as opening at 6am. They are often categorized in degrees of "sleaziness," a strange label that Time Out Tel Aviv bestows in varying degrees on different venues and sleazier is better.

City Center

Right in the middle of City Center and down a dark, unmarked alley is **Radio EPGB** (7 Shadal St., 03/560-3636, 9pm-6am daily, no cover, NIS20 for beer), a hipster dance club and music bar with a quirky atmosphere that includes a pinball machine and punk posters. There are frequent live indie music performances, DJs spinning indie rock and electronic, and the overall atmosphere is very welcoming.

Starting at around 6am and ramping up by 9am, the Tel Aviv after party is largely a creature of Friday and Saturday nights. The **Spice Melange** (113 Hashmonaim St., 052/688-7706, marinaspice@gmail.com, NIS60) has a dress-to-impress atmosphere and food, drinks, and a coffee menu. The enormous dance club **Yaya** (3 Ben Yehuda St. in Migdalor Tower, 052/861-6611, ghozlan@walla.com) has a modern interior, huge outdoor terrace, and a 25-and-up crowd.

South Tel Aviv

The Penguin Club (43 Yehuda Halevi St., 03/566-1450, krembo.galofer@gmail.com, midnight-6am daily, technically member only, NIS50) is a popular underground haunt with electronic and house DJs. It is a good spot to drop by on Wednesday and Thursday nights. The party doesn't really get going until about 2am or later and goes strong until closing time at 6am. Officially it is a member's only club and is only for the 25-plus crowd, but there seems to be some leeway for determined tourists. Just go with a backup plan.

The Block (157 Salame St., inside the Central Bus Station on the 4th Fl., 03/537-8002, www.block-club.com, doors open around 11pm daily, NIS80 and up for DJs) has a high-quality analog sound system and a hefty lineup of international DJs. The urban atmosphere and on-trend customers help its reputation as one of the coolest places in the city to party.

MEGA CLUBS AND DJ CLUBS

Mega clubs and DJ clubs are where to go for some serious dancing and drinking, often in venues that have multiple floors and well-known DJs. The idea with these places is to see and be seen, so getting extra dressed up is a must.

North Tel Aviv

Whiskey a Gogo (3 HaTa'arucha St., 03/544-0633, 9:30pm-last customer daily, NIS45 for cocktails) is a multi-level mega bar with sophisticated decor. Each level has different music for different crowds such as electronica, hip-hop, pop, and rock. Be warned that it's a very trendy spot with a sophisticated crowd and décor; they can afford to be selective about who they let in. So get as done up as possible and don't take no for the first answer if they try to turn you away. Remember that everything in this part of the world is a negotiation.

City Center

A popular late-night hangout is the **The Cat and the Dog** (23 Carlibach St., www.

thecatandthedog.com, about midnight-6am daily, free weekdays, sometimes NIS60-80 weekends). Getting there will require a cab ride if your hotel is anywhere near the seaside, and this place doesn't get going until super-late, around 3am. This DJ club features mostly electronic music and is extremely popular. It's a bit of a mixed scene, so come prepared to experience local flavor.

South Tel Aviv

Just east of trendy Neve Tzedek near Allenby Street, there is a good selection of trendy spots with more sophisticated, polished crowds. The surrounding streets have dance bars that come and go and vary from slick and commercial to alternative. **Lilenblum Street** has a mixture of DJ clubs and bars. Start at the always-popular **Shesek** (17 Lilenblum St., 03/516-9520, 9pm-4am daily, no cover), which is the perfect place for fun. The lounge-bar is situated just behind Rothschild Boulevard and known for its cool factor. Well-heeled locals and tourists mingle here. They have a full bar and you can ask for almost any type of drink, and you can also ask the DJ for almost any type of music. The crowd and the music are both mainstream and more on the mellow side.

Tel Aviv's younger crowd (under 20) loves to hit the huge clubs and dance bars in the area near Ha'Masger to Ha'Rakevet Street. A popular spot is **Haoman 17** (88 Abarbanel St., 03/681-3636, open only on select nights, usually weekends and holidays, call ahead for hours, NIS60-100), a mega club that attracts top DJs from all over the world. It is one of the newest and biggest clubs in the city. There are multiple levels and three main dance areas.

The crowd at **Clara** (1 Kaufmann St. at Dolphinarium Beach, 054/222-2260 or 03/510-2060, www.clara.co.il, 9pm-4am Mon. and Thurs. Apr.-Oct., no cover) is mostly younger with the age range mostly under 30. It is an open-air mega bar right on the beach. Only open in the summer from April-October, Clara usually has a DJ and it has a comfortable atmosphere with tons of couches for hanging out.

GAY AND LESBIAN NIGHTLIFE

Tel Aviv is generally very gay- and lesbian-friendly. In addition, there is a nice selection of places that cater specifically to the gay and lesbian crowd.

Popular among those who know it's there, **Deli Bar** (47 Allenby St., 03/642-5738 or 054/435-2834, 10am-8pm daily, no cover) is reached by passing through a sandwich shop to get to the back where the dancing is happening. Deli features hip-hop and electronica music by some of the city's best DJs and boasts a huge menu of cocktails and imported beers.

Formerly the Maxim Club, **Bootleg** (48 King George St., 03/528-2277 and 052/624-2464, 8pm-7am daily, NIS50 for special DJs) is a gay-friendly stop with a relaxed atmosphere and house music. The crowd is generally comprised of people of all ages, and it has low light and loud music.

Vox (2 Yagea Kapaym, 03/687-0591, www.vox-telaviv.com, 1am-last customer daily, NIS60-100 cover) is a huge club with a large dance floor, several levels, and gay-themed evenings. The dance floor has two huge bars and an overlooking balcony and DJ station. One of Vox's best features is the design, which gives it an intimate atmosphere.

PERFORMING ARTS, VISUAL ARTS, AND CULTURAL CENTERS
City Center

The **Z.O.A. House** (26 Ibn Gabirol St., 03/695-9341, www.zoa.co.il, 24 hours daily) is a charming mixture of cinema, theater, café, and history. With construction that was started in the presence of Israel's first prime minister, David Ben-Gurion, the Zionist Organization of America House now holds a movie theater, a theater for stage, and a ground floor café that is reputed to serve some of the best cappuccino in all of Tel Aviv. There is a surprising array of performances that range from old Shakespeare classics to folk performances that are done in Yiddish.

There are several movie cinemas in the city; you can find current listings by searching online or buying an English newspaper. An easy cinema to reach is **Lez Dizengoff** (50 Dizengoff Center Mall, 03/621-2222, NIS40). Most movie theaters in Israel will have some mainstream movies in English with Hebrew subtitles.

Just behind the Tel Aviv Museum of Art is a large cultural complex that is home to the renowned **Cameri Theatre** (19 Shaul HaMelech Blvd., 03/606-0960, www.cameri.co.il) that puts on Israeli and classic plays, musicals, concerts, and modern theater. In the same complex, the **Tel Aviv Performing Arts Center** (19 Shaul HaMelech Blvd., 03/692-7777, www.israel-opera.co.il), home to the Israeli Opera and the Israel Ballet, offers a wide variety of operatic performances for all ages, and hosts other varied performances almost nightly, year-round. It is particularly known for its dance performances by the Israel Ballet, and hosts all kinds of international performers and festivals throughout the year.

The country's second largest reparatory theater, **Beit Lessin Theater** (101 Dizengoff St., 03/725-5333, www.lessin.co.il) was founded in the early 1980s as a club for Israel's Workers' Union. It is home to Israel's annual **New Israeli Drama Festival** called Open Stage. Numerous award-winning playwrights have shown their work at Beit Lessin or have been discovered on the venue's stage.

The **Habima Theater** (19 Leonardo da Vinci, 03/526-6666, www.habima.co.il) is Israel's national theater, with all productions in Hebrew. Call ahead for productions that are translated simultaneously into English.

South Tel Aviv

A centerpiece of Neve Tzedek is the **Suzanne Dellal Center** (5 Yehieli St., 03/510-5656, www.suzannedellal.org.il), home to modern and experimental productions and top Israeli dance troupes. The carefully restored older buildings that make up the center play host to events, festivals, performances, a restaurant and coffee shop, and a large outer piazza.

© YAIRA YASMIN

Suzanne Dellal Center

ART AND PHOTOGRAPHY GALLERIES
City Center

The **Urban Gallery** (72 and 74 Ben Yehuda St., 03/524-4110, www.urbangallery972.com, 9am-8pm Mon.-Thurs., 9am-3pm Fri., 9am-8pm Sun., free) has two locations in Tel Aviv and one in Jaffa and specializes in classic and contemporary Israeli and international art. It is also home to a large selection of works by famed Israeli artist Menashe Kadishman, known for his offbeat paintings of sheep.

Just south of Dizengoff Center, the **Rothschild Fine Art Gallery** (140 Rothschild Blvd., 052/372-9431, www.rgfineart.com, 11am-6:30pm Mon.-Thurs., 10am-1pm Fri., 11am-1pm Sat., free) features a range of fine art by various Israeli and international artists, and displays mostly paintings.

The well-established and well-known **Gordon Gallery of Contemporary Art** (95 Ben Yehuda St., 03/524-0323, www.gordongallery.co.il, 11am-7pm Mon.-Thurs., 10am-2pm Fri., 10am-1pm Sat., by appointment Sun., free) is

a 45-year-old gallery with multiple locations; 95 Ben Yehuda Street is their largest. The gallery has published two of the most respected and authoritative art books in Israel, and is the father of Israel's first auction house. Today it emphasizes exhibitions of photography, works by top contemporary Israeli artists, and several permanent exhibitions.

The **Rubin Museum** (14 Bialik St., 03/525-5961, www.rubinmuseum.org.il, 10am-3pm Mon. and Wed.-Fri., 10am-8pm Tues., 11am-2pm Sat., adult NIS20, senior NIS10, under 18 free) operates out of the house of famous and popular Israeli modern artist Reuven Rubin and the four floors include works of Rubin, a reading room, a children's gallery, and changing exhibits of other Israeli artists.

Also on Bialik Street, **Bauhaus Foundation Museum** (21 Bialik St., 03/620-4664, 11am-5pm Wed., 10am-2pm Fri.) is a worthwhile stop for architecture buffs. It is a one-room establishment dedicated to the Bauhaus movement through the display of Bauhaus objects and furniture. Housed on the ground floor of a renovated Bauhaus building, it is also home to the Bauhaus Foundation.

The **Zalmania Pri-Or Photo House** (5 Tchernichovski St., 03/517-7916, www.pri-or. com, 10am-6pm Sun.-Thurs., 10am-1pm Fri., free) is home to one of the largest and most important private photography archives in Israel with a collection of historical photographs and over one million negatives. It was established in 1940 by photographer Rudi Weissenstein, who documented the creation of the State of Israel.

Near the Botanical Garden and the Zoological Garden is the **Shpilman Institute for Photography** (27 Shoken St., 3rd Fl., 03/728-3737, http://thesip.org, 4pm-8pm Tues. and Thurs., 10am-2pm Fri.-Sat., free), a major modern photography institute with a newly opened exhibition space. There is a guided tour of the exhibition every Saturday at noon.

Jaffa (Yafo)

An incubator project for Israeli artists, **ST-ART** (8 Hatzedef St., 03/516-9599, www.st-art.co.il, 10am-7pm Tues., 10am-3pm Wed.-Thurs., free) supports mostly young graduates of Israel's leading art schools. It features largely contemporary Israeli art from 1986 onward.

The **Old Jaffa Artists' Colony** (Yefet St. in Jaffa Old Port area, free tour every Wed. at 10am, starts at visitor's center office in Old Jaffa's clock square, 03/603-7700) is a collection of several independent spaces centered around the port area of the old city.

FESTIVALS AND EVENTS
Spring

Tel Aviv comes alive with festivals and events in the spring. The new **White City Music Festival** (Hangar 11 at the Port of Tel Aviv, 03/602-0888, http://tlv-music.netbiz-hosting.net, May, ticket packages from NIS2,500) features major international and Israeli acts covering a range of musical genres including jazz, funk, rock and roll, and ethnic world music.

The **Taste of Tel Aviv Food Festival** (HaYarkon Park, 03/642-2828, www.park. co.il, 8pm-midnight for three days in May, free entry) is the largest food festival in the country.

Also in May is the **Felija Blumenthal International Music Festival** (Tel Aviv Museum of Art, 27 Shaul HaMelech Blvd., 03/620-1185, www.blumentalfestival.com/en, NIS35 and upward per show), a week-long classical array including chamber music, orchestras, solo ensembles, and folk music. Running since 1999, it's known for staging the debut of many Israeli artists who have gone on to become famous.

The only festival of its kind in the Middle East, the annual **Culture of Peace Festival** (Tzavta Theater, 30 Ibn Gabirol St., 03/695-0156, www.havatzelet.org.il under project, three days in May, prices vary) includes Jewish, Muslim, and Christian traditional music.

Summer

The months of June through August are action-packed in Israel and Tel Aviv. The popular **Opera in the Park** (HaYarkon Park, 03/692-7782, www.israel-opera.co.il under Outreach and Education, from 9pm in July, free) showcases performances by the renowned Israeli Opera. Typical crowds to the opera performances are about 80,000 or more from all across Israel, so go early and take a taxi or bus.

The famous **Tel Aviv Pride Parade** (www. gaytlvguide.com/the-guide/pride-parade, June) hosts more than 50 events throughout the week-long festival (which is basically one big, non-stop party), finishing with the Gay Pride Parade. The parade starts at Meir Park and goes to Tchernichovsky Street, then Bograshov Street, and then Ben Yehuda Street and usually finishes around Ben-Gurion Boulevard and moves to Gordon Beach.

Extremely popular, the international **Tel Aviv Swing Festival** (Dance Tel Aviv, 98 Dizengoff St., www.taswing.com, NIS12-NIS420 for individual party tickets and workshops) is a weekend of workshops and events centered on swing that sells out quickly. Festival organizers help attendees find places to stay (including crashing on couches). Workshops start in the late morning and dancing goes until late at night.

The annual **Tel Aviv-Yafo's White Night**

the popular Tel Aviv Pride Parade

festival (www.tel-aviv.gov.il, June) is a celebration of UNESCO's 2003 recognition of Tel Aviv's Bauhaus White City as a World Heritage Site. The one-night festival features dozens of simultaneous indoor and outdoor events throughout the city, including music, art, dance, sports, workshops, and parades.

Fall

As the weather cools down, so do events. There are still some nice picks, including the **International Photography Festival** (locations vary, www.photographyfestival.co.il, Oct., buy tickets by dialing *8780 from Israel or go to www.leaan.co.il, NIS39 and up), a gathering of a couple hundred Israeli and international photographers for a week of workshops and events.

An annual event that marks the opening of Tel Aviv-Yafo's gallery season, the **Loving Art Making Art** festival (www.artyear.co.il, Sept. just before Sukkot, free) is a three-day event that is part of Tel Aviv Art Year. Sixty galleries, museums, and exhibition spaces open to the public for free, leading Israeli artists join in street exhibits, and there are artists' workshops and alternative art spaces.

The **Nike Night Run** (start at Rabin Square, spectators and supporters gather near the intersection of Ibn Gabirol St. and Rokach Blvd., www.nikerunning.co.il/nightrun-telaviv, run from 8pm-10:30pm, Oct., NIS120-180) is a 10K night run from Rabin Square in Tel Aviv's city center to Tel Aviv North Sportek. About 15,000-20,000 runners have participated in recent years.

Winter

The **Uptown-Downtown Festival** (various locations, www.utdt.co.il, dial *9080 in Israel, Dec., ticket prices vary) draws together dozens of musical acts for a week of performances at major clubs around Tel Aviv.

Israel's official **Tel Aviv Fashion Week** (HaTachana, www.tlvfw.com, Nov.) includes receptions, parties, and fashion shows featuring some of the best Israeli designers from the country's lively fashion scene. An alternative fashion week also started running in recent years.

Piano Festival (03/762-6666, http://pianofestival.co.il, Nov.) has programming run completely in Hebrew, but features some big names among Israeli pianists.

In December, **International Exposure** (Suzanne Dellal Center, 5 Yehieli St., 03/510-5656, www.suzannedellal.org.il, tickets vary)

showcases Israeli contemporary dance over the course of several days, with most performances at the Suzanne Dellal Center in Neve Tzedek.

The annual **Jazz Festival** (Tel Aviv Cinematheque, 03/606-0800, www.jazzfest. co.il, Feb., prices vary) has been running for about 25 years and hosts jazz musicians from throughout Israel and the world.

Shopping

Shopping in Tel Aviv is all about what kind of shopping you want to do. Beyond the common souvenir shops, you can find everything from outdoor markets to the showrooms of Israeli designers.

OUTDOOR, OPEN-AIR, AND FARMERS MARKETS
North Tel Aviv

For a down-to-earth experience outdoors at the port, the **Port Market** (Tel Aviv Hanger 12 at the Port of Tel Aviv, 03/544-1505, www. namal.co.il, 8am-8pm Mon.-Sat.) features two levels of foodstuffs for sale. The emphasis is on the "slow food" movement, and options include organic cheese, handmade pasta, gelato, and more. Every Friday an open-air **Farmers Market** (Port of Tel Aviv, 7am-3pm Fri.) opens at the port, expanding the variety of delicious choices.

City Center
◖ CARMEL MARKET

Tel Aviv's most well-known open-air market is **Carmel Market** (entrance to the market is on Allenby St., 8am-dark Sun.-Thurs., 8am-2pm Fri.), named after its location on HaCarmel Street, between Magen David Square at the intersection of King George, Sheinkin, Nahalat Binyamin and Allenby Streets, and also at HaKovshim Garden and the Carmelit bus terminal. It's an outstanding place to experience the local culture and buy fresh produce. Full of everything from spices to dry goods to

clothing, the market is within walking distance to the beach. Vendors call out what they are selling by singing out unique songs, and you can buy everything from freshly squeezed juice to fresh-cut flowers.

There is a wide variety of things in the market to distract and amuse, including street musicians. But the best finds are farther inside the main entrances where there are tons of side alleys selling fresh fish, fruit, vegetables, and exotic spices and nuts.

South Tel Aviv

The spices, nuts, and dried fruits of the **Levinski Market** (Levinski St. in Florentin, 054/226-8089, 8am-6pm Sun.-Thurs., 8am-4:30pm Fri.) make it a popular place for shopping for special treats. It's also the perfect place to do some last-minute souvenir shopping.

SHOPPING DISTRICTS
North Tel Aviv

The retail stores at the **Port of Tel Aviv** (northernmost end of HaYarkon St., 03/544-1505, www.namal.co.il) are on the large side and are mostly chain stores, with a good selection of sporting goods items. The prices are on the high end, but they are also high-quality and include domestic name brands such as Fox, Shilav, and others. Aside from sports-related items, you can also find smaller items like shoes and jewelry.

Connecting Ibn Gabirol and Dizengoff

THE HEART OF ISRAEL'S REMARKABLE FASHION INDUSTRY

One of Israel's most surprising talents is its creative and daring fashion industry. Locally grown designers use creative tactics and approaches to create feminine, elegant, and extremely well-made clothing, shoes, bags, and accessories. Though only a lucky few Israeli designers have managed to go international, the range of items available inside of Israel is incredible.

The hallmark of Israeli fashion is simple and chic designs that feature minimal trimmings or flourishes. The designers let the materials speak for themselves, whether it's a leather handbag or an evening dress. Israeli jewelry is also extremely unique and can be found throughout the country.

Some of the more well-known designers include Lia, Gazelle, D and A, Liat Ginzburg, Sasson Kedem, Yosef, and Zaya by Avital Coorsh. Israel's technological advances have led to the creation of cutting-edge ultrasonic bonding equipment that cuts and seals fabric pieces without sewing a stitch. The method, called seamless construction, has put Israel on the map in the intimate apparel industry sector.

Boutique stores that sell almost exclusively Israeli designers can be found throughout the country, everywhere from trendy shopping districts to major shopping malls. Just ask shop owners selling upper-scale clothing and accessories if they have any items by Israeli designers, and the answer will likely be yes. Many stores are extremely supportive and proud of local designers and will choose to sell their products over imported items.

Tel Aviv is Israel's fashion center, and every year it hosts two international fashion week shows in the fall (a result of an industry-splintered professional relationship). Tel Aviv Fashion Week and Gindi TLV Fashion Week are within one month of each other.

Local designer shops are changing constantly, but former fashion industry professional **Galit Reismann** (054/814-1499, www.tlvstyle.com, tour rates vary based on size of group and length) takes customers on half-day tours (3-5 hours) with personal introductions to designers and personalized shopping experiences.

Streets is **Basel Street,** a popular shopping and hangout area. The heart of the area is **Basel Square,** where you will find some of Tel Aviv's coolest boutique clothing stores. Start at about 34 Basel Street and work your way up or down the block. The farther north you go on Dizengoff Street in North Tel Aviv, the more expensive and fancier the designer boutiques, wedding gown stores, high-end clothing, jewelry, and shoe stores get.

City Center

Parallel to Dizengoff Street is **Bugrashov Street,** which is known for its offbeat and trendy fashion stores and selection of cafés.

Adjacent to Carmel Market, just one street parallel to the east is **Nahalat Binyamin Street,** which has a stretch of cafés, shops, and bars that runs from Allenby Street south into the **Florentin** neighborhood. Florentin

has a mixture of hip designer shops, cafés, and housewares stores.

South Tel Aviv

Unquestionably one of the best places in Tel Aviv for window shopping is the old, European-inspired neighborhood of **Neve Tzedek** (approx. Shabazi St. and north of Jaffa St. between Brant St. and Pines St.), with its high-end shops selling boutique jewelry, antiques, oriental rugs, clothing, and books.

Due west from Florentin is the **Menashiya,** where you'll find the unique shopping experience of **HaTachana** (between Neve Tzedek and the sea, parking entrance at HaMered St. at the corner of Kaufmann St., www.HaTachana.co.il, 10am-10pm Mon.-Sat., pubs, cafés, and restaurants open until midnight or last customer on Fri.), a hip shopping center with restaurants and cafés located at the Old Train

Station Compound. The open space has incorporated elements from the original train station that opened in 1892. You can still see partial train tracks, cars, and freight terminals. You can find unique souvenirs at the **Made in TLV** (03/510-4333) emporium and boutiques. On Thursdays (7pm-midnight), it hosts Israeli designers and artists for an open-air trade show that includes DJ music.

Just a bit southeast of Neve Tzedek across the main drag of Jaffa Street is the neighborhood of **Florentin** (south of Jaffa St. and west of Hertsel St.), which was established in 1927 by Jews who emigrated from Greece. Today it is known as a hangout for hipsters and is full of upper-crust furniture and designer stores.

FLEA MARKETS
North Tel Aviv
The **Artists' and Collectors' Fair** (Port of Tel Aviv, on the pier, 10am-6pm Sat.) is a weekly flea market overlooking the Mediterranean. It's a good place to find locally-made arts and crafts including jewelry and small trinkets. When you're done perusing the market, enjoy the good selection of restaurants nearby.

Jaffa (Yafo)
Probably the most fun you'd have shopping in Jaffa would be at the **Jaffa Flea Market** (east of the clock tower at the southern end of Old Jaffa, intersection of Olei Zion St. and Jerusalem Blvd., 10am-6pm Sun.-Thurs., 10am-2pm Fri.), with its combination of junk and unique finds including copper, antiques, Persian tiles and rugs, and Judaica. Considered one of the major attractions of Old Jaffa, the flea market also has a number of cafés and pubs. During the summer, there's live music on Thursday evenings.

WEEKLY FAIRS AND TRADE MARKETS
City Center
On Thursdays and Fridays, **Dizengoff Center** (intersection of King George St. and Dizengoff

items for sale at a Jaffa flea market

© YAIRA YASMIN

St.) hosts a popular international **food fair** (North building B, ground floor, 03/621-2400 ext. 3003, idan@nihul-dc.co.il, noon-8pm Thurs., 10am-4pm Fri.) for a chance to try a variety of dishes.

Fashionably Late designer market (Dizengoff Square at intersection of Pinsker St. and Dizengoff St., 4pm-11pm Thurs., 050/444-6861) is an open-air showcase of independent designers who put their work out in Dizengoff Square.

Dizengoff Square Vintage and Antiques Market (next to Dizengoff Square at Dizengoff and Reines Sts., noon-10pm Tues., 7am-4pm Fri.) features vendors selling clothes, accessories, books, and arts and crafts.

A section of Nahalat Binyamin Street that runs parallel to Carmel Market is open to foot traffic only and has an outdoor **craft fair** (10am-5pm Tues. and Fri.). Vendors sell wooden toys, jewelry, Judaica, photography, and trinkets of all kinds amid street performers.

SHOPPING MALLS
City Center

Azrieli Mall (132 Menachem Begin Rd., 03/608-1179 www.azrielicenter.co.il, 10am-10pm Sun.-Thurs., 10am-4pm Fri., and 8pm-midnight Sat.) is a huge, multi-level mall that includes a train station stop, a multiplex cinema, and every type of store you can imagine from domestic chains such as Golf to international brands such as The Gap. Convenient and well laid out, it includes coffee shop chains that are located throughout Israel (such as Aroma), cafés, and stands for manicures and pedicures. You can also easily travel from Azrieli by train or bus to and from other parts of the city.

With hundreds of stores, **Dizengoff Center** (50 Dizengoff St., near the intersection with King George St., 03/621-2400, www.dizengof-center.co.il, 8am-2pm daily) straddles two sides of Dizengoff Street and is connected by underground passageways and an overhead bridge. It is the oldest mall in town, and hosts an odd mixture of high-end stores, cafés, and lower-end bargain shops that sell cheap goods; it also has two cinemas. Except for the cinemas, the entire center is closed on Shabbat. It is a good place to visit if you need clothing, makeup, and computer supplies.

Just next to City Hall is **Gan Ha'ir** (71 Ibn Gabirol St., 03/527-9111, most shops 9am-9pm Sun.-Thurs. and 9am-2pm Fri.), a high-end mall centered around an open courtyard. Gan Ha'ir has a number of expensive stores that attract some of Tel Aviv's more sophisticated customers. You can find stores selling food, books, shoes, toys and children's clothing, and more. Inside the mall is a popular Hungarian café called Yehudith's and the rooftop Enav Cultural Center, where lectures, exhibits, concerts, and plays are often held.

Sports and Recreation

Tel Aviv's location on the sea and its sweltering summer days make it an incredibly active place after the sun goes down. Residents are known for showing a lot of skin, being somewhat body-conscious, and dedicated to staying in shape, which makes for a lot of sporting options. For more low-key options like outdoor hangout space, you'll find some of the largest and most well-designed parks in the country.

PARKS AND SQUARES
Dizengoff Square
One of the most easily recognizable landmarks in Tel Aviv, **Dizengoff Square** (intersection of Pinsker St. and Dizengoff St., 24 hours daily, free) is a broad, split-level plaza at the center of the White City with a distinct raised platform above street level and a multicolored fountain in the center. Every Tuesday and Friday,

the **Dizengoff Square Vintage and Antiques Market** (next to Dizengoff Square at Dizengoff and Reines Sts., noon-10pm Tues., 7am-4pm Fri.) sells clothes, accessories, books, arts, and crafts. The city plans to lower the square to street level.

Rabin Square
On November 4, 1995, Prime Minister Yitzhak Rabin was shot and killed by a Jewish assassin upon leaving a mass rally supporting the peace process. After his death, the location of the rally and assassination was renamed **Rabin Square** (69 Ibn Gabirol St., south of City Hall, 24 hours daily, free), and it still serves as a major staging ground for peace rallies, public music events, and annual book fairs. The **Yitzhak Rabin Memorial** (northeast corner on Ibn Gabirol St.) displays 16 basalt rocks from

the famed Dizengoff Square fountain

© YAIRA YASMIN

the Golan Heights sunk into the ground as a symbol of Rabin's roots and bond with Israel.

Meir Park

Featuring a fish pond with floating water flora, a dog run, and huge, old trees **Meir Park** (35 King George St., 24 hours daily, free) is a green sanctuary. It is also home to Tel Aviv's gay community center, which often hosts lectures, sports events, and potlucks. It's a popular spot that's best to avoid at night.

◖ HaYarkon Park

Among Tel Aviv's jewels, **HaYarkon Park** (Port of Tel Aviv and North Tel Aviv at Rokach Blvd., 03/642-2828 or 03/642-0541, www. park.co.il, www.parkfun.co.il, online map: mapcarta.com/26227916, 24 hours daily, free) stretches about 1,000 acres west to east from the Tel Aviv Port to the neighboring city of Ramat Gan. The Yarkon River cuts through the park to the Mediterranean, and it is divided into several sections.

West of Ayalon Highway is an elongated section perfect for long walks, especially in the late evenings because it is well-lit and active. There are two connecting bridges (the Ibn Gabirol Bridge on the west and the Derech Namir Bridge on the east). In this section, on the north side of the river is **Sportek** (Yarkon River north bank, 03/699-0307, www.kir.co.il, 6:30am-10pm daily, prices vary based on activity), a sprawling collection of sports centers and playgrounds with tennis, volleyball, and basketball courts, baseball and soccer fields, rollerblading courts (with equipment for rent), bungee and trampoline jumping, and an Olympic climbing wall. Both sides of the river have bicycle and walking paths.

The eastern side of the park extends into a huge circular pattern and includes a large artificially-constructed lake, a 5-acre **tropical garden** with a micro-climate and orchids, and a 10-acre enclosed **rock garden** (10am-2:30pm Sun.-Thurs., 10am-1:30pm Fri., 10am-3:30pm Sat.), a showcase of Israel's geology and 3,500 species of plants, including 6 acres of cacti alone. On the banks of the Yarkon, **Ten Mills**

(east Yarkon promenade), is a group of old flourmills that operated for centuries, some of them as recently as the 1920s. The mills are situated on landscaped paths near a wooden bridge and an old dam.

Near the lake is **Zapari** (03/642-2888, www. zapari.co.il, call ahead for hours, NIS50), a 7.5-acre oasis of tropical plant life, including banana trees. Zapari is home to a variety of exotic reptiles and birds from around the world, a swan lake with tropical fish and waterfalls, parrots, and a recreation of a traditional African village.

The park hosts concerts and is home to two outdoor concert venues, **Wohl Amphitheater** (03/521-8210) and **Theater in the Park** (03/642-2828).

Just on the edges of the park's eastern side are **Luna Amusement Park** (Merkaz Hayeridim, enter from southern Rokach Blvd. across from HaYarkon Park, 03/642-7080, 10am-8pm Sat. and holidays, NIS80), with a variety of rides for a wide range of ages, and **Memadin Water Park** (near Ramat Gan stadium on eastern side of parking lot across from Luna Amusement Park, 03/642-2777, www.meymadion.co.il, generally 9am-8pm daily but hours and open days vary, Apr.-early Oct., NIS99, after 1pm NIS85).

Hapisga (Summit) Park

Named for its location on the summit of Jaffa mound overlooking the sea, **Hapisga Park** (far southern end of promenade on Jaffa mound) is famed for its vista of Tel Aviv and the shoreline. In August the park's amphitheater hosts evening concerts, and the Zodiac Bridge is a place to make wishes according to your astrological sign.

Ha'atzmaut (Independence) Park

The massive coastal **Independence Park** (240 HaYarkon St.) is just under half a mile long and full of open spaces with breathtaking views of the sea and is gay community-friendly and often used as a gathering spot. The southern end of the park abuts the Marina and is the access point for Nordau and Hilton Beaches.

Charles Clore Park

Recently refurbished, **Charles Clore Park** (12 Kaufmann St., from the south of the Dolphinarium Beach to Jaffa, http://clore-foundation.org.il) has lawns and views of the Mediterranean, access to Charles Clore Beach, and connects Tel Aviv and Jaffa with the Tayalet pathway, which is essentially a promenade.

Ramat Gan National Park

At almost 500 acres, the **Ramat Gan National Park** (access through Ahad Ha'Am St.) is full of lawns, walking and riding paths, a lake with an artificial waterfall, and a Parisian-style garden. At the center is the **Safari Park and Zoo** (1 Ha'Tsvi Ave. in Ramat Gan National Park, 03/630-5328, 03/630-5327, or 03/630-5326, www.safari.co.il, call ahead for hours, adult NIS59, senior NIS52, add NIS7 Safari bus fee for visitors without cars) with about 1,600 animals from all over the world, including 68 species of mammals, 130 species of birds, and 25 species of reptiles. Check out Rotem the Sand Cat, a distinct regional species.

WATER SPORTS
Swimming

The **Gordon Swimming Pool** (14 Eliezer Peri St. at the Tel Aviv Marina, 03/762-3300, www.gordon-pool.co.il, 5am-7pm daily, weekdays NIS45, Sat. NIS50) is an unusual experience with its outdoor, Olympic-size swimming pool filled with saltwater. Heated and open year-round you can get access to the pool and workout equipment on the beach for an additional fee.

Surfing, Diving, Boating, and Beach Sports

For surfing lessons and equipment rentals of various types, the **Surf Point Beach Equipment** (off the promenade between Zrubavel and Nehemia Sts., 03/517-0099, www.surf-point.co.il, 9:30am-6:30pm daily, NIS100/hour or NIS788 for 10 hours) offers surfboard, boat, and windsurfing rentals. **Topsea** (165 HaYarkon St., 050/432-9001,

www.topsea.co.il, 8am-sunset daily, NIS50 and up for rentals, NIS150 and up for lessons) is the oldest surfing center in Tel Aviv. The **Israel Surf Club** (5 Herbert Samuel St., 03/510-3439, http://israelsurfclub.co.il, 8am-8pm daily, NIS100/hour for lessons) near Charles Clore Beach also rents equipment and offers lessons.

For boating, the **Daniel Center** (2 Rokach Blvd., 03/699-0484, www.drc.org.il, 8am-8pm Sun.-Thurs., 8:30am-1pm on Fri.) in HaYarkon Park gives a free introductory **sea kayaking** lesson.

A popular water sport throughout Israel, diving has a number of good places and outfitters in Tel Aviv. The **Tel Aviv Diving Club** (145 Hayarkon St., 054/662-7044, www.divetelaviv.com, 7am-8pm daily, NIS650 including gear rental) is the best place to start for dive lessons, custom dives, and advice.

For sailing information and recommendations, try the **Israel Sailing Association** (03/624-1112).

Hilton Beach, Metsitsim (Sheraton) Beach, Gordon, Frishman, Bugrashov, Jerusalem and Geula all have sand courts available for **volleyball, beach handball, and soccer.** Aviv Beach has a designated area for surfing, kayaking, windsurfing and kite boarding.

TENNIS

The Tel Aviv system for tennis dictates that you reserve a court in advance. There are several around town, including 18 courts at **The National Sports Center** (6 Sheetrit St., 03/649-6464, http://nsc.org.il, tennis 6:30am-10pm Sun.-Thurs., 6:30am-8pm Fri.-Sat., call for prices as they vary by day and time). Contact the informal **Tennis Tel Aviv** (058-603/3370, tennis@tennis-telaviv.co.il) for specific information and recommendations.

GYMS

Many hotels in Tel Aviv, particularly in City Center, are near gyms and some have special arrangements for discount entry for hotel guests. Otherwise, try **Sportek** (HaYarkon Park, Yarkon River north bank, 03/699-0307, www.

Bugrashov Beach

kir.co.il, 6:30am-10pm daily, prices vary based on activity), which includes a rock climbing center. Another option is **Cross Fit Tel Aviv** (167 HaYarkon St. at Atarim Sq., 052/834-1247, www.crossfittelaviv.co.il, 6:30am-10pm daily, NIS200 and up), which is conveniently located just across from the Marina and caters to English-speaking customers.

SPECTATOR SPORTS
There are a couple of major sport arenas in Tel Aviv, including **Yad Eliyahu Arena** (51 Yigal Allon St., 03/537-6376), home to Tel Aviv's Maccabi and Hapoel basketball teams. **Bloomfield Stadium** (8 She'erit Israel St. in Jaffa, 03/637-6000) is the professional soccer arena and also hosts major international performers who draw huge crowds, such as Barbara Streisand. The major sports stadium is **Hadar Yosef Stadium** (10 Sheetrit St., 03/649-7474), which hosts all kinds of sports including soccer.

Accommodations

Tel Aviv's four- and five-star hotels abound, particularly along the coastline. But there are a surprising number of other options throughout the city for every budget, even near the sea. Some pitfalls of Tel Aviv hotels that you'll want to watch out for include rooms that are extremely small but are advertised as suitable for two people, accommodations that are not hostels but have shared bathrooms and showers, and places that might make you try to pay VAT, which is a tax only Israeli citizens or residents are required to pay. There are also often lower rates for tourists, and the best rates are usually found through online travel websites and not through the accommodations themselves. Avoid phone reservations, as you might arrive and find your room has been given away. If you stay in Jaffa, keep in mind you might be awakened by the sound of the post-midnight or 4am calls to prayer. If you are close to a mosque, the singing from the loudspeakers can wake you up very easily. Parking is extremely hard to come by in Tel Aviv, so if you have a rental car, ask in advance about the parking options, as not every hotel offers space.

NORTH TEL AVIV
US$100-150

The small but accommodating **Port Hotel** (4 Yirmeyahu St., corner of 288 HaYarkon St., 03/544-5544, www.porthoteltelaviv.com, US$149 d) is a recently-opened, 21-room hotel with free Wi-Fi, refrigerators, and modern decor and interiors. The hotel has a rooftop lounge area with an outstanding view of the sea. The rooms are simple and very spare on trimmings, but with clean, modern lines. There are numerous nightlife options nearby, and it is just a five-minute walk to the Port of Tel Aviv.

US$150-200

The **Armon HaYarkon** (268 HaYarkon St., 03/605-5271, www.armon-hotel.com, US$165 d) is a small hotel with an unremarkable exterior, but it has all the amenities you need, including breakfast, Wi-Fi, TV, and refrigerator. It's also just a few minutes from the sea and the exciting Port of Tel Aviv with its bars, clubs, shopping, nightlife, and restaurants. It's also a short drive to Israel's domestic airport, Sde Dov, where you can catch flights to the popular southern tourist city of Eilat.

Over US$200

Located right on the edge of the massive Ha'atzmaut (Independence) Park, ◖ **Melody Hotel** (220 HaYarkon St., 03/542-5555, www.atlas.co.il, US$250 d) is within easy walking distance of some of Tel Aviv's most popular beaches. A 2012 Travelers' Choice selection for Trendiest Hotel, this 55-room hotel has views of the sea and the park. The lobby lounge is open throughout the day and, on

Sunday-Thursday, it serves free snacks and drinks in the evening. During warmer months, the 8th-floor rooftop lounge is open. Amenities include LCD TV, Wi-Fi, a safe, fridge, beach towels, bike and beach chair rental, and some discounts for sightseeing tickets and dessert and wine vouchers from the reception desk.

Just down the street, directly across from the Tel Aviv Marina and the Gordon Swimming Pool, is the **Marina Tel Aviv** (167 HaYarkon St., 03/521-1777, www.marina-telaviv.com, US$260 d), a 160-room hotel with sea views and family-friendly rooms that caters to business travelers. Every room has air-conditioning, a bathtub, fridge, safe, and LCD TV. Hangout spaces include a lobby bar, a rooftop sun deck and swimming pool (in season), and a business lounge bar deck. Underground parking is available.

CITY CENTER
Under US$100

Of the many options in City Center, the **Mugraby Hostel** (19 Allenby St., 03/510-2443, www.mugraby-hostel.com, US$70 d) is one of the least expensive hotels if being near the beach is a higher priority for you than privacy and creature comforts. Owned and operated by two brothers, Nimrod and Avi Katorza, the hostel has been in business since 1996 and relocated in 2011. The dorm-style accommodations include shared showers and toilets, linens, kitchen, and lounge with cable TV. The English-speaking staff can offer travel and tour advice, and there is an Internet café on the premises. A nearby laundry service and two 24-hour supermarkets make it convenient for the low-budget traveler.

US$150-200

If you want to roll out of bed and into the sea, **Abratel Suites Hotel** (3 Geula St., 03/516-9966, www.abratelsuiteshotel.com, US$200 d) is a small but good option. With only 24 suites and six standard rooms, the hotel faces the sea and promenade; a room with a sea view costs extra. There is free parking and beach towels, and the entire hotel has central air-conditioning. Rates include breakfast and free coffee, tea, and cookies in the lobby.

An extremely hip option that exudes Tel Aviv's modern style is the **City Hotel** (9 Mapu St., 03/542-5555, www.atlas.co.il, US$195 d). The hotel is known for its cozy but swank atmosphere and excellent restaurant. The 96-room hotel has a bright, modern interior, free Wi-Fi throughout, an outdoor coffee shop on the terrace, room service, free parking, and event space. Guests can use a nearby gym for a fee, and several of the rooms feature a small balcony that can seat up to four. The hotel is a very short walk to the beach, and you can rent a bike or get beach towels from reception. Bed-and-breakfast options are also available for the spacious rooms that have a fridge, safe, and LCD TV.

Part of a regional group of hotels, the **Deborah Hotel** (87 Ben Yehuda St., 03/527-8282, www.arcadiahotels.co.il, US$160 d) is a 69-room establishment just between lively Dizengoff Street and the sea. About two blocks from the sea promenade and the Tel Aviv Marina, Deborah Hotel is kosher and has a hotel synagogue and a Shabbat elevator. Wi-Fi, business traveler services, and a nearby gym at a discount are also available. The interior of the rooms is not spectacular but includes all the basic amenities. The height of the building also allows for some great views of Tel Aviv.

Situated along a row of hotels just one block from the sea and promenade, **TLV88** (88 HaYarkon St., 03/620-4676, www.tlv88.com, US$160 d) is a Bauhaus building from 1936 that gives the feeling of being right on the beach. Renovated in 2012, TLV88 is one of the trendier options in the area, and is self-described as "an intimate boutique hotel with a Monte Carlo style and a French Riviera flavor." The nautical decor of the rooms create a sporty, seafaring atmosphere, and amenities include a 24-hour concierge service and free parking. Every room has a sea or city view, there is a seaside restaurant on the ground floor, and a wide variety of other restaurants and entertainment venues nearby.

◖ **Hotel De La Mer** (2 Ness Tsiyona St., corner of 62 HaYarkon St., 03/510-0011, www.delamer.co.il, US$179 d) is an exclusive European-style boutique hotel. The exterior is restored historic Bauhaus and the interior has been arranged using feng shui techniques. Extremely close to the sea and beach, the units are non-smoking rooms and suites with a range of options, including sea views and in-room whirlpool tubs. The range of services at De La Mer is huge, and includes Wi-Fi, a coffee lounge where you can have breakfast, a sunbathing rooftop terrace, currency conversion, basic postal services, babysitting, clerical services, and 24/7 free coffee and tea service in the lobby. Some rooms have a balcony for an additional charge, and rooms have satellite TV, a writing desk, and a wardrobe closet. You can get adaptors, hair dryers, and irons at the front desk.

Over US$200

Even though it only has 21 rooms, **Dizengoff Suites** (39 Gordon St., 03/523-4363, www.dizengoffsuites.co.il, US$215 d) makes the most of their amazing location close to some of the highlights of Tel Aviv shopping and entertainment. The three available varieties of suites are recently renovated and include a fully equipped kitchenette, mini-fridge, air-conditioning, cable TV, and free Wi-Fi. The elevator can only fit about two people at a time, and there is an unusual card-key system for electricity in the rooms, some of which have a balcony or rooftop terrace. The overall feel is very homey and the staff is friendly and accommodating. An excellent breakfast in the downstairs restaurant with a distinctly Parisian atmosphere, Café Marco, is included.

The brand new 62-room hotel dedicated to Israeli art, ◖ **Artplus Hotel** (35 Ben Yehuda St., 03/542-5555, www.atlas.co.il, US$210 d) is like one big work of art from floor to ceiling and throughout the hotel. Murals on every floor were commissioned by five famous local artists, and the hotel's foyer and lobby feature works by two internationally-renowned Israeli artists, Zadok Ben-David and Sigalit Landau. The overall design is retro modern. It is in easy walking distance to the beach. Amenities include tons of freebies, including parking, bicycle rental, breakfast, refreshments and snacks in the hotel's library every evening, a sun roof terrace, and coupons to local restaurants. Rooms include air-conditioning, a fridge and safe, an LCD TV, and hair dryer.

The atmosphere, location and price of the **Bell Hotel** (50 HaYarkon St., 03/517-4291, www.bellhotel-telaviv.com, US$209 d) are all just right. This seaside boutique hotel is just north of the Dolphinarium and some of Tel Aviv's best nightlife and beach life. A double room includes free parking, Wi-Fi, air-conditioning, fridge, coffee and tea service, and breakfast. The rooms are comfortably and artfully designed to reflect Tel Aviv's vibe of sand and sea, with a sandstone-based color scheme and some rooms with balcony seaside views and whirlpool tubs.

With 227 rooms, the **Hotel Metropolitan and Metropolitan Suites** (11-15 Trumpeldor St., 03/519-2727, www.hotelmetropolitan.co.il, US$219 d) is big enough to give the experience of hotel luxury but still maintains a warm atmosphere. Some of the decor in the rooms is a bit dated, but the lobby bar and restaurant are both modern and open until the wee hours. It is right on the sea. Adjacent to the hotel are sister suites for longer-term stays. With services catered toward business travelers, the hotel has rooms with phones that allow for international calls, a business center (for an extra cost), laundry service, mini bars, and car rental. There is also room service and rooms for guests with disabilities. Guests have free access to a health club and to private parking for a fee. An outdoor pool is open April-October.

SOUTH TEL AVIV
Under US$100
A home-style hostel in the trendy Florentin neighborhood, **Florentine Hostel** (10 Elifelet St., 03/518-7551, florentinehostel.com, US$60 d private room for two, US$25 one dorm bed) has an unusual age restriction that only allows guests between the ages of 18 and 40. Private rooms have a double bed, air-conditioning,

linens, and a shared bathroom and shower. There is also free Wi-Fi, free coffee and tea, a barbeque area, free parking, cell phone and bicycle rental, luggage storage, an indoor lounge, a fully-equipped communal kitchen, and a rooftop terrace. It is within walking distance to Old Jaffa and the flea market, the beach and boardwalk, and the historic but hip Neve Tzedek neighborhood. Near the hostel there are numerous cafés, nightclubs, and pubs.

Part of a small domestic chain, the **Sun Aviv Hotel Tel Aviv** (9A Montefiori St., 03/517-4847, www.sun-aviv.co.il, US$95 d) has just 20 rooms and is located in between Carmel Market, Nahalat Binyamin outdoor mall, and trendy Shabazi Street in Neve Tzedek. A room includes continental breakfast, air-conditioning, mini-bar, satellite TV, laundry service, and car rental. The hotel is decorated in a very spare manner, with few trimmings or luxurious touches. There is a cafeteria on the ground floor, a 24-hour reception desk, and, during the day, cold and hot drinks can be ordered by room service.

Over US$200
Luxurious in a way that is unique to Tel Aviv, the **☾ Neve Tzedek Hotel** (4 Deganya St., off of Shabazi St., 054/207-0706, www.nevetzedekhotel.com, US$760 d) has spacious, airy rooms with endless small touches that make it both visually appealing and comfortable. Some highlights include garden suites with private outdoor garden terraces, plush beds, huge windows, and luxurious furnishings that are both beautiful and comfortable. Opened in 2009 in a historic building, the hotel is near Nana Bar restaurant and Pri Hagefen wine bar, owned by Golan Dor and Tommy Ben-David, neighborhood residents, and the renowned Suzanne Dellal Center, Jaffa, and Zappa Club. In addition to all the usual amenities, a stay here will get you handmade chocolates, cakes, and baked goods; superb cheeses and wines; exotic fruits; spa treatments and kits; beach bags; flowers; house and bath robes; and literature, art, and access to tickets for shows and attractions.

Styled in a decidedly European fashion,

the **Nina Café Suites Hotel** (29 Shabazi St., 03/510-5239, http://ninacafehotel.com, US$250 d) is a luxury boutique hotel in the heart of Neve Tzedek. Both suites and studios are available. All rooms include a mini-bar, cable TV, DVD, Wi-Fi, laundry services, air-conditioning, and breakfast at the nearby Nina Café, or breakfast can be ordered to the room.

Within easy walking distance to the beach and Jaffa and nearby to the trendy and happening HaTachana complex, **The Varsano** (16 Hevrat Shass St., 077/554-5500, http://thevarsano.com, US$475 d) is a stylish and modern luxury boutique hotel that is perfect for longer stays with all the comforts of home. The rooms are designed as suites, with living space and a loft atmosphere, and have fully-equipped kitchens, dining areas, and bedrooms. There is also free Wi-Fi, LCD TV, high-end kitchen appliances, a washer and dryer on premises, and parking (for a fee).

JAFFA (YAFO)
Under US$100
Among some of the more homey picks in Jaffa, the ◖ **Beit Immanuel Congregation and Guest House** (8 Aeurbach St., 03/682-1459, www.beitimmanuel.org, US$92 d) is a good fit for all types of travelers on a budget and is welcoming to couples and families with kids, as well as groups. The small 13-room guesthouse has simple and plain private rooms with bathrooms and dormitory rooms, all with coffee and tea service, air-conditioning, and heat, and some rooms have balconies. Just next to the ancient Jaffa Port and some outstanding (and a bit less crowded) beaches, Beit Immanuel caters to special prayer tour groups or people traveling on short-term religious missions. There is free Wi-Fi in the lobby and a quiet garden area on the ground floor. The included breakfast can be eaten in the garden between May and October. Luggage storage, free secure parking, conference facilities, and a prayer room are available, as well as a Hebrew-language worship service on Friday evenings with English translation.

The **Old Jaffa Hostel and Guesthouse** (13 Amiad St., 03/682-2370, www.telaviv-hostel.com, US$80 d) is in an older building with touches that evoke a distinctly Middle Eastern flavor. Located across the street from the Jaffa flea market, a 10-minute walk from the Old City of Jaffa, and 15 minutes from the Port of Jaffa, the hostel has a sizable rooftop garden and is close to several new cafés, wine bars, pubs, and restaurants. Housed in an old renovated building with high ceilings, colorful floor tiles, and balconies overlooking the flea market, the hostel is closed on national holidays. Amenities include free Wi-Fi, a fee-based Internet station, a fully-equipped kitchen, free coffee, tea and cookies in the morning, and coin laundry service. There is also a storage safe and a code-locked entrance gate.

Over US$200
If you're planning on staying four nights or more in one place, **Andromeda Hill** (3 Andromeda Hill Louis Pasteur St., 03/683-8448, www.andromeda.co.il, US$220 d) is a pick that includes a notably long list of amenities, including a saltwater swimming pool and tremendous views of the sea. Just at the southern tip of Old Jaffa and close to numerous historical sites, beaches, and restaurants, the Andromeda Hill apartment-style stone complex is built on top of a buttress named for Greek mythology's Andromeda. The rooms are modern, simple, and functional, and some of the comforts include a lounge deck, free towel service, a fitness spa, a poolside café, an open promenade and gardens, en-suite kitchenettes, a conference room, parking, and 24-hour security. Some rooms include a balcony. Massage services, a steam room and dry sauna, luggage storage, and Wi-Fi are also available.

TEL AVIV SUBURBS

The largely haphazard way that Tel Aviv was planned and grew (aside from the White City) created, by default, suburbs of the city. These suburbs, which include cities such as **Ramat Gan** in the east, **Holon** in the south, and **Ramat Aviv** in the north, were less outgrowths of Tel Aviv and more something the sprawling city ran into as it grew.

Upon visiting Tel Aviv, there might be a museum or restaurant you want to visit in one of these areas. While they are not part of Tel Aviv proper, they are still very much connected to the city's thriving day and night life.

Ramat Aviv is home to several worthwhile museums, and its position at the north border of HaYarkon Park makes it a natural stop to include if your sightseeing takes you in that direction.

There is enough to see between the Mediterranean Sea and the Ayalon Highway that you don't have to venture into Ramat Gan for fun. But if you happen to work your way to the far eastern side of HaYarkon Park, you'll find the 500-acre **Ramat Gan National Park** (Ramat Gan off of Hwy. 4 near Tel Aviv, 03/631-3964). Inside the park is Safari Park, home to approximately 1,600 animals from all over the world, including 68 species of mammals, 130 species of birds, and 25 species of reptiles.

Also close by is **Meymadion Water Park** (150 Rokach Ave., at Ganei Yehoshua Park, 03/642-2777, NIS99).

Food

You could try a different restaurant for every meal, every day in Tel Aviv and you won't run out of options. The options range from high-end fine dining to casual fare fit for a picnic in the park. One of the hallmarks of Tel Aviv restaurants is that many (particularly the higher-end places) are open only for lunch and dinner. Lunch menus often have a special business menu, which simply means a lower price for an inclusive food and drink option. Most restaurants are open until very late at night, a few are 24 hours, 7 days a week, but fewer open very early in the morning. Unlike Jerusalem, kosher Tel Aviv restaurants are not the majority, and it is fairly easy to find many options open during Shabbat. One thing to keep in mind about the hours that restaurants advertise is that they change, particularly during the winter. If you plan to be early or late to an establishment, call in advance to make sure they will be open.

NORTH TEL AVIV
Italian
A kosher establishment that specializes in thin crust pizza and calzones, **Pizza Fino** (169 Ben Yehuda St., 03/522-8165, noon-midnight Sun.-Thurs., noon-3pm Fri., about 6pm-midnight Sat., NIS60) is a favorite among Tel Avivians who love pizza. Its red brick storefront is situated very obviously at the intersection of Ben Yehuda and Jabotinsky Streets. They have a window for walkup takeout, some indoor seating, and several outdoor sidewalk tables.

Meat and Seafood
A place where everything is centered around seafood, **Mul-Yam** (Port of Tel Aviv Hangar 23, 03/546-9920, www.mulyam.com, 12:30pm-2:30pm and 7:30pm-10:30pm daily, NIS200), which means "facing the sea" in Hebrew, serves only imported fish and seafood and has a tremendous reputation for being the best of the best. Due to the relatively high entrée prices, their business lunch is a popular way to experience the famous restaurant headed by chef Yoram Nitzan. The interior is modest and simple, but it is known as a place that local celebrities and upper-crust Tel

Avivians like to frequent, and it tends to get a bit noisy.

At 🄲 **Gilly's** (Port of Tel Aviv Hangar 15, 03/605-7777, www.namal.co.il, www.gillys. co.il, 10am-10pm daily, NIS100), you must make reservations to experience this Jerusalem transplant known for its savory meat dishes, including a French-style steak. The owner, Gilly Pepperman, is famous for introducing his Jerusalem customers to high-quality, well-prepared meat. The restaurant and bar boast large windows that look out onto the sea and a balcony, and the warm atmosphere and large outdoor seating on the sea somehow manage to evoke a decidedly Jerusalem vibe. Hugely popular for their "Breakfast Royal" (10am-5pm daily), which includes a champagne cocktail, freshly baked bread, eggs, bacon, and more, Gilly presentes menu selections—from appetizers to alcohol and dessert—that are extensive.

Mediterranean and European Fusion

Right on the water at the Port, **White Pergola** (Yordei Hasira 1, Port of Tel Aviv Hangar 4, 03/546-4747, www.hasuka-halevana. co.il, 10am-last customer daily, NIS100), or *Hasukkah Halevana* in Hebrew, is an elegant and popular restaurant that specializes in and is known for its wide array of seafood dishes, but they also serve beef and lamb. Some offerings include lobster, mussels, crab, and shrimp. There is seaside outdoor seating, and part of the restaurant's spacious interior has floor to ceiling blond wood paneling that gives the feel of being inside the belly of a ship. The service can be quite slow, and the wine and alcohol menu is small, but selective.

If you want one of the best outdoor spots on the boardwalk at Tel Aviv's happening port, where you can see and hear crashing waves and the sunset and don't mind being served by a waiter in nothing but a bathing suit, **Speedo Bar** (Port of Tel Aviv Hangar 22, 03/546-1140, www.namal.co.il, 10am-2am daily, NIS70) is your best choice. The menu has a nice variety of lighter items on its bar menu including nachos, egg rolls, and hamburgers, and the breakfast and snack menus are also varied. Main courses are mainly items like schnitzel and other fried food, hamburgers, and some seafood items. The atmosphere is extremely laid-back and the outdoor cushioned lounge chairs will make you want to linger long after you finish.

Also at the Port, **Shalvata Restaurant** (Port of Tel Aviv Hangar 28, 03/544-1279, www.shalvata.co.il, 5pm-11pm Sun.-Thurs., 9am-11pm Fri.-Sat., NIS70) has an unparalleled open seaside atmosphere and is a popular place for events. The bar and restaurant faces the sea with shade from straw parasols and has different sections with varied heights and types of seats, some directly on sand you can dig your toes into. The menu is mainly pizza, pasta, chicken, and hamburgers, and there is a large alcohol, cocktails, and beer menu.

CITY CENTER
American

Known and loved for its hamburgers (which some say are the best in Tel Aviv), **Moses** (35 Rothschild Blvd., 03/566-4949, www.moses-rest.co.il, noon-4am daily, NIS60) is a popular and trendy American-style eatery near the Tel Aviv Stock Exchange, Independence Hall, and a couple of smaller museums and galleries. The slightly pricey combination beef, lamb, and veal hamburger is recommended, but the service is known for being a bit slow, especially in the afternoons. The interior is simple and fashioned after an American diner.

The spacious layout, exposed brick, and huge bar give **Dixie** (120 Igal Alon St., corner of 3 Totzeret Ha'aretz, 03/696-6123, www. dixie.co.il, 24 hours daily, NIS65) a very American (particularly New York City) vibe. Add the large portions of steak, chicken sandwiches, and hamburgers to the mix and you could almost forget you're in Israel. The menu changes three times a year, and a range of wines from leading Israeli and international wineries, beer, and cocktails are available. Known as the grandfather of the 24/7 restaurant concept in Israel, the clientele is very trendy Tel Aviv and it is a favorite of late-night clubbers. The restaurant also delivers takeout orders. Its main downside for visitors to Tel Aviv (unless you're hanging out with locals) is the location, as the main thing nearby is Azrieli Center and HaShalom train station.

Cafés and Bistros

In the style of a New York loft blended with Bauhaus architecture, **Betty White Bistro and Art** (22 Frishman St., 052/884-1146 and 077/510-1171, 8:30am-10:30pm daily, NIS50) has a reputation for being a fun and delicious option just two blocks from the beach. The very trendy, modern, retro decor includes multimedia wall art and lots of white everywhere, and the music ranges from 1960s to electronica but is not overwhelming. This café-style establishment is a good place for a salad or light lunch or breakfast after the beach, or to meet friends for a coffee in the afternoon. There's a decent-size alcohol and drink menu, and absolutely delicious crepes, salmon appetizers, and quinoa salad with lentils, goat cheese, and roasted tomatoes. Betty White also hosts live concerts, art displays, and film screenings.

Situated behind a customized tropical garden patio near Dizengoff Center, **Bar Giora** (4 Bar Giora St., corner of 64 Dizengoff St., 03/620-4880, http://bargiyora.co.il, 10am-last customer Sun.-Thurs., 11am-last customer Fri.-Sat., NIS50) somehow combines a beach atmosphere with the comforts of a bistro. It's a favorite among locals, which adds to its reputation as a neighborhood institution. The multiple level establishment attracts a younger crowd, and has live music in the evenings in the basement level. The menu has a wide range of salads, sandwiches, hamburgers, and Persian, Moroccan, and pasta dishes. There are also a variety of homemade pastries and desserts, and a menu of specials.

Known for its chicken schnitzel, great service, and excellent views of the sea, **Café Metzada** (83 HaYarkon St., with entrance on the promenade, 03/510-3353, 24 hours daily, NIS60) is located just on the promenade and has a relaxed, calm atmosphere with indoor and outdoor seating. The menu and food preparation are simple, but the portions are large and

there are a variety of items such as chicken wings, hamburgers, steak, salad, and desert.

Italian

Considered one of the best Italian restaurants in Tel Aviv, **Rustico** (15 Rothschild Ave., 03/510-0039, www.rustico.co.il, noon-midnight daily, NIS55) has another location (42 Basel St.) and has a selection of fresh pizzas and focaccias that are baked in a large stone oven in view of patrons. They also serve homemade pasta, seafood, and risotto. The rustic Italian countryside interior includes a large bar in the center of the restaurant and windows with views of the avenue. Outdoor seating includes a beautiful wooden porch, but overall it is not the best place for an intimate meal, as it can get very loud and lively, with tables positioned relatively close together.

Meat and Seafood

The combination of a window kiosk on the beach where you can get a margarita and calamari and a Mediterranean-themed indoor restaurant have made **SALT Kitchen and Drinks** (136 HaYarkon St., corner of 2 Gordon St., 057/934-5568, http://salt.rest-e.co.il, 8am-noon Sun., 8am-noon and 7pm-last customer Mon.-Thurs., 8am-2pm and 7pm-last customer Fri.-Sat., beach window kiosk 11am-7pm daily, NIS60 restaurant, NIS30 kiosk) a popular stop for locals and visitors. The creative meat and seafood restaurant's Mediterranean-inspired menu includes items like drum fish with lemony Jerusalem artichokes, and veal sweetbread on black lentils. Situated on the ground floor of the Gordon Boutique Hotel, SALT offers a good view of the beach and promenade. The contemporary interior has a central bar overlooking the terrace and shelves made of ouzo bottles, with large blocks of salt as design accents.

One of Tel Aviv's most famous restaurants, **Manta Ray** (Alma Beach on the Tel Aviv Promenade, west of Charles Clore Park, near the Intercontinental David Hotel at 12 Kaufmann St., 03/517-4773, www.mantaray.co.il, 9am-midnight daily, NIS110) lives up to the hype. A place where Madonna and other stars are said to have eaten, this gourmet seafood restaurant serves items like mullet ceviche and baked blue bream. On weekends, they also serve fresh oysters from Paris. The breakfast menu is available until noon and is surprisingly affordable and very popular (make reservations). The exterior of the building literally looks like a gray, cement hut on the beach, but the interior is spacious and welcoming, even though the clientele and staff tend to be on the yuppie side. It's a great place to have a bit and then hang out on the beach, though there is no swimming.

Mediterranean and European Fusion

A very subdued, classy atmosphere that gives the feel of dining in someone's home is a hallmark of C **Messa** (19 Ha'arbaa St., 03/685-6859, messa@messa.co.il, noon-2:30pm and 7pm-11:30pm daily, bar 7pm-last customer daily, NIS150), a European-style restaurant known for its outstanding service and presentation. The entrance is hidden behind a large door on the corner of a building with a modern exterior; the interior's layout includes a huge, long dining table for numerous customers and a bar. Known to attract customers from the upper echelons of society, Messa's food is based in French Provencal techniques and local ingredients. The restaurant emphasizes using high-quality raw ingredients in their dishes.

Housed in a 129-year-old restored building that once belonged to a Turkish sheik, **Kimmel** (6 HaShachar St., 03/510-5204, www.2eat.co.il/eng/kimmel, noon-11pm daily, NIS120) uses its setting for its take on the "rustic" French country approach to food, drink, and atmosphere, largely succeeding. The arrangement of tables feels a bit like a cafeteria, but the overall warmth of the setting, down to the types of glasses used, overpowers the slightly utilitarian seating arrangements. Vegetables, wine bottles, and antique knickknacks adorn the walls and alcoves, and the dishes place emphasis on cheeses, meat, and fish in rich sauces, herbs, creams, and olive oil. Don't be shy about asking one of Kimmel's friendly waitstaff to explain certain menu items that border on exotic.

Mexican and South American

Named for the Mexican artist, **Frida Kahlo Restaurant Bar** (43 Lindenblum St., 03/566-0481, yoav@fridakahlo.co.il, 7pm-4am Sun., noon-4pm and 7pm-4am Mon.-Thurs., noon-4am Fri.-Sat., NIS100) is just east of Neve Tzedek and some good nightlife spots. The interior is decorated with rich red and orange accents and a circular bar, and the food is a unique Latin-Israeli fusion exacted on meat and seafood dishes with a lengthy alcohol menu. It's a good place for weekday lunch specials and light food and drinks in the evening, and it serves a popular chili con carne hamburger.

If you're in the mood for deliciously satisfying and spicy, spicy, spicy, **Mexicana** (7 Bugrashov St., 03/527-9911, www.mexicana.co.il, noon-midnight daily, NIS60) has Mexican menu that could quell most Americans' cravings for something familiar. The atmosphere is always bustling, especially on Shabbat, when it is one of the few places on its particular stretch of street that is open. The prices are not on the easily affordable end of Mexican restaurants, but one of the best items on the menu, and best priced, is the tortilla soup. The fajitas and chips are also excellent. Despite the outdoor sidewalk seating, the indoor seating area is brightly and cheerfully decorated, but space is rather limited so you could end up at a cozy distance from other diners. The service is unfailingly friendly, upbeat, and accommodating, though you might have to make special requests a few times because they are so busy.

Thai

Thai House (8 Bugrashov St., 03/517-8568, www.2eat.co.il/eng/thai, noon-11pm daily, NIS75) serves up northwest Thai food and classics from the Bangkok and southern islands regions, including curry coconut dishes, street-stall dishes, organic green papaya salad, and farm-grown eggplant. Managed by a husband-wife team with roots in a long line of Thai restaurateurs, the restaurant also offers special fish dishes on request that are not listed on the menu. The somewhat shabby exterior belies the unique bamboo-walled interior that gives the feeling of being in a bamboo hut. Though small, just by reputation for its outstanding authentic Thai food, the restaurant attracts a large number of repeat customers. Reservations are recommended.

Wine and Tapas

Incredibly popular and in a great location near the Tel Aviv Marina, **Wineberg** (106 Ben Yehuda St., 03/522-3939, lunch 11:30am-last customer, dinner 5:30pm-last customer, NIS70) has a rustic, friendly atmosphere replete with a wooden antler head on the wall. Wineberg's food is focused on tapas, cold dishes, meat sandwiches, soup, pasta, and some seafood. Try the lamb siniya, with steamed burghul and eggplant cream, and the gnocchi la romana hot tapas. There is also a large spirits, wine, and beer menu. Wineberg is loved by customers for its winning combination of good food, good atmosphere, and good value for the money.

Mentioned again and again by locals and tourists as a favorite, █ **Vicky & Cristina** (HaTachana Bldg. 17 at 1 Kaufmann St., 03/736-7272 and 057/944-4144, www. HaTachana.co.il/vicky-cristina, 5pm-last customer Sun.-Thurs., noon-last customer Fri.-Sat., NIS90) is a Spanish tapas (Vicky) and wine bar (Cristina), located in a spacious patio under an ancient rubber tree. The atmosphere is intimate and understated, with Latin background music. A wine bar with more than 120 selections (from 7pm daily) is on the back side of the patio with high bar stools and a garden of mosaic-covered sculptures inspired by Barcelona's famous Park Güell.

SOUTH TEL AVIV
Italian

With the reputation as one of the best Italian restaurants in Tel Aviv, **Pronto** (4 Hertsel St., 03/566-0915, www.pronto.co.il, 12:30pm-3pm and 6:30pm-11:30pm daily, NIS90) has had 20 years to establish its stature in the local restaurant scene. A favorite place for doing business and entertaining clients, Pronto has a generous wine menu, and serves mostly pasta for main dishes with a few specialties, including braised duck and lamb chops. The spacious and modern interior includes a small bar and huge floor to ceiling windows that are right on street level.

A favorite standby for a romantic dinner date or an intimate, private meeting, **Nana Bar** (1 Ahad Ha'Am St., 03/516-1915, http://nanabar. rest-e.co.il, noon-last customer Sun.-Thurs., 9am-last customer Fri.-Sat., NIS80) is set in a limestone building with soft light and antique accents in decor designed in the style of Louis XIII. The menu includes fish from the Mediterranean, prime cuts of meat, fresh vegetables from the nearby market, and olive oil from local presses. There is a long bar and an equally long wine list. In warmer weather, there is outdoor seating in a garden courtyard. Local celebrities, diplomats, and heads of state tend to frequent Nana alongside locals and those looking for a picturesque atmosphere.

Japanese

A rare find in the neighborhood where it lives, **Okinawa** (46 Shabazi St., 03/510-1099, www. okinawatlv.co.il, noon-midnight Sun.-Fri., 5:30pm-midnight Sat., NIS60) seems to be the lone sushi bar and Japanese restaurant in the Neve Tzedek area. Serving a sashimi and sushi menu, the restaurant has a relaxed and friendly atmosphere with an accommodating staff, and they have a large cocktail menu to boot. It attracts mostly locals who enjoy sushi restaurants but haven't found a favorite yet.

Meat and Seafood

One of a group of three leading restaurants in Israel, **Herbert Samuel** (6 Kaufmann St. at the Gaon House, 03/516-6516, http://herbert-samuel.co.il, 12:30pm-4pm and 6pm-midnight Sun.-Wed., 12:30pm-midnight Thurs.-Sat., NIS150) is just across the street from the beach and promenade and specializes in meat and seafood dishes. Chef Yonatan Roshfeld has a reality TV show, which contributes to the huge buzz the restaurant enjoys as one of the best in Tel Aviv. Known for its outstanding service, the upscale and contemporary setting includes tables with window views of the sea and a bar. Specialty items on the menu include duck, shrimp lasagna, and an artichoke, chestnut, and truffle soup.

Known for its massive porterhouse steak that weighs in somewhere between 70-170 ounces and piglet in maple sauce and apples, **NG** (6 Ahad Ha'Am St., corner of Yehuda Ha'hasid St., up the staircase, 052/839-3119 and 03/516-7888, www.ngrestaurant.co.il, 6pm-1am Sun.-Thurs., 4pm-1am Fri., noon-1am Sat., NIS110) was voted as Best Meat Restaurant for three years in a row by *Time Out* magazine. Set in picturesque Neve Tzedek, the restaurant's atmosphere is quaint and romantic, with friendly, down-to-earth service (one of the owners might wait on you). There is a generous wine list and selection of several beers from local breweries to round out the hefty food at this self-labeled "meat bar."

Mediterranean and European Fusion

A French gourmet meets Mediterranean fine dining experience and long considered one of Tel Aviv's best restaurants, **Catit** (4 Heichal HaTalmud, 03/510-7001, www.catit.co.il, noon-3pm and 7pm-11pm Sun.-Fri., noon-4pm Sat., NIS180) is a transplant from a small village where it earned a reputation as a must-visit restaurant. It is now one of the most highly-regarded restaurants in Tel Aviv after six years here. Chef Meir Adoni is still known for his unique touch with food, including risotto in wine, veal fillet with Mediterranean olives and za'atar tapenade, and lamb with bulgur and spice seeds. Housed in an historical building with an upscale interior, the venue has an atmosphere that evokes elegant country. Due to its wide reputation, Catit attracts discerning locals and curious tourists alike.

A local favorite, **Suzanna** (9 Shabazi St., 057/944-3060, http://suzana.rest-e.co.il, 10am-2am daily, NIS70) serves Greek and Mediterranean dishes that feature a wide variety of stuffed items. Housed in a distinctive yellow building in Neve Tzedek that includes a very inviting shaded terrace, Suzanna's menu includes traditional Moroccan soup, stuffed vegetables and fruits, stews, and grilled dishes. The outdoor bar is open nightly (7pm-1am).

Wine and Tapas

A warm, muted atmosphere featuring Mediterranean tiles and ropes of hanging garlic is what you'll find at **Tapas 1** (27 Ahad Ha'Am St., 03/566-6966, http://adislifestyle.com, noon-3pm and 7pm-1am Sun.-Thurs., noon-4pm and 7pm-1am Fri.-Sat., NIS60) with its Spanish tapas and other Spanish cuisine. Also known as Ahad Ha'Am Tapas Bar, the restaurant serves dozens of types of tapas and is an extremely popular hangout for young people and culinary enthusiasts. On Mondays specialty seafood dishes are available.

JAFFA (YAFO)
Cafés

The Nalagaat Center's **Black Out Restaurant** (Retsif Haaliya Hashniya at Jaffa Port, 03/633-0808, www.nalagaat.org.il, first sitting 6:30pm, second sitting 9pm Sun., Tues., and Thurs., NIS120) serves meals in complete darkness by waiters who are blind. Also at the Nalagaat Center, **Café Kapish** (Retsif Haaliya Hashniya at Jaffa Port, 03/633-0808, www.nalagaat.org.il, 6pm-11pm Sun.-Thurs., NIS18) deaf and hearing-impaired staff engage with customers using sign language. You can get coffee, beer, wine, and other drinks and snacks.

Seafood

Very popular for its sparkling service and delicious food, **Yona** (Jaffa Port on the Pier, 03/774-2222, www.yona.be, noon-midnight daily, NIS110) has taken the vast interior of an old container warehouse and somehow made it inviting and fun. Huge wooden shipping barrels filled with fresh loaves of bread baked on the premises and lampshades reminiscent of seashells add to the seafaring atmosphere. Not unlike its sister restaurant Manta Ray, Yona is known for its seafood dishes. The restaurant's

TEL AVIV

presentation is based on the "open source" trend that allows customers visual access to the chefs at work. Yona also makes their own yogurt and ricotta, and smokes their salmon and meat on the premises. Vegetarian dishes are also available. There is a large bar and outdoor seating in the summer months with a view of the sunset and fishing boats.

Middle Eastern

It doesn't have a fancy appearance inside or out, but **◖ Itzik HaGadol** (3 Razi'el St., 057/943-8970, www.itzikhagadol.co.il, noon-midnight daily, NIS70) is legendary among generations of local Tel Avivians. Also known as Big Itzik, because of its extension on the other side of the narrow street, it has been in business for decades. Neither the interior nor the general atmosphere boasts warmth and relaxation, but it is impossible to dine here and leave hungry. With an emphasis on meat and mezze (Middle Eastern appetizers and hummus), you can order

lamb chops, goose liver, kebab, grilled eggplant, and more to your heart's content. But watch out for racking up a huge bill and too much food because it accumulates quickly. You will start getting falafel, hummus, and mezze almost immediately after sitting down, so pace yourself and try one thing at a time.

With a name like **Dr. Shakshuka** (3 Beit Eshel St., 057/944-4193, http://drshaksuka.rest-e.co.il, 8am-midnight Sun.-Thurs., NIS45), there is bound to be a lot of hype. But as one of the few kosher Libyan restaurants in town that specializes in very large portions of the staple Middle Eastern egg and vegetable dish called shakshuka, Dr. Shakshuka has somewhat of a corner on the market in their location. Skipping fancy presentation in both their food and decor, the restaurant's interior features old copper items like lamps hanging from the ceiling, exposed stone walls, and large palm plants. Popular with locals and tourists, the atmosphere is 100 percent Middle Eastern.

Information and Services

Tel Aviv caters to tourists and visitors from all over the world, and presents information and services regularly in English, including at ATMs, post offices, and websites.

INFORMATION
Tourist and Travel Information

There are three major tourist information centers, and one of the most centrally located and easily accessible is **HaTachana Train Station Complex Tourist Center** (HaTachana Bldg. 5, 03/776-4005 or 03/516-6188, ext. 3, HaTachana@013net.net, 10am-8pm Sun.–Thurs., 9am–2pm Fri., closed on Jewish holidays). You can also have some fun shopping and eating at HaTachana.

The **Herbert Samuel Promenade Tourist Center** (46 Herbert Samuel St., 03/516-6188 ext. 1, tourist.tlv@barak.net.il, 9:30am-6:30pm Sun.-Thurs., 9am-1pm Fri. Apr. 1-Oct. 31; 9:30am-5:30pm Sun.-Thurs.,

9am-1pm Fri. Nov.1-Mar. 31, closed on Jewish holidays) is a reasonable stop to combine with going to the beach, as it is directly on the promenade and near swimming.

Down in Old Jaffa is the **Jaffa Clock Tower Tourist Center** (2 Marzuk at Azar St., 03/516-6188, ext. 2, jaffainfo11@bezeqint.net, 9:30am-6:30pm Sun.–Thurs., 9am-2pm Fri., 10am-4pm Sat. Apr. 1-Oct. 31; 9:30am-5:30pm Sun.-Thurs., 9am-2pm Fri. Nov. 1-Mar. 31, closed on Jewish holidays).

A new venture of The Association for Tourism Tel Aviv-Jaffa is the **Mobile Segway Information Center** (www.visit-tlv.com, 1pm-7pm daily July-Sept.), which can be seen at various points throughout the city. The segway travels around town, passing through central tourist attractions including the Tel Aviv Marina, the promenade, Jaffa, Neve Tzedek, and Rothschild Boulevard.

Maps

There are some useful online maps of Tel Aviv, including several very detailed options on the **Israel Ministry of Tourism** (www.visitisrael. gov.il) website. They are especially helpful if you have access to a color printer.

Israel Traveler (www.israeltraveler.org) has a handy integrated smart map that allows you to search a location and displays accommodations, food, entertainment, and more in the surrounding vicinity of your search with clickable thumbtacks.

Hospitals and Emergency Services

Very close to the center of Tel Aviv near Hamedim Square is **Ichilov Hospital** (6 Weitzman St., 03/697-4444), which has some of the best facilities in Israel.

For emergencies 24 hours a day and transportation to the nearest emergency room, contact **Magen David Adom** (dial 101 or 03/546-0111, www.mdais.com).

For non-medical emergencies, contact the **Tourist Police** (03/516-5382, corner of Geula and Herbert Samuel Sts.).

Media

The home offices for most of Israel's domestic media companies are located in Tel Aviv, including the general news and interest **Ha'aretz** and **Yediot Ahronoth,** which have editions in English, as well as the English business publication **Globes.** Some publications only found here include **Time Out Tel Aviv.**

English-language radio can be found on 88FM.

SERVICES
Currency Services and Money Exchange

Banks and post offices will change money, but **post offices** (www.israelpost.co.il) charge no commission and have services that include buying foreign currency with a credit card (up to US$1,000), changing traveler's checks for the U.S. dollar and the Euro, and changing cash.

Some post office branches also have Western Union services.

There are also several money changing locations in the center of the city. **Moneygram** (www.moneygram.com) is a popular company that has about three dozen locations throughout Tel Aviv. You can find exact addresses and contact information for Moneygram locations by visiting their website.

Banks and ATMs

All banks have branches or headquarters in Tel Aviv, the financial capital of the country. Most bank branches or buildings are on Allenby Street, Rothschild Boulevard, Herbert Samuel Street, and Yehuda Halevy Street. ATMs are also very easy to find in small shops and near commercial centers. Look for the green and white machines of **Isreal Discount Bank** (27-31 Yehuda Halevi St., 03/514-5555), which generally charge the lowest fee for withdrawing money from a foreign account. ATMs bearing the red, white, and black colors of **Bank Hapoalim** (50 Rothschild Blvd., 03/567-3333) are also fairly easy to find.

For a specific listing of commercial bank addresses, go to the "Aliyahpedia" page on www. nbn.org.il and look under banking.

Postal Service

Post office locations can be found online (www. israelpost.co.il). The main post office branch is on Allenby Street (132 Allenby St.), and there are some conveniently located but smaller branches around town (286 Dizengoff St., 61 HaYarkon St., 3 Zamenhoff St., 3 Mendele St. and 138 Yeffet St. in Jaffa).

Internet

In 2011, Tel Aviv began a free Wi-Fi hotspot program throughout the city, starting with Ben Gurion Boulevard. The hotspots don't allow visits to file-sharing websites and will block you if you try to download files that are too big. If you can't find a city hotspot, most cafés and coffee shops in Tel Aviv have free Wi-Fi. In 2013, the city began spreading a formal

TEL AVIV

network that will eventually include parks, city shores, main streets, and commercial centers.

Embassies

The **American Embassy** (71 HaYarkon St., 03/519-7475, http://israel.usembassy.gov), **Canadian Embassy** (3/5 Nirim St., 03/636-3300, www.canadainternational.gc.ca), and **Embassy of Australia** (Discount Bank Tower, Level 28, 23 Yehuda Halevi St., 03/693-5000, www.israel.embassy.gov.au) are located in Tel Aviv.

Getting There and Around

It's very easy to get to Tel Aviv, to travel within the city, and to take short trips in the vicinity. Tel Aviv itself is only about 20 square miles, and is one hour from both Jerusalem and Haifa, the two other major urban centers of Israel. Public transportation does not run on Shabbat.

GETTING THERE
By Air

Tel Aviv's **Ben Gurion International Airport** (www.iaa.gov.il, 03/975-2386) is about a 15-minute drive from the city center. From the airport, you can get into the city by hotel shuttle, train, taxi, and bus.

The public transportation depot is on the second floor near Gates 21 and 23. Buses go from there to the Egged (www.egged.co.il/Eng) station at nearby Airport City, and then you can transfer to regular Egged bus lines. To get from Airport City to the airport there are free passes.

By Train

Once on the **Israel Railways** train (www.rail.co.il/EN, NIS15), you can be in Tel Aviv's city center in 10 minutes from the airport, and in about 90 minutes from Jerusalem. There are several bus lines that leave about every 20-30 minutes from the airport and stop at four stations.

Tel Aviv's most southerly stop, HaHagana, will get you closest to Jaffa, Florentin, and Neve Tzedek in the south. The next stop, HaShalom, will drop you off at Azrieli Center, and get you near Dizengoff and some of the best beaches in the city. Savidor Station gets you in proximity of Jabotinsky Street and the Marina and Old Port. University Station is quite far north and actually gets you just outside of the city.

You can buy a daily or multi-journey ticket; kids under five travel for free.

By Car

If you are driving into Tel Aviv, you are going to take Highway 1 from Jerusalem and Highway 2 from Haifa. You will run through the center of the city on Ayalon (North or South), also known as Highway 20. Ayalon has about half a dozen exits that lead to different parts of the city.

By Share Taxi

Sherut, or share taxis, also travel to and from Tel Aviv and are your best (and almost only) option during Shabbat. A *sherut* from Jerusalem is about NIS30 or less, and leaves from the base of Zion Square, seven days a week. The end point for most *sherut* is the Tel Aviv Central Bus Station (106 Levinski St.), just east of Neve Tzedek and Florentin. If you are paying close attention and know where you are, you can call out to the *sherut* driver at certain points along the route to hop out after they have exited the freeway and are in Tel Aviv. If you are on the freeway and have some type of emergency and need to get off the bus, it's also acceptable to ask the driver to pull over and they will if there is a place to stop.

By Bus

The green-and-white **Egged** (www.egged.co.il/Eng) buses travel into south Tel Aviv to the Central Bus Station. From Jerusalem's Central

Bus Station, it is about an hour ride without traffic. Try to avoid making the trip on a Friday afternoon, as the traffic is usually the worst at that time. Once in Tel Aviv, there are tons of taxis outside the front doors of the bus station.

GETTING AROUND
Driving

Tel Aviv is relatively easy to navigate by car. Since the western border of the city is the Mediterranean, and Ayalon Highway essentially forms the eastern border, you always have landmarks for orientation. You might come across some Orthodox Jewish areas that frown upon driving on Shabbat, but you most likely won't have anything thrown at your vehicle like you might in similar areas of Jerusalem.

The parking system in Israel is universal: gray curbs are free parking, blue and white stripes are paid (look for the pay station and keep change on hand), and red and white stripes mean no parking.

Aside from renting a car at the airport, there is a group of car rental company offices on HaYarkon Street just north of Frishman Street. They include **Eldan** (114 HaYarkon St., 03/527-1166, www.eldan.co.il), **Avis** (113 HaYarkon St., 03/527-1752, http://avis.co.il), and **Shlomo Sixt** (122 HaYarkon St., 03/524-4935, www.shlomo.co.il).

Public Transportation

The city bus line, **Dan** (03/639-4444, www.dan.co.il/english) operates a series of very convenient lines throughout the city, and they have detailed information on their English language website. They shut down for Shabbat.

Taxis

Recommended by the Tel Aviv Tourism Bureau are **Gordon Taxi** (03/527-2999), **Habima Taxi** (03/528-3131), and **Kastel** (03/633-2253).

Rental Bikes

One of Tel Aviv's coolest features is **Tel-o-Fun** (www.tel-o-fun.co.il/en), a bicycle rental system. You can pick up and drop off a rented bike at any point throughout the city. There is no law in Tel Aviv that requires bicyclists to wear a helmet.

Shabbat and Holidays

For the most part, most venues in Tel Aviv are open on Shabbat and holidays, but public transportation shuts down. You can find *sherut* (share taxis) at the Central Bus Station (106 Levinski St.) that will take you to a variety of places for a price, including to Jerusalem. They leave when the taxi is full, not on a set schedule.

TEL AVIV

HAIFA AND THE NORTH COAST

The north coast of Israel has a subtle, seductive charm that makes it extremely easy to lose yourself for several days. Whether you are in Haifa, Akko, Caesarea, Zichron Ya'akov, Nahariya, or Rosh Hanikra, there are options for indoor and outdoor activities and excursions, a surprising number of high-end boutique hotels, and some world-class wineries.

© GENEVIEVE BELMAKER

HIGHLIGHTS

LOOK FOR 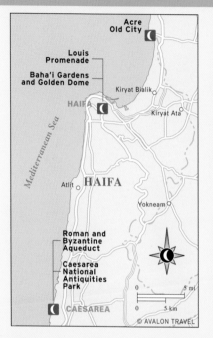 TO FIND RECOMMENDED SIGHTS, ACTIVITIES, DINING, AND LODGING.

dens, but it's not until you see them that you understand why. A marvel of terraced garden landscaping and a reminder of the power of faith, they stand out among Haifa's sights (page 159).

Louis Promenade: There's no better place to get your first glimpse of Haifa than from the Louis Promenade. It's difficult to tear yourself away from the gorgeous vistas of the Port of Haifa and the lower city (page 166).

Acre Old City: If you make only one side trip on the north coast, go to the Old City in Akko (Acre). The centuries-old structures and odd, winding streets illuminate layers of history critical to understanding the region (page 175).

Caesarea National Antiquities Park: Not far from Tel Aviv, you'll find surviving examples of Roman civilization, including an amphitheater, the hippodrome, and Hellenistic and Crusader ruins (page 185).

Roman and Byzantine Aqueduct: The aqueduct outside of Caesarea is an excellent place to combine sightseeing with outdoor play. The ancient aqueduct creates a sort of barrier for the popular beach, which is an easy place to slow down and enjoy wading or swimming in the sea (page 186).

Baha'i Gardens and Golden Dome: Everyone talks about the Baha'i dome and gar-

One of the best jumping-off places for exploring the region is Haifa, Israel's third-largest city, situated on the coast a short drive north of Tel Aviv. The city, which is built up on the side of Mount Carmel (a fairly typical practice), seems to revolve around the massive, dominating Baha'i Gardens and Golden Dome socially, economically, and spiritually. Haifa is full of scenic vistas around every corner, excellent restaurants of all kinds, and a range of interesting activities such as long walks on the promenade by the beach and world-class museums. It is also home to the "MIT of Israel," the Technion, and is known as a tolerant and inclusive place,

where Arabs, Jews, and Christians live together peacefully.

Not far from Haifa are some of Israel's most memorable coastal spots, including Akko (a UNESCO World Heritage Site), Caesarea and the ruins of the Roman aqueduct, and the artist village of Zichron Ya'akov. A notable stopping point that is a bit off the beaten path is the little seaside town of Nahariya, where you'll find some of Israel's best surfing year-round and townspeople who will warm your heart with their hospitality.

Throughout the coastal region north of Tel Aviv, there is such a wide variety of things to see

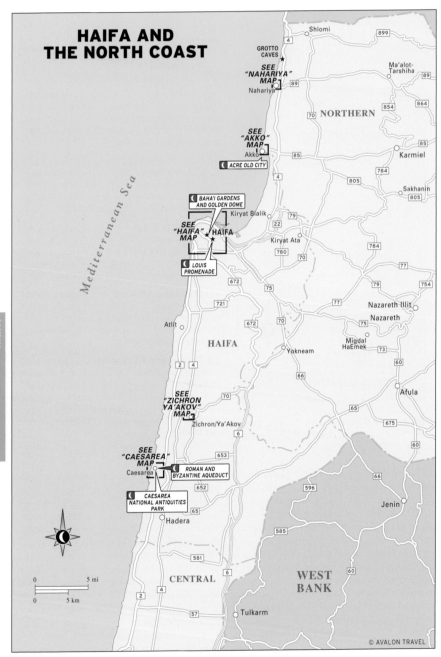

HAIFA AND THE NORTH COAST

HAIFA

Mediterranean Sea

Shlomi

GROTTO
CAVES

**SEE
"NAHARIYA"
MAP**

Nahariya

Ma'alot-
Tarshiha

NORTHERN

Karmiel

**SEE
"AKKO"
MAP**

Akko

☾ ACRE OLD CITY

Sakhanin

☾ BAHA'I GARDENS
AND GOLDEN DOME

Kiryat Bialik

**SEE
"HAIFA"
MAP**   ★ HAIFA

Kiryat Ata

☾ LOUIS
PROMENADE

Atlit

HAIFA

Yokneam

Nazareth Illit

Nazareth

Migdal
HaEmek

**SEE
"ZICHRON
YA'AKOV"
MAP**

Zichron/Ya'Akov

Afula

**SEE
"CAESAREA"
MAP**

Caesarea

☾ ROMAN AND
BYZANTINE AQUEDUCT

☾ CAESAREA
NATIONAL ANTIQUITIES
PARK

Hadera

Jenin

WEST
BANK

CENTRAL

Tulkarm

© AVALON TRAVEL

0   5 mi

0   5 km

and do, it's hard to leave once you're here, so try to keep things open-ended. You might plan to spend just one night in Nahariya, but once you're riding a free bike rental from your hotel down the miles-long promenade by the beach, plans could change.

ORIENTATION

Haifa is Israel's third-largest city and is directly north of Tel Aviv by about one hour and northwest of Jerusalem by about two hours. The city is built on and around Mount Carmel, and is full of winding, steep streets and main roads that sweep around the base of the mountain, following the shore of the sea.

Haifa is the gateway to the Galilee and Israel's north coast, and makes an excellent base for excursions within an hour radius, including north to Akko, Rosh Hanikra, Nahariya; south to Zichron Ya'akov, Caesarea, and Tel Aviv; and east to Nazareth.

PLANNING YOUR TIME

You will need at least two nights for Haifa alone. Depending on how many trips you want to make to the surrounding areas, four nights and five days in the area is best. Anywhere in between 2-5 days will give you a good but quick sampling of the area.

The trick to seeing and experiencing a satisfying amount of Haifa is to plan your time according to which neighborhoods you are traversing. The neighborhoods and related sights are situated like steps up and down Mount Carmel.

A good approach is to plan a walking route that eventually leads to a resting place, such as following the Louis Promenade to the Baha'i Gardens as far down as you can go and ending up at the base of the gardens in the German Colony. You can also plan a route around the city's subway stops for easy getting in and out.

Haifa

One of Haifa's main distinguishing features is its reputation as a model of peaceful coexistence among different faiths and ethnicities within Israel; you'll often hear Israelis remark on it. When you're in Haifa, you can feel it. At the foot of the Baha'i Gardens and Golden Dome,

significant for followers of the Baha'i faith, you can hear the bells of a nearby Christian church and see Arabs and Jews eating in the same restaurants in the German Colony.

The life of the city revolves around several major points, including the famed Baha'i

HAIFA'S TOPOGRAPHY AND NEIGHBORHOODS

The first time you enter Haifa you understand why it has been dubbed the San Francisco of Israel. The city's winding streets are extremely steep in the places where the city climbs up Mount Carmel. There are three major tiers of the city. The lowest is the old city center, **Wadi Salib,** which extends to **Wadi Nisnas** and is commonly called downtown. The area is the city's center of Arab life and culture.

The next tier up is the **Hadar** neighborhood, which dates back to the 1900s and is about halfway up Mount Carmel. Hadar is home to a

large Jewish synagogue and block after block of closely-situated, lower-end shops of all kinds. During Shabbat, part of a major street near the synagogue is closed to traffic and the entire area shuts down from late Friday afternoon until well after dark on Saturday night.

One of the most prestigious areas in town that is also highest up on the mountainside is **Carmel,** which includes the French Carmel, Merkaz HaCarmel, Romema, Carmeliya, and more. Carmel is home to some of Haifa's finest restaurants with the most remarkable views.

HAIFA

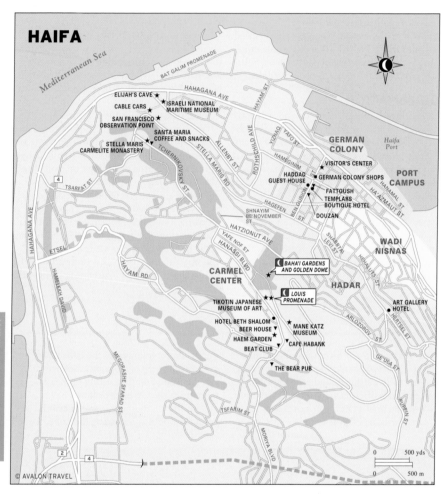

HAIFA

ELIJAH'S CAVE ★
CABLE CARS ★
★ ISRAELI NATIONAL
MARITIME MUSEUM
SAN FRANCISCO ★
OBSERVATION POINT
SANTA MARIA
COFFEE AND SNACKS
STELLA MARIS ▼
CARMELITE MONASTERY

Mediterranean Sea
BAT GALIM PROMENADE
HAHAGANA AVE

GERMAN
COLONY
VISITOR'S CENTER
HADDAD
GUEST HOUSE ★ GERMAN COLONY SHOPS
FATTOUSH
TEMPLARS
BOUTIQUE HOTEL
DOUZAN

Haifa
Port

PORT
CAMPUS

WADI
NISNAS

CARMEL
CENTER
■ BAHA'I GARDENS
AND GOLDEN DOME ★
★★ LOUIS
PROMENADE
TIKOTIN JAPANESE ★★
MUSEUM OF ART

HADAR

ART GALLERY
HOTEL

HOTEL BETH SHALOM ●
BEER HOUSE ▼ ★ MANE KATZ
MUSEUM
HAEM GARDEN ▼
BEAT CLUB ▼ CAFE HABANK

▼ THE BEAR PUB

0   500 yds
0   500 m

© AVALON TRAVEL

Gardens and Golden Dome, the beaches, and the distinct neighborhoods on multiple ascending tiers from the seaside to the top of Mount Carmel. Many areas of Haifa remain open on the weekend (except for the Hadar district), so there are many options of things to do, see, and experience on Friday and Saturday.

HISTORY

The earliest evidence of human settlements in the region of Haifa goes back to the 14th century BC. Haifa is mentioned in 3rd century BC

Jewish Talmudic literature as a small fishing village and the home of several Jewish scholars. The Haifa of that time is believed to have existed from the Jaffa Street Jewish cemetery to Ramban Hospital.

Its seaside position and port encouraged the capture and governance of Haifa by a variety of rulers throughout the ages, including Byzantine, Arab, Crusader, Mamluk, Ottoman, and Egyptian.

In 1909, around the same time that Haifa was emerging as a major industrial port and

© GENEVIEVE BELMAKER

the skyline of Haifa

center of population, the city became a central place for followers of the Baha'i faith, when the remains of their religious leader, the Bab, were moved to nearby Akko (Acre) and a shrine was built on Mount Carmel by 'Abdu'l-Baha. Today Haifa is a central site of worship, pilgrimage, and administration for the Baha'i religion.

After the Israel War of Independence in 1948, Haifa became a gateway for waves of Jewish immigrants from all over the world coming to the newly established Jewish state. Several neighborhoods sprang up very quickly as a result to accommodate the new residents, and, by 1970, Haifa's population was about 200,000. With the fall of the former Soviet Union, a huge influx of 35,000 more immigrants came to the city.

SIGHTS
◖ Baha'i Gardens and Golden Dome

Haifa's Baha'i World Center includes the golden Shrine of the Bab, terraced gardens, and administrative buildings, covering the northern slope on Mount Carmel all the way to the foot of the mountain at the German Colony. The **Baha'i Gardens and Golden Dome** (Baha'i World Center, 80 Hatzionut Ave., 04/831-3131, www.ganbahai.org.il/en, Inner Gardens 9am-noon Tues.-Thurs., Outer Gardens 9am-7pm daily, closed Wed., free entrance and free tours) is so massive and dominating that it acts as the unofficial center of Haifa.

An extended staircase that goes up the side of Mount Carmel is divided into 19 terraces and the golden Baha'i Shrine of the Bab is situated in a dominating position in the middle. The golden-domed shrine marks the burial place of one of the two prophets of the Baha'i faith, and can be seen from multiple points throughout the city.

The garden is an intricate work of art that exudes a calm and peaceful atmosphere. Entrance to the outer gardens can be accessed from the top and bottom entrances, and free guided tours in English begin at noon from the top entrance.

© GENEVIEVE BELMAKER

view of the Baha'i Gardens and Golden Dome

The smaller but also very pretty and peaceful Baha'i gardens in Akko are the resting place and former residence of the second prophet of the Baha'i faith.

Mane Katz Museum

Located in a small and distinguished house with views of the Bay of Haifa, the **Mane Katz Museum** (89 Yafe Nof St., 04/911-9372, www.mkm.org.il, 10am-4pm Sat.-Thurs., 10am-1pm Fri., adult NIS30, child NIS20, senior NIS15, combined Haifa museum ticket NIS60) is tucked away at the southern end of Louis Promenade. The museum was the home of the artist Mane Katz at the end of his life, and features some of his work. Also on display are Jewish religious and ceremonial pieces, and works by Marc Chagall.

Haifa City Museum

The **Haifa City Museum** (11 Ben Gurion Ave., 04/911-5888, www.hcm.org.il, 10am-4pm Mon.-Thurs., 10am-1pm Fri., 10am-3pm Sat., adult NIS30, child NIS20, senior NIS15, combined Haifa museum ticket NIS60) is a good place to get some background on the history of Haifa. Located in a former Templar school building in the historic German Colony, the museum has been undergoing renovations and additions in stages. The museum's changing exhibitions focus on topics of regional interest including architecture, history, and residents.

Stella Maris Carmelite Monastery

Whether you go to see the **vistas** or the **Stella Maris Carmelite Monastery** (top of Stella Maris Rd., off of Tchernikovsky St. and adjacent to the upper station of the Haifa cable car, 04/833-7758, 6am-noon and 3pm-6pm daily, free), heading to the top of Mount Carmel on Stella Maris Road is well worth it. The Carmelites are a religious order of the Catholic Church that took their name from Mount Carmel, where they originated. From about 1631 onward, the monastery was built and destroyed several times. The current structure was opened in 1836, and the

© GENEVIEVE BELMAKER

the interior of Stella Maris Carmelite Monastery in Haifa

interior is full of beautiful, detailed paintings that grace the small but exquisite interior's vaulted ceiling.

San Francisco Observation Point

The blue dome cage of the **San Francisco Observation Point** (across from Stella Maris Carmelite Monastery on Tchernikovsky St., free audio guide at site) provides a gorgeous view. A recording, in multiple languages, provides detailed background information on the area.

Israeli National Maritime Museum

It can be a bit confusing to find, but the **Israeli National Maritime Museum** (198 Allenby St., 04/853-6622, www.nmm.org.il, 10am-4pm Sun.-Thurs., 10am-1pm Fri., 10am-3pm Sat., adult NIS30, child NIS20, senior NIS15, combined Haifa museum ticket NIS60) features a collection that cover 5,000 years of maritime history of the Mediterranean basin, the Red Sea, and the Nile. The museum has three levels with permanent and changing exhibitions,

and is an interesting window into the region's maritime history. It is just down the road from the more obscure Clandestine Immigration and Naval Museum (204 Allenby St.), which can be confusing. Look for the large ships on display outside to lead you to the general area of the museums.

Elijah's Cave

Basically across the street from the Maritime Museum, and situated about midway up the mountainside toward Stella Maris, is the humble religious and spiritual destination of **Elijah's Cave** (230 Allenby St., 04/852-7430, 8am-5pm Sun.-Thurs., 8:30am-12:45pm Fri., free). Expect to see people here praying, as it is an important site to followers of Christianity, Judaism, and Islam. Ceremonies are also sometimes held here on religious days, and it is widely accepted to be a cave where the prophet Elijah lived. The site is accessible from the top of the mountain at Stella Maris, but much easier to reach from Allenby Street, and there are separate male and female entrances.

Cable Car

If you have no fear of heights, the **Cable Car** (top entrance at Stella Maris Carmelite Monastery area at Tchernikovsky St. and bottom entrance at Bat Galim Promenade, www.tour-haifa.co.il, 10am-6pm daily, NIS29 round-trip, NIS19 one-way) affords great views of Haifa, Carmel Mountain, and Haifa Port. The slightly rickety and globe-shaped cars dangle from cables that go up and down the mountainside on a regular basis during the day. The bottom car can be found nearby the Clandestine Immigration and Naval Museum and its huge outdoor ships. The lower cars drop you off at the slightly-worse-for-wear Bat Galim beach and promenade. The upper cars are a quick walk from the Stella Maris Carmelite Monastery. The top terminal also has three restaurants with amazing views that are somewhat pricey but popular among locals.

German Colony

Good for simply strolling about and taking in a variety of scenery and restaurants, the **German Colony** is the area roughly between the base of the Baha'i Gardens and the Port. Numerous buildings here were built during the 1800s by the German Templars, and the area provides a calm and charming respite from a day of more intense sightseeing. There are guided tours in multiple languages through the German Colony; check with the **information center** (48 Ben Gurion St., 04/853-5606, www.tour-haifa.co.il, 9am-5pm Sun.-Thurs., 9am-1pm Fri., 10am-3pm Sat.).

Madatech: National Museum of Science, Technology, and Space

Slightly expensive, but a good option if traveling with kids, **Madatech: National Museum of Science, Technology, and Space** (25 Shmariyahu Levine St., 04/861-4444, www.madatech.org.il, 11am-3pm Sun.-Thurs., 11am-6pm Sat., adult NIS75, under 18 NIS65) is a hands-on, experiential science museum that is not far from the Baha'i Gardens and bustling Hanassi Boulevard. Housed in a restored

Haifa's cable cars carry people up and down the mountainside.

© GENEVIEVE BELMAKER

HAIFA

THE INFLUENCE OF THE GERMAN TEMPLARS

Throughout Haifa and the north coast, the influence of the German Templars can still be seen in the form of entire neighborhoods that exhibit graceful architectural design and exude an atmosphere of antique elegance.

German Templars of the late 19th century who settled in what was then Palestine are not the same thing as the Templar knights, a monastic military order of the 12th century that guarded European pilgrims in the holy land. Today there are Templars neighborhoods in Jerusalem, Tel Aviv, and Haifa.

The German Templars neighborhood in Haifa (called the German Colony, just like in Jerusalem) is not large, but its unique character has

been carefully preserved and walking tours regularly explore it. It runs from the foot of the Baha'i Gardens roughly to the port between Rothschild and Ben Gurion Streets.

Haifa's German Colony has been recently restored in a major undertaking by the city and is one of the best places in the city to have a relaxing meal (the businesses are open seven days a week), especially in combination with a visit to the Baha'i Gardens. It is also home to some of the city's best boutique hotels.

The oddest aspect of the German Templars' history is that around the time of World War II, they were sympathetic to the Nazis and were ultimately expelled from Palestine.

historic 1912 building, the museum includes dozens of exhibits and several 3-D movies.

Reuben Hecht Museum Haifa

A small museum on the University of Haifa campus, the **Reuben Hecht Museum Haifa** (University of Haifa, Mt. Carmel, 04/825-7773, http://mushecht.haifa.ac.il, 10am-4pm Sun.-Mon. and Wed.-Thurs., 10am-7pm Tues., 10am-1pm Fri., 10am-2pm Sat., guided tours for groups, free) will satisfy the archaeologist in any traveler. Some of the exhibits create the experience of being in a town under siege by the Romans. The Canaanite mummies and remnants of an ancient ship that was discovered underwater in the 1980s are interesting touches, as is the exhibit of l'Ecole de Paris artwork. The museum affords a wonderful vista of Haifa and a chance to wander about the university campus.

TOURS
Route of 1,000 Steps

If you are in very good shape, adventurous, and good with maps, you can try the **Route of 1,000 Steps,** a self-guided tour that goes from the top of Mount Carmel down through several major neighborhoods of the city, ending at the German Colony. The route starts

from Savyonim Lookout Point near Yefe Nof Street. You want to be in the vicinity of the Crowne Plaza Hotel Haifa (124 Yefe Nof St.) to get started. There are four routes along the way that are marked by steps and are color-coded.

Free Tours

Many hotels in Haifa offer free tours as a courtesy to their guests. Tour times and availability vary; so when you check in, ask the front desk of your hotel if they have anything available and what the tour schedule is. It is worthwhile to try and book a hotel that offers free tours, as buying a private tour is expensive.

Private Tours

The Haifa Tourism Board offers some tours, but the schedules change and are often only on the weekend. If you are interested in arranging a private tour, stick with a licensed guide. One option, **Eva Israel Tours** (052/247-7469, www.eva-israeltours.com), arranges tours to suit your taste. Contact them in advance for specifics.

ENTERTAINMENT AND EVENTS

Haifa is home to a wide variety of things to do when the sun goes down, from wine tastings (wine lovers will enjoy the surprisingly wide variety of regional wines), to live music, to festivals and the largest movie theater in Israel.

Cinema
YES PLANET

Billed as the largest movie theater in Israel, **yes PLANET** (55 HaHistadrut St., 04/841-6898, http://yesplanet.co.il) has two dozen screens. Like most movie theaters in the country, it shows contemporary American and European films in English with Hebrew subtitles. Always check the film in advance for the language, though, even if the actors are familiar.

Live Music, Clubs, and Bars
THE BEAT CLUB

Part of the variety of options for day and night on Hanassi Boulevard, the **Beat Club** (124 Hanassi Blvd., 04/866-2244 and 04/810-7107, www.beat.co.il, daily, cover varies) is a top live performance club in Haifa and the north, with live musical performances of the leading domestic artists daily. Beat Club sometimes hosts international acts.

SYNCOPA

Recommended by locals who like to party (in typical laid-back Haifa style), **Syncopa** (5 Khayat St., 04/866-0174, 8pm-last customer daily, NIS30) is a bar with a crowd that is generally over 25. Mostly playing funk music, the bar has a softly-lit interior and is a popular spot for simply hanging out.

THE BEER HOUSE

Known for its wide variety of 120 beers and its central location in the Carmel neighborhood just below Ha'em Park, the **Beer House** (116 Hanassi Blvd., 04/822-9750, 3pm-last customer Sat.-Thurs., 7pm-last customer Fri., NIS50) is worth stopping by. The interior is nothing fancy, but the service is friendly and there is a decent food menu that features meat dishes.

THE BEAR INN PUB

Easy to spot on busy Hanassi Boulevard, just near a Carmelit station, **The Bear Inn Pub**

(135 Hanassi Blvd., 04/838-1703, 5pm-3am Sat.-Wed., 11pm-4am Thurs.-Fri., NIS60) is a popular local spot for a drink. They offer a fairly extensive alcohol menu and a wide variety of beers, and have a rich, woody interior that looks and feels like an English pub. Most of the customers are locals and expatriates, and the large alcohol menu attracts a more mature crowd. They serve standard pub food, but the range of choices includes everything from a burger to salmon carpaccio.

Festivals
FIRST FRUITS WINE AND CHEESE TASTING FESTIVAL

Held annually around May or June, the **First Fruits Wine and Cheese Tasting Festival** (Haifa Auditorium Park near the Haifa Cinematheque in the Hacarmel neighborhood, 04/853-5606, www.tour-haifa.co.il, 6pm-11pm daily) showcases regional wineries, wines, and foodstuffs with an emphasis on Haifa and the north. In addition to wines from vineyards of all sizes, there are booths of boutique cheese makers, chocolatiers, olive oil, and wine accessories; workshops and lectures are also given.

PUPPET FESTIVAL

The end of August brings the completely free **Puppet Festival** (Haifa Auditorium in Central Carmel, 052/389-7487, yaeln@012.net.il, free) that includes children's performances, puppet shows, outdoor events, and an exhibition of masterpiece artistic puppets.

HAIFA INTERNATIONAL FILM FESTIVAL

Held in late September or early October, the **Haifa International Film Festival** (multiple venues, 04/801-3471, www.haifaff.co.il/eng) has been operating for about 30 years. It includes events, lectures, and awards.

FESTIVAL OF FESTIVALS

This popular December festival is a multicultural food and folklore festival that bills itself as the only one of its kind in the Middle East. Also known as the Holiday of Holidays,

ISRAEL'S NATIONAL TRAIL IN HAIFA

If you look closely you will see signs in Haifa for the Israel National Trail (*Shevil Israel* in Hebrew, www.israelnationaltrail.com and www.israeltrail.net), a hiking footpath that runs 580-620 miles (depending on the routes) from the Red Sea in the south to the border with Lebanon in the north.

The trail, which takes about 45 days to complete, can be seen at various points in Haifa, where it can be identified by subtle trail markings of three stripes of white, blue, and orange. It is listed among the National Geographic's World's Best Hikes.

The trail also passes through Jerusalem, Tel Aviv, Nazareth, the Negev, and the Sea of Galilee.

the **Festival of Festivals** (04/853-5606, www.tour-haifa.co.il, 9am-8pm Thurs.-Sat.) for several weekends throughout December makes use of the numerous religious holidays that occur among different faiths and cultures in the region in the month of December. The festival is held in the Wadi Nisnas neighborhood of Haifa, between the neighborhoods of Hadar and the downtown area around the German Colony. The main staging areas are on Khoury Street, Hatzionut Street, Shabbtai Levi Street, and HaWadi Street.

SHOPPING

Haifa has some of the best shopping malls in the country. It also has specific districts that are dedicated to shopping. There is so much to see and do in Haifa, though, that the thought of going shopping probably won't occur to you unless you need something.

German Colony

Along Ben Gurion Boulevard in the **German Colony** are a variety of high-end shops, art galleries, souvenir shops, coffee houses, and restaurants housed in historic 19th-century Templar buildings. Most of the shops are open by 10am and close around 8pm on weekdays, with some closed or operating on more limited hours on Friday and Saturday.

Merkaz Panorama

Conveniently located on Hanassi Boulevard, within an easy walk to all the hotels in the area, **Merkaz Panorama** (109 Hanassi Blvd., 04/837-5011, 9am-8pm Sun.-Thurs., 9am-2pm Fri.) is a small, upscale shopping mall that offers a surprising variety of clothes, shoes, and coffee shops with sandwiches and salads.

SPORTS AND RECREATION

As a coastal city, Haifa is home to numerous parks, promenades, and outdoor activities. Its proximity to Mount Carmel also affords good hiking opportunities.

Parks, Gardens, and Beaches

DADO BEACH

You might want to take a car or taxi to get here, but **Dado Beach** (southwest Haifa coast) is the best place in town for enjoying the beach, whether or not you go in the water. The promenade is long, there are beach chairs with shade, and it has numerous options for eating. It's even pleasant in good winter weather.

SCULPTURE GARDEN

At the **Sculpture Garden** (Mitzpor Shalom or Peace Park, upper section of Hatzionut Ave., corner of Shnayim Be'November St., www.malbinsculpture.com, 8am-6pm daily, free), 29 bronze sculptures by Israeli artist Ursula Malbin line the walkways and are scattered about the lawns. The garden has a sweeping view of Haifa, the Mediterranean Sea, and the hills of the Galilee and Lebanon on a clear day. It is a 10-minute walk to the mid-section level of the Baha'i Gardens.

〔 LOUIS PROMENADE

One of the best places in the city for a long walk full of incredible vistas of Haifa, the port, and the lower city, **Louis Promenade** (off of Yefe Nof St. in the Carmel district) runs through the center of the Carmel district parallel to Yefe Nof Street. There are plenty of places to sit and enjoy the view, take photographs, and enjoy the scenery. It is close to the main cluster of hotels on Hanassi Boulevard, which makes it an easy walk if you're staying in the area.

Along Yefe Nof Street just off of the promenade, there are a couple of small, but nice museums, including the **Tikotin Museum of Japanese Art** (89 Hanassi St., 04/838-3554, www.tmja.org.il, 10am-4pm Sun.-Wed., 10am-7pm Thurs., 10am-1pm Fri., 10am-5pm Sat., adult NIS50, child and senior NIS25) and the **Mane Katz Museum** (89 Yafe Nof St., 04/911-9372, www.mkm.org.il, 10am-4pm Sat.-Thurs., 10am-1pm Fri., adult NIS30, child NIS20, senior NIS15, combined Haifa museum ticket NIS60). If you follow Yefe Nof Street by foot for about 15 minutes or less past the end of the promenade, you'll find the upper entrance to the Baha'i Gardens.

HANGING BRIDGES AT NESHER PARK

If you have the means to get here, the **Hanging Bridges at Nesher Park** (Carmel National Forest, arrive from Haruv St. in Nesher off Rte. 4, 04/823-1452, www.parks.org.il, NIS38) can give you the experience of being up in the trees. Not for the faint of heart or those who are afraid of heights, the bridges are suspended between canyons in the midst of the forest. There is a picnic and play area for kids, and it's about 25 minutes by car almost directly southeast out of Haifa.

HECHT PARK

The largest area of greenery inside Haifa city limits, **Hecht Park** (Ha'hagana St., www.tour-haifa.co.il) is at the north end of Dado Beach and promenade and hugs the coast with continuous views of the sea. The park has a path

Louis Promenade affords spectacular vistas of Haifa.

© GENEVIEVE BELMAKER

for walking and running that spans an almost two-mile perimeter.

X-PARK

Attracting every skill level, from families to professionals, the **X-Park** (southern entrance to Haifa in the Congress Center, 054/788-3812, www.xpark.co.il, call for pricing as it depends on activity) includes a skating park complex, an Olympic climbing wall, a rope park, paintball, and more. If you have extra time in the Haifa area or want to do something active on your way in or out of the city, this is a good option.

ACCOMMODATIONS

There are many hotel options in Haifa and the north coast, ranging from five-star luxury resort hotels, to bed-and-breakfast options, to very simple and affordable hostels. The only note of caution is to beware of booking a room in the Hadar district over the weekend. Though there are some affordable options there, the entire area shuts down from late Friday afternoon through late Saturday evening, and you'll be hard-pressed to even find a place to eat.

Under US$100

With 50 rooms and its slightly removed position from the hustle of central Haifa, the **Haifa Marom Hotel** (51 Palmach St., 04/825-4355, marom.hotelasp.com, US$85 d) is situated in a peaceful location amidst pine trees on top of Mount Carmel, with a sun deck and surrounded by gardens. The plain but comfortably furnished rooms are air-conditioned and all include a bathroom, free Wi-Fi, phone, and satellite TV. Deluxe rooms have a whirlpool bath. Other amenities include free covered parking and 24-hour room service. The hotel has dining rooms, large halls for conferences and events, a gym, and a spa. It is in close proximity to the Technion and Haifa University, the Horev Center, the Grand Canyon Shopping Center, and the City's Sports Hall.

Situated in a renovated Arabic-style building in downtown Haifa, the **Port Inn** (34 Jaffa Rd., 04/852-4401, http://portinn.net, US$99 d) is a cross between a hostel and a motel, with 18 vacation apartment rentals, room rentals, and dormitory rentals to choose from. The Inn's central location is close to the Haifa Port passenger terminal, the Haifa Merkaz-Hasmona train station, and the Carmelit subway. It is also near the Baha'i Gardens, the German Colony, and numerous restaurants. The Inn is decorated in a simple, homey manner and with a common lounge area with a multilingual satellite TV, a kitchen with free coffee and tea all day, and a lush tropical garden area for sitting and relaxing. There are coin-operated washing machines.

Located near the National Museum of Science, the Hadar Shopping District, and the Carmelit subway, the **Loui M. Apartments** (35 HeHaluts St., 054/837-1342, http://loui-hotelhaifa.com, US$72 d) is a 14-room motel with a simple, boxy exterior and a plain interior with rooms and studios laid out with the feel of apartments. Rooms include an LCD TV, a small dining area, and a private bathroom. The building has a roof terrace and is about 10 minutes from Haifa Port.

US$100-150

The family-run **Hotel Beth-Shalom** (110 Hanassi Blvd., 04/837-3480, www.beth-shalom.co.il, US$110 d) is a small 10-room hotel tucked away on busy Hanassi Boulevard that caters to pilgrims. It is conveniently located near a number of sites, shopping, food, and an area of town that stays open during the weekend. The rooms are very small, spotlessly clean, and every inch is so well-utilized that you have room for everything. The staff is extremely warm and accommodating, and there is some space at the front of the hotel for parking. Some rooms include a small balcony with a bit of canopy from the trees. Wi-Fi costs US$5 from the front desk.

The **(Art Gallery Hotel** (61 Hertsel St., 04/861-6161, http://haifa.hotelgallery.co.il, US$115 d) is a 40-room boutique hotel designed around the theme of art and scenery, and art galleries are integrated into the interior. The Bauhaus building has a clean, modern interior, 24-hour concierge service, and parking is available. Two computers with Internet are available in the lobby and there are free guided tours of the hotel art galleries. Though small by American standards, all of the rooms include free Wi-Fi, air-conditioning, LCD cable TV, and wooden floors, while suites feature a separate sleeping area, a balcony overlooking the city, and a spa bath. The 24-hour fitness center overlooks Haifa Bay and the hotel offers free tour services. Slightly off the beaten path, the hotel is an excellent choice for a bit of luxury at an extremely affordable price, especially if you are traveling with a car. Beware about booking here over the weekend, though, as you'll be in an area that shuts down on Friday and Saturday.

Situated in the bustling downtown Turkish market area, the **1926 Designed Apartments** (36 Moshe Aron, 054/539-9040, http://1926. co.il, US$118 d) is a very small eight-room apartment suite that comes highly recommended by travelers for its location, modern atmosphere, and central location. The building is within easy walking distance from the Carmelit, direct buses throughout Haifa, Haifa Port, the Dagon Grain Museum, and the History of the City of Haifa Museum. The modern, bright, and pretty apartments in the renovated building include a sitting area with a sofa; a kitchen with a refrigerator, microwave, hotplate, electric kettle, cutlery, and dishes; air-conditioning; a 32-inch screen cable satellite TV; and free Wi-Fi Internet. Each studio apartment can accommodate two or three people.

The **Theodor Hotel** (63 Hertsel St., 04/867-7325, www.theodorhotel.co.il, US$115 d) is a 98-room hotel in Haifa's Hadar neighborhood (the neighborhood shuts down on the weekend). The hotel has free Wi-Fi, small collections of books on all 11 floors, and a very comfortable, spacious lobby that feels more like a coffee shop. The modern, bright and comfortably furnished rooms are geared toward couples and include cable TV, a hot water kettle for tea and coffee, a safe, air-conditioning, and telephones for direct inbound calls. The hotel is slightly off the beaten path, but has views of the Carmel Mountains and Haifa Bay, and includes a lobby

bar, restaurant, lobby TV, and laundry services. You can also buy postage and change money at the front desk. Hotel staff can assist with arranging for a doctor or babysitter, and there are on-site spa treatments.

The small and rustic **Haddad Guest House** (26 Ben Gurion St., 077/201-0618, www.haddadguesthouse.com, US$110 d) makes up in services what it lacks in flash. Some of the 13 rooms have a view of Mount Carmel, the Baha'i Gardens, or Haifa Bay. Rooms have a double or twin beds, a closet, private shower and toilet, a small, fully-equipped kitchen, a small TV, hair dryer, and air-conditioning. An extra bed can be added to a room on request. Guest services include Wi-Fi, laundry, and office services. Haddad's interior is extremely simple and a bit utilitarian, but it is located in the heart of the main street of the German Colony, the center of Haifa's nightlife, art gallery scene, shopping, museums, and cafés and is 15 minutes by foot to the Baha'i Gardens. Ask the front desk for discount coupons for nearby restaurants.

US$150-200

Just a 15-minute walk from the Baha'i Gardens in the center of Carmel neighborhood and a few minutes from the Carmelit subway, the slightly aged **Nof Hotel** (101 Hanassi Blvd., 04/835-4311, www.nofhotel.co.il, US$157 d) has very basic interior decor with some rooms that are in need of renovation and others that have been renovated. Also, only some rooms have Wi-Fi; be sure to request a room that has been renovated and has Internet. Most of the 91 rooms have outstanding views of Haifa Bay, the Baha'i Gardens, and the western Galilee. Parking is free and there are coffee shops, restaurants, and stores nearby. Inside the hotel is a cafeteria, a piano bar with live music, and a kosher Chinese restaurant. Room amenities include cable TV, a hair dryer, a direct-dial phone, air-conditioning, and a mini bar. Lobby services include a coffee and tea corner, computers with Internet for free use, and personal safes at reception. The hotel can also assist with car rental, laundry services, and taxis.

The **Colony Hotel Haifa** (28 Ben Gurion St.,

04/851-3344, www.colonyhaifa.com, US$195 d), known for its friendly staff and convenient location, is a 103-year-old restored boutique hotel in Haifa's historic German Colony. The building's lovely exterior is limestone with green shuttered windows, and inside there are 40 rooms and mini-suites with tiling accents and comfortable, modern furnishings that give an overall feel of historic luxury. The hotel's terrace overlooks the Baha'i Gardens, which is a straight 10-minute walk up Ben Gurion Street. The hotel has a 24-hour lobby bar, a spa room, gardens, and free Wi-Fi in all the rooms. Concierge services help with reserving tours, laundry services, and takeout orders from nearby restaurants. The hotel is also near cafés, shopping, and Haifa Port.

There is something unforgettable about the **Templars Boutique Hotel** (36 Ben Gurion St., 077/500-3110, www.templers-haifa.com, US$179 d), and it's not just that it has one of the best locations in the German Colony. The privately-owned boutique hotel is set back a bit from the main street and has a huge private parking lot in the back, and an indoor-outdoor café with a gorgeous patio and covered tables in the front. Some of the beautiful, classy, modern rooms feature massive free-standing bathtubs, whirlpool tubs, or huge showers, alongside luxurious and comfortable decor with sitting chairs and large, soft beds. Just at the foot of the Baha'i Gardens, the building dates back to 1870 and won first place in the German Colony's recent building renovation competition. Each room is designed in a different style, and the hotel offers last-minute deals and free Baha'i Gardens walking tours. It is near public transportation and all rooms have a kitchenette, a coffee and tea maker, a flat-screen satellite TV, free Wi-Fi, and air-conditioning.

Over US$200

In the typically luxurious style of Israeli bed-and-breakfasts, the family-owned **Baha'i Gardens Zimmer** (25A HaGefen St., 050/763-5339, www.bahaizimmer.co.il, US$250 d)

© GENEVIEVE BELMAKER

The Colony Hotel Haifa in the German Colony

delivers beautiful accommodations in an equally beautiful setting. Near the Baha'i Gardens in a small stone house in the German Colony, the bed-and-breakfast only has three rooms; so book in advance. The units are air-conditioned apartments with a hot tub, a 40-inch flat-screen TV with cable, free Wi-Fi, and a furnished patio or balcony. Each apartment has a fully-equipped kitchen and a dining area with a bar. Accommodations include a breakfast voucher, free parking by reservation, free Wi-Fi, and there are also massage services. Ranked class A in the IBB chart by the Israeli Ministry of Tourism for 2013, Baha'i Gardens Zimmer also includes a bar, 24-hour front desk, a sun terrace, hot tub, and laundry services.

Villa Carmel Boutique Hotel (1 Heinrich Heine St. off 30 Moriah Blvd., 04/837-5777, www.villacarmel.co.il, US$220 d) is a 15-room boutique hotel with a modern, sleek interior that includes comfortable couches in the rooms and a pretty dining room. Situated in the middle of Haifa's prestigious Carmel district, the Villa was built as Haifa's most luxurious hotel in the 1940s, and has been renovated with modern conveniences. Surrounded by a small glen of trees, the hotel was a regular choice of Israel's first prime minister, David Ben Gurion, and his wife. The hotel is quite far off the beaten path and tucked away in a residential neighborhood. It's a good fit if you're looking for an immersed escape. Room amenities include Egyptian cotton linens, cozy beds, free Wi-Fi, a desk and phone with conference call capability, and wide-screen HD TVs. Most rooms have a whirlpool bath or computerized jet shower. The hotel has a restaurant, lush garden, rooftop sundeck with a large whirlpool tub and sauna, and massages by appointment. There is also a fully-equipped business center and private meeting space with screen and projector.

FOOD

Haifa's food scene offers two unique experiences: Druze cuisine and winery restaurants. Aside from that it also offers a wide variety of seafood restaurants, pubs, and standard Israeli fare of salads, toasted cheese sandwiches, and meat dishes. There is a decidedly Russian influence to some of the restaurants, including in the style the food is prepared and the amount of meat dishes offered.

Bistro

The open, split-level, loft-like floor plan of **Sinta Bar** (127 Moriya Blvd., 04/834-1170, www.sinta-bar.co.il, noon-11pm daily, NIS 90) gives this meat-lover's paradise in Haifa's Ahuza district a cool and relaxed atmosphere. At a decade old, the restaurant is considered one of Haifa's longer-running institutions and is a very short drive from the Carmel district. Serving up seafood and meat dishes with a nice selection of desserts made in-house, it is a low-key and classy option for dinner, especially if you're staying on the mountain.

Coffee Shops and Cafés

If you find yourself at the **Stella Maris Carmelite Monastery,** you won't miss the obviously-positioned **Santa Maria Coffee and Snacks** (entrance to Stella Maris Carmelite Monastery on Tchernikovsky St., 04/859-7518, 8am-8pm daily, NIS55) at the entrance. Relaxed and casual in both its atmosphere and location, it makes a terrific place to have a leisurely cup of coffee and enjoy their famous apple strudel. They also have a nice selection of sandwiches, desserts, and breakfast items. The staff is incredibly friendly and upbeat, and there is a beautiful view of the open sky and sea.

With its fresh, bright atmosphere and emphasis on the healthiest of dishes including some gluten-free food options, **Café Louise** (58 Moriya Blvd., 04/834-9950, www.cafelouise.co.il, 10am-10pm Sun.-Thurs., 9am-3pm Fri., NIS60) has another location in Haifa at the Grand Canyon Mall and one in Tel Aviv. The seafood and meat dishes are punctuated with some vegan menu choices and detailed touches like whole wheat pasta. Catering to the health-conscious of Haifa, it offers a nice alternative to somewhat standard options at cafés that include things like salads and bread.

With their claim to fame that they were the

first coffee shop/café in Haifa, **℄Café HaBank** (119 Hanassi Blvd., Carmel Center, 04/838-9623, www.rest.co.il, 8:30am-midnight Sun.-Thurs., 8:30am-after midnight Sat., NIS60) is a kosher restaurant that serves up fairly standard, but really delicious, fare that includes salad and meat dishes. Seating is creatively arranged with an outdoor patio, an inside greenhouse-like area, and an inner area with a bar, flat-screen TVs, and fish tanks. They make their desserts (try the banana crumble or the huge slice of unbaked cheesecake) and are known for their lamb pastry dish (NIS76). The crowd is very local and pretty subdued, and the staff is friendly and laid-back.

One of many seaside cafés along the promenade at Dado Beach, **Camel Restaurant** (Dado Beach, 04/852-2990, 9am-2am daily, NIS55) is easy to spot with its huge yellow sign. Like many of the restaurants along the strip, it has a spacious, simple interior. They don't mind sandy feet and there is tons of outdoor seating. The café also has plenty of beach seating with comfy, cushioned chairs and umbrellas for seating even in the winter months. It's a great place to get a large pizza that's enough for three or four people, and the staff is friendly and accommodating.

Italian
Inspired by Tuscany, the upscale **Hanamal 24** (24 Hanamal St., 057/944-2262, http://hanamal24.rest.co.il, noon-midnight Mon.-Sat., NIS110) has several different rooms throughout the restaurant's space, including a lounge, piazza, and wine cellar. Touches of brick in the flooring and rich, warm wood tones throughout give it a welcoming atmosphere. Some highlights of the dinner menu include shrimp over eel gratin, a bacon-wrapped pork filet, and other meat and seafood dishes. The extensive wine list includes choices from Israel and beyond.

Latin
You wouldn't expect to find Cuban-themed food in the German Colony in Haifa, but **Havana** (25 Ben Gurion St., 053/809-4797,

10am-3am daily, NIS70) somewhat fits the bill. With a richly decorated atmosphere that includes comfy pillows and hookahs, soft lighting and wood finishes, Havana has a very relaxing and warm atmosphere. Most of the menu items include meat and fish dishes, and an occasional pasta dish. They cater to Haifa's hipper and younger crowds. As long as you don't go expecting to find fried plantains and refried beans, you won't be disappointed.

Mediterranean
The key word when describing **Tsfarim 1** (1 Tsfarim St., 04/811-2235, www.zafririm1.co.il, noon-last customer daily, NIS55) is "cool." Everything from the atmosphere to the menu presentation and the unique preparation of dishes makes it a lively option for breakfast or lunch. Situated in the Carmel district, Tsfarim 1 serves up dishes with a Mediterranean flair, such as the Taboon chicken and Baladi eggplant. The restaurant's exposed brick interior walls and black-lacquer tables with overhead lighting give it an overall feel of a New York spot you might find in SoHo.

Middle Eastern
Just next to the slightly gritty Hadar district of town is the heavily Arab section of town, Wadi Nisnas, and several options for falafel, hummus, *shwarma,* and the like. Around the area of Hanevi'im and Hehaluts Streets is a nice selection of falafel shops and stands, most of which are open from late morning (10am) to evening (about 9pm).

One of the most popular spots in the German Colony for both its food and atmosphere, **℄Fattoush** (38 Ben Gurion St., 04/852-4930, 8am-1am daily, NIS65) serves up a nice variety of Middle Eastern food and the best cappuccino in town, hands down. The massive outdoor and patio seating and the cave-like interior of the restaurant are both decorated with tons of tiny touches, including colorful beads and glass lamps and brass finishings that make you feel that you are in an

HAIFA

© GENEVIEVE BELMAKER

outdoor seating at the popular Fattoush restaurant in Haifa

exotic locale. The pace of the restaurant is very busy, but that's to be expected. A handwritten sign at the entrance states that all types of people of all backgrounds and beliefs are welcome.

At the family-run, French-Arab fusion restaurant **Douzan** (35 Ben Gurion St., 04/852-5444, 10am-midnight daily, NIS55) the whole aim is to make customers feel at home and relaxed. Decorated with whimsical touches that include old clocks, musical instruments, and velvety cushions, it is known for its surprising specialties that include small meat pies with pine nuts (called *sfeeha*).

An excellent choice for Arab food, including hummus, in the midst of the German Colony, **Allenby Restaurant** (43 Allenby St., 04/852-9928, 7am-7pm Sat.-Thurs., 7am-5pm Fri., NIS45) is simple with few frills and fast, efficient service. The exterior and interior are also simple and unassuming, with a plain storefront and a more cafeteria-like interior. Catering to a more mature, working-class crowd, the restaurant is famous for the various presentations and side dishes that accompany its hummus, vegetable dishes, and Turkish coffee.

Winery Restaurants and Wine Bars

Just up the street from the cute Ha'em Park near the Carmel district is the **Wine Bar** (107 Yefe Nof St., 077/500-4895, noon-midnight Mon.-Sat., NIS70). It is relatively new and has a huge wine selection and range of prices. The lovely selection of meat and fish dishes includes traditional dishes with an original twist, including the shrimp risotto.

INFORMATION AND SERVICES

Haifa is a tourist destination even for Israelis and is well-equipped for visitors.

Tourist Information

You will see signs for it all over town, but there is only one **Haifa Tourist Information Office** (48 Ben Gurion St., www.tour-haifa.co.il/eng, 9am-5pm Sun.-Thurs., 9am-1pm Fri.,

Douzan restaurant in Haifa's German Colony

10am-3pm Sat.), conveniently located in the German Colony. The basement office is full of flyers, maps, and information about the area. The real wealth of information, though, can be found in the staff who work here: They will give you as many details as you can handle.

Online Resources

The most robust website for online resources about Haifa and the surrounding areas is the **Haifa Tourist Board** (www.tour-haifa.co.il/eng). Don't worry about downloading their tourist guide, though. You will get offered the compact printed version at every turn once you are in Haifa.

Also useful is the **Haifa Aliya Website** (www1.haifa.muni.il/aliya) with tons of information on services, transportation, and the makeup of different neighborhoods.

Hospitals and Emergency Services

Fairly centrally located and with an emergency room, the **Bnai Zion Medical Center** (47 Golomb St., 04/837-1973, www.b-zion.org.il) is located between the Hadar and Carmel districts.

You can also call **Magen David Adom** (04/851-2233) 24 hours a day for emergency services, including for an ambulance to the nearest emergency room.

Police

The tourist police in nearby Tel Aviv can be reached by phone (03/516-5382) if the need arises, and they should be able to direct you to the appropriate location or service.

ATMs, Banks, and Currency Exchange

The most robust areas in town for ATMs, banks, and money changing services are on Hanassi Boulevard near Yefe Nof Street and Ha'em Park, as well as on Ben Gurion Street in the center of the German Colony.

Inside the **Panorama Mall** (109 Hanassi Blvd., 04/837-5011, 9am-8pm Sun.-Thurs., 9am-2pm Fri.) is a currency exchange desk.

PUBLIC TRANSPORTATION SURPRISES

A pleasantly surprising aspect of Haifa, Israel's third largest city, is that it features some unique public transportation options that cannot be found anywhere else in Israel.

The first surprise is that during **Shabbat,** there is some public transportation running, something that not even Tel Aviv can claim. Public bus service on the green Egged buses still runs, though on a less frequent schedule.

The second surprise is that Haifa is home to Israel's only subway, the **Carmelit.** Even though the Carmelit's range and distance is extremely limited (it goes in a straight line from the lower city to the upper city in just six stops), it offers a convenient transportation option.

The route the Carmelit travels goes straight through a major section of Haifa's tourist areas, and is a less-intimidating option for a first-time visitor than taking a bus or taxi.

Haifa's final public transportation surprise is the **cable car** that traverses the side of Mount Carmel at a daring angle. It leaves every 15 minutes or less and has one stop at the top of the mountain and one stop at the bottom. It is yet another option for tourists looking for the quickest and least expensive route between some of the city's attractions, including Stella Maris Carmelite Monastery, San Francisco Observation Point, Elijah's Cave, and the Israel National Maritime Museum.

GETTING THERE AND AROUND

Most visitors to Haifa arrive by car or the national Israeli intercity train. Egged buses that travel all over the country also go here. Once here, you can get around by city bus, taxi, or Israel's only underground subway train—the Carmelit.

By Car

Driving into Haifa is fairly simple, but once you get into the city you really need to have a GPS to navigate around Mount Carmel and through the winding, hilly streets. Take Highway 2 straight north from Tel Aviv, or Highway 1 to 2 or 6 from Jerusalem. Highway 2 is a very pretty drive along the coast in good weather, and you can even see some ancient ruins if you're watching closely.

There are three car rental companies lined up next to each other at the northern entrance to the city. **Avis** (34 HaHistadrut St., 04/861-0444, http://avis.co.il) is a familiar option, and if they cannot accommodate you, the competition is literally next door, including **Eldan** (164 HaHistadrut St., 04/841-0910, www.eldan.co.il) and **Shlomo Sixt Car Rental** (48 HaHistadrut St., 04/872-5525, en.shlomo.co.il).

By Bus

There are buses leaving multiple times a day from Jerusalem, Tel Aviv, and elsewhere to get you into Haifa. There are five stations within the city, and you could end up on the wrong side of town if you don't know where you're going. It's about a two-hour ride from Jerusalem and can be crowded on Thursdays and Fridays, especially in the late afternoon.

From Jerusalem, take **Egged** bus (www.egged.co.il, NIS42) number 940 or 947 from the Central Bus Station.

Once here, there are public buses (Egged) that run all over the city and even operate on the weekend, though not as frequently.

By Boat

Some visitors to Haifa arrive and stay for a day or two due to a scheduled stop on their cruise ship or boat trip. The Port of Haifa is in the downtown area and is about a 10-minute drive or 30-minute walk to the German Colony.

By Train

The **Israel Railways** (www.rail.co.il) train station is a 70-minute ride from Tel Aviv and three-hour ride from Jerusalem.

By Cable Car

If you find yourself at Haifa's Bat Galim Promenade on the waterfront and want to get up the side of the mountain to see Stella Maris Carmelite Monastery, the **Cable Car** (top station on Tchernikovsky St. opposite the Stella Maris Carmelite Monastery, bottom station at the northern end of Bat Galim Promenade, www.tour-haifa.co.il, 10am-6pm daily, NIS29 round-trip, NIS19 one-way) is the quickest and cheapest way to go. The ride only takes about seven minutes one way, but the dangling cars are slightly rickety and it is very high up.

By Subway (Carmelit)

Haifa proudly boasts the only subway in Israel, but in practice the area the **Carmelit** (http://carmelithaifa.com, 6am-midnight Sun.-Thurs., 6am-3pm Fri., after sunset-midnight Sat., single ticket about NIS7) covers is very limited. It is most convenient if you're traveling in a straight line between the different stations at the lower city, Wadi Nisnas, and straight up the mountain until Hanassi Boulevard. In all there are only six stations. You can buy a single, daily, or 10-ride ticket.

Akko (Acre)

Akko is small, pretty, and full of interesting nooks and crannies. Repeatedly conquered and occupied by different civilizations throughout the ages, the Old City of Akko (also called Acre) is a UNESCO World Heritage Site. To visit Akko's Old City and wander through the ancient halls of stone with their massive, arching ceilings is to step into the past.

Also a favorite spot to get world-class seafood (one of the region's most famous seafood chefs operates here) and within easy driving distance of Haifa, Akko is the perfect place to spend the afternoon and take in a meal.

SIGHTS
Baha'i Gardens

Smaller than its Haifa counterpart but similarly designed and landscaped, the **Baha'i Gardens** (just off Hwy. 4 when entering Akko, 04/831-3131, www.ganbahai.org.il/en/akko, Inner Gardens 9am-noon Fri.-Mon., Outer Gardens 9am-4pm daily, free) is the resting place of the founder of the Baha'i religion, and the location of the house where he lived during the last years of his life. The immaculate, circular gardens create a peaceful cocoon of tranquility.

◖ Acre Old City

Akko's magnificent **Acre Old City** (southern end of HaHagana St. that follows the

water, www.akko.org.il/en, NIS15 and up for sites, combination ticket options available, ticket office at the Enchanted Garden) is a UNESCO World Heritage Site and comprised of a complex network of buildings, sites, and museums that would take about two

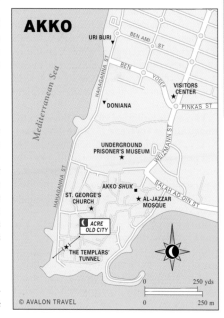

HAIFA

AKKO

URI BURI
BEN AMI ST
HAHAGANA ST
BEN
YOSEF
VISITORS CENTER
Mediterranean Sea
DONIANA
PINKAS ST
WEIZMANN ST
UNDERGROUND PRISONER'S MUSEUM
HAHAGANA ST
AKKO SHUK
SALAH AD-DIN ST
ST. GEORGE'S CHURCH
AL-JAZZAR MOSQUE
ACRE OLD CITY
THE TEMPLARS' TUNNEL
0   250 yds
0   250 m
© AVALON TRAVEL

© GENEVIEVE BELMAKER

Acre Old City

days to tour completely. The Crusader city is a network of walls and fortresses, knights' halls, and beautiful, golden stone that seem to whisper stories from its past as you walk through the main complex of halls, buildings, and courtyards. There are some areas that are in the process of ongoing renovations, but the collective impact is akin to stepping straight into the past.

The main buildings of the Old City, the **Hospitaller's Fortress** (8:30am-6pm Sun.-Thurs., Sat., and holidays, 8:30am-5pm Fri. and holiday eves) and its courtyard, were the main fortress of a monastic military order that was established to treat the sick in the Holy Land. The order had its headquarters in Akko from 1191 to 1291.

Fascinating and a bit haunting is the **Underground Prisoner's Museum** (The Citadel, tour reservations in advance at 04/991-1375, 8:30am-4:30pm Sun.-Thurs., 8:30am-1:30pm Fri.), which features tons of life-size, bronze statues of prisoners and other characters who played roles in the prison's history, positioned throughout different rooms.

The **Al Basha Turkish Bath** (8:30am-6pm Sun.-Thurs., Sat., and holidays, 9am-5pm Fri. and holiday eves) also features bronze, life-size statues of people going about their business in the bathhouse, including props and scenes of what life was like in the intact six rooms.

It takes about a 20-minute walk through back streets to reach **The Templars' Tunnel** (8:30am-5:30pm Sun.-Thurs., Sat., and holidays, 8:30am-4:30pm Fri. and holiday eves), used by the monastic military order called Templars that guarded European pilgrims while they were visiting the Holy Land. The main fortress of the Templars was built at the western end of the tunnel, and the tunnel extends for 350 meters underground.

The route to reach the tunnel is not well-marked, and it is necessary to ask for directions along the way. Set out by about 2pm to give yourself enough time to find the tunnel, explore it, and find your way back. You must have a ticket to enter, which you can purchase at the main ticket booth of the Old City.

Churches and Mosques

There are several ancient churches and mosques in Akko, most of which can be found on the very well-organized website for the Old City (www.akko.org.il/en). One of the churches considered among the most beautiful in the Levant is **Saint George's Church** (04/991-0563, call in advance for a visit), a Greek Orthodox Church that was likely Akko's first Christian house of worship built during the Turkish period.

Dominating and beautiful, the **Al-Jazzar Mosque** (04/991-3039, NIS10) is brilliant green and white and looks stunning from a distance. The entrance to the mosque, one of the second largest in Israel, is up some steep steps just at the beginning of the pathway that leads to the Templars' Tunnel. According to an Arabic inscription above the front door, the mosque was inaugurated around 1781. The interior has beautiful pillars and arching below a second-floor open walkway, with inlaid inscriptions on the circumference of the inner building. There are no specific hours, but try to visit between 9am-4pm Saturday-Thursday, and avoid Fridays.

THE WORLD OF OLD ACRE

In 2010, UNESCO declared Old Acre (Akko) a World Heritage Site of outstanding universal value, and with good reason. The designation is international recognition of Old Acre's history as home to a number of different cultures throughout the centuries, and guarantees a certain degree of protection and preservation for the sake of global humanity.

Old Acre is an historic, walled, port city that has been populated—without interruption—since the time of the Phoenicians (about 1500-300 BC) until modern day.

Old Acre's position on a peninsula with a natural bay made it internationally important during the time of the Crusaders. Its strategic port became a center for international trade. In the 18th century, it became the capital of the region's Ottoman Empire after a long period of decline.

One of Old Acre's most impressive monuments to its storied history are the remains of the Crusader City (AD 1104-1291) that have stayed almost completely intact above and below the modern street level. Since the 18th century, Old Acre in its current state has fit the characteristics of a fortified Ottoman city with typical urban elements of a citadel, mosques, *khans* (roadside inns), and baths.

© GENEVIEVE BELMAKER

the interior of the Old City at Akko

ENTERTAINMENT AND EVENTS

Renowned domestically and internationally, Akko's **Festival of Alternative Theater** (Acre Old City, during the intermediate days of the Sukkot holiday in the fall, www.accofestival. co.il, NIS40-75) has been held every year since 1979 in the Old City. The festival's events include plays, street performances, booths, and fire demonstrations. The main events are held in the Hospitaller's Fortress.

SHOPPING

Akko's two main shopping areas can be found easily by looking for the green and white Al-Jazzar Mosque. Get to the far eastern side of the Old City, and as you face the mosque, go to the left and you'll find some shops and stores that sell a variety of items like food and basic amenities. Go to the right (with the mosque on your left) and you'll pass through a small plaza that leads into the *shuk* (outdoor market).

ACCOMMODATIONS

Places to stay in Akko are very few and largely limited to luxury accommodations that might not be open in the low season. It is a very short drive from Akko to other nearby cities and towns that offer more options for places to stay at a range of prices.

Over US$200

If you plan to spring for a night in Akko, try **The Efendi Hotel** (Louis XI St., P.O.B 2503, Acre Old City, 074/729-9799, www.efendi-hotel.com, US$390 d), a five-star luxury boutique hotel with just 12 rooms in the historic Old City. The hotel has views of the historic city walls and the Mediterranean Sea. Built from two ancient houses that were combined and restored over a period of eight years, the hotel has rooms spread out over three levels with different designs and some feature illustrations, preserved wood, sea views, and views of the ancient city of Akko and the scenic mountains of the western Galilee. Hotel services include a spa room, a 400-year-old Turkish bath, a wine bar, and a cellar from the Crusader era. Rooms feature Egyptian cotton linens, goose down pillows and blankets, robes and slippers, marble-lined bathrooms with large showers, freestanding bathtubs, and towel warmers. There is also free Wi-Fi, a mini-bar, and an espresso machine.

FOOD
Middle Eastern

A good place to stop off for lunch, **Hummus Said** (middle of the Old City market area, off of Salah ad Din St., 04/991-3945, 6am-2:30pm Sun.-Fri., NIS25) serves up piles of pita, pickled dishes, and other appetizers, as well as hummus. It has a small, humble interior with just a few tables, and is extremely popular among locals and tourists. Expect a crowd if you go during the height of mealtime.

For a more upscale experience, **Mobarsham** (4 HaHagana St., waterfront, 057/944-1472, http://mobarsham.rest-e.co.il, 10am-midnight daily, NIS85) has a spacious interior that is very simply decorated. Serving seafood, meat, and a variety of Mediterranean-style salads and appetizers (*labaneh,* eggplant with tahini, and Turkish salad), Mobarsham also has some unusual offerings including fried Arabic cheese, lamb kebab, and red striped mullet fish.

Seafood

Set up in an old Turkish house converted into a restaurant and facing the Mediterranean, **Uri Buri** (11 HaHagana St., waterfront, 04/955-2212, http://uriburi.co.il, noon-11pm Wed.-Mon., NIS110) specializes in unique and masterful seafood preparation and presentation thanks to their iconic chef-owner Uri Yurmias. The interior is set up with individual rooms with Arab decor for an intimate atmosphere with limited seating. Reservations are recommended. Outdoor terrace seating facing the sea is also available in good weather. The dishes are inventive—Creole shrimp with spicy sauce and mangoes and fried calamari rings with three dips—and the half-orders allow you to sample more.

Also on the waterfront and situated on the third floor of the building, **Doniana** (6 HaHagana St., waterfront, 04/991-0001, noon-midnight daily, NIS60) is an Arab-style fish and meat restaurant with an atmosphere defined by its views of the sea and the city. The mezze (appetizer) selection has an extensive number of dishes and can be filling enough for a meal, especially around midday.

INFORMATION AND SERVICES

Akko is a tourist destination, and once you get anywhere near the Old City and Al-Jazzar Mosque, it is well-equipped to meet your needs.

Old Acre Visitors' Center

Just to the right as you enter the Enchanted Garden, the **Old Acre Visitors' Center** (1 Weizmann St., 04/995-6706, 8:30am-4pm Sun.-Thurs. and Sat., 8:30am-3:30pm Fri. and holiday eves) has some useful maps and a seven-minute free introductory movie about Akko in English.

Online Resources

By far the best website about Akko, put up by the Old Acre Development Company, is www.akko.org.il/en. The website includes maps, site introductions, operating times, and background information.

ATMs and Money Exchange

The plaza in front of Al-Jazzar Mosque has a convenient combination of an ATM, bank, and money exchange service.

Police and Emergency Services

Just around the corner from the Al-Jazzar Mosque you'll find the extremely friendly and accommodating volunteer **tourist police** (9am-5pm daily).

GETTING THERE AND AROUND

Akko is very easy to reach by car by way of Highway 4 from either the north or the south. There is plenty of parking around town and plenty of signage in English to direct you to the Old City.

If you are taking a bus (www.egged.co.il), from Haifa take bus numbers 251 and 271. Coming from the north, take bus numbers 501 and 360. Once in the city, you can get from city center to the Old City on bus numbers 61 and 62.

The **Israel Railways** (www.rail.co.il) Akko train station is an 80-minute ride from Tel Aviv and up to 3.5 hours from Jerusalem; from the station, it is a 15-minute walk to the Old City.

Nahariya

Nahariya is a surprising little town where everyone knows each other. The town is brimming with sweet details, including a river that runs through the center of town, and is lined with decorative street lamps. It's the perfect place to spend a couple of low-key days and get in some surfing, swimming, bike riding, and long walks. Nahariya's city center is compact and quaint, with a nice selection of restaurants, shops, and scenery. The most enchanting aspect by day or night is the Ga'aton River that runs through the center of town and is bordered by graceful trees and a white railing. It is one of the most pleasant strolls in Israel.

SIGHTS
Promenade

Pleasant even in the winter, Nahariya's long **promenade** (off of HaMa'apalim St.) is very close to the town's center and has space for running, biking, and strolling. The buildings along the promenade are well maintained, and at some points there are restaurants and coffee shops. The promenade extends south for about five miles, almost to Akko.

Grotto Caves at Rosh Hanikra

A 10-minute drive from Nahariya are the gorgeous, sparkling blue **Grotto Caves** (Rte. 4 to the northernmost part of Israel, 073/271-0100,

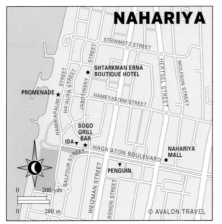

HAIFA

www.rosh-hanikra.com, 9am-6pm Sun.-Thurs., 9am-4pm Fri. and holiday eves, 9am-6pm Sat. and holidays Apr.-Oct.; 9am-4pm Sun.-Fri. and holiday eves, 9am-6pm Sat. and holidays mid-Oct.-Mar.; adult NIS45, child and senior NIS35) at Rosh Hanikra. About 220 yards of walking track leads down to the natural grottoes, which are lit. Located at Israel's northernmost point at the border with Lebanon, the grottoes also have a few other attractions, including a promenade, a cable car, and sea-view restaurants. The entire site of the grottoes is set up so you can experience both the grottoes and the sea at an extremely close proximity through a network of paved walkways and cable cars. Note that it's not particularly accessible to people with disabilities.

The Lieberman House Museum

Showcasing the history of the city of Nahariya and housed in the former house of one of the town's first settlers, **The Lieberman House Museum** (21 Hagedud St., 04/982-1516, nahariyamuseums@gmail.com, 9am-1pm Sun., 9am-1pm and 4pm-7pm Mon., 9am-1pm Tues., 9am-1pm and 4pm-7pm Wed., 9am-1pm Thurs., 9am-noon Fri., 10am-2pm Sat., free) includes an archive of photos, posters, announcements, and correspondence from Nahariya's past and the Lieberman house's past, dating from pre-1948 through today.

SHOPPING
Nahariya Mall

The very small **Nahariya Mall** (2 Irish St., Ein Sara, 04/992-9977, www.nahariya-mall.co.il, 10am-9:30pm Sun.-Thurs., 9am-2:30pm Fri.) sells a variety of shoes, bags, and clothes, and has a surf shop that sells equipment and might be willing to rent pieces out.

SPORTS AND RECREATION

There are several outdoor and recreational sports in and around Nahariya, including swimming, bicycling, surfing, and hiking.

Surfing

A popular pastime in Nahariya is surfing, particularly at **Sokolow (Sokolov) Beach** (Nahum Sokolow St. at the beach end of HaGa'aton Blvd.). The beaches are clean and easily accessible. On a day with good waves (even in the middle of a workday during the week), you can expect to see at least a dozen surfers in the water. Sokolow is considered a very consistent break, with waves that can get up to about seven feet or higher.

Swimming

Look for HaGa'aton Boulevard and follow it to the sea and you'll find plenty of spots to swim. If you need a landmark on the shore, look for the large structure that looks like boat sails. Some of the beaches cost a small fee (about NIS10) and others are free.

You'll likely see locals swimming in areas with warnings posted to not swim there, but don't be tempted to follow suit. The undertow of the Mediterranean can be very strong, even in shallow water and on a calm day. Stick to areas that are designated beaches with lifeguards. Try your luck at **Galei Galil Beach.**

Bicycling

A favorite pastime in Nahariya, bike riding is a good way to take in a lot of the seaside and hop into a café for lunch without tiring yourself out. Try the front desk at the centrally located Shtarkman Erna Boutique Hotel for **bicycle rentals** (29 Jabotinsky St., 04/992-0170, www.sernahotel.co.il).

© GENEVIEVE BELMAKER

The Ga'aton River runs through the center of Nahariya.

ACCOMMODATIONS

Though small, Nahariya has a relatively large number of accommodations that vary from cheap motels to upscale boutique hotels. There is no reason to settle for something you're unhappy with if you wind up staying here for a night or two. Most hotels are within very easy walking distance of the beach and promenade.

US$100-150

Near the popular Galilee Beach and the train station, the ☾ **Shtarkman Erna Boutique Hotel** (29 Jabotinsky St., 04/992-0170, www. sernahotel.co.il, US$128 d) is a classy, understated 26-room boutique hotel. Originally opened in 1959 and since renovated and remodeled, this multi-generation, family-run hotel has air-conditioned rooms with free Wi-Fi, cable TV, a telephone, and a small fridge. Some rooms have a spa bath, drinks are served in the hotel's private garden, bicycles are available for free, and there is free parking. The owners that run Shtarkman are quintessential locals and know every possible detail about their town and the surrounding area. Excursions can be arranged through the hotel staff, and guests get discounts on local restaurants and tickets to nearby historic Akko. In the month of August, guests get free entrance to a private beach and country club with swimming pools and tennis courts. Some of the rooms are on the small side by American standards, but every inch of the place makes you feel perfectly at home, including the lavish breakfast that's included in your stay.

Travel Hotel at Kibbutz Gesher Haziv (Kibbutz Gesher Haziv on HaOranim St., just north of Nahariya, 04/995-8568, www.zimmeril.com, US$140 d) is a bed-and-breakfast situated north of Nahariya near the cliffs of Rosh Hanikra and a short drive from Achziv Beach. Located on a kibbutz overlooking the Mediterranean, the atmosphere of Gesher Haziv is pure Israel countryside. All 32 rooms are plainly decorated but have a warm atmosphere and include private bathrooms, air-conditioning, a television, refrigerator, microwave, and free coffee and cookies. There are several nature reserves nearby that can be explored by foot, donkey, horseback, or by jeep with a guide and driver. Located in the western Galilee, a main center of Crusader activities, the kibbutz

HAIFA

© GENEVIEVE BELMAKER

the popular Galei Galil Beach in Nahariya

makes it convenient to explore Crusader castles at Montfort and Yechiam and the underground Crusader city in Akko. The kibbutz offers discount coupons for all attractions and restaurants in the area, free Wi-Fi in common areas, and free entrance to their pool, sports facilities, and children's playgrounds.

Camping

Just a bit north of Nahariya is the popular **Achziv National Park** (about three miles north of Nahariya on the way to Rosh Hanikra, 04/982-3263, www.parks.org.il, sign in and out for camping is by noon, NIS35, child NIS18), which has space for camping as well as beautiful, secluded beaches. There is also a Crusader fortress in the area and the ruins of ancient Achziv.

FOOD

Dining options in Nahariya are surprisingly plentiful, easy to access, and provide a variety of options, even late at night.

American

The **Sogo Grill Bar** (1 Jabotinsky St., corner of HaGa'aton Blvd., 04/900-0001, salit_amar@hotmail.com, 9am-3am daily, NIS55) is a restaurant by day and a dance bar by night. The interior is huge and spacious, with a massive bar and modern finishes on all the decor. The food is a fairly standard fare of burgers, sandwiches, and salads. If you're looking for some nightlife, this is a good place to start.

Cafés

One of the oldest restaurants in town, **Penguin** (21 HaGa'aton Blvd., 04/992-8855, 9am-midnight daily, NIS55) is easy to find with the life-size penguins at the front door. The interior is simple, spacious, clean, and classy, with tons of outdoor seating and a nice wine and liquor selection. Their signature dish is schnitzel, and they also serve a wide variety of sandwiches and do a typical hearty Israeli breakfast.

Fine Dining

An upper-crust dining experience can be had at the chef restaurant **Ida** (48 HaGa'aton Blvd., 057/944-3732, 9am-11pm Sun.-Thurs., 10am-11pm Sat., NIS90) in the former home of the first mayor of Nahariya, Gershon Tatz, for whose wife Ida the restaurant is named. The classy, subdued atmosphere is accented with touches like floor-length curtains and cushy, leather-upholstered chairs. The restaurant sits on the banks of the Ga'aton River. Dishes include a variety of fish, meat, and seafood entrées, including grilled veal liver in wine sauce and the catch of the day from the fish menu.

INFORMATION AND SERVICES

As a small, coastal town, Nahariya has all the basic services you might need. The residents are extremely friendly and most speak English. If you have questions, you should feel comfortable to ask anyone you encounter.

Online Resources

The best source of online information about Nahariya is the **Israel Ministry of Tourism** website (www.goisrael.com). Also full of useful information is the family-run **Shtarkman Erna Boutique Hotel**'s website (www.sernahotel.co.il), which has tons of tips and information about tourism in the area.

ATMs and Currency Exchange

Your best bet for an ATM and for changing money is the **Nahariya Mall** (2 Irish St., Ein Sara, 04/992-9977, www.nahariya-mall.co.il, 10am-9:30pm Sun.-Thurs., 9am-2:30pm Fri.).

Police, Emergency, and Tourist Services

Dial 100 for the **police** and 101 for **emergency**

medical services from any phone. Dial *3888 from any phone for tourism, the Israel Police, the Ministry of Interior services, the Airport Authority, and more.

GETTING THERE AND AROUND
By Car

You can reach Nahariya very easily by taking Highway 4 north. It's about 40 minutes from Haifa and just over two hours from Jerusalem. Once here, it's a remarkably easy place to navigate, with tons of free parking. It's basically impossible to get lost with the Ga'aton River as a guidepost in the center of town.

By Bus

The **Egged** bus (www.egged.co.il) number 960 takes about 3 hours from Jerusalem (NIS60 one-way) and bus number 910 takes about 3.5 hours from Tel Aviv (NIS69.50 one-way). Both have transfers in Haifa.

Once in Nahariya, several Egged bus lines operate throughout town.

By Train

The **Israel Railways** (www.rail.co.il) train takes about three hours from Jerusalem (NIS61 one-way), and about 90 minutes from Tel Aviv (NIS44.50 one-way).

Netanya

A seaside resort spot that is known for its oddly 1970s-themed atmosphere and popularity among French visitors, Netanya is not a major destination for Israelis or overseas visitors. However, it is just about equidistant between Haifa and Tel Aviv, and offers an alternative for exploring some low-key spots or just relaxing on the beach without the crowds you find in Tel Aviv.

SIGHTS
Parks and Nature Reserves

Netanya has several natural attractions in its

vicinity that the Tourist Information Office should be able to tell you about. The **Utopia Tropical Orchard Park** (Kibbutz Bahan, 09/878-2191, www.utopiapark.co.il/english, adult NIS59, child NIS44, senior NIS54) is a good option because it can be reached by bus from the Netanya Central Bus station (#33 Native Express). Kibbutz Bahan, home of the park, is the last stop on the line. The park is an incredible, lush oasis near Netanya that boasts waterfalls, a massive indoor greenhouse with tropical plants, and a deck area for eating and drinking. A late morning or

© BELYAEV VIACHESLAV/123RF.COM

fountain in Netanya

HAIFA

afternoon visit to Utopia could be a welcome respite, especially during Israel's hot, muggy summer months.

SPORTS AND RECREATION
Beaches
One of Netanya's cool features is that it has eight beaches. At the most central, **Sironit Beach** (base of Rishonim Promenade), there is a **transparent elevator** down to the beach. Buffered by piers, the water is safe for swimming almost the entire year. In the summer months, nearby restaurants provide entertainment and there are sports tournaments and games on the beach.

Hiking
Israel's **National Trail** (www.israelnational-trail.com and www.netanya.muni.il) passes through Netanya, winding through some scenic areas that include the urban **purple Iris reserve,** several of the area's beaches, and the cliffs next to the city. The entire trail is about 620 miles from the Red Sea to the border with Lebanon.

INFORMATION AND SERVICES
The **Tourist Information Office** (12 Ha'azmaut Sq., 09/882-7286, 8am-4pm Sun.-Thurs., 9am-2pm Fri.) is right at the town center and offers information about Netanya and the surrounding area.

The **Netanya Board of Tourism** (www.gon-etanya.com) has a great website that provides a lot of basic information for visitors.

GETTING THERE AND AROUND
Israel Railways (www.rail.co.il) has a train station in Netanya. The train ride is about 30 minutes from Tel Aviv (NIS15.5 one-way) and two hours from Jerusalem (NIS36.5 one-way).

Netanya is a 30-minute drive from Tel Aviv just off of Highway 2, or 45 minutes off of Highway 4.

From Jerusalem, take **Egged** bus (www.egged.co.il) number 947 from the Central Bus Station (NIS30 one-way), which takes about 90 minutes. From Tel Aviv, take bus number 641 (NIS18 one-way), which takes close to 2 hours.

Caesarea (Qesarya)

Caesarea is two towns: the ancient city and the modern, rural town that is a favorite vacation home spot of wealthy Israelis. The ruins of ancient Caesarea can be seen alongside the modern town. The main highlight is the Antiquities Park.

SIGHTS
◖ Caesarea National Antiquities Park

The **Caesarea National Antiquities Park** (off Hwy. 2 near Kibbutz Sdot Yam, 04/626-7080, www.parks.org.il, 8am-6pm Sun.-Thurs., 8am-5pm Fri. Apr.-Sept.; 8am-4pm Sun.-Thurs., 8am-3pm Fri. Oct.-Mar., NIS38) is unique in

that it has buildings from different historical periods. Spanning a time period of about 2,300 years, the park covers an area of about 125 acres and includes archeological remnants from the Hellenistic period (the 3rd century BC) to the Crusader period (the 12th century AD), during a time when Caesarea was a port city and Israel's capital.

Named for Augustus Caesar, who gave the city to King Herod, Caesarea was built up by Herod to include venues for entertainment, bathhouses, and places of worship. Touring through the Antiquities Park allows you to wander in between ancient buildings and ruins,

© GENEVIEVE BELMAKER

the ancient Roman and Byzantine Aqueduct at Caesarea

including the **Hippodrome** and the still used **Roman Amphitheater.**

Situated inside the national park, the **Caesarea Port** (04/626-8882, www.caesarea.com) is an intoxicating mixture of ancient and modern, including the ancient **Crusader City.** Aside from the ancient port itself, there is a beach, restaurants, galleries, and more. Here you can also find the multimedia **Travel Through Time** (long building next to the jetty, English presentation every 15 min.) that tells Caesarea's history in three stations: a short movie of the city's history from ancient times through today; a 3-D interactive presentation on the impact of different historical figures; and a computer-generated show that depicts the city's construction masterpieces throughout history from the time of Herod onward.

Caesarea Antiquities Museum

Just at the southern entrance of Caesarea is the **Caesarea Antiquities Museum** (Kibbutz Sdot Yam, 04/636-4367, www.parks.org.il, 10am-4pm Sun.-Thurs., 8am-1pm Fri., NIS13), home to tons of treasures from the Mediterranean Sea and the surrounding area, including ancient coins, late Roman sculptures, Roman and Byzantine gems and jewelry, and pottery. Many of the finds here were dug up from the ground in the surrounding area by residents on the kibbutz over the past several decades.

◖ Roman and Byzantine Aqueduct

More part of the scenery than a destination, the **Roman and Byzantine Aqueduct** (shore of the Mediterranean Sea) is just a few miles east of modern Caesarea proper. It runs along the seashore in a stunning display of ancient engineering.

There are several portions of the aqueduct, some of which are underground. You can see another portion of the aqueduct along Highway 2 between Caesarea and Haifa. The portion nearest Caesarea was built by the Romans in the 2nd century AD and was repaired many times, so portions of the still-remaining aqueduct are different ages.

The raised stone aqueduct was used to bring water to the old city of Caesarea, and a large portion of it is still intact. The incredible architecture and engineering of the aqueduct is apparent despite its somewhat crumbling facade. But overall, it has held up remarkably well and is still incredibly beautiful, especially against the backdrop of the Mediterranean Sea. It stops short of reaching Caesarea because part of the aqueduct has not survived.

If you're adventurous and in good enough shape, you can climb up on top of the aqueduct at Aqueduct Beach, and walk along the top.

Birds Mosaic Floor

Believed to be part of a large villa dating back to the 6th or 7th century BC, the **Birds Mosaic Floor** (about 0.25 miles from the Antiquities Park, free) was likely part of a large, open courtyard. Several other parts of the villa had mosaic floors and have also been discovered at the site. The area is open, you can walk on the mosaic, and it is easy to spot.

Tours

For a guided day trip to Caesarea plus a couple of other areas, **Egged Tours** (www.eggedtours.com, Sun., Tues., and Fri., US$109 from Jerusalem, US$98 from Tel Aviv) has a one-day tour that also includes Akko and Rosh Hanikra. The tours depart from Jerusalem at 5:50am and from Tel Aviv at 7:15am.

ENTERTAINMENT AND EVENTS

Particularly in the summer, Caesarea is fun to experience in the evenings with its natural ambience of the ancient port and outdoor seating at cafés. It's not Tel Aviv, but it has a nice rhythm to it.

Concerts at the Roman Amphitheater

During the summer months, the ancient **Roman Amphitheater** (Caesarea National Antiquities Park, 04/626-7080, www.parks.org.il) holds outdoor concerts in a magical, unforgettable setting. There is no official website

for upcoming concerts, but you can try searching **Eventim** (www.eventim.co.il) close to the date you are interested in.

Festivals

Every year during the months of July and August on Tuesday nights, different events are held at the port near the art gallery market and food stands for **Caesarea Nights.** Events, which include movie screenings, are scattered throughout the port area.

SHOPPING

A great place to shop for gifts and souvenirs is the **Caesarea Port.** A highlight is the **Draydel House** (The Port, 04/626-1144, www.draydel-house.com, 10am-6pm daily) home to ceramic artist Eran Graveler, who sells ceramics and Judaica items. His crowning glory is his famed collection of over 300 different ceramic draydels, and in early 2013 he opened a second location in Tel Aviv.

SPORTS AND RECREATION

Caesarea's main distinction for sports enthusiasts is its 18-hole international golf course, the only one of its kind in Israel. It also has some nice beaches and places for water sports, including diving.

Parks and Beaches

One of the best beaches to visit in the Caesarea area is **Aqueduct Beach** (free), which you will see signs for as you drive through town. There is free parking, but there are no restrooms or places to change.

Golf

The **Caesarea Golf Club and Professional Golf Course** (Golf Neighborhood, 04/610-9600, golf@caesarea.com, 6am-6:30pm Tues.-Sun. summer, 6am-5pm Tues.-Sun. winter, NIS480 for 18 holes) was established in the 1960s by the Baron Edmond de Rothschild family and is the only international golf club in Israel. The grounds of the club include training ranges, a perfectly groomed course, a pro shop, and a gourmet restaurant. In 2009, the course was redesigned by internationally renowned golf course designer Pete Dye.

Diving

The **Old Caesarea Diving Center** (The Port, 04/626-5898, www.caesarea-diving.com) is in a unique location on the ancient ruins of Herod's now-submerged port. The center operates the **Underwater Archaeological Park** with preserved underwater treasures and marine flora and fauna. Both certified and inexperienced divers are welcome, and you can get guided and independent diving and snorkeling, lessons, and gear for rent.

ACCOMMODATIONS

It is a tempting place to stay overnight, but Caesarea is strangely lacking choices for accommodations, particularly in the summer months. The only real hotel in the area is the extremely expensive Dan Caesarea.

The two best options if you want to stay in the area for a few nights are to go to nearby Zichron Ya'akov or to get a vacation rental. **Aloha Caesarea Vacation Rentals** (054/425-8045, www.aloha.co.il, US$150 d and up) can accommodate a variety of needs and groups. They also have accommodations in nearby areas.

FOOD
Cafés

Port Café (The Port, 04/610-0221, www.port-cafe.co.il, 8:30am-last customer daily, NIS65) has a great view. It's a good bet for breakfast omelets and other egg dishes, salads, tapas, pizza, and seafood entrées. The exterior has an ancient stone look and the interior furniture gives the feeling of being on a ship, with heavy, worn wooden tables, deck, and railings. The café has an extensive wine and alcohol menu, including cocktails.

Seafood

Around the corner from Port Café is **Helena** (The Port, 053/809-4915, www.2eat.co.il/eng/helena, noon-11pm daily, NIS100), a gourmet

restaurant run by two leading chefs in Israel that overlooks the sea and the port. The interior is extremely simple with hardwood floors, ceiling fans, and a massive outdoor deck seating area that is mostly covered from the hot sun. The menu's Mediterranean style features mainly seafood dishes, including a rich bouillabaisse. They also do a nice fish fillet that is served on a bed of gnocchi with cream sauce, mushrooms, and spinach.

INFORMATION AND SERVICES

The **Caesarea Development Corporation** (www.caesarea.com) has a fairly useful website with plenty of photos and basic information about visiting the area.

GETTING THERE AND AROUND

It is very easy to get to Caesarea by car, but there is no direct train here and the bus involves a transfer at a junction.

By Car

Take Highway 2 about 30 minutes past Tel Aviv and follow the exit signs for Caesarea. Follow the road until you see the anchor sculpture, turn right, and go to the end of the road to the visitors' parking lot.

By Bus

From Jerusalem, take the **Egged** bus (www.egged.co.il) number 972 from Jerusalem to Hadera (about an hour and 45 minutes, NIS30), and then transfer to the **Nateev Express** (www.nateevexpress.com) bus number 76 or 77.

By Train

From Jerusalem it is a 2.5-hour train ride on **Israel Railways** (www.rail.co.il) to the Binyamina station (NIS44.5 one-way). From Tel Aviv it is only 30 minutes (NIS25) to Binyamina. From the train station, take one of the waiting taxis to your destination (approx. NIS40). It's about a 15-20-minute taxi ride.

Zichron Ya'akov

Situated on a mountainside overlooking the sea, Zichron Ya'akov is a sweet oasis just off the highway that makes for a perfect place to stop for a meal or stay for a night. As a moshav, it has the feel of a village and the town center's pedestrian mall has been done to in a European style with a pedestrian restaurant and shopping area.

SIGHTS
Town Center
The main point of interest in town is the quaint, idyllic **Town Center** (Hameyasdim St.), also known as the Midrahov. Once you're in Zichron Ya'akov, just follow the many signs to find the Midrahov, or ask anybody who passes by. The place is so small you can't get lost.

Once here, you can easily spend a leisurely afternoon or evening enjoying a meal and coffee, browsing through the many interesting shops, and listening to street musicians perform.

First Aliyah Museum
It is very, very small, but the **First Aliyah Museum** (2 Hanadiv St., 04/629-4777, 9am-2pm Mon. and Wed.-Fri., 9am-3pm Tues., NIS10) is interesting for a quick pass through, and is directly across from the gorgeous Gan Tiyyul (Strolling Garden). The museum tells stories of immigrants who came to Palestine, particularly Zichron Ya'akov, in the first wave of Jewish immigration that began in 1882. There are multi-media presentations, sculptures, photographs, and English descriptions of the exhibits on two floors in the tightly packed quarters.

Carmel Wine and Culture
Housed in a wine cellar that was built in 1892 by Baron Edmond de Rothschild, the **Carmel Wine and Culture** (Derech Ha'Yekev/Winery St., 04/639-1788, www.carmelwines.co.il, 9am-5pm Sun.-Thurs., 9am-2pm Fri. and holiday eves, NIS22 and up for tastings) is a must-see for any wine enthusiast. The complex includes a wine shop, a visitor's center, a restaurant, two specialist tasting rooms, a small cinema, and a barrel room in one of Rothschild's historic underground cellars. A variety of tastings are available, some of which require reservations.

HAIFA

© GENEVIEVE BELMAKER

Zichron Ya'akov Town Center

HAIFA

SPORTS AND RECREATION
Parks and Beaches

At the southeastern entrance to Zichron Ya'akov is **Ramat Hanadiv Nature Reserve** (Rte. 652 between Zichron Ya'akov and Binyamina, 04/629-8111, www.ramat-hanadiv.org.il, 8am-4pm Sun.-Thurs., 8am-2pm Fri., 8am-4pm Sat., crypt closed on Sat., free), a memorial garden and a nature reserve that is also the final resting place of Baron Edmond de Rothschild and his wife. The reserve has four circular routes with gorgeous vistas. There are also archaeological relics scattered throughout and the Ein Tzur spring. The park also has its own kosher dairy restaurant (04/844-9979).

There are a few beaches nearby, but the closest authorized one is **Dor Beach** (just off Hwy. 4, NIS10), which is very clean, pretty, and sandy.

ACCOMMODATIONS
US$150-200

Distinguished partly because of its almost complete lack of competition and partly because of its charm, the (**Hotel Beit Maimon** (Zahal 4 St., 04/629-0390, www.maimon.com, US$181 d) is located in the hills of lovely and picturesque Zichron Ya'akov, just half an hour south of Haifa. The small, 25-room hotel has an on-premises restaurant, room service for drinks, and some rooms with breathtaking views of the Mediterranean Sea. Every room has air-conditioning, a 32-inch LCD TV, direct-dial telephone, Wi-Fi, a refrigerator, and bathroom with shower. Some rooms have a connecting door and a large whirlpool bathtub overlooking the sea. There is also an outdoor whirlpool tub on the second floor.

Over US$200

Though the number of rooms is extremely limited at only four, **The Castle** (Old Tel Aviv Haifa Rd. 4-10, Kerem Maharal, 054/720-0661, www.thecastle.co.il, US$350 d) makes up for in uniqueness what it lacks in available rooms. The 900-year-old Crusader fort from the 11th century is just 30 minutes south of Haifa near the coast, and caters to travelers

© GENEVIEVE BELMAKER

First Aliyah Museum

seeking a unique vacation. The only structure in Israel from this period that is privately owned, The Castle was built as a home for the ruler of the area, and has been painstakingly restored. Two suites have a balcony and two have a garden. The interior features massive stone bathtubs, and paintings and artwork created by one of the owners. There is free Wi-Fi throughout (when it's working), free parking, 24-hour concierge service, a dining area, a fully-equipped shared kitchen, and a panoramic balcony with an incredible view of the countryside. Nearby activities include horseback riding, cookout facilities, bicycle rental, and picnic lunches.

FOOD

Throw a rock in the town center and you'll hit a restaurant, coffee shop, pub, or café of almost every size and type. The hard part is choosing.

On Hanadiv Street, try **Ayalet and Gili Restaurant** (23 Generous St. off of Hanadiv St., 077/403-0455, 10am-last customer Sun.-Thurs., 9am-one hour before sundown Fri.,

NIS60), which bills itself as authentic Israeli food made with love. Their menu includes soups, vegetarian platters, and chicken and beef dishes. The side dishes and salads are decidedly Mediterranean, and include items such as bulgur and quinoa. The bright, cheerful, and homey environment gives the feeling of sitting down at the dinner table just next to your mother's kitchen. Live music is also featured on a regular basis.

INFORMATION AND SERVICES

Just next to the Founder's Monument on Hameyasdim Street is the **Gidonim Tourism Information Centre** (04/639-8811, gidonim@ bezeqint.net, 8:30am-1pm Mon.-Thurs.), where you can inquire—in advance—about arranging a tour in English.

The **Tourism Development Agency of Zichron Ya'akov** (www.zy1882.co.il) has some useful information.

Hanadiv Street pedestrian mall is the best place to find most services, including ATMs.

GETTING THERE AND AROUND

Zichron Ya'akov is relatively easy to reach, especially if you remember that the spelling of the town's name changes from sign to sign as you drive. It is well known, though, so there is no problem asking for directions.

By Car

If traveling by car, take Highway 2 to Route 70 and the exit for Zichron Ya'akov. It is about an hour from Tel Aviv. From Jerusalem, take Highway 6 to Route 70, which takes about 90 minutes.

By Train

Binyamina Train Station is about a 12-minute drive from Zichron Ya'akov. The **Israel Railways** (www.rail.co.il) train takes 2.5 hours from Jerusalem (NIS80 round-trip) and 50 minutes from Tel Aviv (NIS35 round-trip).

By Bus

The bus from Jerusalem (www.egged.co.il) to Zichron Ya'akov transfers at Tel Aviv and stops at the Binyamina Train Station and takes 2.5 hours (NIS42 one-way). From Tel Aviv it is a 90-minute ride (NIS24 one-way) that also lands you at the train station. From there you will need to take a taxi.

THE GALILEE AND THE GOLAN HEIGHTS

Northern Israel has vast spaces of nothing, punctuated by significant cultural and religious sites such as Nazareth, Tiberias, and Capernaum, to name a few. This is one of the most beautiful parts of the region and is a perfect place to escape for an excursion into the countryside. Aside from religious attractions, Northern Israel has beautiful scenery, world-class wine,

© GENEVIEVE BELMAKER

HIGHLIGHTS

LOOK FOR ◖ TO FIND RECOMMENDED SIGHTS, ACTIVITIES, DINING, AND LODGING.

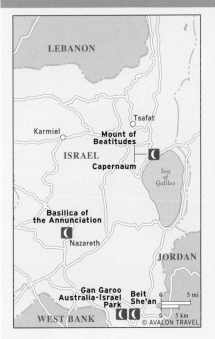

◖ **Mount of Beatitudes:** The site where Jesus gave the Sermon on the Mount near Tiberias is one of the most peaceful spots in all of Israel (page 202).

◖ **Capernaum:** The ruins and church at Capernaum, a city where Jesus once lived and taught, weave a magical web of mystery on the shores of the Sea of Galilee (page 203).

◖ **Basilica of the Annunciation:** This cavernous, modern church in Nazareth yields a wealth of lovely details, including a huge collection of wall mosaics from all over the world depicting the Virgin Mary and Jesus (page 212).

◖ **Beit She'an:** Tucked into a crevice between the borders with Jordan and the West Bank, magnificent Beit She'an has massive and remarkably well-preserved Roman columns (page 219).

◖ **Gan Garoo Australia-Israel Park:** Animal lovers will enjoy the pure fun that awaits them at the Gan Garoo park, where kangaroos and other Australian animals live (page 220).

archaeological and historical sites, outstanding sports and recreation, and interesting people.

East of Haifa is Nazareth, the town where Jesus lived for much of his life. Also built up the side of a mountain, upper Nazareth has some of the steepest and narrowest roads in the region. The Old City of Nazareth is full of interesting sights including an outdoor market, but the main attraction is the Church of the Annunciation, a modern Catholic church built over the ruins of Byzantine and Crusader churches.

Though the Golan Heights (both upper and lower) and the Galilee are full of hiking, biking, camping, and swimming spots, the anchor of the region is the Sea of Galilee. The

ancient sea is the main water source for Israel, and home to a number of significant sights, including the ancient town of Tiberias and the ruins at Capernaum, where Jesus once taught and lived. It was near Capernaum that Jesus gave the Sermon on the Mount and turned a few fish and loaves of bread into enough food to feed thousands. There are so many legends and history in the Golan and Galilee that after spending a few nights here, it's easy to slip into an introspective, philosophical state of mind and begin to forget about the rest of the world.

ORIENTATION

The Sea of Galilee (Kinneret in Hebrew) is home to one of the lowest-lying lakes in the

© GENEVIEVE BELMAKER

Pilgrims and tourists view the ancient synagogue at Capernaum.

world. It is full of religious history, legends, and significant sites as well as incredible archaeological sites. The two main cities in the region are Nazareth, which is basically in the middle of the Galilee, and Tiberias, which is on the western shore of the Sea of Galilee. The Sea of Galilee is only about 31 miles around. The eastern shore is in the Golan Heights and the western shore is in the Galilee.

Much of the region has year-round hiking trails, hot springs, and different types of ecotourism. The main baptismal site for pilgrims in the Jordan River is here, at Yardenit. The entire region seems vast on a map, but in reality it is relatively easy to get from one point to another by car or bus, particularly with recent improvements in the roads.

PLANNING YOUR TIME

Set aside 3-5 days and nights to explore the Golan and the Galilee. A rental car is highly recommended in the interest of time and for the flexibility of seeing different sights, but you can also get around to most areas by bus.

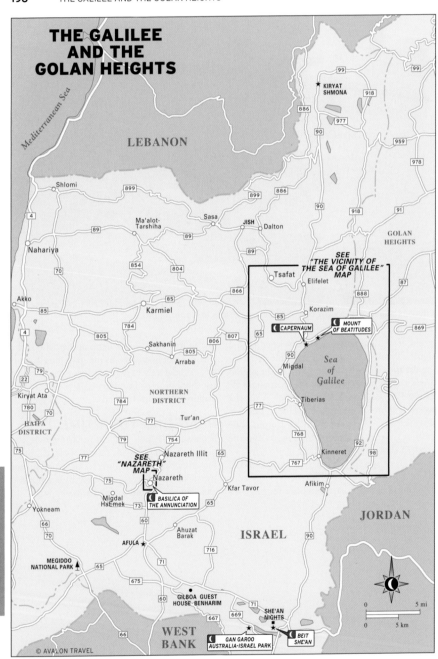

THE GALILEE AND THE GOLAN HEIGHTS

THE GALILEE

THE UNDEFINED TERRITORY OF THE GOLAN HEIGHTS

© GENEVIEVE BELMAKER

the top of Mount Hermon in summer

Depending on who you ask about the status of the Golan Heights, you'll get a different answer; the geography alone can be confusing.

The area known as the Golan Heights runs from Mount Hermon in the north, at the intersection of the borders of Lebanon, Syria, and Israel, to the south at Hamat Gader and the intersection of the borders of Jordan, Israel, and the West Bank. The western side of the Golan Heights hugs the shoreline of the Sea of Galilee and the 1949 Israel-Syria armistice line. On the eastern border of the Golan Heights is the complex, layered border of the 1974 ceasefire maintained by the United Nations Disengagement Observer Force, then a DMZ buffer zone, and then the official border of Syria.

Israel considers the Golan Heights of significant strategic importance for three reasons: the presence of a defensible land border, a buffer for northern Israel from artillery fire, and access to the country's most significant water source of the Sea of Galilee. In 1981, Israel officially put the Golan Heights under Israeli law, jurisdiction, and administration, but its status as part of Israel is not universally accepted in the international community.

THE GALILEE

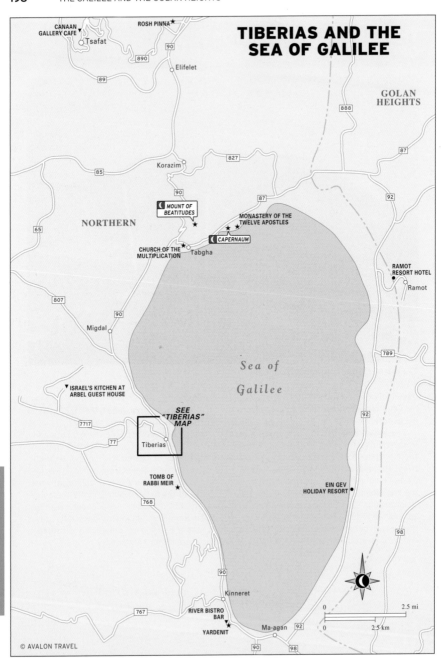

TIBERIAS AND THE SEA OF GALILEE

CANAAN GALLERY CAFE

ROSH PINNA

Tsafat

90

890

Elifelet

89

GOLAN HEIGHTS

888

87

827

Korazim

92

85

90

87

NORTHERN

MOUNT OF BEATITUDES

MONASTERY OF THE TWELVE APOSTLES

CAPERNAUM

65

CHURCH OF THE MULTIPLICATION

Tabgha

RAMOT RESORT HOTEL

Ramot

807

90

Migdal

789

Sea of

Galilee

92

ISRAEL'S KITCHEN AT ARBEL GUEST HOUSE

SEE "TIBERIAS" MAP

7717

77

Tiberias

TOMB OF RABBI MEIR

EIN GEV HOLIDAY RESORT

768

98

90

Kinneret

767

RIVER BISTRO BAR

YARDENIT

Ma-agan

92

98

90

0   2.5 mi

0   2.5 km

THE GALILEE

Tiberias and the Sea of Galilee

Tiberias is a medium-size town of about 40,000 on the western shore of the Sea of Galilee and the largest town on the Galilee. It caters to domestic and international tourists, though some of its ancient sites are abandoned or not well preserved. It has been continuously occupied for thousands of years, and has historical and religious sites of Christian, Jewish, and Muslim origin in the town and nearby. The majority of the population is Jewish, and at more than 656 feet below sea level, it is the lowest city in Israel and gets extremely hot and humid in the summer.

The Sea of Galilee has an extremely narrow strip of land along most of the eastern shore that is on the Israeli side of the 1949 Israeli-Syrian armistice line. Most activities on the eastern shore include water sports and outdoor adventures. Past the 1949 line toward Syria is the territory known as the Golan.

HISTORY

Believed to be one of the earliest settlements dating back to the early Bronze Age in the land known today as Israel, Tiberias was named in honor of the Roman emperor in AD 18. Following the destruction of the Second Temple in Jerusalem, many Jews fled to Tiberias and the city eventually became an important center of religious Jewish learning. Tiberias is where the Mishnah, a commentary on the Torah, is believed to have been put together by powerful rabbis of the day. The Jewish Great Rabbinical Court was also located in Tiberias.

Key to the city's development is the nearby natural hot springs, renowned for its curative and therapeutic properties. Throughout the ages, Tiberias became known as one of Judaism's four holy cities.

The area around the Sea of Galilee is also deeply important to Christians. At a certain

© GENEVIEVE BELMAKER

the Sea of Galilee from the shores of Capernaum

THE GALILEE

point in his life, Jesus is believed to have moved his base of activities to the northern shore of the Galilee, where several widely recognized miracles took place, including the multiplication of the bread and fish for the masses, and walking on water. The significance of Jesus' activities here led to the establishment of many churches in the area after Christianity began to spread.

SIGHTS

Many of the more remarkable and interesting sights in Tiberias are just to the north, while the main attractions of the town itself center around the beautiful, long waterfront promenade with its many restaurants and cafés. Near the black, basalt walls of the old city you'll see some ruins that are abandoned and lack any explanation of their history. Most of the sites in the area are Christian holy sites and burial sites of Jewish sages.

Tomb of Rabbi Akiva

Just up the mountainside behind the Kiryat Moshe neighborhood of Tiberias is the small, domed **Tomb of Rabbi Akiva** (off Yohanan Ben Zakai St., on Trumpeldor St. north of town center, 24 hours daily, reception hours vary, free), a Jewish sage born in AD 50 who was killed for supporting the Bar Kochba revolt. The tomb has long been a pilgrimage site, where devout believers pray for rain during drought years.

Tomb of Maimonides

Near the Tomb of Rabbi Akia is the final

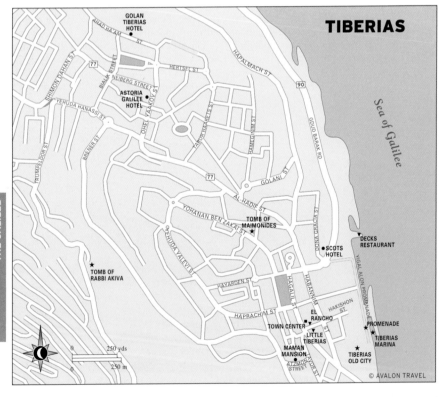

THE BLACK STONES OF TIBERIAS

While visiting Tiberias and the surrounding region, you'll likely notice that many of the buildings are constructed with an unusual black stone. The stone is volcanic black basalt, typical of the region and common in Tiberias and nearby, particularly in the older buildings.

The old tradition of using black basalt stone to construct buildings is fading away in modern times due to the need for buildings to be more durable and less susceptible to damage during earthquakes. Though the black basalt is beautiful and unique, it is not as safe or durable as modern building materials.

The old city of Tiberias is easy to distinguish from the newer area of the city by the clear demarcation of medieval black basalt walls and the contrasting white plaster in between the stones.

resting place of a popular sage and philosopher. The **Tomb of Maimonides** (just off of off Yohanan Ben Zakai St., north of Tiberias town center, 24 hours daily, free) is known as a place to pray for good fortune, especially for a family. Also known as Ramban, Maimonides was employed in the court of the revered Muslim leader Saladin as his physician. The site features a symbolic walkway to the tomb with seven columns on each side with religious inscriptions and a stream of water next to them. There is a large metal structure covering the tomb complex that symbolizes a crown, a mark of respect in Jewish tradition.

Tomb of Rabbi Meir

The resting place of another sage and one of Judaism's holiest sites is the **Tomb of Rabbi Meir** (south end of Tiberias near Ha'Marchatzaot Rd., just below the Tiberias hot springs, 8am-5pm Sun.-Thurs., 8am-2pm Fri., free), a Sephardic tomb with a blue-domed roof that overlooks the Galilee. Meir's nickname Ba'al Haneis means "miracle worker," based on a legend that he saved his sister-in-law from the Romans with a single prayer. Jews around the world give charity in Rabbi Meir's name, and his tomb is a popular place for religious Jews to celebrate the first haircut of their three-year-old boys and pray for divine intervention. Every year, one month after Passover and four days before the holiday of Lag b'Omer, thousands of believers flock to the tomb and light huge bonfires.

Marina and Old City

Along the shore of the Sea of Galilee in Tiberias is the lively and bustling **marina** that is full of restaurants, shops, and beautiful views. The boats docked in the marina used to sell regular rides across the Sea of Galilee, but in recent years the tradition has declined and now it is almost impossible to hire a ride on the water.

The **old city** sits at the southern end of town and consists of a partial wall and a few buildings mixed in with the modern architecture. The end of the old city marks the beginning of the promenade.

Dona Gracia Hotel and Museum

A former castle holds the **Dona Gracia Hotel and Museum** (3 Haprachim St., 04/671-7176, www.donagracia.com), dedicated to a Jewish woman named Dona Gracia, who used her wealth to save many Jews from the Spanish inquisition and establish a Jewish city in Tiberias. The different halls of the museum tell Gracia's story using scenery, visuals, and audio, and the main exhibit uses miniatures to depict different scenes. It is possible to request to dress in one of the hotel-museum's 16th-century-style costumes for a souvenir picture.

Tabgha

Tabgha is a Greek word that means seven springs. In a cove on the northwestern shore of the Sea of Galilee is **Tabgha** (Rte. 87, Ginosar), known for being where many miracles recorded in the Bible occurred, including the miracle of

THE GALILEE

© GENEVIEVE BELMAKER

the interior of the Church of the Multiplication

Jesus multiplying three loaves of bread and two fish into enough to feed 5,000.

The event is marked by the **Church of the Multiplication** (04/670-0180, 10am-5pm Sun., 8:30am-5pm Mon.-Sat., free), a Christian church with a very simple interior that is a replica of a 4th-century basilica, with an outer courtyard and fish pond. The highlights of the church include a famed mosaic floor of a basket of bread flanked by two fish, and a rock underneath the church's main altar, which is believed to be the actual rock that Jesus blessed and broke the bread on.

From the church you can walk along a promenade about 200 yards to the very simple and boxy black basalt **Church of the Primacy of St. Peter** (04/672-4767, 8am-noon and 2pm-5pm daily, free), the site where Jesus is said to have appeared to his disciples after his resurrection and forgiven Peter for denying him on the night of his trial. The church is built over a flat rock called the Table of Christ where it's believed a fire was lit for Jesus to have breakfast with his disciples. The church is also at the

site where the miraculous catch of fish is said to have occurred.

◖ Mount of Beatitudes

Situated atop the **Mount of Beatitudes,** where Jesus is believed to have given the sermon on the mount, is a gray-domed **Roman-Catholic church** (Rte. 8177, off Rte. 90, 04/679-0978, 8am-noon and 2:30pm-5pm daily Apr.-Sept., 8am-noon and 2:30pm-4pm daily Oct.-Mar., NIS5 parking per car), surrounded by colonnaded walkways at the end of a garden.

The gardens are dotted with fountains and decorative tablets inscribed with excerpts from the sermon, and the hillside slopes down toward the Galilee, forming a natural amphitheater. This is where people believe Jesus gave the sermon, and there are plenty of benches and places to sit in the gardens and look out over the sea and quietly contemplate the surroundings.

The interior of the church is small and simple but very beautiful, with a beautiful gold-ceilinged dome and a colonnaded portico that looks out over the Galilee. The site is run by

© GENEVIEVE BELMAKER

"LET ANYONE WHO THIRST COME TO ME AND DRINK WHOEVER BELIEVES IN ME AS SCRIPTURE SAYS RIVERS OF LIVING WATER FLOW FROM WITHIN JML" (Jn. 7:37)

a tablet with the teaching of Jesus in the garden of the Mount of Beatitudes

incredibly warm and friendly nuns who are available to answer questions.

ℂ Capernaum

A large parking lot by the Galilee and a long path leads to **Capernaum** (off Rte. 87 north of Tiberias, 04/672-1059, 8:30am-11:30am and 3:30pm-4:45pm daily, NIS3), one of the most astonishing sites in the area. Something about the ruins, which include remarkable foundations and colonnades and even seats of an ancient synagogue, evoke a living feeling of the ancient past.

Not far from the foundation of the synagogue is the remains of a large limestone relief that used to be on the exterior of the synagogue. The detailed carved pictures on the stone include typical religious Jewish symbols and images of a synagogue.

Capernaum is the town where Jesus is said to have lived for three years and performed numerous miracles, including healing Peter's mother-in-law and raising the synagogue leader's daughter from the dead.

A modern church sits above the ruins of a church that was built on the site of Peter's house. You can see the ruins of the old church and its mosaic floor through a glass viewing floor. Throughout the site you can see small pieces of white paper with prayers written on them that have been folded up and placed in areas that are considered holy.

Capernaum is relatively small and easy to walk about; it includes an information desk and a snack shop. Modest dress is required: Keep your shoulders and legs covered.

Monastery of the Twelve Apostles

Just down the road from Capernaum is the Greek Orthodox **Monastery of the Twelve Apostles** (Rte. 87 at Kfar Nahum Junction, 04/672-2282, capernaum1@gmail.com, 10am-5pm daily but call in advance because hours vary, free), noticeable by its unusual pink domed roof. The church isn't large, but its interior is remarkably detailed, and every inch of the walls seems to be adorned with paintings of the 12 apostles and scenes from their lives.

THE GALILEE

ruins of the ancient synagogue at Capernaum

THE GALILEE

interior of the Monastery of the Twelve Apostles

Yardenit

At the point where the Jordan River starts to flow out of the Sea of Galilee is the **Yardenit** baptismal site (Kibbutz Kinneret off Rte. 90, 04/675-9111, www.yardenit.com, 8am-6pm Sun.-Thurs., 8am-4pm Fri. Mar.-Nov., 8am-5pm Sun.-Thurs., 8am-4pm Fri. Dec.-Feb., last baptism one hour before closing, closed on Yom Kippur, free entrance, $10 robe rental). A large limestone building marks the entrance, and baptisms can be performed in the river or in the baptismal pools, though you should bring something to wear underneath if you plan on wearing a baptism robe. There are changing facilities, a gift shop, and snacks on site. The general atmosphere of Yardenit is a bit commercial and touristy, though scores of pilgrims do visit every year to enter the waters. This is one location on the Jordan River that claims to be the site where Jesus was baptized by John.

ENTERTAINMENT AND EVENTS

There is not a lot to speak of when it comes to entertainment and events in and around Tiberias. It is a fairly low-key area, but one exception is the annual **Jacob's Ladder Festival** (Ginosar, 04/685-0403, www.jlfestival.com, May, NIS225 and up), a three-day festival of food, wine, and live music in Ginosar, just a 15-minute drive up the Galilee shore from Tiberias.

SHOPPING

Tiberias is a good place to do a bit of shopping if you need clothes, shoes, or other basic items.

Once you get to the **Town Center** (you'll know it by the long outdoor chairs and counters under the covered sidewalk promenade), you can find a surprising variety of shops and stores at reasonable prices. Near the marina and promenade, the shopping is concentrated around the town's main streets, Hagalil and HaBannim. You can find everything from shoe stores to small grocery stores to national chain stores such as Fox, and souvenir shops.

SPORTS AND RECREATION
Parks and Nature Reserves

Boasting 17 natural hot springs that have long been renowned for their health benefits, **Hamat Tiberias National Park** (Rte. 7677, 20 minutes south of Tiberias, 04/672-5287, 8am-5pm daily Apr.-Sept., 8am-4pm daily Oct.-Mar., last entry one hour before closing, adult NIS14, child NIS7) is worth venturing out of Tiberias to see. Inside the park you will find a synagogue with a mosaic floor built between 286 and 337 BC, and the **Hammam Suleiman Museum** inside an ancient Turkish bathhouse at the entrance.

Beaches

There are two important things to note about the beaches on the Galilee. One is that even if you are a strong swimmer, stick to designated beaches that have lifeguards. Even though it just looks like a big lake, there is a notoriously strong undertow and swimmers at unsupervised beaches have drowned. The other thing is that in recent years there has been a proliferation of privatized beaches, so many beaches are completely restricted. Others charge for entrance. Wherever you are in the area, just ask locals in the shops and restaurants for directions to the best beaches.

Noting the dangers and restrictions of beach access in the area, most swimming beaches are located on the eastern shore of the Galilee. Among them are the well-maintained **Ein Gev Beach** (Kibbutz Ein Gev, Gev on the eastern shore of the Sea of Galilee, 04/665-8008, adult NIS30, child NIS25), adjacent to a restroom, lockers, and changing rooms. Another option just south of Tiberias is the very popular **Tzemach Beach** (southern tip of the Sea of Galilee off Hwy. 90, 04/675-2440 or 052/303-3777, 9am-5pm Sun.-Thurs. or call in advance for groups on weekends, NIS 55, NIS70 for night and day lodging). There are tons of events here in the summer, beach umbrellas, and water sports galore, and it's an easy drive if you're staying in a hotel in Tiberias.

THE GALILEE

© GENEVIEVE BELMAKER

Shops line the covered plaza on the main street in the Town Center of Tiberias.

THE GALILEE

On the Water

In the past couple of years, it has become increasingly difficult to spontaneously hop on a boat in the Tiberias marina for a ride around the Sea of Galilee, especially in the low season. Your best bet is to inquire at one of the upscale hotels, such as the Scots Hotel, on the waterfront, about possible boat trips. Otherwise, you can try **Jesus Boats** (Tiberias Marina, 057/775-8562, www.jesusboats.com, inquire for price).

Expeditions

Just south of Tiberias you can take a carriage ride into the Galilean countryside for a two-hour adventure with **Jordan Carriages** (near the entrance to Kibbutz Kinneret off Rte. 90 south, 052/370-1662, merkavot@nana.co.il, year-round, adult NIS60, child NIS50, book in advance). The carriages are not plush by any means, but the experience includes stops along the way in the Jordan Valley for things like baking pita bread, walks across rope bridges, and other activities.

It gets super hot and humid during the summer months, but riding a **bicycle** around town is highly recommended as a fun way to see the area. Some hotels rent out bicycles by the day, try the **Aviv Hotel and Hostel** (66 HaGalil St. in town center, 04/672-3510, NIS40 and up). Just remember to start early and drink a lot of water.

There are a wide variety of other sporting and countryside adventures that you can take while in the area of Tiberias and the Sea of Galilee. A long list of possibilities can be found at www.zimmeril.com.

ACCOMMODATIONS

The town of Tiberias alone has a range of about 30 different accommodations, from youth hostels to luxury hotels, with most options on or within easy walking distance to the beach or the promenade, restaurants, and shopping. Near Tiberias, around the shore of the Sea of Galilee, other options range from *zimmers* (rooms to rent) to camping.

© GENEVIEVE BELMAKER

Jesus Boats offers trips on the Sea of Galilee.

Under US$100

Located in Old Town Tiberias, **Maman Mansion** (Atzmon St. in Schunat Achva Atzmon, 04/679-2986, www.maman-mansion. co.il, US$83 d) doesn't have much, but what they have is pretty choice, including an outdoor pool, a great view of the Sea of Galilee, bike rentals, and free parking and Wi-Fi. The small hotel houses 23 rooms in a 19th-century building. The rooms are bright, air-conditioned rooms with a TV. There is also a garden and chapel.

It is very bare bones on creature comforts, but **Aviv Hostel** (66 Hagalil St., 04/672-3510, www.aviv-hotel.co.il, US$60 d) fits the bill nicely for a clean, quiet, centrally-located place to stay in Tiberias. The hostel shares restaurant facilities with its more upscale sister hotel next door, where your included breakfast is served from a massive, gourmet spread. The rooms include a kitchen with a small fridge, private bathrooms, free parking, and balconies and views of the Sea of Galilee. It's a pretty good bang for your buck, especially if you're on a tight budget.

US$100-150

For the price, the family-run **Restal Hotel** (Yehuda Halevi St., 04/679-0555, www.restal. co.il, US$135 d) is a comfortable fit for a couple nights' stay in the center of Tiberias. The recently refurbished hotel has an outdoor swimming pool and modern decor with wood floors and a flat-screen TV in the rooms. The hotel is on the larger side, with 174 rooms, a bar, a 24-hour front desk, and a fitness center. There is free Wi-Fi in all public areas.

On the hillside in central Tiberias and close to shops, restaurants, and 20 minutes by foot to the Sea of Galilee, the **Berger Hotel** (27 Neiberg St., 04/671-5151, www.bergerhotel. co.il, US$107 d) is a medium-size hotel that feature balconies with view of the city in most of the rooms. Kitchenette rooms are available on request at booking, and rooms include cable TV with international channels, a private

THE GALILEE

bathroom, and a telephone for incoming calls. There is also a restaurant, 24-hour front desk, and free Wi-Fi in public areas.

Overlooking Tiberias, the **Astoria Galilee Hotel** (13 Ohel Yaakov St., 04/672-2351/2, www.astoria.co.il, US$103 d) is one of the oldest hotels in Tiberias, and about 20 minutes by foot to the seashore. The hotel has 88 rooms, free Wi-Fi, and modern updated rooms. There is also an outdoor pool, table tennis, and a sauna. The location makes it convenient to hop out of town and explore nearby sights and towns, including Safed and the Jordan River.

On the eastern shore of the Galilee, the **Ein Gev Holiday Resort** (Kibbutz Ein Gev, 04/665-8035, tourist department 04/665-8030, www.eingev.com, US$104 d) not only has extremely reasonable rates and is in an idyllic location, it can accommodate families and groups. Ein Gev, with a total of 166 rooms, is set up as a series of cabins spread over the grounds plus 40 rooms situated around the hotel's reception area in the main building. Ein Gev's specialty is organized tours for international visitors. Situated in the oldest kibbutz on the Galilee, their restaurant is famous for their St. Peter's fish. They offer free Wi-Fi, comfortably furnished (though not fancy) rooms, and special offers throughout the year on their website. There is a game room, a playground, a spa treatment room, and beachfront access.

Karei Deshe Youth Hostel & Guest House (D.N. Hevel Korazim, 02/594-5633, www.iyha.org.il, US$100 d) is a youth hostel on the western shore of the Galilee with a private beach, just about 20 minutes north of Tiberias. It has an inner courtyard, buffet breakfast, basketball court, and Wi-Fi. Rooms here book incredibly far in advance, even during the low season. It is near the Yardenit baptismal site at the Jordan River and hot water springs. The rooms come either as dormitories or private rooms with private bathrooms. There is a walking path nearby that leads through four major sites in the area: the Church of the Multiplication, the Mount of Beatitudes, Capernaum, and the Monastery of the Twelve Apostles.

US$150-200

With an outdoor pool overlooking the Sea of Galilee and a hot tub, the **Golan Hotel** (14 Ahad Ha'Am St., 04/671-1555, www.golanhotel.co.il, US$150 d) is just at the northern end of Tiberias. There's also a fitness center with a gym and sauna where guests can book massages and other treatments. With almost 100 rooms, the Golan Hotel also has a 24-hour front desk, garden, and terrace.

Just about 15 minutes north of Tiberias, the **Nof Ginosar Hotel** (off of Rte. 90 north just before Ginosar, 04/670-0320, www.ginosar.co.il, US$200 d) is a resort-style hotel on the western shore of the Galilee with a private beach and extensive grounds that are part of Kibbutz Ginosar. The hotel is arranged in an unusual style with a 161-room hotel plus a holiday village nearby with 75 ground-floor rooms spread out throughout the area and an outdoor pool. The complex also has basketball and tennis courts and a jogging track that runs along a river. The friendly, English-speaking hotel staff can also help arrange excursions into the surrounding area.

Over US$200

Ramot Resort Hotel (eastern Sea of Galilee, 04/673-2636, www.ramotresort.com, US$210 d) is more like a resort compound of cabins than a hotel. Just at the foot of the Golan, the hotel has 123 rooms spread out through cabins and chalets on grounds that overlook the Galilee through a canopy of palm trees. The rooms in the cabins are like small houses, with most of the amenities of home, including a kitchen, coffee service, a flat-screen TV, and huge, comfy beds. The area has hiking trails, and you can drive about 30 minutes south around the shore of the Galilee to reach Tiberias. The hotel sells out for the coming summer at least six months or more in advance.

One of the most prestigious and popular hotels in Tiberias, ◖ **The Scots Hotel** (1 Gdud Barak Rd., www.scotshotels.co.il, 04/671-0710, US$375 d) is situated just steps away from the promenade that runs along the Sea of Galilee. It is in a historic building that used to be a

The Scots Hotel

hospital, and has been remade into a medium-size hotel with some rooms that have views of the water. The hotel's restaurant serves gourmet food, and there is a wine cellar and art gallery on site. You can also take advantage of the outdoor pool, in-room breakfast, currency exchange desk, and an ATM. Wi-Fi costs an extra US$18.

It only has 11 rooms, but the **Shirat Hayam Boutique Hotel**'s (Yigal Alon Promenade, 04/672-1122, US$270 d) pretty exterior and charming location on the Tiberias promenade makes it a hot commodity. The rooms and suites all have an LCD cable TV, a fridge, and a tea kettle. The 19th-century building has been equipped to also allow for hot tubs and balconies in some suites and there is room service and a 24-hour front desk.

Beach Camping

The shores of the Sea of Galilee make a great place for camping, especially during the summer months when the weather is extremely warm. Most of them have some kind of entrance fee, which varies, but is generally about NIS20 per night. It is best to call the campground in advance and verify their entrance fee and hours of operation.

Along the eastern shore of the Sea of Galilee, some campsites that include amenities like running water, toilets, and showers are **Gofra Beach** (04/673-1942), **Halukim Beach** (04/673-2185), **Duga Beach** (04/673-1214), and **Sussita Beach** (04/665-8199).

At the northern end of the Sea of Galilee is **Amnon Beach** (northern tip of the Sea of Galilee near the Amnun 2000 Recreation Village, 050/710-3420), and on the western shore is **Tamar Beach** (western shore of the Sea of Galilee, near Ginosar and 15 minutes north of Tiberias, 04/679-0630 and 050/585-2101).

FOOD
Fine Dining

If you're looking for gourmet dining and romantic atmosphere at its very best while in Tiberias, **Decks Restaurant** (Gdud Barak St., Tiberias,

THE GALILEE

© GENEVIEVE BELMAKER

Decks Restaurant has a fine spot on the water.

© GENEVIEVE BELMAKER

04/672-1538, decks@barak.net.il, 7pm-after midnight, Sun.-Thurs., one hour after sunset-after midnight Sat., NIS100, reservations needed) should be your first stop. Their meticulous attention to detail includes grilling meat cooked over citrus, olive, and other kinds of wood. The restaurant's interior features a long deck that extends out over the Galilee; the deck is covered in the winter. It's an especially good place for a romantic meal, though it's easy to rack up a large bill.

Israeli Kitchen Cooking

A wide variety of customers from locals to tourists frequent **Little Tiberias** (2 HaKishon St., Tiberias, 04/679-2806, http://littletiberias.rest-e.co.il, noon-midnight daily, NIS80). Tucked into a building that forms part of the wall of the old city, it is just off the town's main street and next door to a score of other options. The interior is modern and has a homey feeling. One of their specialties is a beef stroganoff. The types of dishes that are served here include standards that can be found in Israeli kitchens: schnitzel, cucumber and tomato salad, pita, and more.

Kibbutz Dining

Located on one of the oldest kibbutzim in the area, Kibbutz Ein Gev's restaurant **Marinado at the Port** (Kibbutz Ein Gev, 057/944-4106, http://marinadoattheport.rest-e.co.il, noon-last customer Sun.-Thurs., noon-one hour before sunset Fri., NIS90) has an incomparable view if you dine outside. Not only are you sitting on the waterfront, you are in a semi-private, idyllic setting. The restaurant itself is nothing fancy in its interior and general presentation, and serves the typical seafood fare of the area, including whole St. Peter's fish. There is tons of seating indoors and outdoors. The only real problem with Marinado is that it's difficult to tear yourself away, especially if you go around sunset.

Mediterranean

A family restaurant and one of the best known in town with an extremely loyal customer base, **Avi's Restaurant** (1 HaKishon St., Tiberias, 04/679-1797, noon-midnight Sun.-Thurs., one hour after sunset-midnight Sat., NIS55) serves Israeli-style meat and vegetarian dishes, and free mezze (appetizers). Their specialty is meat dishes and the owner will probably send more food to your table than you can eat. The homey environment of Avi's (which is the name of the owner) includes arched windows, stone walls, stained glass windows, and a large aquarium.

Though you probably wouldn't want to leave Tiberias just to eat here, **Israel's Kitchen at Arbel Guest House** (Arbel Village just west of Tiberias on Rte. 7717, 04/679-4919, 7:30pm-last customer daily, www.4shavit.com/infoen.htm, NIS120, call in advance for reservation) is fine dining in a country farmhouse atmosphere, set in a small village north of the city. Known for their delicious meat dishes and fresh ingredients in an idyllic garden setting, Arbel mainly exists to feed their guests, but will usually accommodate outside customers.

Middle Eastern

A Lebanese restaurant with friendly staff that caters to families, **Ktze Hanahal** (Kibbutz Ginosar, off Rte. 90 north, 04/671-7776, 9:30am-9:30pm Sun.-Thurs., 9:30am-midnight Fri.-Sat., NIS70) is situated in the middle of a kibbutz about 15 minutes north of Tiberias. The restaurant's dishes blend local Galilee-style food with Lebanese home cooking. The food is served in large portions, which are best enjoyed family style.

If you're heading out of Tiberias, just 15 minutes to the north is the Lebanese-style **Tanureen** (off Rte.90 north at Migdal Crossroads, 04/671-2896, noon-midnight daily, NIS85), which serves seafood and meat prepared in a distinctively Middle Eastern style. Some of their specialties include grilled eggplant and Lebanese-style kebab. The restaurant's interior is spacious, modern, and upscale. It's perhaps not exactly what you'd expect to find off the beaten path.

Another one of Kibbutz Ginosar's offerings is **Katzeh Ha'Nahal** (Kibbutz Ginosar entrance on Kinneret Rd., off Rte. 90 north, 04/671-7776, noon-midnight daily, NIS70), dubbed authentic Lebanese and Jordanian cuisine even by the locals. The specialty of Katzeh Ha'Nahal is their kebab preparation, put together while you watch. A fun feature of the restaurant is the playroom where weary parents can deposit their kids; the atmosphere is generally family friendly and simple.

Seafood

Both family run and family friendly, **Galei Gil Restaurant** (Old Promenade, Tiberias, 04/672-0699, 11am-3pm Sun.-Thurs., 7pm-last customer Fri.-Sat., NIS60) is one of the oldest seafood restaurants in Tiberias, and is known for its Tilapia fish cooked over coals. Conveniently located in the town center on the shores of the Galilee with a view of the water, it has a welcoming and warm atmosphere. The menu is reasonably priced, and you should easily get your fill of food.

Steaks and Burgers

Specializing in South American-style meats, the kosher **C El Rancho**'s (3 HaKishon St., 04/672-0946, www.2eat.co.il/elrancho, noon-last evening customer Sun.-Thurs., noon-3pm Fri., NIS80) claim to fame is that they serve the best steak in Israel, and everyone knows it. While their steak is very well done, it is typical by American standards. The friendly staff is accommodating and upbeat, and the interior is huge with exposed brick walls and wood touches, giving it a ranch house feeling. The final touch is bottles of Israeli wine on display.

If you happen to have taken an afternoon to visit the baptismal site at Yardenit, stop off at the **River Bistro Bar** (Yardenit, Kibbutz Kinneret, 057/944-3619, onhadas@walla.co.il, 7pm-3am daily, NIS75) afterward for dinner. The combination of going to a riverside bar and grill after visiting the possible baptismal site of Jesus might seem odd, but it is one of the few decent options in the area. The interior has high, cabana-like ceilings and tables are lined up against huge windows. The centerpiece is the bar, with its wide variety of alcoholic drinks and several types of beer on tap. The kitchen at the River Bistro Bar is obsessed with hamburgers, so your best bet here is probably a burger and a beer.

INFORMATION

The most useful online information about Tiberias, the Golan, and the Sea of Galilee can be found on the websites of the **Israel Ministry of Tourism** (www.goisrael.com) and the **Golan and Galilee Tourism Foundation** (www.gogalilee.com). The independent, tourist-minded **Go Visit Israel** (www.govisitisrael.com) has tons of useful information in a simple format. The website is a bit harder to navigate, but **Zimmer** (www.zimmer.co.il) has extremely helpful information from locals.

GETTING THERE AND AROUND
By Car

Tiberias is located about two hours north of Jerusalem by car. Most of the drive is along Highway 6, which skirts the West Bank. It is about 90 minutes from Tel Aviv, also mostly along Highway 6.

Once you are in the area, Tiberias makes an excellent base to travel to other sites and towns along the shore of the Sea of Galilee, which has a circumference of only about 31 miles. With a car, you can easily leave your hotel in the late morning, see several sites at a leisurely pace, and be back in time for an early dinner. Tiberias itself is not that large and is very easy to navigate.

By Bus

You can travel to Tiberias from Jerusalem by **Egged** bus (www.egged.co.il, bus 963 or 962, NIS42 one-way) in about 2.5 hours. From Tel Aviv (bus 835 or 841, NIS42 one-way), it is approximately a three-hour trip.

Once in Tiberias, there are city buses and some bus companies that operate exclusively in the north of Israel. In Tiberias call *6686 from a local phone, or check out a useful alternative (in English) for buses anywhere in the country, **Bus.Co.Il** (www.bus.co.il), which provides detailed transportation information and timetables for Tiberias and the surrounding areas.

Nazareth and Vicinity

Nazareth is an important city to both religious Christians and Arabs, and its main draw for visitors is religious sites. Built up the side of a mountain, Nazareth's streets become increasingly steep and narrow the higher up you go, and it is an incredibly difficult city to navigate. With a predominately Arab population, Nazareth is also home to good Middle Eastern restaurants, an Arab *shuk* (outdoor market), and an old city region.

SIGHTS
The Old City Market

In the course of visiting sites in Nazareth, you'll find yourself in the **Old City,** which includes a **market** (04/601-1072, board@nazarethboard.org, 9am-5pm Mon.-Fri., 9am-2pm Sat.) and a grouping of about 100 very impressive **Ottoman period homes.** You might also come upon the 18th-century **Saraya or Government House** (top of Aliyah Bet St.), built by a famous governor of the Galilee in 1740 as his summer home and currently undergoing renovations to become the Museum of Nazareth.

Nazareth Village

A careful recreation of life in Nazareth during biblical times, **Nazareth Village** (5079 St. in the Old City, opposite the French Hospital, 04/645-6042, www.nazarethvillage.com, 9am-5pm Mon.-Sat., last tour at 3pm, adult NIS50, child NIS22, senior NIS34) is something similar to a living and breathing museum with guides in period dress who lead you through what life was like 2,000 years ago in Nazareth.

◖ Basilica of the Annunciation

The **Basilica of the Annunciation** (southwestern corner of the Old City, 04/657-2501, www.basilicanazareth.org, 8am-5pm Mon.-Sat.

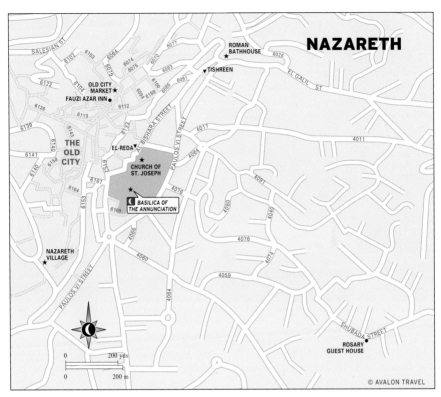

NAZARETH

ROMAN BATHHOUSE

TISHREEN

EL GALIL ST

OLD CITY MARKET
FAUZI AZAR INN

SALESIAN ST

THE OLD CITY

EL-REDA

CHURCH OF ST. JOSEPH

BASILICA OF THE ANNUNCIATION

AL-BISHARA STREET

PAULUS VI STREET

NAZARETH VILLAGE

PAULUS VI STREET

SHUBADA STREET

ROSARY GUEST HOUSE

0   200 yds

0   200 m

© AVALON TRAVEL

Oct.-Mar., 8am-6pm daily Apr.-Sept., modest dress, free) is one of the largest churches in the Middle East. It is a bit difficult to find it on your own, as it's located about halfway up the mountainside of very steep and narrow roads. It's best to reach it with a tour group or via a taxi.

The Catholic church was established in 1969, and built on the site of what is believed to be the Virgin Mary's original home. The cavernous, two-story church engulfs a cave and the remains of previous churches, including a stone wall behind the cave from a 12th-century Crusader church. There are two stories to the church, with the upper level overlooking the main worship area.

One of the most engaging and dynamic features in the church, on the walls and throughout the massive courtyard surrounding the building, is an extensive collection of mosaic paintings from all over the world, each depicting scenes of the Virgin Mary with baby Jesus.

St. Gabriel's Church

One of the loveliest among the many churches in town, the Greek Orthodox **St. Gabriel's Church** (Paulus VI St., 04/656-8488, www. nazarethinfo.org, 8am-noon and 2pm-5pm Mon.-Sat., free) is just at the entrance to the city as you are coming from the north. This is the spot where, according to the Greek Orthodox tradition, Gabriel announced the future birth of Christ to the Virgin Mary. The church has a high, arched ceiling, and between the colonnades the ceiling is painted with religious images against a blue backdrop.

THE GALILEE

© GENEVIEVE BELMAKER

The Basilica of the Annunciation, one of the largest churches in the Middle East, was built on the site believed to be the original home of the Virgin Mary.

Church of Saint Joseph

The **Church of Saint Joseph** (northwestern corner of the Old City near the Basilica of the Annunciation, 04/657-2501, www.nazarethinfo.org, 8am-5pm Mon.-Sat. Oct.-Mar., 8am-6pm Mon.-Sat. Apr.-Sept., free) is said to be built over the carpentry workshop of Joseph, Jesus's father. The Franciscan church now on the site was established in 1914 over the ruins of older churches and the lower level has an ancient water pit, mosaics, caves, and barns from ancient Nazareth of the 1st and 2nd centuries BC.

Roman Bathhouse

The beginnings of the Cactus souvenir shop in 1993 brought with it the discovery of the **Roman Bathhouse** (Mary's Well Square under the Cactus souvenir shop, 04/657-8539, www.nazarethbathhouse.org, 9am-7pm Mon.-Sat., NIS120 for private tours of up to four people), a 2,000-year-old bathhouse under the

shop. Excavations have revealed underground heating tunnels, a hot room, and furnace. The tour fee includes refreshments.

Megiddo National Park

One of Israel's several UNESCO World Heritage Sites, **Megiddo National Park** (Megiddo and Yokne'am Junctions on Rte. 66, 04/659-0316, 8am-5pm daily Apr.-Sept., 8am-4pm daily Oct.-Mar., last entry one hour before closing, NIS27) surrounds the ancient ruins of the biblical town Megiddo. A historically strategically important city that went from ruler to ruler throughout the ages, it is today a national park that makes for a relatively easy hike. Abandoned after the Persian period, Megiddo is identified with Armageddon, the scene of the battle of the End of Days according to Revelation 16:14-21. The park includes a souvenir shop, a museum with an audiovisual presentation, and guided tours by reservation. The site is good

© GENEVIEVE BELMAKER

© GENEVIEVE BELMAKER

Two of the depictions of the Virgin Mary and baby Jesus in the Basilica of the Annunciation are part of a collection from all over the world.

for visits year round and it takes about one to two hours to tour it.

Mount Precipice

Just about 1.5 miles outside of Nazareth is **Mount Precipice** (second exit off Rte. 60 south out of Nazareth), also known as the Mount of the Leap of the Lord, one of the city's highest points. Mount Precipice is where the people of Nazareth took Jesus to be thrown off the cliff. There is a viewing platform to see the landscape below, and at the same spot is the **Cave of the Leap,** a 50,000-year-old cave that has the remains of 13 human skeletons and over 15,000 artifacts from the Stone Age.

Zippori National Park

About three miles west of Nazareth is the well-laid out **Zippori National Park** (2.5 miles east of Hamovil junction on Rte. 79 between Hamovil junction and Nazareth, 04/656-8272, 8am-5pm daily Apr.-Sept., 8am-4pm daily

Oct.-Mar., last entry one hour before closing, adult NIS27, child NIS14), which is home to the ruins of a Crusader castle, foundations of a Byzantine church, and an excavated 4,500-seat Roman amphitheater. It is also home to several mosaic floorings, including the Mona Lisa of the Galilee, a remarkable depiction of a woman made from mosaic tiling. There is a visitor's center at the entrance. As you leave the park you can explore the water channel and cistern.

ACCOMMODATIONS US$100-150

Fauzi Azar Inn (6091 Al-Bishara in Old City Nazareth, near Tishreen Restaurant, 04/602-0469, www.fauziazarinn.com, US$115 d) is a small, 10-room guesthouse in Old City Nazareth that exudes Arab charm because of its location and the architecture of arched outer colonnades and cave-like rooms. Housed in a 200-year-old Arab mansion, the inn has free Wi-Fi, a common area terrace, and

THE GALILEE

air-conditioning. Located near the *shuk,* vegetable market, restaurants and coffee shops, and the Basilica of the Annunciation, it works well as a base to explore Nazareth.

Tabar Hotel (5053 El Mutran St., 04/608-5400, www.tabarhotel.com, US$130 d) is a 90-room, five-floor hotel on a hillside of a largely residential area overlooking the city of Nazareth. The hotel has a modern, clean, simple interior and every room has free Wi-Fi, air-conditioning, and private balconies with views of the city and the Jezreel Valley. The hotel has a restaurant and coffee bar, and is within walking distance to the Old City markets.

A bit off the beaten path, **Rosary Guest House** (6141/2 El-Dabas St., 04/655-4435, www.rsisters.com, US$130 d) is a restored monastery with 24 air-conditioned rooms that all have a balcony with garden views and a private bathroom. The Church of the Annunciation is a 10-minute walk away. The rooms are simply furnished, and there is free Wi-Fi and a TV in the shared lounge. You can book tours directly at the guesthouse and there is a chapel on site.

US$150-200

The **Golden Crown Old City Hotel** (16 Galilee St., 04/650-8000, www.goldencrown.co.il, US$150 d) is close to most major attractions in the Old City and has all the comforts of a mid-size hotel, including gorgeous city-view rooms with satellite TV, a restaurant, and free private parking. The rooms are sleek, modern, and upscale with free Wi-Fi, room service, and the option of having the included breakfast brought to your room.

Over US$200

Gardenia Nazareth Hotel (off of Old Afula Route Nazareth Rd., 073/211-5200, www.gardeniahotel.co.il, US$234 d) is a mid-size luxury hotel on the outskirts of Nazareth. The hotel's pastoral atmosphere, amidst pine trees and gardens with views of the Jezreel Valley, Mount Tabor, and Gilboa Heights, is only a 10-minute drive from crowded Nazareth. The hotel's rooms are comfortably equipped with large,

soft beds and updated, modern interiors. There is free Wi-Fi in public areas, a large outdoor pool, restaurant, playground, complimentary newspapers, and 24-hour front desk service.

FOOD
Middle Eastern

Just uphill from the Basilica of the Annunciation, **El-Reda** (21 Al-Bishara St., Old City Nazareth, 04/608-4404, 7pm-2am Sun., 1pm-2am Mon.-Sat., NIS55) is an Arab-style café with a great view and an atmosphere of authenticity. Dishes prepared by the owner, Dehar Zaidani, reflect his enthusiasm for regional cuisine. The slightly bohemian atmosphere of the El-Reda is amplified from time to time with live music and poetry.

Not far from Mary's Well is **Tishreen** (56 Al-Bishara St., 04/608-4666, noon-midnight daily, NIS110), an upscale Middle Eastern restaurant in Nazareth's Old City serving seafood, vegetarian dishes, and some tasty Arab-style pizza. Popular among locals for leisurely lunches and dinners, Tishreen's interior is muted and low-key.

A gorgeous, massive, stone-walled interior is the first thing you notice upon entering **Sudfeh** (Al-Bishara St., 04/656-6611, www.sudfeh.com, noon-midnight Mon.-Sat., 6pm-midnight Sun., NIS80), which is inside a former stone Arab house. The lively restaurant-bar has a creative selection of salads and local flavors in a European-style package. At just a 10 minutes' walk from the Basilica of the Annunciation, Sudfeh is an affordable, yet upscale, dining option that sometimes hosts live performances by local musicians.

When you're in the mood for a huge spread of Middle Eastern food, head to **Diana** (51 Paulos VI St., 04/657-2919, www.2eat.co.il/eng/diana, noon-midnight daily, NIS70), where you'll find unusual twists to common dishes, such as kebab on cinnamon sticks. Some of the ingredients used in the dishes are local to the Nazareth region. The lamb is particularly succulent and tender. Diana is a bit hard to find, so don't be shy about asking for directions, as it is well known.

© GENEVIEVE BELMAKER

the crowded hillside of Nazareth

GETTING THERE AND AROUND

By Car

Nazareth is located just under two hours north of Jerusalem by car. Most of the drive is along Highway 6, which skirts the West Bank. It is about an hour and 20 minutes from Tel Aviv, also mostly along Highway 6.

Driving within Nazareth is an incomparable nightmare, unless you are accustomed to extremely steep, narrow streets that are sometimes not clearly marked as one-way. Using a GPS in Nazareth to navigate can make matters worse because certain parts of the city are so tightly packed. Nazareth Illit, or Upper Nazareth, and the Old City area have many of the more

troublesome streets but also many of the major sights. If you must drive to Nazareth, park near the entrance to the city and take taxi cabs to your destinations.

By Bus

Getting to the center of Nazareth, near the Basilica of the Annunciation, from Jerusalem by **Egged** bus (www.egged.co.il, bus 955, NIS42 one-way) is just under 2.5 hours. From Tel Aviv, it takes three hours (bus 702, NIS37.5 one-way).

Once in Nazareth, you can take city buses **Bus.Co.Il** (www.bus.co.il) to get around. But it is always best to ask for specific information at the front desk of any hotel in town.

THE GALILEE

The Galilee

There are numerous sites and things to do scattered throughout the Galilee, but the main attractions are outdoor activities, such as hiking.

SIGHTS
Tsfat (Safed) and Vicinity

Tsfat (off Rte. 89 west, 04/692-4427, www.safed.co.il) is an ancient town in the Upper Galilee 3,200 feet above sea level with commanding views of the Golan, the Hermon, Lebanon, and Syria. About 40 minutes north of Tiberias, Tsfat is a great place for short hikes to archaeological sites, such as **Montfort Castle** (24 hours daily), the Crusader fortress at the top of the town. Tsfat is also considered the center of Jewish mysticism and one of Judaism's holy cities.

Jish

A small town about 40 minutes northwest of Tiberias, **Jish** (from Tiberias, take Rte. 90 and then Rte. 89) sits near Dalton Lake and has a few archaeological sites, two historical synagogues, and a unique mausoleum and burial caves.

Rosh Pina

A 120-year-old moshav situated on the northeastern slope of Mount Canaan overlooking the Hula Valley and the Golan, **Rosh Pina** (Rte. 90 about 30 minutes northeast of Tiberias) has a well-developed tourism industry that caters to high-end customers. It has a variety of restaurants and hotels. Farmers started the moshav in the late 1800s with the support of Baron Edmond de Rothschild. The town makes a good base for touring the upper Galilee and the Golan. Its historic **town center** has some spots worth exploring, including an audiovisual presentation about the town's history at the **House of Officials** (center of Rosh Pina, HaChalutzim St., also known as the Old Rosh Pina Office, 04/693-6603, 8:30am-5pm Sun.-Thurs. and 8:30am-1pm Fri.-Sat., NIS15).

Kiryat Shmona

In the heart of the Hula Valley, **Kiryat Shmona**'s (take Rte. 90 north, one hour from Tiberias) main attraction is the **scenic cable car** (Kibbutz Manara, Rte. 90, Kiryat Shmona, 04/690-5830, 9:30am-5pm daily Mar.-July and Sept.-Oct., 9:30am-7pm daily Aug., 11am-4pm daily Nov.-Feb., NIS59 weekdays and NIS69 weekends, last car is half an hour before closing). It is the longest cable car in Israel, going

THE JESUS TRAIL

Throughout the Galilee, there are scores of sights that were significant in the course of the life and teachings of Jesus. Even sights that have more obscure connections to Jesus are advertised as places where relatives of Jesus lived, worked, or were born. Some of the most significant points along the trail are Nazareth, Cana, Migdal, Tabgha, and Capernaum.

It is possible to have a guided experience along what has become known as the Jesus Trail, and literally walk in the footsteps of where Jesus is historically recorded to have lived, traveled, and spread his teachings.

The website **Jesus Trail** (http://jesustrail.com) provides a significant amount of information about hiking routes between biblical sites significant to Jesus and his activities in the Galilee region. A combination of ecotourism and religious tourism, the Jesus Trail covers several significant points between Nazareth and Capernaum. You can also take a self-guided tour that includes hiking guidance and pre-arranged accommodations along the way for six days and five nights.

© KOBBY DAGAN/123RF.COM

the ruins of Beit She'an

from Kiryat Shmona up to the cliffs of Kibbutz Manara. At the observation point at the top of the cable car is a restaurant, hiking path, and sports center.

◖ Beit She'an

Just at the southern edge of the Galilee where it meets the West Bank is 6,000-year-old **Beit She'an,** home to **ancient ruins** that are scattered throughout the modern city and home to **Beit She'an National Park** (off Shaul HaMelech St., Afula, www.parks.org.il/ ParksENG and www.gogalilee.org, 04/658-7189, 8am-5pm Sat.-Thurs. Apr.-Sept., 8am-4pm Sun.-Fri., 8am-5pm Sat. Oct.-Mar., NIS25).

Another of Israel's UNESCO World Heritage Sites, Beit She'an is one of the oldest cities of the Ancient Near East and sits at the crossroads to the Fertile Crescent. Incredibly, about 20 layers of settlement have been found at Beit She'an that go as far back as the 5th millennium BC. Beit She'an rose to its height under the Romans and the Byzantines before

being destroyed by an earthquake in AD 749. The colonnaded streets, a bathhouse, theater, and shrines were reconstructed in Beit She'an National Park.

You can pick up a free map at the entrance, and tour around this remarkable archaeological site that was known as Scythopolis during the late Roman and Byzantine periods (2nd-6th centuries AD). Excavations that started here in the 1960s revealed a **Roman Amphitheater.** More recent work to uncover the city has revealed a beautiful **downtown,** with colonnaded main streets, a central plaza, fountain, a Byzantine bathhouse, and more.

In the evenings, a few hours after the park closes, the park hosts a multi-media **night show** for an extra fee. The night show comes with the added benefit of enjoying the park when the sun and the temperature, which can get up to over 100°F in the summer, have gone down.

Beit Alpha Synagogue and Mosaic
The 6th-century **Beit Alpha Synagogue and Mosaic** (Kibbutz Heftziba, Rte. 669,

04/653-2004, 8am-4pm daily and until 5pm in the summer, adult NIS18, child NIS9) features a magnificent mosaic floor. It is considered simplistic compared to other mosaics in the region, but it is one of Israel's great archaeological treasures. One of the first archaeological discoveries in modern Israel, the mosaic has images from the zodiac arranged in reverse order, which does not correspond to the region's seasons.

◀ Gan Garoo Australia-Israel Park

One of the more unusual places you'll find in Israel is the four-acre **Gan Garoo Australia-Israel Park** (Kibbutz Nir David, off Rte. 669 at Gan Ha-Shlosha, 04/648-8080, 9am-4pm Mon.-Fri., 9am-5pm Sat., NIS40) in Beit She'an Valley. The park is full of a variety of Australian animals including kangaroos, flying foxes, cassowaries, koalas, and more.

In typical Israeli fashion, the operation isn't too tightly controlled, which makes it possible to mingle a bit with the animals and get a close look at wildlife that you might never see otherwise. The park is a nice change of pace from the ancient ruins, parks, and religious sites that dominate the area. It is also great fun for kids, though you might want to closely supervise any children with you.

ENTERTAINMENT AND EVENTS

The annual **She'an Nights Festival** (Beit She'an Foundation for Culture and Tourism, 04/658-8892, www.gogalilee.org, prices vary) is not to be confused with the She'an Nights multi-media show that runs in the evenings on a regular basis in Beit She'an National Park. The festival is held annually, usually around the time of Sukkot (Oct.) and includes food, wine, street performers, and music.

SPORTS AND RECREATION
Parks, Nature Reserves, and Mountains

Full of different outdoor pursuits from hiking to paragliding, **Mount Gilboa** is at the southernmost part of the Lower Galilee. Some of its features include the **Gilboa Iris Nature Reserve** (Mar.-Apr.), **hiking trails,** and a **scenic road** (Rte. 667) that includes places to stop and look at the vista.

Hula Nature Reserve (Upper Galilee, 04/681-7137 and 04/693-7069, www.agamon-hula.co.il, 9am-4pm Sun.-Thurs., 6:30am-4pm Fri.-Sat., depending on activity NIS20 and up) is a world-class site for observing nesting and migrating birds in a natural habitat. The reserve is right in the heart of the Hula Valley, and offers a wide range of activities for nature lovers, including guided night tours.

Noted for its exceptionally breathtaking view, **Mount Tabor** is about 30 minutes east of Nazareth, and is said to be the place of Jesus's transfiguration. On the mountaintop is the **Basilica of the Transfiguration** (04/673-2283, www.goisrael.com), a complex that includes a Greek Orthodox church and a gorgeous Franciscan church with a colonnaded interior of white stone and high ceilings. There are also Crusader and Byzantine ruins on the mountaintop.

More than just a nice, long cable car ride over the hills, **Manara Cliff** (Rte. 90, Kiryat Shmona, 04/690-5830, www.cliff.co.il and www.zimmeril.com, 10am-4pm Mon.-Thurs., call in advance because prices and hours of operation vary) is like a huge indoor-outdoor playground that also offers mountain slides, scenic trains, and bungee trampolines. Situated in the Upper Galilee with a view of the Hula Valley, a restaurant, and a sports center, Manara Cliff also offers a guided hiking tour of the area.

About 10 minutes from Tsfat, **Bat Ya'ar Ranch** (04/692-1788, www.batyaar.co.il) offers a variety of ranch-like activities, including short horseback rides, family activities, and a ranch house-style restaurant.

ACCOMMODATIONS
US$100-150

About 30 minutes east of Nazareth and west of Tiberias, the **Tabor Land Guest House** (Kfar Kisch, 050/544-1972, www.taborland.com, US$100 d) boasts views of the Jordanian Gilead Mountains to the east and Mount Tabor to the west. The accommodations are extremely simple with four rooms (some dormitory style). There is free Wi-Fi throughout the premises. The location is a good jumping-off point for hikes in the Lower Galilee. Guests can use the kitchen, garden, terrace, and living room with a TV and DVD player.

US$150-200

In a small village near Gan Garoo, Harod Spring Nature Reserve, and the incomparable Beit She'an National Park, **Gilboa Guest House Benharim** (top of Gidona Village, 050/336-0061, www.gilboaguesthouse.com, US$173 d) is a very simple, eight-room establishment with free Wi-Fi, an outdoor area equipped for barbecues, and an on-site wellness center. The plainly-decorated rooms have views of the Gilboa Mountains and include a TV. Some rooms are dormitory style with a shared bathroom, and there is a fully-equipped common kitchen and reading area.

Over US$200

Country luxury is the specialty of **Noach Batavor** (Kfar Kisch, 052/283-7397, www.zimmeril.com, US$236 d), located in the Kfar Kisch Moshav, and catering to couples. Three luxury wooden cabins include hot tubs, panoramic views of Mount Tabor, free Wi-Fi, and an LCD TV and DVD player. Every cabin has a kitchenette and luxury amenities like robes and slippers. The moshav has an olive oil plant with guided tours and tastings. Nearby attractions include the church on top of Mount Tabor and the Nahal Tabor Nature Reserve. It is a great area for outdoor sports including canoeing, hiking, biking, and horseback riding.

With only four rooms, booking a room well in advance at the extremely popular **Artists' Colony Inn Zefat** (9 Simtat Yud Zayin, Safed, 04/604-1101, www.artcol.co.il, US$210 d) is a must. The bed-and-breakfast is in a fully renovated stone villa with rooms that have been converted into comfortable, modern suites that include free Wi-Fi. Located in the artist colony district of the ancient city of Safed, the villa has a garden and terrace with views. All suites have a flat-screen TV, and there are free coffee and

snacks in the lobby. The International Centre for Tzfat Kabbalah is a 5-minute walk away, and it is 25 minutes by car to the Sea of Galilee.

FOOD
Cafés

The steady stream of tourists to Safed ensures that there are several options for places to eat, but none are quite as charming as the ◖ **Canaan Gallery Café** (47 Beit Yosef St., Safed, 04/697-4449, 10am-6:30pm Sun.-Thurs., 10am-3pm Fri., NIS30). Replete with music, art, and a scenic view, Canaan functions mainly as a coffee shop with some light food choices including sandwiches.

A relatively new kid on the block, **Haari 8** (8 Haari St., Safed, 04/692-0033, www.safed.co.il, 10am-10pm Sun.-Thurs., 10am-3pm Fri.) is a standout for its unusually warm and friendly service. This Mehadrin Kosher (extra Kosher) restaurant is just at the edge of the Old City. It is a convenient stop for an American-style hamburger for lunch after a morning of touring. The menu has other options, but the hamburger is the main attraction.

Mediterranean

If you're in the mood for an expedition that ends with a unique dining experience, try **Goats with the Wind** (near Moshav Yodfat, Har Hashabi, 050/532-7387, www.goatswiththewind.com, 10:30am-3pm daily, call one day in advance for reservations, NIS85), an organic cheese and goat farm and restaurant in the heartland of the Upper Galilee. The restaurant is at the end of a dirt track. It is privately owned and operated, so you get a truly unique, Israeli experience. The goat cheese comes from goat milk on the farm and is presented elegantly. All seating is on private verandas where you can feast on dishes like tomato and eggplant salad, *labaneh,* fried eggplant, cabbage salad, and other Mediterranean delights.

Steak and Seafood

In the middle of the pastoral Galilean countryside is **Dag al HaDan** (Tel Dan in Kiryat Shmona, 04/695-0225, www.dagaldan.co.il, noon-last customer daily Sept.-June, 9am-last customer daily July-Aug., NIS90), a kosher dairy restaurant next to the Dan River. The restaurant's emphasis is on fish, especially trout, which is fitting because its name means fish on the Dan River. You can also get mezze (appetizers), sandwiches, and other standard Mediterranean café fare, and the layout is housed in a rustic, barn-like structure with plenty of seating.

With a reputation as an outstanding place to get a steak, **Hatachana** (1 HaRishonim St., Metula town center, 04/694-4810, noon-10pm daily, NIS90), which means the mill, raises its own cattle and serves up a variety of meat dishes including T-bone steaks, lamb chops, and hamburgers. It tends to get packed with meat lovers, so reservations are recommended.

GETTING THERE AND AROUND
By Car
The Upper and Lower Galilee make up a broad swath of land that is relatively easy to cross by car, and many of the roads and highways between towns and cities have been recently or are in the process of being widened and improved. It takes about 90 minutes to get to the Lower Galilee from Jerusalem and a little over an hour from Tel Aviv.

Once in the Galilee, because of the empty expanses between towns and cities, you might encounter people hitchhiking by pointing their index finger toward the ground. It is legal to hitchhike in Israel and frequently used for transportation in more deserted areas, but the typical cautionary notes about hitchhiking or picking up hitchhikers still apply.

By Bus
As in the rest of the country, the easiest and most convenient bus service around the Galilee is **Egged** (www.egged.co.il), which lists schedules, bus numbers, and times in English. You can also check **Bus.Co.Il** (www.bus.co.il).

The Golan Heights

The Golan is situated in the northernmost region of Israel and shares borders with Lebanon and Syria. It is a popular domestic weekend getaway spot, and is also popular for hiking and other outdoor pursuits. The Golan Heights is home to fine wineries and apple and cherry orchards, and is the source of much of the beef and dairy in the region.

SIGHTS
Druze Villages
Throughout the internationally disputed territory of the Golan there are several **Druze villages** inhabited by a total of about 20,000 Druze, an Arab people of Syrian descent who have Israeli citizenship. The Druze have a reputation as warm and willing hosts to visitors and make up about half of the population of the Golan.

Druze villages include **Ein Kinya** (near Mt. Hermon next to the Sahar River), which is the smallest but the most popular among tourists. The other villages are **Majdal al-Shams** (near intersection of Rte. 98 north and Hwy. 989 north), **Bukata** and **Misada.** You can freely enter any of the villages, which are safe and generally welcoming to visitors.

Katsrin
The capital of the Golan Heights, **Katsrin** (take Rte. 87 north to Hwy. 9088 west, www.igalil.org.il/Eng), or Qatsrin, was founded in 1977 and is considered the tourism center of the region.

The town's features include the **Golan Archaeological Museum** (Rte. 87, Merom Golan, 04/696-2412, 8am-5pm Sun.-Thurs., 8am-3pm Fri., 10am-4pm Sat., NIS24 with the Ancient Katsrin Park). The modern, well-maintained museum is small but laid out well. It has a short film and exhibit about the Golan. You can also learn about the destruction of Gamla,

Apples are boxed up in the Golan Heights, the main apple producer in the region.

a stronghold during the First Revolt against Rome that the Romans destroyed in AD 67.

In the immediate vicinity is the **Ancient Katsrin Park** (Rte. 87, Merom Golan, 04/696-2412, 9am-4pm Sun.-Thurs., 9am-2pm Fri. Sept.-May; 9am-6pm Sun.-Thurs., 9am-4pm Fri., 10am-4pm Sat. June-Aug., NIS24 with the Golan Archaeological Museum). The park features the remains of a 3rd century Jewish village, including an ancient synagogue. Two reconstructed houses are set up with props of common objects that might have been used when the village, which was likely struck by an earthquake, was inhabited.

Golan Heights Winery

The producer of several popular domestic brands, the world-famous **Golan Heights Winery** (Rte. 87, south of Katsrin, 04/683-8435, www.golanwines.co.il, 8:30am-5:30pm Sun., 8:30am-6:30pm Mon.-Thurs., 8:30am-1:30pm Fri. and holiday eves, NIS20) is less than two miles from Katsrin. It features a visitor's center that offers tours (book in advance)

and a gift shop with the full range of wines and wine accessories.

Dolmens (Prehistoric Megalith Tombs)

As you are traveling about the Golan, you will likely see **dolmens,** or prehistoric megalith tombs, that date to about 30 BC and are believed to have been used for burial by nomadic tribes, and then possibly reused for secondary burial long later. The dolmens look like flat rocks stacked on top of each other and stacked in partially freestanding formations; they appear in the middle of desolate areas.

SPORTS AND RECREATION
Parks and Nature Reserves

At the foot of Mount Hermon is the Banias Spring that leads through a canyon to the magnificent Banias Waterfall. It's all part of **Banias Nature Reserve** (east of Kibbutz Snir on Rte. 99, 04/690-2577 for spring, 04/695-0272 for waterfall, 8am-5pm Sat.-Thurs. and 8am-4pm Fri. and holidays Apr.-Sept., 8am-4pm

THE GALILEE

THE MYSTERIOUS DRUZE

The people of the Golan Heights, in particular the Druze, are in turn just as complex as the division of borders and land. Previously Syrian residents, the Druze in the Golan follow a mystical religion that is largely secret and has its own courts, laws in personal matters, and leadership.

The approximately 20,000 Druze in the Golan (the majority population in the region) have a unique status as a minority group, and have been serving in the Israeli military and border police since 1948, even though their passports read "undefined" as their nationality. The Druze culture is Arab, but they don't follow mainstream Arab culture, and have held high-level positions in the political, public, and military life of Israel.

The Druze religion allows for women to attain high positions, and its major aspects are considered secret, though they will allow that they believe in reincarnation.

Druze villages are renowned for their hospitality and warm welcomes, and are located mainly in the Galilee and the Golan. The largest Druze village in Israel is in Daliyat el-Carmel, on Mount Carmel in the heart of the Carmel National Park, just southeast of Haifa. In the Golan, the center of Druze life is the village of Majdal al-Shams, with a population of 8,000 at the foot of Mount Hermon. Misada, Bukata, and Ein Kinya are also important Druze villages in the Golan.

Sat.-Thurs. and 8am-3pm Fri. and holidays Oct.-Mar., adult NIS27, child NIS14, combination tickets available for Nimrod Fortress and Banias for adult NIS38, child NIS19). The reserve has some very scenic trails that are highlighted with archaeological ruins.

Within the reserve there are several sites to visit, depending on which route you take. Once called Caesarea Philippi, you can take a 45-minute trail to go through **Roman and Crusader ruins,** including a Roman bridge. Farther along is the **waterfall** and a backtrack route will take you toward **Agrippas' Palace.**

The relatively easy two-hour hike in **Nimrod Fortress National Park** (Rte. 989 between Kiryat Shmona and Mt. Hermon, 04/694-9277, 8am-5pm Sat.-Thurs. and 8am-4pm Fri. and holidays Apr.-Sept., 8am-4pm and 8am-3pm Fri. and holidays Oct.-Mar., adult NIS21, child NIS9, combination tickets available for Nimrod Fortress and Banias for adult NIS38, child NIS19) leads to the unique offerings of a vulture nesting site and a secret passageway at Nimrod Fortress. Situated above Banias Spring

on the slopes of Mount Hermon, the 13th-century fortress was gradually built up over time and the hiking path passes by a huge gate, an ancient toilet, guard towers, and cisterns.

Not what you'd expect to find in the Middle East, but when in season, **Mount Hermon** (off of Rte. 98, www.skihermon.co.il, 8am-4pm daily, adult NIS49, child NIS42) has a functioning ski resort complete with a ski lift. If you don't ski, you can play on snow sleds, ride the cable car, or hang out in the restaurant. In the summer, the area has gorgeous vistas of Syria, Lebanon, the Galilee, and the Hula Valley, and you can take guided tours, ride mountain sleds, and tool around the mountain bike park.

Gamla Nature Reserve (Rte. 869 from Gamla Junction to Daliyot Junction on the eastern side of the Sea of Galilee, 04/682-2282/3, 8am-5pm and 8am-4pm Fri. and holidays Apr.-Sept., 8am-4pm and 8am-3pm Fri. and holidays Oct.-Mar., adult NIS27, child NIS14) has relatively easy hikes that vary from 1-4 hours. The site includes observation plazas, a snack bar, and binoculars for rent. The

ISRAEL'S WINE COUNTRY

The history of wine in Israel is a long one. For thousands of years, Jews have been using wine for mostly sacramental purposes. The development of wine and the wine industry today has reached the point that some wines made in Israel are recognized internationally and even win international awards. There is the added element in Israel of a wide variety of kosher wines.

Israeli wine country is concentrated in a few areas: in the foothills of Jerusalem and the surrounding areas, the Negev Desert, the Golan, and the Galilee. Unfortunately the industry is still young enough that wine-related tourism hasn't developed to the point where you can take a wine tour of any regions. But you can make arrangements through a tour guide, by request, to visit different wineries.

Many wineries have visiting centers and offer the chance to take a tour and have tastings for about NIS40.

In the Golan Heights, the center of tourism, Katsrin, is also the center of the regional wine industry, led by the **Golan Heights Winery** (www.golanwines.co.il), which is considered by many to be the grandfather of Israel's modern-day wine industry. The visitor's center offers a variety of tours and tastings in multiple languages, and has a gift shop.

In the Upper Galilee, particularly in the area of Carmel Mountain, there are a variety of wineries of all sizes. An excellent website that gives an overview of Israel's wine country is **Israeli Wines** (www.wines-israel.co.il/len), where you can get current news and information about the industry as well as product information.

© GENEVIEVE BELMAKER

Many wineries in the Golan Heights offer tours and tastings.

THE GALILEE

© GENEVIEVE BELMAKER

the ski lift at Mount Hermon in the summer

and buses to and from Tel Aviv and Jerusalem stop nearby.

The Society for the Protection of Nature in Israel (SPNI) has field schools throughout Israel and the Golan, and they make a great option if you are looking for something affordable, conveniently located, and only need the most basic in amenities and comfort. Even in the high season of summer, the **Golan SPNI Field School** (Katsrin, 04/696-1234, field school reservations hotline 03/638-8688, www.teva.org.il, US$131 d) is affordable. The simple, ground-floor accommodations are surrounded by trees, and it caters to groups of travelers, including touring and Birthright groups, so you might have a lively crowd here with you. Every room is air-conditioned and can hold about six people. Breakfast is included in the price.

Part way up Mount Hermon sits the **Chalet Nimrod Castle Hostel** (Nachal Nimrod, 04/698-4218, www.bikta.net, US$149 d) with varied types of cabins that were built by the owners, Guy and Lilach. The independent cabins are void of technology and surround a central lodge where you can get breakfast (for an extra fee) and maps and travel guides to the surrounding area. The whole vibe of the chalet is peace and calm, and its location on the Golan Trail makes for easy access to hiking. The cabins are air-conditioned and include a kitchenette.

reserve is famed for its Griffon vulture observation point and views of an ancient city and the remains of a Byzantine church. It is also home to one of the most ancient synagogues in Israel.

ACCOMMODATIONS
US$100-150

One of the more unique experiences you might have in accommodations, **Ghengis Khan in the Golan** (Givat Yoav, Neot Golan, 052/371-5687, www.gkhan.co.il, US$102 d) is a popular specialty lodging spot with just five rooms along the Golan Trail. Family run with handmade tents and free Wi-Fi, it is a contradiction between technology and nature. It provides an area to cook out, a garden with seating, and a shared kitchen with an option to buy food supplies. The tents are equipped with mattresses, pillows, and private or shared bathrooms nearby. Nearby excursions include horseback riding, hiking, and jeep trips for hire. The Galilee is just 15 minutes by car,

US$150-200

Just east of the Galilee and the famous Kibbutz Ein Gev, **Between Water and Sky** (Neot Golan, 054/488-2299, www.neot-golan.a-is-rael.com, US$199 d) caters to couples looking for a romantic getaway and has a limited three suites that come with a hot tub, a flat-screen TV with satellite, a furnished balcony with views of the Sea of Galilee, free Wi-Fi, a minibar with free non-alcoholic drinks, and a DVD library. Basically every element of pampering is covered here, even flowers, chocolate, wine, and cookies are waiting when you arrive. There is an olive press on the property that can be toured to see how olive oil is made. It's five minutes from the Sea of Galilee.

Over US$200

Best for families and couples, the **Sanabl Druze Hospitality Center** (Ein Kinya Golan Heights, Nimrod, 050/577-8850, www.zimmeril.com, US$275 d) is a small religious property in the Druze village of Ein Kinya in the Golan Heights. It includes a Druze restaurant (ask for the Druze stew) and options for suites and villas that all have a TV and DVD player. There are also cooking facilities and a traditional Druze buffet breakfast is included. There is free parking and Wi-Fi, and you can arrange for horseback riding, hiking, and jeep excursions through the center. If there's snow, it's a five-minute drive to skiing on Mount Hermon. It's also near Banias Nature Reserve and Nimrod Fortress National Park.

To the north of the Galilee with just four suites, **Tenebagolan Suites Zimmers** (293 Gan Hashiqmim, Had Nes, 04/697-0027, www.tenebagolan.co.il, US$260 d) is a luxury experience that caters to people who want a rustic experience with individualized pampering. Every suite has a hot tub, a terrace view of the Golan Heights, and a flat-screen TV. You can borrow a bicycle for free, and there is also free Wi-Fi. A common kitchen is open for use, and a prepared Israeli breakfast is included. It is 5 minutes to the Galilee and about 30 minutes from Tiberias.

One of several luxury accommodations on the Ramot Moshav, **Naomi's Place** (Kochal, Moshav Ramot, 04/673-2157, www.zimmeril.com, US$250) is a bed-and-breakfast in the midst of a date plantation. The four wood cabins are set on spacious grounds that include a swimming pool, playground, and an area to cook out. About 5 minutes from the Galilee and 20 minutes from the holy city of Safed, it is very close to hiking trails. Every cabin has a cozy, warm interior with soft lighting and large, luxurious beds, a private garden, hammock, a kitchenette, and fireplace. Though breakfast is provided, there are also restaurants nearby.

Conveniently located near a bus stop and just five minutes from the Golan Heights Winery, **Vila Golan** (Inbar St. on the outskirts of Katsrin, 050/957-5758, www.zimmeril.com, US$220 d) is a very small luxury bed-and-breakfast in the sweet little town of Katsrin. The four suites all have a fully loaded kitchenette, a huge bed, a TV-DVD player, and free Wi-Fi. You get a free bottle of wine on arrival and breakfast is included. There is an option for a room with a hot tub. The town's country club gives guests of Vila Golan a discount, and it's near the Golan Heights Winery and a short drive to the Galilee.

FOOD
Farm Restaurants

Near the entrance to the Hula Nature Reserve is **Dubrovin Farm Restaurant** (Rte. 90, Merom Golan, grounds of Dubrovin Farm, 04/693-7371, dubrovinfarm@bezeqint.net, call in advance for reservations as hours vary, NIS125) on the grounds of a reconstructed farm founded in 1909, complete with a farmhouse and small museum (04/693-7371, NIS12). The restaurant serves a prix-fixe menu featuring meat dishes and non-dairy ice cream for dessert. It is best enjoyed by groups.

Local Delicacies

Specializing in the use of almost exclusively local ingredients, **Yogi Chef** (Emir Junction West off Hwy. 978 in the Food and Arts Complex at Wasset Tourism Center, 04/689-3630, www.yogichef.co.il, 1pm-11pm Thurs.-Sat., NIS80) is worth stopping by. Each dish is a small work of art, and they are known for their steaks and tomato-orange soup. Run by Boston-trained chef Yotam Givol, they also serve local wines and offer culinary tours and cooking classes.

Middle Eastern Fusion

If you get as far north as Majdal al-Shams near the Syrian border, check out the local sophisticate, **Undefined** (Majdal al-Shams main road, 050/764-1699, 11am-10pm daily,

NIS50), named for the description that most Syrian Druze have on their IDs for nationality. Serving an interesting mix of Asian and Middle Eastern dishes, steaks, and fresh fruit desserts, the café setting has a friendly atmosphere that sometimes hosts live acoustic performances.

Moshav Dining

Extremely convenient if you happen to stay at the nearby Moshav Ramot hotel and with a simplistic, but warm, atmosphere and very extensive regional wine menu, **Moshbutz** (third turn inside Moshav Ramot, eastern shore of the Galilee, 04/679-5095, http://mushbutz.rest-e.co.il, 6pm-last customer daily, NIS80) takes its name from the combination of the words moshav and kibbutz, reflecting its roots in connection with the moshav. Try to get a seat near the windows and enjoy the view of the eastern shore of the Sea of Galilee. They do serve dishes such as hamburgers, but the beef is aged and may not appeal to an American standard. A better bet is the beef stew in wine stock or the pork spareribs (a rare find in this part of the world).

GETTING THERE AND AROUND
By Car

If you can manage it, the best way to get around the Golan Heights is by car. Any other independent mode of transportation might prove a bit tricky. One option is to rent a car in Tiberias from **Eldan Car Rental** (1 HaBannim St., 04/672-2831, www.eldan.co.il), the largest domestic car rental company in Israel.

By Bus

Egged buses (www.egged.co.il) do travel into the Golan, and a trip to Katsrin (Qatsrin), a city about 40 minutes north of Tiberias is possible. To Katsrin from Tel Aviv is about 3.5 hours (bus 843, NIS44 one-way), and from Jerusalem it is closer to 4 hours (bus 966, NIS44 one-way). Once you are in the Golan, there are Egged routes that traverse between the towns on a regular basis.

EILAT AND THE NEGEV

The southern half of Israel is home to the vast Negev Desert that is sparsely populated but filled with a myriad of significant and interesting sights. The Negev is the largest desert in Israel, and accounts for more than half of Israel's land. It is home to the ancient city of Beer Sheva, numerous Bedouin tribes, and some of Israel's most popular ecotourism destinations.

© GENEVIEVE BELMAKER

HIGHLIGHTS

LOOK FOR ◖ TO FIND RECOMMENDED SIGHTS, ACTIVITIES, DINING, AND LODGING.

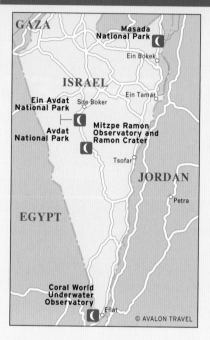

◖ **Masada National Park:** Arguably the most dramatic vista in the region is from atop Masada National Park, a hilltop fortress of Herod the Great that served as the last stand for a band of rebel Jews facing off against the Roman army (page 234).

◖ **Ein Avdat National Park:** The always-flowing stream at this park is a highlight of easy-to-navigate desert trails engineered to protect the natural environment. It is a prime ecotourism site (page 243).

◖ **Avdat National Park:** Adjacent to Ein Avdat, Avdat National Park is home to one of the most famous Nabataean cities, situated along the ancient incense route (page 244).

◖ **Mitzpe Ramon Observatory and Ramon Crater:** Mitzpe Ramon is the site of the largest of three massive geological craters in the Negev, as well as numerous hiking routes (page 244).

◖ **Coral World Underwater Observatory:** See scores of rare, colorful tropical fish at this underwater world just a few miles outside of Eilat (page 255).

Although the Negev is rather sparsely populated, it has numerous outstanding options for a range of activities such as desert hikes, camping, and off-road adventures that include riding on dirt bikes and ATVs. Some of the region's more notable ecotourism experiences include unique accommodations, like environmentally-friendly, custom-designed desert huts and camel rides.

At the northeastern side of the Negev is the Dead Sea, the lowest point on earth, famed for its therapeutic waters and warm air. The Dead Sea is beloved for its mud, which you can take directly out of the sea and spread on your body. The tourism demand in the Dead Sea region means that there are a wealth of hotels, many of them luxury, that cater to guests looking to do nothing but relax and unwind. It is also a fairly easy drive from Jerusalem, making it the perfect side trip for a day or overnight trip.

Along the western shore of the Dead Sea are the stunning ruins of Masada, believed to be a former mountaintop fortress of Herod the Great, where a group of rebel Jews took their last stand against Roman soldiers. On a clear day, you can see the expanse of the Dead Sea below.

At the southernmost tip of the Negev is Eilat, famed for its water recreation sports. It is one of the most popular vacation destinations

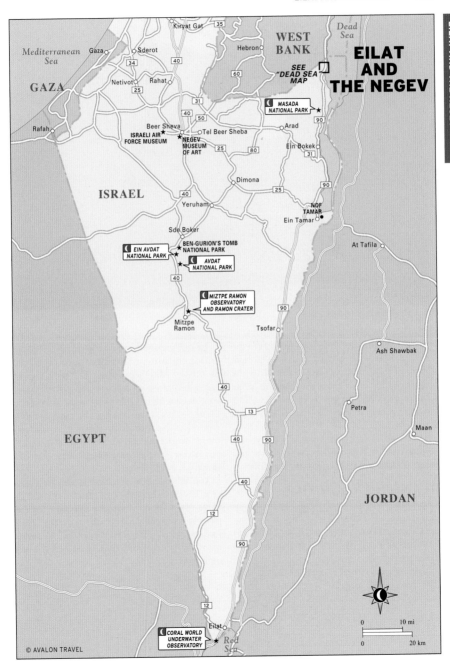

© AVALON TRAVEL

© GENEVIEVE BELMAKER

ruins at Masada National Park

in Israel and also one of the hottest places in the country, especially in the summer. A unique feature of Eilat is its tax-free status. It is the only place in Israel without the standard Value Added Tax (VAT) on goods and services. It is also the gateway to Petra, Jordan, which is just across the border.

If you have the time, energy, money, and willingness, there are many sights to see and adventures to be had in the south and Eilat.

PLANNING YOUR TIME

The south is full of vast spaces of desert, punctuated by a few major destinations, including the Dead Sea, Beer Sheva, and Eilat. The minimum amount of time you should plan to spend in the south is four days, which should give you just enough time to experience the best of what the region has to offer.

Be cautious when you make any travel plans during the summer months, especially in the months of May-September. The temperature can be brutally high at times (above 105°F), and combined with the humidity in the area of the Dead Sea it can make even the most exciting trip miserable, especially if you're not accustomed to the climate. It can also be dangerous if you don't drink enough water or avoid the sun.

You should allow at least two days for Eilat, as it is very far south, and most activities involve water sports. It is also the most logical place to jump off for a day trip to nearby Petra, Jordan, and the famed archaeological site there, for which you should allow at least one overnight stay.

The Dead Sea

The lowest point on earth, the Dead Sea draws tourists from all over the world to indulge in its rich mud and relax in its spas. The high salinity of the waters of the Dead Sea, in which nothing lives, makes it possible to easily float on the water. Surrounding the Sea are a few smaller towns and clusters of hotels and restaurants, with one large strip of mostly luxury hotels and restaurants that cater to tourists.

ORIENTATION

Once one complete body of water, the Dead Sea is now split into a northern and southern portion because of the exploitation of the Sea's

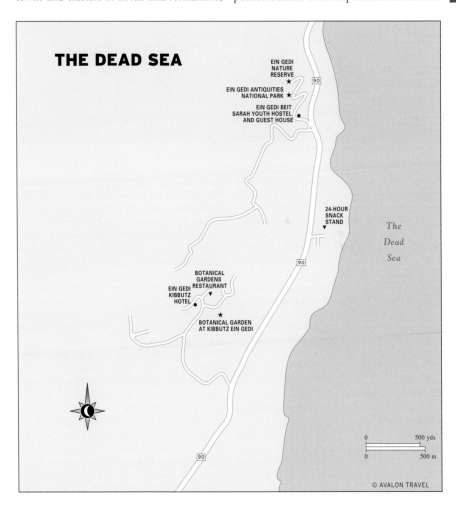

THE DEAD SEA

EIN GEDI NATURE RESERVE
90
EIN GEDI ANTIQUITIES NATIONAL PARK
EIN GEDI BEIT SARAH YOUTH HOSTEL AND GUEST HOUSE

24-HOUR SNACK STAND

The Dead Sea

90

BOTANICAL GARDENS RESTAURANT
EIN GEDI KIBBUTZ HOTEL
BOTANICAL GARDEN AT KIBBUTZ EIN GEDI

0   500 yds
0   500 m

90

© AVALON TRAVEL

© ALEKSANDR PENIN/123RF.COM

The high salinity of the Dead Sea makes floating easy.

resources, which are so popular in health and beauty products. Most of the larger northern portion is within the West Bank on the western shore and within Jordan on the eastern shore. Look across the Sea at night and you will see the lights of Jordan twinkling not far away.

The first destination just across the West Bank border is Ein Gedi, home to an ancient spring and waterfalls and a couple of accommodation options. The southern half of the Dead Sea is where you'll find the major grouping of hotels and activities catering to tourists in Ein Bokek and just to the south. Between Ein Gedi and Ein Bokek are various beaches and spas.

SIGHTS
◖ Masada National Park

There are many mysteries surrounding **Masada National Park** (approximately one hour south of Jerusalem via Rtes. 1 and 90, 03/539-6700 and 08/658-4207/8, reservation center for sound and light show 08/995-9333, www.masada.org.il and www.parks.org.il, 8am-5pm daily Apr.-Sept., 8am-4pm daily Oct.-Mar.,

last entry one hour before closing and one hour earlier on Fri. and holiday eves, NIS27-72 depending on cable car ticket choice), chief among them is what exactly happened to the Jewish inhabitants who were surrounded by the Roman army, besieged for months, and ultimately committed suicide to avoid capture.

Another one of Israel's UNESCO World Heritage Sites, Masada is breathtaking for the view of the Dead Sea and the impossibly steep ascent that you can make by cable car or by foot. The entrance fee to the park also includes camping fees.

Masada sits at the top of a high peak above the Dead Sea. What is left today are remnants of the once-magnificent court that was originally built by King Herod. You can rent an audio guide to the site, which seems like nothing more than dusty, hot archaeological remains on top of a huge hill unless you look closely and take your time. The best way to get into the spirit of Masada is with a tour guide (inquire in advance) who can take you through the various points and answer questions.

© GENEVIEVE BELMAKER

Masada National Park with the Dead Sea in the distance

On a clear day, the view of the Dead Sea from Masada is incredible, and you can see it from the top of Masada or from the cable cars that take you up and down from the visitor's center. You can walk up via the path on the side of the mountain, but that can be a dangerous endeavor in hot weather: People do get heat exhaustion and dehydration while on the trail. Whether you go up by cable car or trail, take water and drink continuously.

You might not be in the mood for more historical information when you finish, but don't miss the inventive and informative **Yigal Yadin Masada Museum,** (08/658-4207/8 and 08/658-4464, museum.m@npa.org.il, 8am-4pm Sun.-Thurs., NIS20 or combined ticket) just past the very classy gift shop. Entrance to the museum is included with the price of your ticket, and you'll get an automatically-activated audio guide to accompany you through the choice, well-displayed artifacts and life-size recreations of people in scenes related to Masada. It brings the entire experience to life, and is one of the coolest museums you'll see in Israel, even though it's quite small.

Ein Gedi Nature Reserve

About 20 minutes down the road from Masada in the direction of Jerusalem is **Ein Gedi Nature Reserve** (off Rte. 90, 08/658-4285, www.parks.org.il, 8am-5pm daily Apr.-Sept., 8am-4pm daily Oct.-Mar., with additional entrance restrictions, adult NIS27, child NIS14), a charming, conveniently located reserve that is brimming with the deer-like ibexes, small hyrax, and natural pools of water that has been flowing for about 2,000 years.

There are three main trails in and you can take a short, relatively easy hike from the park entrance straight up to the second natural pool of water and swim and cool off under the waterfall. It's not deep enough for a serious swim, but it seems like heaven on a hot day. Go early in the morning before huge groups descend on the popular trails from around noon onward.

You can also see the remains of an ancient irrigation system, and there is a snack bar and

© GENEVIEVE BELMAKER

a cable car at Masada National Park

souvenir shop at the entrance, but beware that rangers patrol the area for people eating inside the reserve; you could get fined if caught eating food here.

Ein Gedi Antiquities National Park

Inside of the Ein Gedi Nature Reserve, just north of the main parking area, is the **Ein Gedi Antiquities National Park** (off Rte. 90, 08/658-4285, www.parks.org.il, 8am-4pm Sat.-Thurs., 8am-3pm Fri., included with admission to the nature reserve) with its 1,200-year-old mosaic floor left over from the remains of an ancient Jewish synagogue from the 3rd century AD. The complex is shaded and has places to sit. The mosaic floor has mysterious inscriptions that include a warning to not reveal the local secret (likely a reference to the production of a local persimmon perfume).

Qumran National Park

In 1947, a Bedouin goat herder discovered the first seven scrolls of what became known as the Dead Sea Scrolls in a cave inside of what is now **Qumran National Park** (13 miles east of Jerusalem via Hwy. 1 to Rte. 90, 02/994-2235, 02/654-1255 for guided tours, www.parks.org.il, 8am-5pm daily Apr.-Sept., 8am-4pm daily Oct.-Mar., last entry one hour before closing, adult NIS21, child NIS9). In the 1950s, 10 more caves with manuscripts were discovered. Though it took time to understand what the scrolls were, the findings rocked the worlds of archaeology, anthropology, and religion. Made by Jews between 200 BC and AD 70, the scrolls fill in important details about ancient scribal practices, traditions, and techniques of biblical interpretation.

Today you can tour the Qumran complex, the remains of an ancient city of a strict religious sect called the Qumrans, including the nearby 11 caves and underground tunnels.

Botanical Garden at Kibbutz Ein Gedi

Just inside Kibbutz Ein Gedi is the **Botanical Garden** (off Hwy. 90 alongside the Dead Sea at Tamar Regional Council, 08/659-4726, www.

ein-gedi.co.il, anytime, free), which makes for incredible nighttime tours with its diverse plant life and selection of flowers that bloom in the night. People from the kibbutz actually live within the garden and it has more than 1,000 varieties of flora from all over the world. They give tours for groups and individuals.

ENTERTAINMENT AND EVENTS
Festivals

Every year the **Tamar Festival** (multiple venues, www.tamarfestival.com, Oct., NIS150-220) lasts for several days in October during the Sukkot holiday and features performances by local and international artists. Events during the day include hikes, tours, and children's activities. The festival is known for its choice lineup of activities and music featured in various venues in the south of Israel, including the Botanical Garden at Ein Gedi, the Kikar Sdom villages, and Masada. If you plan ahead and pay a bit extra, you can camp in the midst of the event.

Sports Challenges

With a lineup that includes a mountain bike marathon and moonlit running, the two-day **Veolia Desert Challenge** (050/883-3008, www.desertchallenge.co.il) is for extreme sports lovers who also love the desert. The event also includes family activities, camping accommodations, and a general atmosphere of enjoying the desert through experiencing extreme sports.

The **Dead Sea Half-Marathon Race** (www.eingedi-run.co.il, Feb.) has been going strong for three decades. The run takes place near Ein Gedi at a time when the local temperature is more bearable, and includes gorgeous views of the Dead Sea along the way.

SHOPPING

Once you are anywhere near the beaches of the Dead Sea, there are gift stores and shops everywhere people gather, mostly selling Dead Sea-related beauty and skin products, revered for their quality and benefits. The most extensive network of shopping, though, is in the area of **Ein Bokek,** just off of Route 90.

The dark side of Dead Sea products is the lack of regulations surrounding the removal and use of natural resources from the Dead Sea. The exploitation of resources from the Dead Sea has been connected to environmental problems in the area and there are lingering questions over legal claims to the land.

SPORTS AND RECREATION

The main attraction in the Dead Sea region is undoubtedly the Dead Sea itself. The lowest point on earth and filled with waters in which nothing is living, the Dead Sea is renowned for its rich mineral deposits and general health benefits.

There is a great deal of controversy surrounding the use of materials from the Dead Sea and other issues with development and exploitation of resources in the area. The Sea is slowly disappearing and there is a major swath in its center where land is now exposed, splitting the Sea into a northern and southern portion.

At many points in the Sea, you can enter the waters and rub the reputedly therapeutic mud on your body and face. Take care if you have any cuts on your body, as the salty waters will go straight into the wound and cause horrible stinging pain.

The major beaches are well-apportioned with showers, changing rooms, snack bars, lounge chairs, and shade. The less-used beaches still often have showers, but might be lacking the mud to rub on the body.

Beaches

Just near Kibbutz Mitzpe Shalem is **Mineral Beach** (Rte. 90 near Kibbutz Mitzpe Shalem, 02/994-4888, 9am-5pm Sun.-Thurs., 8am-5pm Fri.-Sat., NIS50 weekdays, NIS60 weekends and holidays) with its well-kept shores, shaded sulfur pool, plenty of mud for rubbing, and a health center that offers treatments and massages. There is also a passable cafeteria, showers, changing rooms, storage, an indoor freshwater pool, and more.

Just off Route 90, about 90 minutes south of Jerusalem, is the extremely well-developed area of **Ein Bokek** that includes two beaches with shades and chair for rent, about a dozen luxury hotels, several clinics and spas, hot springs, shopping malls, and restaurants and bars. There is also the option for free camping here.

A bit more country in its atmosphere and related amenities is **Ein Gedi Beach** (off Rte. 90, 8am-5pm daily Apr.-Sept., 8am-4pm daily Oct.-Mar., free), just down the road from Kibbutz Ein Gedi off Route 90 on the way to Masada. There is a large parking lot and beach access, though in parts the way is steep and rocky to get to the water. A narrow strip of sandy beach includes red parasols for lounging and paid toilets and showers. A snack stand at the entrance of the parking lot is open 24 hours and is the only store of any kind for miles around. Outside of its official operating hours, you can come anytime and can also camp overnight for free.

The northernmost of the Dead Sea beaches that is closest to Jerusalem, about a 40-minute drive, is **New Kalia Beach** (02/994-2391, www. dead-sea.org.il, 8am-6pm daily Apr.-Sept., 8am-5pm daily Oct.-Mar., adult NIS40, child NIS30). The beach has a covered snack and drink bar, which plays loud music, changing rooms, showers, beach chairs, and umbrellas. It is slightly disconcerting to see the minefield warnings just a stone's throw from the beach, but there is plenty of mud and the general atmosphere is very mellow. A Bedouin tent area, camping facilities, and a Dead Sea products gift shop are also available.

Spas and Health Resorts

Famed for its health benefits, the Dead Sea region has a wide range of spas, stretching from the Kibbutz Ein Gedi area all the way to Ein Bokek. Any hotel in the area will know of nearby spas and their reputation, but you can also try Ein Gedi **Sea of Spa** (Kibbutz Ein Gedi, 08/659-4934, www.eingediseaofspa.co.il, 8am-5pm daily Oct.-Mar. and 8am-6pm Sun.-Thurs,. 8am-5pm Fri. Apr.-Sept.), with its natural hot springs, sweet water pool, natural cosmetic mud, beach, and body treatments center.

Camel Rides

En route to the Dead Sea, you'll encounter a few places that offer **camel rides** for a fee, usually somewhere around NIS50. The camels are usually kept waiting in some kind of a parking lot or very close to the road for long periods of time, and there are little to no government regulations about the treatment and care of the animals.

ACCOMMODATIONS

There are a wide variety of accommodations in and around the Dead Sea region, ranging from camping to five-star hotels. The fanciest hotels are grouped in and around Ein Bokek, on the southern end of the waters. This area is built up with restaurants, shops, and spas. At night, the area looks a bit like Las Vegas. There are also a number of options in the area of Ein Gedi and Masada, which have about 20 minutes of road in between them. Other options are at Almog, Kalya, and Arad, which are not as close to the beaches, but still keep you in the vicinity.

Under US$100

The **Ein Gedi Beit Sarah Youth Hostel and Guest House** (Ein Gedi, 02/594-5600, www. iyha.org.il, US$87 d) looks a bit like a military barracks when you first approach the heavy iron gate surrounding the outside, but once you're in, it's rather nice. Several buildings are spread out across a small expanse of ground and it is very spare, but the simple rooms are clean and roomy enough, and several even have nice patios with a fantastic view of the Dead Sea, which is just right across the road. It is also a five-minute walk to the entrance of Ein Gedi Nature Reserve. Free Wi-Fi and breakfast are included, and there is a huge lounge area by the 24-hour front desk.

The **Masada Guest House and Youth Hostel** (Masada at Ein Bokek, 08/995-3222, www.iyha.org.il, US$98 d) is a relatively large building for a hostel that looks like it was carved out of the hillside. It has a private swimming pool (in season) and is just near the entrance to Masada National Park. All 88 rooms have a private shower and bathroom, air-conditioning, and a mini bar. There is also a large dining room and an Internet station available, and breakfast is included.

A charming option if you want to be in the desert but don't need to be next door to the Dead Sea is **Villa 1000** (Baraket 43 in Arad, www.zimmeril.com, US$94 d). The place is tiny, with only nine rooms, but it's set in a garden with a cookout area, there is free Wi-Fi throughout, and all of the rooms are equipped for cooking. Arad is a good jumping off point for the Dead Sea and the Negev, which are both about 30 minutes away.

US$100-150

A villa that has been converted into three separate units, **Zimmer Mantur** (Mivtza Lot 30, Arad, 054/766-9308, www.zimmermantur. com, US$125 d) has a guest garden, cookout facilities, and the rooms have balconies with views of the garden or the nearby valley. Free Wi-Fi and a flat screen TV come with the room, and there's easy access to nearby jeep excursions in the Negev or the Judean Deserts.

US$150-200

At the very southern end of the Dead Sea just next to the salt pools is **Nof Tamar** (Ein Tamar, 052/886-8632, US$158 d). The very tiny, three-room property has views of the Negev Desert from air-conditioned log cabin chalets that have world-class amenities including satellite TV, whirlpool bathtubs, verandas, and kitchenettes. It is about 30 minutes from Masada and an hour from Beer Sheva.

Simple but cozy, **Gil's Guest Rooms** (Neve Zohar, Ein Bokek 107, 052/270-2502, www. einbokek.com/gil, US$169 d) is a viable option for accommodations if you want to be in the Ein Bokek area but want to pay a little less. There's free Wi-Fi, satellite TV, and you can get breakfast and dinner on site. It's not fancy, but the rooms are a good size and the staff is helpful in navigating around the Dead Sea area.

Just a two-minute walk from the beach, **Isrotel Ganim Hotel** (Ein Bokek, 08/668-9090, www.gardenshotels.com, US$194 d) is a 200-room hotel with a massive, sprawling

layout, spa treatments, two indoor swimming pools, an outdoor pool, and a children's pool. All of the rooms overlook the Dead Sea. The breakfast buffet is included.

Over US$200

The **Ein Gedi Kibbutz Hotel** (Kibbutz Ein Gedi, 08/659-4222, www.ein-gedi.co.il, US$239 d) is set within a kibbutz that boasts a botanical garden and a huge outdoor swimming pool with changing rooms and showers. The hotel also has a private beach and there is a nearby spa with mineral pools. It is a 10-minute drive from the Ein Gedi Nature Reserve and 15 minutes from Masada. All of the rooms have tea and coffee service and satellite TV. The on-site restaurant serves a huge buffet dinner on Friday night, and there is a small bar and information center with area information in the hotel's main lobby.

Daniel Hotel Dead Sea (off Rte. 90, Ein Bokek, 08/668-9999, www.tamareshotels.co.il, US$302 d) is a full-fledged luxury hotel with all the trimmings in its 302 rooms with desert and Dead Sea views. The hotel also has swimming pools, a conference center, and a health club with a gym, sauna, whirlpool, and steam room.

FOOD

The Dead Sea area is marked by long stretches of road where there is nothing to eat, punctuated by groupings of areas where you can get food. A couple of websites that offer listings of restaurants are www.einbokek.com and www. deadsea.co.il.

Ein Gedi

There are very few food options in the Ein Gedi area, but you do have a **24-hour snack stand** (NIS20) just across from the Ein Gedi Nature Reserve that sells items like sandwiches and soda. Just outside the entrance to the reserve is a small **convenience store** (08/659-4915, 8am-5pm daily Apr.-Sept., 8am-4pm daily Oct.-Mar., NIS20) that sells mostly snack items and drinks.

Another option is the **Botanical Gardens**

Restaurant (Kibbutz Ein Gedi, 08/659-4221, www.ein-gedi.co.il/en, 7am-10am and 6:30pm-8:30pm daily, NIS75), a fairly nice restaurant with a huge amount of space that feels a bit like a cafeteria and an all-you-can-eat buffet. The setting is gorgeous though, amidst the Kibbutz Ein Gedi botanical garden, and it is just off the hotel's lobby, where there is also a small bar and lounge area. The restaurant is kosher, but they do serve dinner on Friday night with a huge buffet.

Ein Bokek

If you find yourself in the Ein Bokek area, your best bet for finding some decent food will probably be at one of the large hotels or one of the shopping centers. If you want something on the beach, the generic beach restaurants and snack stands are easy to find.

For very simple coffee, sandwiches, and salads, you can go to the local branch of **Aroma** (Petra Shopping Center, circular shopping center in the middle of Ein Bokek, 08/995-4021, www.aroma.co.il/en, 8am-11pm daily, NIS35). There isn't much atmosphere, but it is open daily and is a relatively predictable experience with free Wi-Fi to boot. Once you are at the shopping center, there are other options as well.

At the Leonardo Hotel Inn is the Bedouin tent restaurant and bar, **Taj Mahal** (Leonardo Hotel Inn, 053/809-4823, www.taj-mahal.co.il, noon-2am daily, NIS70), where you can sit on cushions and puff on a hookah water pipe. The restaurant has a fairly limited food menu, with mostly some simple steak and chicken dishes and salads, but they do have an extensive beer, wine, and alcohol menu. Their schedule varies despite their published hours, especially in the off season, so call before going to make sure they are open and serving food.

In the lobby of the Isrotel Hotel is the **The Ranch House Restaurant** (Isrotel Hotel Dead Sea, off Rte. 90, Ein Bokek, 08/668-9666, 7pm-11pm Sun.-Thurs., 6:30pm-11pm Sat., NIS110), serving American-style dishes, and open mainly for dinner. The atmosphere is spacious, modern, and relaxing and their specialty is serving cuts of meat by weight.

South Dead Sea

At the very southern end of the Dead Sea are a few options for food in an area called Neot HaKikar, but most of these venues require reservations. One of them is **Secrets my Mother Told Me** (off Rte. 90 at Sodom Sq., 052/899-1199), which serves breakfast, lunch, and dinner, but you must call in advance for reservations. They serve buffet-style spreads and are best for groups of four or more.

GETTING THERE AND AROUND

It is a world away from Jerusalem, but the Dead Sea area is remarkably easy to get to by car and bus. Once here, you can traverse the entire shore of the Sea along Route 90 in about 80 minutes. It is about 45 minutes to the northernmost area, Kalya, and another 30 minutes to Ein Gedi Nature Reserve, and another 25 minutes to the major hotel and restaurant area of Ein Bokek. From Ein Bokek you can get to the very southern end of the Dead Sea at Neot Hakikar in another 30 minutes.

By Car

From Jerusalem, take Highway 1 east to Route 90 and follow the signs to the Dead Sea. You will drive for about an hour, part of the way in the West Bank, until you get to Ein Gedi, which is just over the border from the West Bank on the Israeli side. From Tel Aviv, take the same route, except add a bit more time along Highway 1. It's approximately a two-hour drive, give or take, depending on traffic.

Once you are in the area, it is very easy to get about by car. There is only one main road (Rte. 90) and everything is clearly signposted or obvious from a distance. For example, it is impossible to miss the massive grouping of hotels at Ein Bokek.

By Bus

Buses go to the Dead Sea on a very regular basis from Jerusalem via **Egged** buses (www.egged.co.il, bus numbers 421, 486, 487, NIS37.5), and it takes about 90 minutes to reach Ein Gedi. The bus stops are situated along Route 90, and a good stop to begin with is at the Ein Gedi Beit Sarah Youth Hostel and Guest House because it is immediately adjacent to Ein Gedi National Park.

From Tel Aviv, take off from the Arlozorov Terminal (bus number 421, NIS47) for the trip that takes about 2.5 hours. Watch out for other routes from Tel Aviv that require transfers.

Once you get off the bus, you'll be very close to the Ein Gedi Nature Reserve and it will be easy to get back on the bus and continue southward. Beware that the Ein Gedi Beit Sarah Youth Hostel and Guest House won't let you in their gate if you are not a registered guest, though.

The Negev

Seemingly rather bare to the eye, the Negev is full of all kinds of wildlife that you can easily see close up, which is part of what makes it a popular destination for nature-related hikes and other activities. It is also the gateway to Eilat, the southernmost city in Israel.

ORIENTATION

The largest city in the Negev, Beer Sheva is incredibly ancient: It was founded over 3,700 years ago. Developed into a more modern city by the Ottomans and then the British, the Beer Sheva of today is a mixed city of immigrants—Jews, Arabs, and Bedouins—from dozens of countries. Home to the University of the Negev, it also makes a logical base for starting adventures in the region, particularly to Arad or Dimona (both about 40 minutes away).

About 40 minutes due south from Beer Sheva is the historic Kibbutz Sde Boker, former home of Israel's first Prime Minister David Ben-Gurion. The kibbutz and nearby

an ancient well outside the city gate of Beer Sheva

Midreshet Sde Boker are centers for ecotourism in the region, and are a good stop on the way to see Mitzpe Ramon, Ein Avdat National Park, and the ancient Nabataean city of Avdat.

SIGHTS
Beer Sheva

Modern Beer Sheva is not the most remarkable-looking place, but it has a number of interesting and valuable stops, including a couple of good museums. Among them is the **Negev Museum of Art** (60 HaAtsmaut St., 08/699-3535, www.negev-museum.org.il, 10am-4pm Mon.-Tues. and Thurs., noon-7pm Wed., 10am-2pm Fri.-Sat., NIS15) in Beer Sheva's Old City in a 1906 building that was home to the Turkish governor. The recently renovated building has two galleries with contemporary exhibitions of photography, sculpture, prints, and paintings, and hosts live concerts in the summer.

At the edge of town is the ancient **Tel Beer Sheba** (off the Beer Sheva-Shoket junction on Rte. 60 just south of Omer, 08/646-7286, www.parks.org.il, 8am-5pm daily Apr.-Sept., 8am-4pm daily Oct.-Mar., adult NIS15, child NIS7), most of a city that dates back to the 10th century BC. You can walk around what is left of the ancient streets and buildings, and really see the layout and imagine what it was like to live here. The Tel is considered to be

of unparalleled importance in relation to the study of biblical-period urban planning and biblical history and, as such, was designated by UNESCO as a World Heritage Site. If it's in the summer months, go as early in the morning as possible and take a hat and water. There is no shade, except for the little bit in the observation tower, which you can climb up.

Just outside of town is the **Israeli Air Force Museum** (Hatzerim Air Force Base, Rte. 2357 about 5 miles southwest of Beer Sheva, 08/990-6853, www.iaf.org.il, 8am-5pm Sun.-Thurs., 8am-1pm Sun., NIS30), which features exhibits of Israeli aviation history, including over 140 aircraft and anti-aircraft, and among them missile launchers are on display.

Situated in the Lahav Forest near Kibbutz Lahav, about 12 miles north of Beer Sheva, is the **Museum of Bedouin Culture at the Joe Alon Center** (Rte. 40 to Dvira Junction, then follow signs for Joe Alon Center, www.joealon.org.il, 08/991-3322, 9am-4pm Sun.-Thurs., NIS20). The museum is the only one of its kind in the region, documenting the unique aspects of Bedouin culture as it transitioned from a nomadic to modern lifestyle. The museum is the central focus of the Joe Alon Center, situated inside of a round building that resembles a tent. The Bedouin's story of transition is told through a series of

THE PEOPLE OF THE NEGEV

One of the most unique characteristics of the Negev is the people who live here and have lived here throughout history. In ancient times, Nabataean traders developed several cities along their profitable trade routes here. Abraham made his home in the very ancient city of Beer Sheva. Others who have lived in the vast desert region throughout the ages include Arab nomads, Canaanites, Philistines, Edomites, Byzantines, Ottomans, and Jews. The ancient economy of the Negev was based largely on sheep herding, agriculture, and trade.

The modern Jewish settlement of the Negev

started a century ago with about a dozen settlements. Israel's first Prime Minister, David Ben-Gurion, was a major advocate of settling in the Negev after moving to Kibbutz Sde Boker.

Among the modern residents of the Negev are Arab Bedouins. As you travel through the Negev and the south of Israel, you'll notice quite a number of semi-permanent Bedouin encampments or clusters of makeshift homes dotting the desert landscape. The Bedouin were once a nomadic people who have largely settled down and integrated into modern culture, but some of their nomadic tendencies survive.

THE ANCIENT INCENSE ROUTE

For seven centuries, the mysterious Nabataeans established and worked their incense trade over a network of routes that totaled more than 1,200 miles. The Nabataean incense trade route, which extended from Yemen and Oman in the Arabian Peninsula to the Mediterranean, operated from the 3rd century BC to the 4th century AD. The main trade route was from Petra, the capital city of the mighty Nabataeans in Jordan, just across the border of modern-day Israel.

The portion of the route in the Negev Desert included the four Nabataean towns of Halutsa, Mamshit, Avdat, and Shivta. The ruins of fortresses, agricultural landscapes, and advanced irrigation systems that remain are evidence of the incredible profits that were made in the trade of frankincense and other valuable incense and spices.

The water collection and irrigation systems of cisterns, reservoirs, dams, and channeling made large-scale agriculture possible in the towns along the incense route that were supported by the wealth of the incense trade. The most outstanding evidence of the water systems can be found in the vicinity of Avdat and the central Negev.

The incense route is a UNESCO World Heritage Site and considered a testimony to ancient technology and innovation used to successfully settle and support human life in the extremely harsh desert setting.

---

life-size mannequins and admission includes a cup of coffee in a Bedouin tent if you're game.

Sde Boker and Ein Avdat

Head about 40 minutes directly south of Beer Sheva along Route 40 and you'll come upon **Kibbutz Sde Boker** and the ecotourism and historical sites close by to it. The kibbutz has a winery and gift shop, but the main attraction is **Ben-Gurion's Hut** (Kibbutz Sde Boker, 08/656-0469, www.bgh.org.il, 8:30am-4pm Sun.-Thurs., 8:30am-2pm Fri., 10am-4pm Sat. and holiday eves, last entry 30 minutes before closing, NIS10), the home of Israel's first prime minister, David Ben-Gurion, and his wife Paula, left just as it was when he died in 1973. The house is referred to as a hut because of its modest appearance. Ben-Gurion, who idealized the Negev as the frontier land of Israel, lived in the house with his wife when Sde Boker was just a young kibbutz. A building next to his house has an exhibit—a short historical animated film—about Ben-Gurion's connection to the Negev.

Only leaving the kibbutz just before his death, his and his wife's final resting places are about five minutes south at **Ben-Gurion's** Tomb National Park (off Rte. 40 near Ben-Gurion College, 08/655-5684, www.parks.org.il, always open, free). Their gravesites overlook a stunning desert view that includes the Tzin Canyon and the Avdat highlands right in the midst of the Negev.

C EIN AVDAT NATIONAL PARK

Just about 10 minutes to the south of Ben-Gurion's tomb is the gorgeous **Ein Avdat National Park** (off Rte. 40, 08/655-5684, www.parks.org.il, 8am-5pm daily Apr.-Sept., 8am-4pm daily Oct.-Mar., last entrance one hour before closing, adult NIS29, child NIS15, combination ticket with Avdat National Park adult NIS46, child NIS24), which features the Nakhal Zin canyons, springs, waterfalls, and various native plants and animals.

Ein Avdat is also home to the mysteriously ever-flowing waters of the Avdat Spring that have cut a deep, narrow canyon through the rock. For the adventurous travelers, it makes an excellent place to wade on a hot day or even take a swim.

The park features a well-designed trail that protects the natural habitat, and you can see all kinds of wildlife if you take your time and stay relatively quiet. The most commonly seen

© ALEX GULEVICH/123RF.COM

Ein Avdat National Park

animal is the ibex, a mountain goat that is end-lessly fascinating as it scales the steep desert cliffs with ease.

◖ Avdat National Park

Avdat National Park (off Rte. 40, 08/655-1511, www.parks.org.il, 8am-5pm daily Apr.-Sept., 8am-4pm daily Oct.-Mar., last entrance one hour before closing on Fri. and holiday eves, adult NIS27, child NIS14, combination ticket with Ein Avdat National Park adult NIS46, child NIS24) is home to one of the most fa-mous Nabataean cities along the incense route that they used to transport incense, spices, and perfumes.

Avdat had its high point when it flourished around 30-9 BC, and it was subsequently de-stroyed and rebuilt, rising and falling until the Arab conquest in the 7th century AD.

Some of the most remarkable aspects of the ruins include the restored gateway on the acropolis, the Roman bathhouse and watch-tower, the 4th-century churches, and caves that served as burial places, storage, and cisterns.

Avdat has a visitor's center with more infor-mation about the site, including a short film about the incense route and related spices. The site is a key stop for travelers interested in understanding more about how the ancient spice route worked, its social and economic functions, and its significance regionally and globally.

◖ Mitzpe Ramon Observatory and Ramon Crater

Just 30 minutes south of Sde Boker is the **Mitzpe Ramon Observatory and Ramon Crater** (Rte. 40, 08/658-8691, www.parks. org.il, 8am-4pm Sat.-Thurs., 8am-3pm Fri. and holiday eves, one hour later in the sum-mer, NIS44), where the largest of three mas-sive geological craters in the Negev can be seen. The Ramon Crater Nature Reserve (Makhtesh Ramon Nature Reserve) is part of a complex that includes a visitor's center with a bookstore and hiking information.

In the nature reserve are a variety of hik-ing trails, the more advanced trails of which

looking down at the Ramon Crater

can take up to three days to traverse. You can arrange hiking expeditions of all kinds through the nature reserve, and even experience Bedouin tents, rappelling, and more.

The visitor's center is an excellent place to learn about the area and put questions to the Israel Nature Reserves Authority staff working here, as well as ask about hiring guide services. There are also slide and film shows and a museum with exhibits of the area's natural habitat. Make sure to keep a map with you at all times when hiking in the area, and keep water and a hat with you.

Bedouin Tents and *Khans*

Throughout the Negev you'll see extensive groups of humble, semi-permanent Bedouin dwellings dotting the landscape. You can have a closer encounter with Bedouin culture by visiting a **Bedouin tent** and ***khan*** (roadside inn) in Sefinat Hamidbar, Khan Hashayarot, and Khan Beerotayim. The tents and *khans* (which can be good for overnight camping or a rest stop) can be found at the Mashabei Sadeh

junction, near the ancient city of Avdat and the village of Ezuz. It's best to visit 10 am-4 pm daily. There's no formal fee but you will be encouraged to spend money on either food or crafts and should come prepared to spend at least NIS30-40.

Along the Incense Route

Near the modern day city of Dimona are the highlights of the 1,500-mile **Ancient Incense Route** that was used by merchants and traders in ancient times. A section of about 100 miles cut through what is today known as Israel and ended at the Port of Gaza. Today you can visit some of the stops on the route, declared UNESCO World Heritage Sites in 2005.

At **Mamshit** (Rte. 25, about 5 miles southeast of Dimona, 08/655-6478, www.parks.org.il, 8am-4pm daily Apr.-Sept., 8am-4pm daily Oct.-Mar., last entry one hour before closing, adult NIS22, child NIS10) there is a reconstructed city with streets, arched structures, mosaics, a large house, and ruins of an inn, churches, a bathhouse, rainwater collecting pools, and other structures. Mamshit was the site of the discovery of a trove of almost 11,000 silver coins. Beyond visiting the park, you can camp here overnight.

Beyond Mamshit, are the sites of **Avdat,** which includes the ruins of a fortress, churches, homes, a bathhouse, and a workshop. Then there was **Shivta** (08/655-5684, www.parks.org.il) and the northernmost stop of **Halutsa,** where you can find the ruins of a theater and a church.

ENTERTAINMENT AND EVENTS
Festivals

In the spring, the big show in the south is the **Zorba the Buddha Festival** (08/632-6508, www.zorba.co.il, late Mar.-Apr.), which runs for four or five days and has a strong spiritual, Buddhist slant. The festival takes advantage of the desert landscape to showcase musical performances, theater, movement exhibitions, meditation, and dance. It's the kind of festival that organizers ask you to

imagine sipping a cup of Chai tea in a desert setting: complete mellowness in the heart of the desert.

For fans of indie rock music and camping in the desert, **In-D-Negev** (Mitzpe Gvulot, Rte. 234 to Ze'elim Junction, http://indnegev.co.il, Oct., NIS90-220) is three days of music, camping, and celebrating with a general spirit of togetherness and inclusion. The festival organizers even make allowances for kids, with activities and a play area. There is usually a crowd of about 4,000 people.

SHOPPING

The best and the majority of shopping in the Negev outside of Eilat is in Beer Sheva. The most unique aspect you'll likely encounter at the **Beer Sheva Bedouin Market** (south of the David Hacham Blvd. and HaMelacha St. intersection, southwest of the Old City in Beer Sheva, 8am-4pm Thurs.) is Bedouin women completely covered in black. The majority of items for sale are racks and racks of discount clothing, as well as a few stalls for items like

the Beer Sheva weekly market

THE POWERFUL AND MYSTERIOUS NABATAEANS

Much has been written and said about the empire of the ancient Nabataeans, but they, and their former capital city in Petra, Jordan, remain shrouded in an air of mystery.

The Nabataeans were master traders, builders, and experts of ancient technology for creating ingenious water systems to support and sustain desert life. Bolstered by the wealth they earned over 700 years of their hugely profitably incense trade route, they established a society and culture in the harsh desert.

Natural disasters wiped out part of the Nabataean history in their capital city of Petra, limiting definitive information about certain aspects of their culture. One thing that is known is that their traders traveled in caravans across vast distances in the deserts, transporting spices,

incense, and perfumes, which were shipped out of the port at Gaza. As time passed, the way stations that grew out of their passage back and forth through the Negev Desert grew into cities where terraced agriculture and sophisticated irrigation practices helped them thrive.

The remains of the four Nabataean cities of Halutsa, Mamshit, Avdat, and Shivta are significant archaeological sites, but the most remarkable and breathtaking remnants of the Nabataeans is the ancient city of Petra, in Jordan.

The Roman Empire attempted more than once to conquer the Nabataeans, and in AD 106, they finally succeeded. The caravan cities, particularly Avdat, fell into decline after the Romans conquered them.

---

water pipes, toys, and candy. If you take your time, you can find some Bedouin craft items for sale, and it can be a great place to mingle with locals.

As the major metropolis for many smaller towns in the south, Beer Sheva has several strip malls that include outlet stores and a little bit of everything. There are several strip malls around town, but the biggest is collectively referred to by locals as **Big** strip mall; it's just at the outskirts of town.

About 20 minutes northwest of Beer Sheva is the **Desert Embroidery Store and Visitor's Center** (Lakiya, off Rte. 31 north from Beer Sheva, 08/651-3208, www.desert-embroidery. org, 9:30am-1:30pm Sun.-Thurs., 10am-4pm Sat., closed on Muslim holidays, call in advance), where you can buy colorful and attractive hand-embroidered items like bags, wallets, and the like. The store is run by the Association for the Improvement of Women's Status Lakiya branch. The visitor's center specializes in traditional Bedouin hospitality, where you can sit on woven cushions and have a light lunch. Again, call in advance to alert them you are coming, especially if you have a large group or are planning on eating lunch here.

SPORTS AND RECREATION
National Parks and Nature Reserves

More than a park, **Timna National Park** (about 17 miles north of Eilat off Rte. 90, 08/631-6756, www.parktimna.co.il, 8am-4pm Sun.-Thurs. and Sat., 8am-3pm Fri. and holiday eves Sept.-June; 8am-1pm Sun.-Mon. and Wed.-Sat., 8am-1pm and 5pm-8pm Tues., with guided sunset tours by reservation, July-Aug.; park entrance: adult NIS44, child NIS39) is an entire experience that includes hot air balloons and famed touring routes, including the incredible natural rock formations of Solomon's Pillars. There are also family activities by the lake, a restaurant and souvenir shop, and sunset and night tours.

Not far from Timna and a good combination trip is the **Hai Bar Nature Reserve** (20 miles north of Eilat on Rte. 90, 08/637-6018, www.parks.org.il, 8:30am-5pm Sun.-Thurs., 8:30am-4pm Fri.-Sat., NIS39, Predators Center only NIS25) that includes a small petting zoo, an African village, and a play archaeology dig for kids. It is just under five square miles, and if you have a rental car you can rent a tour CD and drive through the park, dodging friendly ostriches as you go. The adjacent **Predators Center** is about 7.5 square miles and is home to local birds and animals of prey, including the only remaining lappet-face vultures in Israel.

Bike and Jeep Tours

The Negev is an excellent area for sporty adventures like bicycle riding tours, which can be booked through a company like **Desert Eco Tours** (052/276-5753, www.desertecotours.com). You can tour major sites in the region by bicycle on one- or two-day trips. The company also offers jeep tours, which is an excellent way to see the area, especially if you aren't used to hiking in the heat, and if you can handle the bumpy terrain.

Archery

If you're up for learning something new while traveling, the **Desert Archery Park** (Mitzpe Ramon, 050/534-4598, www.desertarchery.co.il, prices vary) might be of interest. You can take a hike through the desert while shooting a bow and arrow and taking in the scenery.

ACCOMMODATIONS

If you end up spending a few nights in the Negev, it's the perfect place to take advantage of some of Israel's most unique overnight stays, including desert camping and Bedouin lodging.

Under US$100

Near the ancient incense route, the Gidron Stream, and just three miles from Moshav Hatzeva, **Ras Hashita** (Meshek 85, Hatzeva, 052/366-5927, US$30 d) is a very rustic and inexpensive stay in the midst of the Arava Desert. Guests stay in tents in the middle of a small complex that has space for 16 different accommodations, and share an outdoor bathroom. There is also a public tent for hanging out on mats and swinging in hammocks. There is a shared kitchen, and you're allowed to cook out on the premises. Hiking trips in the desert and other excursions can be arranged from here.

Offering a truly unique place to stay, **Negev Camel Ranch** (Rte. 25, southeast of Dimona,

08/655-2829, www.cameland.co.il, US$56 d) is a working farm that raises camels for riding. It's the perfect place to experience a camel desert ride and excursion into the desert. Near Mamshit, the ranch has very simple desert huts for sleeping, and shared bathrooms, with towels and bedding provided. Dinner, which is only served until 7pm and is an extra US$15, is a traditional vegetarian meal that includes lentils, rice, and bread with dates and tea for dessert. You can also visit the farm and the camels for free if you're not game to stay here.

Set on the northern ridge of the Ramon Crater, **Mitzpe Ramon Youth Hostel** (4 Nahal Nikrot, Mitzpe Ramon, 08/658-8443, www.iyha.org.il, US$98 d) is a typical, blandly-decorated but clean hostel with a good number of rooms (almost 50), which is handy in the busy summer season when most hostels book months in advance. There are private bathrooms with showers available, and breakfast is included. If you're heading out to do some hiking, the hostel can help arrange for lunch to take, and can also assist with jeep and camel tours.

Set in Mitzpe Ramon, the very tiny **Green Backpackers** (10/6 Nahal Sirpad, 08/653-2319, www.thegreenbackpackers.com, US$71 d, cash payments for in-person payment and no breakfast included with online booking) is an ecotourism hostel that caters to backpackers and is run by guides. The hostel only takes adult guests, and has free Wi-Fi in common areas, a shared kitchen, and shared TV-DVD and computer station. Near the Ramon Crater and the Israel National Trail, the hostel is near public transportation. You can get travel advice, maps, and rent gear here.

You'll be hard-pressed to find something as unique as the **Desert Days Eco Lodge** (off the Arava Rd. near Zukim village, 052/617-0028, www.negevecolodge.com, US$99 d, often has 2-night weekend minimum during high season). Designed by Tel Aviv transplants who built the place themselves, the nine "eco-huts" in the Arava Desert look like they sprung straight up from the desert itself. Every hut mirrors and blends with the desert

DESERT ECOTOURISM

One of the most interesting and attractive parts of touring the south of Israel is the option for experiencing what is known as desert ecotourism. In a general sense, desert ecotourism includes options for accommodations that employ sustainable practices and in many cases are built by hand to blend with the desert environment. Accommodations might also be very rough and on par with camping, including options for staying in tents with outhouses and very minimal creature comforts, as well as staying in Bedouin tent encampments.

Other aspects of desert ecotourism include farms and animal reserves that allow visitors to see desert animals up close; Bedouin arts and crafts tours; archery; and bicycling. Most aspects of desert ecotourism emphasize minimal impact on the environment but maximum exposure and experience.

A very useful website for desert ecotourism information in the south and throughout Israel is **Ecotourism Israel** (www.ecotourism-israel.com). If you are looking for guided tour options, try **Desert Eco Tours** (www.desertecotours.com).

environment; they have solar panel-generated electricity, and used water is recycled into the desert. Huts include free Wi-Fi and there is an outdoor swimming pool and a communal *khan* (roadside inn) for guests to mingle with each other and learn about the area.

US$100-150

Right in the middle of Moshav Hatzeva, **Desert Routes Inn** (Moshav Hatzeva, 052/366-5927, shvilimbamidbar@gmail.com, US$134 d) is a small inn with less than a dozen rooms near the border with Jordan in the Arava Desert. The inn is the perfect combination of desert hospitality blended with modern conveniences. The cozy rooms have small but comfortable beds, and the common areas of the inn are designed with exotic, but simple, touches that include woven sitting mats around huge tables, hammocks, and semi-covered outdoor patio seating. The rustic desert experience is buffered by the amenities of free Wi-Fi, a hot tub, private patios with desert views, a swimming pool on the moshav, and shuttle service to and from Hatzeva Junction, where buses going to Jerusalem and Tel Aviv stop.

A 30-minute drive from the Dead Sea, **Drachim Guest House** (1 Hanasi Blvd., Dimona, www.drachim.org, 08/655-6540,

US$118 d) is a spacious property with 59 rooms that is something between a hotel and a hostel. Drachim's perks include a semi-Olympic indoor swimming pool, a spa, gardens, free Wi-Fi, and a cafeteria where the included breakfast is served. The rooms are simple but homey, and the whole place is set up for the traveler who wants a taste of comfort and luxury without going broke.

The **Desert Olive Farm** (Ramat Negev, Sde Boker, 052/558-3065, www.zimmeril.com, US$134 d) achieves the perfect combination of a desert experience with all the luxury touches that Israeli *zimmers* (rooms to rent) are known for, including whirlpool bathtubs. You can stay in a cabin, tent, or suite; note that if you stay in a tent, all of your bathroom facilities are under the stars. The farm is 20 minutes from Mitzpe Ramon, 40 minutes from Beer Sheva, and it is just absolutely gorgeous and enchanting.

The mid-size **Ramon Suites Hotel** (8 Nahal Meishar St., Mitzpe Ramon, www.ramonhotel.co.il, 08/658-8884, US$145 d) is basic, nice, and modern, and offers suites that have kitchenettes. The three-floor hotel has 34 rooms with free Wi-Fi and the option of using a laptop for no extra charge, tea and coffee service, and spacious rooms. The highlight of Ramon Suites' location is that it's at the doorstep of the

Ramon Crater Nature Reserve, and the hotel will give you a free bike to take a ride there.

US$150-200

Don't let the hot tub and nice wine selection fool you: **Boker Valley Vineyards Farm** (Rte. 40 between Tlallim and Sde Boker, 08/657-3483, US$172 d) is pure rustic Negev Desert accommodations. The five sweet cabins are set around the property of Negev Farms, a working wine producer with vineyards and organic olive trees. Each cabin has a refrigerator, coffee and tea service, and there is a cookout area. You can eat dinner at the farm if you arrange it in advance; it's near Avdat National Park. Neve Midbar thermal baths gives discounts to guests.

Over US$200

A little piece of luxury in a desert setting, **Desert Home** (70 Ein Shaviv St., Mitzpe Ramon, 052/322-9496, www.baitbamidbar. com, US$215 d) is known for its designer interior that includes bleached wood floors and carefully designed rooms painted in beautiful, calming colors. You might not need the fireplace, but the five rooms all also come with free Wi-Fi, furnished balconies, a kitchenette, a satellite TV, and daily room service of the included breakfast. One last perk is the garden hot tub.

Home to a luxury hotel and one of the best restaurants in town, **Chez Eugène** (8/1 Har Ardon St., Mitzpe Ramon, http://mitzperamonhotel.co.il, 08/653-9595, US$265 d) is very small with only half a dozen rooms, but it has a range of high-tech amenities including free Wi-Fi, a CD and DVD player, iPod docking station, and a Playstation 3 console. Wines from the hotel's vineyards are served in the restaurant, and tours and excursions (including a night walking tour) can be organized through the concierge.

Camping

There are a wide variety of camping options in the Negev. Stick to designated camping areas and pay the entrance fee or you might get fined by a park ranger. The most useful website for camping information is the Israel **Nature and Parks Authority** site (www.ecotourism-israel. com). You can search parks by region and the listings all include camping information.

FOOD
Beer Sheva

A favorite standby among locals **Saba Giabetto** (28 Rager St. Rasco Center, 08/627-2829) is known for its homey atmosphere (Saba means grandfather in Hebrew), tasty sandwiches, and sassy menu that has fun facts and information about the restaurant.

Situated near the Museum of the Negev and the Old City, **Arabica** (12 Hertsel St., 08/627-7801, http://arabica-rest.co.il , 11:30am-last customer Sun.-Thurs., 11:30am-an hour before sunset Fri., hour after sunset-last customer Sat., NIS80) serves Middle Eastern fusion cuisine in a modern, upscale atmosphere. The menu is arranged under categories of price that start at NIS69 and go up to NIS125, and include meat and seafood dishes. It is very popular and you might find yourself in for a long wait unless you make reservations.

Situated close to city center and hotels, **Casa do Brasil** (1 Montefiore, 08/627-3330, www. casadobrasil.co.il, noon-midnight Sun.-Thurs., noon-4pm Fri., 30 minutes after sunset-last customer Sat., NIS50) is all about serving up nice, big cuts of beef in a casual, party-like atmosphere. A domestic chain with three locations, the Beer Sheva branch has a very spacious, simple interior and outdoor seating.

The cheap prices at **Metah Midbar** (Mercuz-HaNegev Building off of Yitzhak St., 054/633-6020, noon-midnight Sun.-Fri., 1pm-midnight Sat., NIS35) come with a price: a sometimes rowdy crowd of students from the nearby Ben-Gurion University campus. The best menu items include standbys like the hamburger and the chicken salad. They also have Wi-Fi and outlets behind the bar, so it's a great place to stop if you want to check email or other things online.

WINERIES OF THE NEGEV

It might seem surprising to hear of wineries that exist in a vast, harsh desert, but nonetheless they are here, in the pioneering spirit that is such a defining characteristic of the Negev and its people.

One of the more well-established is the **Sde Boker Winery,** run out of Kibbutz Sde Boker, where Israel's first prime minister and advocate of desert life, David Ben-Gurion, lived with his wife.

Another winery, **Carmey Avdat,** has its vineyards in the ancient, already-existing terraces that are part of the ruins of an agricultural settlement that is about 1,500 years old. They use the annual flash floods to irrigate.

Near the Dead Sea is **Yatir Winery,** whose vineyards are in the largest planted forest in Israel, the Yatir. Their wines are sold at the exclusive London department store Selfridges and they are known for their white wines.

Two others are **Boker Valley Vineyards** and **Neot Semedar.**

Dimona

Not far from the ancient Nabataean city of Mamshit, Dimona is a smaller town that offers a few very simple options for food, including the typical national chains of CaféCafé and Aroma, both in Peretz Center.

A bit of a change of pace from hummus and pita, **Pizza Bachchan** (3 Herzl Blvd., 08/657-0550, www.piza-pazzaz.co.il, NIS80) serves up gourmet pizza with hearty amounts of toppings. It is part of a domestic chain of pizzerias. They will deliver if you are staying at a nearby hotel. The price varies according to what kind of toppings you get, but you can generally expect to pay about NIS80 for a two-topping, medium pizza.

Mitzpe Ramon

Probably your best bet in the Negev, outside of Beer Sheva, for a range of dining options, Mitzpe Ramon is also near the famed, must-see Ramon Crater.

One of the fanciest places in town, **Chez Eugène** (8/1 Har Ardon St., 08/653-9595, http://mitzperamonhotel.co.il, 7pm-10pm Sun.-Thurs., noon-4pm and 7pm-10pm Fri., noon-10pm Sat., NIS90) is part of a boutique hotel with the same name. The restaurant interprets some classic dishes through the lens of local flavors and traditions, including handmade sausage, seafood dishes with cauliflower

cream sauce, and coconut pudding with balsamic syrup for dessert and Negev boutique beer. The restaurant's setting in the modern Chez Eugène boutique hotel in the area known as the Spice Quarter keeps the whole experience elegant but local.

Hakatze (2 Har Ardon St., 08/659-5273 and 050/756-5063, noon-8pm Mon. and Wed.-Fri., NIS40) is a simple restaurant just at the edge of town that makes home-style Israeli food with an emphasis on grilled meats and typical Middle Eastern side dishes, including pita bread. An unusual, but nice touch, are the English magazines that can be read in the back of the restaurant.

A combination coffee shop and gift shop, **Hadasa'ar** (6 Har Boker St., 08/940-8473, 8am-8pm Sun.-Thurs., 8am-4pm Fri., NIS40) also sells organic groceries and operates as a semi-cooperative. It's a good place to stop off if you just want something quick and light, and maybe a souvenir for the road.

Situated inside the Ramon Inn, the **Ramon Inn Restaurant** (1 Ein Akev, 08/658-8822, breakfast 7am-9am and dinner 7:30pm-9:30pm daily, NIS120 fixed price) does a huge buffet that varies by the day and includes a wide variety of dishes of local flavor (which means spicy in some cases). It's a bit of a rush for food when the dining room doors open. You need to have a reservation if you are not a guest at the hotel,

Watch out for camels while driving through the Negev.

© ALBERTO AROCHAS/123RF.COM

but it is guaranteed to be filling. They also serve a buffet breakfast.

Sde Boker

Situated in a fairly isolated spot, the area around Sde Boker has some phenomenal sites to visit, but very few options for restaurants. It's a good area to carry some food to go with you from Mitzpe Ramon or wherever you are coming from.

In an area where there are very few options for something simple, the **Sde Boker Field School** (Midreshet Ben-Gurion, www.boker. org.il/english) has a decent option: a snack shop with shaded outdoor seating with an incredible view of the Negev Desert. Right next door to Kibbutz Sde Boker and not far from the Ramon Crater, it's situated in the perfect spot to just stop, have a quick bite, and move on. If you've brought snacks with you and just want a place with outdoor picnic tables and free parking, it's also convenient for that. Don't miss the view from the observation deck about 100 yards away from the picnic tables.

GETTING THERE AND AROUND

The area of the Negev is vast and spread about with large distances in between sights and places to eat and sleep. It's possible to get around by bus and train, but there is generally very little traffic and it also makes for fairly easy and enjoyable driving if you have a car.

By Car

The main city of the Negev, Beer Sheva, is about a two-hour drive from Jerusalem, mostly along Highway 6. Though it looks circuitous on a map, the best and fastest road out of Jerusalem is immediately west and then south, rather than straight south, which will add about 20 minutes to your drive time.

From Tel Aviv you can reach Beer Sheva in less than 90 minutes, mostly along Highway 6.

By Train

The **Israel Railways** (www.rail.co.il) traverses through several points in the Negev, including Beer Sheva. There are no trains from

Jerusalem to the south, but there are trains from the south back to Jerusalem that take about 2.5 hours (NIS39 one-way). From Tel Aviv, it is about 80 minutes to Beer Sheva (NIS30 one-way).

By Bus

By far the most convenient way to get to the Negev and to travel around in the area is by **Egged** bus (www.egged.co.il). From Jerusalem it is about two hours (bus numbers 446 and 470, NIS30 one-way) to Beer Sheva and from Tel Aviv it is about 90 minutes (bus number 370, NIS17 one-way). Once in the area, **Metrodan** buses get you around locally. They do not have a website in English, but you can find related information on a compilation website (www.bus.co.il).

Eilat

As far south as you can go in Israel is the resort town and diving destination of Eilat. Summer temperatures in Eilat reach well over 100°F, but in the midst of winter and early spring it is very pleasant.

Eilat has grown up around the axis of the Red Sea. Most major destinations, activities, restaurants, accommodations, and sites in Eilat are somewhere on or near the shore of the Red Sea.

If you're driving, it is almost impossible to get lost in Eilat, and it's full of massive round-abouts that make driving in a foreign country less intimidating.

SIGHTS

Eilat's main draw is its world-class diving, its beaches, and the many opulent hotel and spa options. There are a few standout places to have fun, especially if traveling with kids.

© GIDON BELMAKER

The Port of Eilat is popular with boating and water sports enthusiasts.

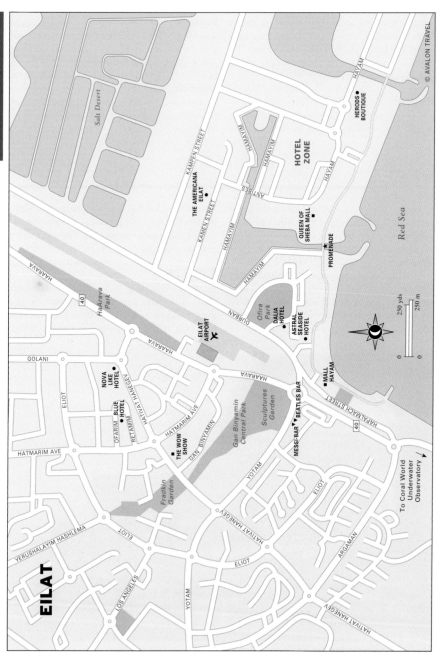

© AVALON TRAVEL

EILAT

Salt Desert

HaArava Park

Red Sea

HOTEL ZONE

HERODS BOUTIQUE

QUEEN OF SHEBA MALL

PROMENADE

THE AMERICANA EILAT

KAMEN STREET

KAMEN STREET

HAMAYIM

HAMAYIM

HAMAYIM

HAMAYIM

HAMAYIM

HAMAYIM

ANTIBES

HAYAM

HAYAM

DURBAN

Ofira Park

DALIA HOTEL

ASTRAL SEASIDE HOTEL

MALL HAYAM

HAPALMACH STREET

EILAT AIRPORT

HAARAVA

HAARAVA

HAARAVA

40

GOLANI

ELIOT

NOVA LIKE HOTEL

OFARIM · BLUE HOTEL

RETAMIM

HATIVAT HANEGEV

HATMARIM AVE

HATMARIM AVE

GAN BINYAMIN

THE WOW SHOW

Gan Binyamin Central Park

Sculptures Garden

MESSI BAR · BEATLES BAR

HATMARIM AVE

Fradkin Garden

YERUSHALAYIM HASHLEMA

ELIOT

LOS ANGELES

YOTAM

ELIOT

YOTAM

HATIVAT HANEGEV

ELIOT

ARGAMAN

HATIVAT HANEGEV

40

To Coral World Underwater Observatory

250 yds

250 m

0

0

Dolphin Reef Diving Center

The **Dolphin Reef Diving Center** (Metsarim St. on South Beach, 08/630-0100, www.dolphin-reef.co.il, 9am-5pm Sun.-Thurs., 9am-4:30pm Fri.-Sat. and holidays, adult NIS64, child NIS44) is Israel's version of swimming with the dolphins. At the center, bottlenose dolphins can be visited from the floating piers and observation points. Guided swims are also available. Included with the entrance fee is a full day's access to the park and observation points, including beach access, but there is no lifeguard. There's an extra charge for access to the snorkeling and diving center, relaxation pools, the children's activity center, and the underwater photography center. The center also has a restaurant and there is a bar on the beach.

◖ Coral World Underwater Observatory

Hours of pure fun and enjoyment are just five miles from Eilat's city center at the **Coral World Underwater Observatory** (Rte. 90, 08/636-4200, www.coralworld.com/eilat, 8:30am-5pm Sat.-Thurs., 8:30am-4pm Fri. and holidays, NIS79, NIS89 including Oceanarium), distinguishable by the structure pointing into the sky.

Throughout the complex, which includes a cafeteria, you can look through a dozen different windows to see bright, rare fish, including a dark room for viewing glow-in-the-dark sea life and phosphorescent fish. For an extra charge, you can go for an underwater dive in a 100-ton yellow submarine.

It's easy to spend half a day at the Observatory and Oceanarium, especially if you time your visit around daily events like the 11am shark feeding, 3pm Amazon animal feeding, a trip to the Oceanarium's simulated-motion theater, a trip up to the observatory tower where you can see the neighboring countries of Jordan and Egypt, and a visit to the café.

King's City

A bit opulent and slightly over the top, the biblical theme park **King's City** (East Lagoon in North Beach area, 08/630-4444, www.

You can spend hours at the Coral World Underwater Observatory.

kingscity.co.il, NIS125) is still good fun with all of its rides, games, and mostly air-conditioned facilities. Depicting stories of King Solomon, Queen Sheba, and others, the park includes high-tech features and interactive aspects that range from 3D movies to mazes. There are plenty of places to grab a quick bite in the park, so it's an especially easy option if visiting with a family group.

ENTERTAINMENT AND EVENTS
Festivals and Shows

If you are in Eilat in the dead of winter, the **Red Sea Winter Jazz Festival** (www.redseajazzeilat.com, Jan.) is a combination of music, culture, and events. It's been running for just a few years and is an offshoot of the **Red Sea Jazz Festival** (www.redseajazzeilat.com, July) that takes place in the summer. Both span several days and are considered the best festivals of their kind in all of Israel, attracting international acts and the best domestic artists. Concerts are held in three venues, one of which overlooks the Red Sea. Package deals on hotels, flights, and shows can be found on the festival website.

For a performance full of acrobatics, dance, and lighting effects all to a soundtrack, **The WOW Show** (Royal Garden Hotel, 1 Kampen St., North Shore, 08/638-6701, www.isrotel.com, shows run 11am-8:30pm Mon.-Sat., NIS75-110) is a fun way to while away the time. The thematic performance changes every year and sometimes includes dancing, comedians, and other performing artists.

Bars, Pubs, and Clubs

The **Three Monkeys Pub** (23 Pa'amei HaShalom St., Royal Beach Promenade, 08/636-8888 and 053/809-4596, 9pm-late night daily) is Eilat's oldest and most well-known sports bar and live performance venue with beach seating and a generally laid-back atmosphere. There's a huge cocktail, beer, and alcohol menu and light food options.

With its impossibly long bar and slick red-and-black interior, the **Beatles Bar** (1 Yotam,

4th Fl., 077/430-1458 and 052/801-3939, shay.dvd@gmail.com, restaurant 7pm-11pm daily, dance bar 11pm-4am daily, NIS80) oozes cool. If you come earlier in the evening you can get a burger and if you stay late you can dance the night away. The restaurant, which includes beach service, turns into a dance club in the wee hours.

Popular with both locals and tourists, **Messi-Bar** (1 Yotam, middle floor, 052/351-7336, 9:30pm-late night Tues.-Sun., minimum age 25 years) features all kinds of rock music in both English and Hebrew. The extremely casual atmosphere plays on the town's beach vibe, with sturdy, tall wooden tables and room for dancing.

SHOPPING

Eilat's special offering to shoppers is that there is no Value Added Tax (VAT) on items in stores. The selection of stores is similar to what you'll find in the rest of Israel, but stores are geared toward drawing customers in for deals with special late-night sessions and an extra-soothing level of air-conditioning to escape the heat.

Shopping Malls and Centers

For everything you could possibly want to buy, **Mall Hayam** (1 HaPalmach, North Shore, 08/634-0006, 9:30am-11:30pm Sun.-Thurs., 9am-one hour before sunset Fri.) is Eilat's biggest and Israel's most profitable mall. The mall has everything from a game center to international and domestic clothing chains to food. The multi-level mall also has a fantastic view of the Red Sea.

In close proximity to a number of hotels, the **Queen of Sheba Mall** (North Beach promenade near the Hilton, 10am-midnight daily) is 43,000 square feet of commerce with a view of the Eilat marina and places to grab a quick bite to eat.

Eilat's version of Rodeo Drive or a Parisian avenue is **La Boulevard** (5 Antiv, North Shore, 08/638-6666, 9am-11pm daily), a shopping center that comes with street lamps, wood benches, air-conditioning, and cover from the sun. The products are high-end, international brands of jewelry, fashion, sporting goods, and a French-inspired bakery.

SPORTS AND RECREATION

The main sporting attraction and a major draw to the area in general is diving. Other popular water-related activities in Eilat include glass-bottom boats and the many beaches in the area.

Beaches

There are a variety of beaches in Eilat that offer something for everyone, including water sports, parties, restaurants, and night clubs. At **HaShchafim (or Herod's) Beach** (north Eilat near Herod's Hotel) you can see movie screenings. **HaZahav Beach** (near the hotel promenade between the Isrotel Royal Beach Hotel and Dan Hotel) is synonymous with romance and has great atmosphere for just kicking back. **Dolphin Reef** (on Eilat-Taba Rd. after the Dead Sea Works potash plant) is the place to swim with the dolphins. **Royal Beach** (in front of the Royal Beach Hotel off of Pa'amei HaShalom

St.) is the best bet if you want to dine on the sand.

Diving and Water Sports

Over 100 types of stony coral and 650 species of tropical fish grace the **Coral Beach Nature Reserve** (Coral Beach opposite the Eilat Field School, 07/637-6829, www.parks.org.il, 9am-5pm daily, adult NIS35, child NIS18) at the southern end of Eilat. The centerpiece of the reserve is a 1,200-meter-long, densely populated coral reef that runs parallel to the beach.

The **Royal Water Sports** (Shvil Hayam St., 08/646-6881, 8:30am-7:30pm daily) is a sports club on Royal Beach with banana boats, tubing, jet water-skiing, kayaking, and paddle boats.

One of the best diving schools in the country, **Aqua Sport** (Mitsrayim Way, 08/633-4404, www.aqua-sport.com, 9am-4pm daily) has been in business for more than four decades and can accommodate divers of every level. They also rent equipment and have showers, bathroom facilities, and Bedouin tents.

© GIDON BELMAKER

One of Eilat's most popular activities is scuba diving.

Introductory dives for people ages 8-88 are offered daily.

Opposite of the Coral Beach Nature Reserve is **Diver's Village** (Mitsrayim Way, 08/637-2268, www.diversvillage.co.il), which has been operating for 20 years, rents diving and snorkeling equipment, and gives lessons. Introductory and refresher lessons are available, and there are showers and toilets, a snack bar, and three guest rooms. Introductory dives are available to kids as young as 7.

Glass-Bottom Boats

For a glimpse into the underwater world of the Red Sea without putting a toe in the water, you can ride on one of the **Israel-Yam** (North Shore at the marina between Caesar Hotel and Sheraton Moriah Hotel, 08/633-2325, www.israel-yam.co.il, prices vary, boats depart from the marina at 10:30am, 1pm, and 3:30pm) 72-foot yachts. The boats include a sundeck, a dance floor for private parties, and a snack bar. The lowest level has a long, rectangle-shape window for the underwater viewing floor. A two-hour ride includes a tour past the Coral Reef and the Japanese Gardens, along the Israeli-Jordanian border, and a dolphin watch on the Israeli-Egyptian border at Taba.

ACCOMMODATIONS

Eilat's status as a major domestic and international tourist destination means that there is a plethora of upper-end hotels and hotel chains. Many of the nicer hotels require a two-night minimum stay when booking on the weekend, and the fairly standard feature of Israeli hotels to include breakfast isn't universal in Eilat. Check in advance about included breakfast, as it might be by request only. Most hotels are grouped around the beaches and diving areas.

Under US$100

One of the most affordable places to stay in pricey Eilat is the **Sea Princess Motel** (136 Retamim St., 08/910-2330, www.pninathaya-meilat.co.il, US$85 d), next to the Eilat Bus Station and 10 minutes to major shopping, including Mall Hayam. With about three dozen

private rooms and dorm rooms that all have a TV, a fridge, and microwaves, the Sea Princess has free Wi-Fi in common areas, a TV in the lobby, and a garden. The front desk is 24 hours, and you can go by foot to the nearest beach, which is about 15 minutes away.

US$100-150

Still affordable and with a few extra perks, the **Blue Hotel** (123 Ofarim St., 08/632-6601, http://bluehotel.co.il, US$120 d) has a 24-hour front desk, newspaper service, and rooms with a terrace. As a guest you also have access to renting out a bicycle, a tour desk, and Wi-Fi is free throughout the hotel. Recent renovations add to the general ambience of the hotel, which is very breezy and tropical. It's possible to book a package stay at the hotel for diving.

In a great location at the center of the hopping North Beach area, the **Dalia Hotel** (4 Tarshish St. at North Beach, 08/633-4004 and 057/941-8896, www.daliahotel.co.il, US$125 d) is close to the beach, shopping, and the promenade. Though it's on the smaller end with only 60 rooms, the hotel has a swimming pool and sun deck, a children's pool, a pub, a coffee bar, and a restaurant. There is also access to tourism information, and laundry and baby-sitting services. The rooms are slightly spartan and on the small side, but they include a small fridge and table with chairs.

One of the coolest features of **Holitel La Playa Hotel** (3 Simtat Shfifon off of Kamen St., 08/939-4555, www.holitel.co.il, US$145 d) is the palm tree-encircled outdoor swimming pool. The hotel, which is near Eilat Airport, is decorated in Moroccan style, and all of the rooms have a TV, sofa, and coffee and tea service. Near city center and the beach, La Playa is a larger hotel with over 200 rooms, a spa, a cinema, a library, pool tables, video games, and a mini market. When you're tired of the beach, you can order food and drinks poolside or hang out in the hotel's bar for a drink. If you book on the weekend, there is a two-night minimum stay.

The layout of **The Americana Eilat** (7 Kamen St. at North Beach, 08/630-3777, www.

americanahotel.co.il, US$122 d) is slightly motel-ish with three stories and rooms that open directly to the outside, but the amenities and price make it a worthwhile stay. There are a variety of room types among the 140 rooms that include some with balconies and a view of the pool, kitchenettes, connecting rooms, and extra-large family rooms. The rooms are bright and comfortably furnished and include free Wi-Fi, a fridge, hair dryer, and cable TV. There is also a sauna and hot tub, shaded children's pool, a supermarket, a spa club, and a restaurant and nightclub at the hotel. Not far away is the promenade and waterfront.

Tucked right into the middle of central Eilat, the **Rio Hotel** (9 Hatmarim Ave., 08/630-1111, www.riohotel.co.il, US$129 d) is a boutique establishment with a trendy, upscale interior that includes a bar, restaurant, and small pool. Very close to the airport and bus station, guests here get access to the neighborhood disco at Hotel Mega, and a free glass of wine with dinner at the hotel restaurant.

US$150-200

Truly just a hop, skip, and a jump to the beach, **Prima Music Hotel** (Turkiz St. at Almog Beach, 08/638-8555, www.prima-hotels-israel. com, US$170 d) is just five minutes from Coral Beach. The hotel's bright, tropical interior is designed on a musical theme complete with a music room with vintage records that guests can play, giving it a quirky touch. Other features include a common area sea view terrace and some rooms with a sea view, cable TV, and CD sound systems. A stay here includes a huge buffet breakfast, bicycle rentals, and the option of a dinner buffet. It's also close to scores of restaurants at Almog Beach Marina. The Olympic-size swimming pool has a view of the Red Sea and there are tennis and volleyball courts on the hotel grounds.

Trendy and very family friendly, the **Nova Like Hotel** (6 Hativat Hanegev St., 08/638-2444 reception, 03/542-5555 reservations, www.atlas.co.il, US$158 d) is a recently renovated larger hotel with two-room suites and large studios that all have a kitchenette. The

rooms surround a pool, and many include a balcony with a pool view. There's also a kids' pool, sun deck, lobby lounge and bar, bicycle rental, and live entertainment during the high season. About 10-15 minutes by foot gets you to the main Eilat beaches. Rooms include free Wi-Fi and direct-dial telephones.

Boasting one of the best poolside views of the Red Sea in town, the (**Astral Seaside Hotel** (North Beach St., 08/636-7444, www. astralhotels.co.il, US$190 d weekdays, US$228 d weekends, hotel requires two-night stay on weekends) has a massive wooden poolside sundeck and lounge chairs. The spacious rooms are beautiful, bright, and modern and some include floor-to-ceiling windows with a terrace and sea views. The medium-size hotel also has a children's club, evening shows in high season, and in-room Swedish massages by request. There's free lobby Wi-Fi, a synagogue, spa, lobby bar, and it's just minutes away from the sea.

Near Taba Beach and Coral Beach, the multi-storey **Herods Boutique** (23 Pa'amei HaShalom St., North Shore, 08/638-0010 and 03/511-0000, www.herodshotels.com/en/ eilat, US$193 d) has views of the lagoon and the Edom Mountains. Home to a wide variety of activities geared towards kids, the hotel's rooms include a special channel on the TV for kids, mini-bars, coffee and tea service, and an option for connecting doors. The interior design has slightly opulent touches, and many of the rooms have a balcony with a view. The hotel also boasts the largest conference center in Eilat and has a swimming pool. The hotel is at the end of the promenade, but be careful when booking, as there are several hotels in Eilat with the word Herod in the title.

Nearby North Beach and Dolphin Reef, **Vista Hotel** (17 Kamen St., North Shore, 08/630-3030, www.vistaeilat.co.il, US$160 d) is also near Aqaba Fort and Aqaba City Center Shopping Mall. The hotel has a marina, an outdoor pool with a bar, free Wi-Fi in public areas, a fitness center, a restaurant, and an indoor bar. The hotel is smallish, with about 84 rooms, but the interior layout has a very spacious, modern, clean feeling. The rooms are on the smaller side, but most of them have a cityscape or water view, and include a TV, free newspapers, a fridge, and free Wi-Fi. The front desk can help with tickets and tours, business services, and currency exchange. Some cool touches are the waterfall in the pool and the arcade for kids.

Just a few miles outside of Eilat, **Eilot Kibbutz Country Lodging** (Kibbutz Eilot about 3 miles north of Eilat, 08/635-8816, www.eilot.co.il/en, US$165 d) offers an option for experiencing the area in a more pastoral setting. The hotel is small, with only 40 rooms, but has an indoor and an outdoor pool, a garden with facilities for cookouts, rooms with balconies, and a petting zoo for kids.

Over US$200

Luxury accommodations in Eilat is a serious business, and the **Magic Sunrise Club Eilat** (Kibbutz Eilot, 03/511-0098 and 08/630-5333, www.fattal-hotels.com, US$220 d) is a prime example of the all-inclusive options that are available. Near North Beach, Dolphin Reef, and Aqaba City Center Shopping Mall, this large hotel includes everything but free Wi-Fi. There are a range of dining options, from coffee to a full restaurant, concierge service, and a 24-hour front desk. Rooms have mini-bars, safes, satellite TV, balconies, direct-dial phones, and some ground-floor rooms open to a broad lawn. The interior design is quite spare but very nicely done with a Spanish theme, and the rooms are very spacious. Almost everything you could need is at this hotel.

One of the top luxury options in town, **Le Meridien** (1 HaPalmach St., North Shore, 08/638-3333, www.starwoodhotels.com/lemeridien, US$252 d) is a large, European-style hotel with 245 rooms and nearby beach access. Some rooms include balconies, sea views, and a private hot tub on the balcony. From 5pm-11pm the lobby has free drinks and appetizers. The outdoor pool overlooks the sea and has direct access to the promenade.

Expensive but worth every penny, the **Club Hotel Eilat** (2 Kheil HaHandasa Blvd. off of Habaz St., 08/636-1666, www.

clubhotels-israel.com, US$315 d) is more like an oasis compound of luxury than a hotel. The main attraction is the massive outdoor pool that includes water slides, waterfalls, and the shade of palm trees. The hotel also has a synagogue, spa and sauna, restaurant, arcade, gym, and 40 acres of grounds. The nautical interior design of the massive, 700-room hotel almost gives the feel of being in cabins on a cruise ship. When you get tired of playing at the hotel, the beach and lagoon are within easy walking distance.

Famed for its high-quality guest service, the **Rimonim Eilat Hotel** (Tarshish St., North Shore, 08/636-9369, http://english.rimonim.com, US$408 d) is literally one minute away from the Red Sea beach, and is right in the middle of Eilat's main shopping district. Every room has a balcony that overlooks the sea and the hotel's large outdoor pool. There is a lobby bar, restaurant, gym, and spa. The rooms are modern and designed with bright colors and extra touches like a dining bar, a large-screen TV, and sliding glass doors that lead to the balcony.

Home to the well-known nightly WOW show, the **Royal Garden Hotel** (1 Kampen St., North Shore, 08/633-7010, www.isrotel.com/royal_garden, US$360 d) caters to people on family vacations with roomy suites that are decorated with wood accents and cozy interiors that feel more like home than a hotel room. The gorgeous, lagoon-like outdoor pool and water park has a snack bar and the hotel is near the boardwalk and beach. Be warned that the hotel does not provide pool towels or have a restaurant, but every room has a kitchenette complete with utensils and a dining area.

The **U Coral Beach Club Resort** (Almog Beach, 08/635-0000, www.leonardo-hotels.com, US$330 d) is an all-inclusive option that has its own beach, swimming pool, and spa center. The hotel features include a bar with the option for lounging on the outdoor deck with a drink and on-site live stage performances. This 281-room hotel offers free shuttle bus, a gift shop, a poolside bar, and rooms with all the amenities you could possibly need, decorated in a simple, modern, upscale style. Dry cleaning and laundry service, room service, babysitting, and a hair salon are also available.

FOOD
Cafés and Coffee Shops

Set in the heart of the high-end Royal Garden Hotel shops avenue, **Café Boulevard** (5 Antibes, 08/638-6699, 8am-11pm daily, NIS45) is set up as a classic café with items in a case on display and a massive, spacious interior with small tables and sofas. Known for the quirky pictures they create in customers' latte foam, Boulevard usually features a Friday night live performance and has a decent alcohol menu.

The place to go for dessert and coffee is **Chocola** (6 Hatmarim Ave., 08/637-2555, www.chocola.co.il, 8am-8pm Sun.-Thurs., 8am-4pm Fri., NIS35), a French boutique bakery and patisserie that serves some of the most beautiful creations you've ever seen.

The neighborhood **Café Bzi** (11 Hatmarim Ave., 08/637-0948, 8am-midnight Mon.-Thurs., 8am-3pm Fri. closed from 6pm-8pm Mon.-Thurs., NIS45) has a family-friendly atmosphere and serves up standard Israeli coffee shop fare, with the added feature of being the local *shakshuka* joint. Bzi also advertises that you can request changes and additions to menu items, a fairly unusual feature in Israel.

The Kakao Espresso Bar (3 Antibes, 08/633-4496, www.kakao.co.il, 9am-midnight daily, NIS55) is part of a domestic chain that's been around since 2004 that serves up health food and light meals as well as coffee and pastries. Kakao is loved for its Belgian waffle dessert and friendly service, and has a gorgeous, elegant interior. The Eilat branch is pleasantly located right near the lagoon and also serves a nice selection of alcohol.

More than just a café-bakery, **Shibolim** (39 Eilot in Town Centre, 08/632-3932, www.eilat-city.net, 7am-9pm Sun.-Thurs., 7am-2pm Fri., NIS40) serves a range of rustic, homemade bread and pastries with homemade jams and dips. It's conveniently located in the town center and the extra touches make

their version of Israeli breakfast exceptionally delicious.

Dining and Dancing

Situated right in the middle of Ofira Park, **Park Avenue** (24 Tarshish St., 08/633-3303, www.park-avenue.co.il, 7pm-4am daily, NIS75) is part high-end restaurant and part dance bar that caters to the beautiful and trendy crowd of Eilat. The bar food of wings and calamari has a decidedly Mediterranean twist, and their steak and meat dishes come with hefty sides like mashed potatoes and sauce.

Italian

With a simple atmosphere and an open kitchen, **Angelina** (3 Antibes, 053/809-4348 and 08/636-3439, www.angelina-rest.co.il, 7pm-11pm Sun.-Thurs., 8pm-11pm Sat., NIS50) specializes in all manner of pizza and pasta, including a delectable zucchini, sweet potato, and feta cheese pizza pie and a spinach and gorgonzola cheese pasta dish. The chairs and general atmosphere are definitely pizzeria, but it's a nice option for a hearty Italian meal at a very affordable price, and it is right by the water with promenade seating.

Seafood

Preceded by its sterling, decades-long reputation as being one of the best seafood places in town, **Last Refuge** (Turkiz St. at Coral Beach near the underwater observatory, 072/216-0093 and 08/637-2437, www.rol.co.il/sites/eng/hamiflat, 12:30pm-11pm daily, NIS130) has colorful nautical interior decor and boasts a gorgeous view of the Red Sea. Some of their menu features include fish, mussels in garlic and cream, grilled lobsters, and seafood platters.

A relatively new kid on the block, **Pago Pago** (99 HaMayim, 08/637-6660 and 08/633-7747, www.pagopagorest.com, 12:30pm-11:30pm daily, NIS75) is situated right on the beach with a view of the Red Sea in a very sleek, modern building. The menu includes steak and seafood dishes as well as custom desserts. Try the shrimp calamari Marseille or Spanish mackerel with yogurt. The restaurant is not huge, but the dual-level layout includes a long bar and a warm atmosphere with wood flooring.

For a more informal and less expensive, but still very worthwhile seafood restaurant, **Denis-Kingdom** (12 Kamen St. next to Herod's Hotel, 052/555-6561 and 08/637-9898, noon-11pm Sun.-Thurs., noon-2:30pm Fri., 8pm-11pm Sat., NIS80) is a good option. Run by an Eilat fish farm that specializes in sea bream, you can have fish that you see swimming in the tanks on your plate, on demand, and cooked to order. Some tastier options include sea bass, bream, and fish soup. The portions are generous and come with side dishes like baked potatoes. The children's seafood options include carefully deboned filets. Don't miss the round wine room with a huge selection of regional wines.

A casual, trendy atmosphere with black leather chairs, dark wood tables, and expansive outdoor seating are the hallmarks of **Boston Fish and Grill** (21 Pa'amei HaShalom, 08/633-3007 and 08/633-7177, www.boston-grill.co.il, noon-midnight daily, NIS100). Run by five chefs of German, French, English, Norwegian, and Scottish heritage, the eclectic menu features New England dishes with the regional influence of each chef.

South American

If you make it a bit off the beaten path of city center in search of a hearty meat meal, go to **Little Brazil** (3 Eilot, 08/637-2018, brazil.eilat@gmail.com, 12:30pm-11pm daily, NIS120), an all-you-can-eat, South American Churrasco-style meat restaurant. The atmosphere is warm and friendly and because of the location you'll get a mix of locals and tourists. But you'll also get so much meat from the roaming waiter, called a Pasador, you won't want to eat again for days.

INFORMATION AND SERVICES

The tourism and information services in Eilat are some of the best in Israel since it is such a popular destination.

The well-equipped and helpful **Municipal Tourism Corporation Eilat** (2 Yotam St., 08/636-7890, rstourism@eilat.muni.il, 8am-5pm Sun.-Thurs.) is an operation of the City of Eilat and caters to international tourists, with a large amount of information in English.

The **city's official tourism website** (www.redseaeilat.com) is a very well done website with anything and everything you could want to know about Eilat. It includes listings of every kind of service imaginable.

The **city of Eilat** (www.eilat-city.net) also has a very useful and easy to use website.

In an emergency, contact the **Eilat Tourist Police** (08/636-7209 or 106) and emergency medical services **Magen David Adom** (08/637-2333 or 101).

There are about half a dozen currency exchange locations around town, including **Money Gold** (Mall HaYam, 08/634-0049, open during mall hours) and **Nawi Money Exchange** (8 Antibes St., Hilton Queen of Sheba promenade, 050/388-3111, 10am-midnight Sun.-Thurs., 10am-4pm Fri.).

GETTING THERE AND AROUND

Getting to Eilat seems daunting from the vantage point of Tel Aviv or Jerusalem, but once you're on the way, it's a fairly straight and uneventful (though lengthy) trip if you are going by car or bus.

By Car

From Jerusalem, it is a minimum four-hour drive to Eilat. Late at night there is very little traffic and you don't have the burden of the hot sun beating down on your vehicle or fighting with the air-conditioning. The roads are not lit for most of the way, and there is a great deal of blackness as you drive through the mountainous areas near the Dead Sea and through the Negev Desert. However, every turn along the road is very clearly marked, especially in the areas where it is a two-lane highway.

From Jerusalem, you will follow Route 90 south as far as you can go until you reach Eilat.

If you drive during the day, it's a good idea to take the whole day and incorporate a stop or two along the way at the Dead Sea.

From Tel Aviv, take Highway 6 to Route 40 south for about four hours. The route from Tel Aviv takes you past the incredible crater at Mitzpe Ramon and cuts straight through the desert with long stretches of nothing but a gas station every now and then.

Once you're in Eilat and driving about, you'll easily get the hang of navigating the plethora of enormous roundabouts that control traffic. The city is well sign-posted and there is plenty of parking.

By Bus

The bus trip from Jerusalem to Eilat is just under five hours on an **Egged** bus (www.egged. co.il, bus number 444, NIS78 one-way). From Tel Aviv to Eilat, it takes well over five hours (bus numbers 390 and 394, NIS78 one-way).

Once you're in Eilat, the only public transportation service in town is Egged.

By Air

It is possible to reach Eilat by plane. The **Eilat Domestic Airport** (08/636-3800, www.iaa. gov.il) takes flights from Arkia, El Al, Israir, and Sun Dor airlines. The airport is small and convenient, and flying is a good option if you plan to also take in a trip to Petra, Jordan, while you're in the area. Most tour companies will pick you up directly from the airport if you arrive on a morning flight.

THE WEST BANK

In spite of the complicated legal and political situation in the West Bank, it remains home to some important archaeological and spiritual sites – holy to Arabs, Jews, and Christians. It also includes significant, ancient biblical cities such as Jericho, Bethlehem, Hebron, and Nablus (Shechem in Hebrew), alongside more modern cities like Ramallah and Ariel.

© GENEVIEVE BELMAKER

HIGHLIGHTS

LOOK FOR ◖ TO FIND RECOMMENDED SIGHTS, ACTIVITIES, DINING, AND LODGING.

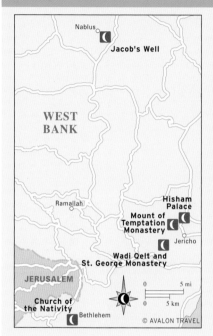

◖ **Church of the Nativity:** This ancient church in Bethlehem, believed to be the birthplace of Jesus, has an atmosphere of mystery and wonder on the inside (page 269).

◖ **Jacob's Well:** Way off the beaten path, Jacob's Well is where Jesus is said to have once stopped for a drink of water. It is housed deep under a massive church that's set amidst vast, lushly landscaped grounds (page 277).

◖ **Mount of Temptation Monastery:** High above Jericho is the place where Jesus is said to have been tempted by Satan. This spot is now home to a monastery, which you can reach by a cable car that travels over the Biblical-era ruins of Jericho (page 280).

◖ **Hisham Palace:** A mosque, massive mosaic floors, decorative touches, and fountains are the highlights of these ruins near Jericho, still in the process of being restored and preserved (page 282).

◖ **Wadi Qelt and St. George Monastery:** Hike a canyon next to flowing streams that leads to an ancient Greek Orthodox monastery (page 282).

THE WEST BANK

Situated roughly between Jerusalem and Jordan, the West Bank is an area of about 2,200 square miles. The landscape is a patchwork of olive and lemon tree groves, Arab villages, and Jewish settlements, with the occasional checkpoint or fence with concertina wire. While the West Bank is not part of Israel proper, different interpretations of borders and the presence of Jewish settlements have seriously complicated its status both regionally and internationally. Israel maintains a strong military presence in many areas, particularly in areas where there are Jewish settlements.

Some parts of the West Bank are completely under Palestinian control, some under shared control with Israel, and some are completely under Israeli control, known as Areas A, B, and C, respectively. Many people also refer to the area collectively as Palestine or as Judea and Samaria. It's important to understand whether you are in Area A, B, or C, as it will impact how you move about and what the generally accepted customs are. Some areas of the West Bank are extremely religiously conservative (such as Hebron), and other areas are tricky to navigate unless you connect with an international relief group of some kind (such as in Nablus).

When traveling in the region, keep in mind that it is important to wear more conservative

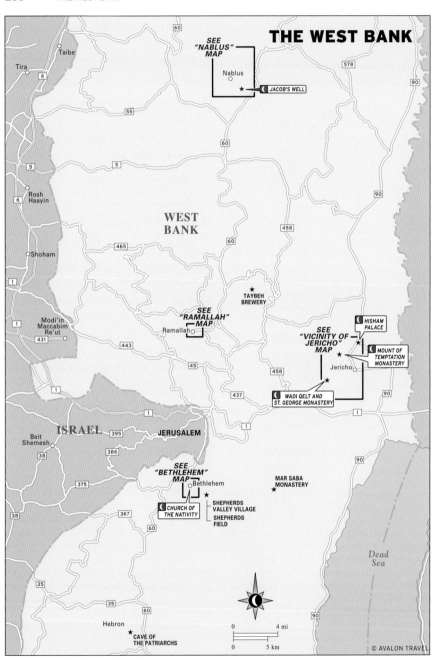

clothing (especially women), which generally means nothing too tight or revealing, and it's best to keep arms and legs covered.

Complications and special considerations aside, the West Bank is one of the most fascinating areas of the region. It is a bit on the wild side, and evokes a feeling of being in untamed territory. But it's also an easy place to connect with the rich historical past. Looking out over the rugged, sparsely populated landscape with its patchwork of gray-green olive trees and minarets, it is easy to see why so many people of different faiths want to maintain a connection to this part of the land.

HISTORY

The recent history of the West Bank is the most relevant for the purpose of travel. The current border of the West Bank was created in a 1949 armistice agreement that divided the newly created Jewish state from the other parts of the Mandatory Palestine.

In the 1948 War of Independence, Israel took control of the western part of Jerusalem, and Jordan took control of the eastern part, including the Old City, home to dozens of sites that are deeply important to the Christian, Jewish, and Muslim faiths. Until 1967, the West Bank was ruled by Jordan.

The West Bank of today is divided into three zones: Palestinian Authority-controlled (Area A); joint Palestinian Authority and Israeli-controlled (Area B); and Israeli-controlled (Area C). In the last 20 years, the steadily increasing population of Israeli citizens living in the West Bank has further complicated an already complex labyrinth of checkpoints, fences, settlements, and Arab villages and towns.

The status of both Jerusalem and the West Bank are two of the most contentious issues that have impeded progress towards a peace agreement between the Palestinian Authority and Israel.

ORIENTATION

The West Bank is the area to the west of the Jordan River and east of Israel. To enter or exit the West Bank, you will have to pass through checkpoints. The West Bank extends just to the north of Jenin, covers much of the Dead Sea, and its southernmost point is just 25 minutes from Beer Sheva, the largest city in the Negev.

PLANNING YOUR TIME

In spite of the tangled legal situation, the West Bank remains home to some important historical and religious sites and it is worth spending a couple of days exploring the more notable sights.

Visiting Bethlehem with a tour guide is a good way to explore the various religious and cultural sites. Hire a guide in Jerusalem; the odds of getting ripped off are too high if you hire someone in Bethlehem.

Bethlehem

Bethlehem is a city of 75,000 people that depends largely on tourists and pilgrims who are attracted by its religious and historical sites, chief among them the place where Jesus was born. It is 15 minutes from Jerusalem and is completely controlled by the Palestinian Authority. It is illegal for Israelis to enter Bethlehem.

SAFETY

Bethlehem is 15 minutes from Jerusalem's city center and entrance is through a fairly strict checkpoint. You must bring your passport with you and be prepared for a wait when leaving the city. Though it is basically safe, check your embassy website before going.

Once in Bethlehem, you will notice a number

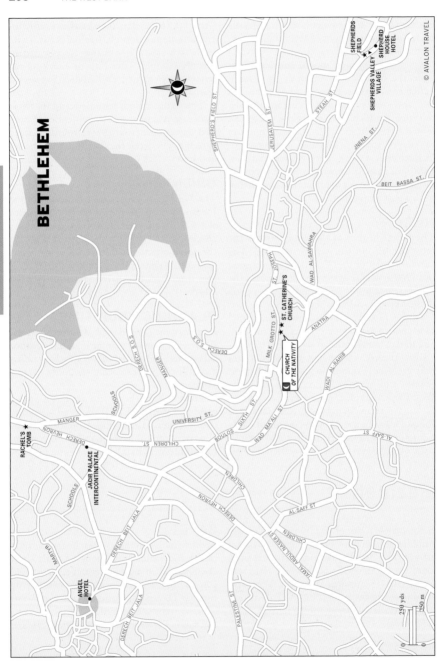

BETHLEHEM

© AVALON TRAVEL

SHEPHERDS FIELD ★
SHEPHERD HOUSE HOTEL
SHEPHERDS VALLEY VILLAGE

SHEPHERD'S FIELD ST.
JERUSALEM ST.
STEAH ST.
JNENA ST.
BEIT BASSA ST.
WAD AL SAWAHRA
ST. JOSEPH
MILK GROTTO ST.
ST. CATHERINE'S CHURCH ★★
CHURCH OF THE NATIVITY
ANATRA
WADI AL RAHIB
DERECH S.O.S.
DERECH S.O.S.
MANGER
SCHOOLS
UNIVERSITY ST.
MANGER
RACHEL'S TOMB ★
DERECH HEVRON
SCHOOLS
JACIR PALACE INTERCONTINENTAL
CHILDREN ST.
BOULOS
SIXTH ST.
WAD MA'ALI ST.
AL SAFF ST.
CHILDREN
DERECH HEVRON
AL SAFF ST.
CHILDREN
AMAL ABDUL NASER ST.
AS SABAH
DERECH BEIT JALA
PALESTINE ST.
MARTYRS
ANGEL HOTEL
DERECH BEIT JALA

250 yds
250 m

of heavily armed Palestinian Authority troops standing on the street. Though they may look intimidating, they are actually extremely friendly to tourists and are a great resource for information.

Despite the paranoia some people have about visiting here, it is an extremely safe and friendly city, though if you are driving you might get lost, even with a GPS.

SIGHTS
Manger Square
The heart of Bethlehem's Old City and the jumping-off point for the town's most popular attractions and events is **Manger Square** (center of Bethlehem off of Manger St.). A large number of hotels and places to eat are also located here.

◖ Church of the Nativity
Not overly impressive from the outside, the **Church of the Nativity** (Manger Sq. in the Old City, 02/274-2440, church hours are 6:30am-7:30pm daily Apr.-Sept., 5:30am-5pm daily Oct.-Mar.; grotto hours 6am-noon and 2pm-7:30pm daily Apr.-Sept., 5am-noon and 2pm-5pm daily Oct.-Mar.; Sun. church is open for holy mass and grotto is open only in afternoon, free) is imposing and impressive once you duck through the low main entrance door. Located basically at the center of Bethlehem in the Old City, it is one of the oldest working churches in the world, and was constructed by the Roman Emperor Constantine in the 4th century AD. The modern church is under the control and guardianship of the Greek Orthodox Church, the Roman Catholics, and the Armenians.

The church building is over the grotto where Mary is believed to have given birth to Jesus. The interior is dark with shafts of light streaming through the high windows, pillars, and low-hanging ceremonial lamps. The entire atmosphere is quite solemn and mysterious.

Due to its popularity among tourists and pilgrims, you might run into people selling their tour guide services just outside the entrance of the church. They charge upward of NIS80 or more. If you hire a guide, it's best to go with them to the site and make arrangements in advance.

To get to the grotto, you need to go down stairs where you'll see a 14-pointed silver star with the inscription *Hic de Virgin Maria Jesus Christus Natus Est* (Here Jesus Christ was born to the Virgin Mary). Nearby is the **cloister of St. Jerome,** who is known for translating the Bible into Latin.

St. Catherine's Church
The location of the annual Catholic midnight Christmas mass that is broadcast on television globally, attached to the Church of the Nativity, is the Roman Catholic **St. Catherine's Church** (Manger Sq. in the Old City center, 6am-noon and 2pm-7pm daily Apr.-Sept., 5:30am-5:30pm daily Oct.-Mar., free). The late 19th-century church was built by Franciscans and has a series of grottoes that were once used as places to live.

© BORYA GALPERIN/123RF.COM

Manger Square

THE SETTLEMENT ISSUE

© GENEVIEVE BELMAKER

a typical, well-developed Jewish settlement in the West Bank

One of the most confusing and complicated issues in the West Bank is about settlement: groups of Jews who have settled in homes throughout the region. The population of Jewish settlers in the West Bank is approximately 350,000 and growing. That number does not include the almost 300,000 Jews who live in East Jerusalem and developments around the Jerusalem area.

Their presence in some parts of the West Bank is illegal. The continued support (and in some cases encouragement) of settlements by the Israeli government is interpreted by many as an act of bad faith in the peace process with the Palestinian Authority. The Israeli government does forcibly remove settlements when they are on land controlled fully by the Palestinian Authority. Some settlers live peacefully next to their Arab neighbors, whose villages often surround them, but there have been many cases of violence from both sides.

The range of types of settlements is enormous, and can be anything from a small group of 10 families living on a hilltop in fairly make-shift accommodations to well-established cities with a full infrastructure and municipal government services. In areas that are not fully under Israeli military control, the government provides armed soldiers for protection, builds roads, and provides basic services such as electricity.

The issue of settlements is extremely contentious both domestically and internationally. The unsatisfactory resolution of the situation and continued building of new settlements is regarded as a major impediment to peace between Arabs and Jews in the region. The very existence of Jewish settlements throughout the West Bank creates a serious problem in the question of the formal establishment of a Palestinian state. If the armistice line that demarcates the West Bank were to become the legal border of a Palestinian state, a quarter of a million Jews would find themselves living in a foreign country.

Several books have been written on the topic; one of the most recent is called *Lords of the Land* by Idith Zirtal and Akiva Eldar.

© MOSCOWBEAR/123RF.COM

interior of the Church of the Nativity

Rachel's Tomb

The third-holiest site to the Jewish religion, **Rachel's Tomb** (Jerusalem-Hebron Rd. near the entrance to Bethlehem, 7:30am-4pm Sun.-Thurs., 7:30am-3:30pm Fri.) is the burial site of Rachel, wife of Jacob, who died giving birth to his second son. Over the years, the domed structure of the tomb has been gradually enclosed in a walled compound due to the deteriorating security situation in the area. Access to the tomb is very limited, and it might not be possible to enter unless you are with a tour group that has been pre-approved.

Mar Saba Monastery

Only men are allowed to enter, but the 5th-century Greek Orthodox **Mar Saba Monastery** (about 9 miles from Bethlehem, 02/277-3135, 8am-5pm daily, free) is a beautiful building that has existed continuously for 1,500 years and overlooks the Kidron Valley. There is no electricity or running water in the monastery and it is full of passages, alcoves, cells, and stairs that add to its ambience.

ENTERTAINMENT AND EVENTS
Christmas Eve

One of the main events in Bethlehem is **Christmas eve,** which includes a midnight mass in St. Catherine's Church; visiting the birthplace of Jesus in the Church of the Nativity; and celebrations and live music in Manger Square, around the stage and enormous Christmas tree that are set up for the event.

SHOPPING

There is a surprising amount of shopping to be had in Bethlehem, but the main area that most people have the time for is directly surrounding **Manger Square.** There are several shops that cater to pilgrims and sell postcards and handmade trinkets, boxes, and nativity scene pieces made from olive wood, many with inlaid mother of pearl. Shop owners try to sell the pieces for very high prices, but feel free to bargain with them if you're interested in something.

Also interesting and with a local twist is

© GENEVIEVE BELMAKER

postcards for sale near Manger Square in Bethlehem

the **Palestinian Heritage Center** (Maha Saca, Manger St., 02/274-2381, www.phc.ps, 10am-8pm Mon.-Sat., call ahead to confirm if open), which sells embroidery and other handcrafted products. The center employs women from refugee camps in the West Bank.

Just off of Manger Square is a pedestrian street full of shops selling all kinds of goods, from hand-woven rugs to soda. The shopkeepers try to sell products for a price that is based on the product's status as an antique. If you plan on shopping here, do not pay the first price you're offered; instead, be willing to walk away to get the lowest possible bid from the vendor.

A great place to shop for locally-made products and get travel guide services to area sights is the **Bethlehem Fair Trade Artisans** (Milk Grotto St., 02/275-0365, www.bethlehemfairtrade.org, 10am-5pm Mon.-Sat.). Contact them for more information about their tour guide services and educational programs about their products and the area.

ACCOMMODATIONS

Bethlehem is highly accustomed to pilgrims and tourists of an international caliber and is set up with a range of accommodation options from five-star hotels to hostels and guesthouses.

Under US$100

If you are on a budget but still want to be close to the action, **Al-Salam Hotel** (Manger St., opposite the Church of the Nativity, 02/276-4083/4, samhotel@p-ol.com, US$55 d) has the location and price that outweigh the very sparse setup. Every room has a bathroom, shower, TV, and phone. The hotel is on the small side with only about two dozen rooms and very plain, spare furnishings. It is a good option if you are making a last-minute booking and want a budget price.

With a great atmosphere and an affordable price, the **Angel Hotel** (184 Al-Sahel St., Beit Jala, 02/276-6880, www.angelhotel.ps, US$90 d) is one of Bethlehem's more well-known and popular places to stay. It is a bit off the beaten

THE WEST BANK VS. PALESTINE

The language used to describe the land to the east of Jerusalem commonly referred to as either the West Bank or Palestine can be extremely confusing.

The west in the name refers to its western proximity to the Jordan River, as it used to be part of the Hashemite Kingdom of Jordan. A reference to the area as Palestine is more of a political statement than a formal name. The hope for many is that this will change, however.

One glimmer of hopeful change came in November 2012, when the United Nations granted Palestine non-member observer status, while still urging efforts for a formal, two-state solution between Israel and the Palestinians. At the time of publication, no such solution had been reached.

The most politically neutral way to refer to the region is to call it the West Bank.

path in nearby Beit Jala, but the hotel has a rooftop restaurant with incredible views, free Wi-Fi, a breakfast buffet, and a bar with an outdoor terrace. The rooms are decorated very simply with tile flooring and have basic amenities.

The **Bethlehem Star Hotel** (Freres St., 02/274-3249, www.palestinehotels.com, US$69 d) is super plain and known as a favorite spot for journalists to stay. Close to Bethlehem's city center, the hotel has a fantastic view of the city from its breakfast room, and there is also a rooftop restaurant and Wi-Fi.

US$100-150

The mid-size **Shepherd House Hotel** (Shepherds Field St., 02/274-0656, 02/274-0657, or 02/274-0658, www.shepherdbethlehem.com, US$120 d) is in a pastoral setting and a short drive to the Church of the Nativity and other Christian sites. The hotel has a 24-hour front desk, dry cleaning and laundry service, free Wi-Fi, and some of the more than 100 rooms have a balcony with a view of the lovely mountain landscape that surrounds Bethlehem. The exterior of the building is simple, but the rooms are comfortably furnished and spacious, and the elegant lobby is full of comfortable chairs and nice corners to sit.

US$150-200

The **Jacir Palace Intercontinental** (Jerusalem-Hebron Rd., 02/276-6777, www.ihg.com,

US$196 d) gets its name from its former status as a palace. The perfectly beautiful, classy hotel has a soothing atmosphere and is full of elegant touches. Even if you're not a guest here, it's worthwhile to have a cappuccino in the lobby coffee shop amidst the massive stone pillars and skylight atrium. All of the 250 rooms at the Jacir are decorated in a warm, yet elegant fashion with comfortable touches like loveseats and coffee tables, bathtubs, balconies overlooking the hotel grounds, and a sitting area with satellite TV. The hotel has a restaurant, coffee shop, gym, bar, and pool. Make reservations as far in advance as possible; it is by far and away the nicest place in town and books early, especially during December. It is a short drive to the Church of the Nativity.

About as close as you can get to Manger Square is **Manger Square Hotel** (Manger St., 02/277-8888, http://mangersquarehotel.com, US$150 d), an upscale hotel with 220 rooms that caters to international visitors. The hotel has a spacious lobby and dining room that serves buffet-style meals, free Wi-Fi throughout, and modern rooms with wooden furniture, satellite TV, and a minibar. Though it is just steps from the main tourist attractions of Bethlehem, the hotel may entice you to stay inside and relax at the bar or get room service.

FOOD

If you visit Bethlehem for just the day, the easiest place to get something to eat is in one of

AREAS A, B, AND C

The West Bank is divided into three sections: Palestinian Authority-controlled (Area A); Palestinian Authority and Israeli military joint control (Area B); and Israeli military-controlled (Area C). If you looked at a map of the West Bank that was coded according to these three areas, you would see a complex division of territory and control. The divisions are part of the reason that while traveling through the West Bank, there are checkpoints, fences, and gates in certain areas.

An easy way to remember who is in control where goes something like this: the Palestinian Authority (PA) has an A in its acronym, and controls Area A. Both the PA and Israel control area B and the word "both" starts with B. By process of elimination, Area C is fully-Israeli controlled.

It is important to take into account safety precautions before you go to any area in the West Bank and know whether you are going to Area A, B, or C. For example, Nablus is in the very center of a large Area A section and the city of Ariel (which started as a small settlement) is in an Area C section.

Some Arab villages and Jewish settlements are partially in more than one area, or in an area that is not controlled by their respective government. Most of the West Bank is Area C and every major Arab town in the region, even if it is in Area A or B, is surrounded on almost every side by Area C territory.

the restaurants that surround the plaza area of Manger Square. Another option, though pricier, is any of the nicer hotels, as most have some kind of dining options, especially in the evenings. If you are traveling with a tour group, the tour will probably make arrangements with a particular place in advance, eliminating the guesswork for you.

Cafés and Coffee Shops

Just downhill from Manger Square is the sweet little **Dar Jdoudna Coffee Shop** (Manger Sq. in the Old City, 02/274-3212, 9am-8pm Mon.-Sat., NIS40), housed in an old textile factory building with an olive oil press. It's a good place to have a coffee with something sweet. Dar Jdoudna means "our grandfather's house," which is symbolic of the Palestinian expression of returning to their ancestral homes.

Italian

For some really delicious pizza made with high-quality ingredients, **Mundo Restaurant** (Manger St., 02/274-2299, 11am-11pm daily, NIS55) is family friendly and a popular spot for both tourists and locals. They serve all kinds

of other Italian food, mostly pasta dishes, and the interior of the restaurant is lined with floor to ceiling wood. An entire wall is comprised of huge windows that afford a fantastic view of the area.

Middle Eastern

Also in Manger Square and known for their very consistent and delicious falafel, **Afteem Al-Yafawi** (Manger Sq. in the Old City, 02/274-7940, afteemrestaurant@yahoo.com, 8am-9pm Mon.-Sat., NIS60) is a family-owned restaurant that has been in business since 1948. The restaurant is in an old Arab-style building of stone, and they serve generous helpings of hummus, falafel, and other traditional Middle Eastern foods.

You can experience Bedouin hospitality at **Shepherds Valley Village** (Shepherds Field St., Beit Sahour, 02/277-3875, 11am-5pm Mon.-Sat., NIS55). You can lunch inside a huge Bedouin tent on mezze (appetizers) and grilled meat and vegetables, with a view of the area that, according to tradition, is where the shepherds saw the star above Bethlehem that led them to baby Jesus.

For an experience that will get you some

interaction with locals, **Ka'abar** (Beit Jala St., near Municipality Bldg., Beit Jala, 02/274-1419, 11am-9pm Mon.-Sat., NIS40) is in the village just west of Bethlehem called Beit Jala. Ka'abar grills chicken outdoors, but has no menu. When you order, you get a prix fixe menu with meat and five side dishes and mint tea to finish. It's just a taxi ride from Manger Square.

INFORMATION AND SERVICES
Tour Guide
Visiting Bethlehem with a tour guide is a good way to experience the city and avoids many of the hassles you might encounter on your own. **(John) Hanna Awwad** (PO Box 51340, Jerusalem, 91513, 02/289-9305 or 054/445-2824, awwadhanna@yahoo.com) is based in Jerusalem, which is best because you would not want to go to Bethlehem and then try to hire a guide–the odds of getting ripped off are too high. John is so well-known and connected in Jerusalem that if he happens to not be available, he will be able to recommend an alternative.

GETTING THERE AND AROUND
There are several ways to get into Bethlehem and all of them involve going through a checkpoint.

Checkpoint
The main checkpoint entrance to Bethlehem is 15 minutes from Jerusalem city center at the end of Hebron Road. Going into the city is easier than getting out because the guards check the cars going into Jerusalem a bit more closely.

Taxis and Share Taxis
Taking a taxi into Bethlehem might prove difficult. The easiest thing to do is take a taxi to the checkpoint, walk through, and find another taxi on the other side. It is a bit confusing where the checkpoint is exactly because there is a serious lack of signs into or out of the city. Just follow the general flow of traffic, or keep asking until you get the right directions.

Damascus Gate Buses and Taxis
If you go to Damascus Gate in Jerusalem near

THE WEST BANK

ALTERNATIVE TOURS

In recent years, there has been a proliferation of alternative tour companies, offering other options than the standard tour guide or group. Many of the alternative tours emphasize a participatory experience, such as helping to pick olives during the harvest, or have a political agenda or slant. Either way, they can give you a fresh perspective on the West Bank.

One of the most popular and well-known social enterprise alternative tour companies is **Green Olive Tours** (03/721-9540 in Israel, 612/276-2077 in the U.S., www.toursinenglish.com). The company gives tours that deal with the culture, history, and political geography of the West Bank for groups and individuals. The work the company does also aims to support the local population in the areas it tours by working with local tour guides, overnight host family stays, and encouraging the purchase of local crafts.

Another option is the well-established and reputable **Alternative Tourism Group (ATG)** (74 Star St. in Beit Sahour, 02/277-2151, www.atg.ps), a Palestinian NGO that specializes in taking a critical look at the historical, cultural, and political situation in the West Bank. The company is based in Beit Sahour, near Bethlehem.

Though Green Olive Tours and ATG are separate companies, they sometimes work in cooperation with one another.

the Old City, you should be able to find a bus or *sherut* (share taxi) that will take you to Bethlehem. Just be confident about what you're doing, and don't get tricked into being driven for a fixed price by a taxi: Insist that they use the meter; it's the law.

Buses

You can also take a Jerusalem city bus straight down Hebron Road (buses 71, 72, 73, 74) to the end, walk through the checkpoint, and pick up a taxi on the other side. Bus routes change, so check in advance what goes in that direction.

Nablus and Vicinity

Mentioned many times in the Bible by the name Shechem, and once a flashpoint of violence during the Second Intifada, Nablus in the past 10 years has been steadily growing and stabilizing. There is also a sizable *shuk* (outdoor market) here, An-Najah National University, and

Nablus is famed as the home to the best version of the Arab treat, *knafe,* that you will ever eat.

Situated at the center of the Palestinian-controlled area of the West Bank, Nablus is avoided by most Israelis and, in times of regional unrest, scheduled tours to the area are

KNAFE

© GENEVIEVE BELMAKER

a *knafe* shop in the Old City of Nablus

Whatever else you eat, go in search of *knafe* (pronounced ka-nah-feh), a flat Arab cheese and biscuit-type creation cooked up on large, shallow pans and served fresh out of the oven. There are several shops in the Old City that sell

it; ask anybody to point you in the direction of the nearest *knafe* shop. Just be warned: the variation of *knafe* in Nablus is considered the best of the best, so once you have it here, you will be hard pressed to find its equivalent.

usually cancelled. If you can manage the trip, Nablus has a unique charm and very warm residents; but check your embassy's website for any travel warnings before going.

SIGHTS

There are very few sights in Nablus unless you are interested in an intensive tour with highlights of the complicated political situation and some modern history about what happened during the Second Intifada and afterwards. Once you are here, however, it's a fun place to stroll, buy some souvenirs for a great price, and try *knafe*.

Old City Market

The center of Nablus is home to the **Old City,** which serves as a destination for shopping, eating, and sightseeing. There are six quarters to the very densely populated Old City: Yasmina, Gharb, Qaryun, Aqaba, Qaysariyya, and Habala. You can find six Turkish baths here and a few historic monuments. Note the fading posters plastered about the area and remembrance plaques of people who died during fighting with Israeli forces, including occasional bullet holes on walls and unrepaired windows.

Mount Gerizim

Overlooking Nablus is **Mount Gerizim,** home to the last remaining community of Samaritans, who are guardians of some of the region's strictest and most ancient religious traditions. They believe that the earth of the mountain they live on was used by God to create Adam, and thus is extremely holy to them. The area has numerous archaeological ruins. It is possible to visit the area, including the Samaritan community that lives here, but you should arrange for a guide familiar with the area to take you. On Passover, you can see a traditional lamb sacrifice at the community center.

◖ Jacob's Well

Well worth the side trip of about 10 minutes by car from Nablus city center, **Jacob's Well** (off of Rte. 5487 at the entrance to Nablus, 09/237-5123, 9am-noon and 2pm-4pm daily,

Jacob's Well just outside of Nablus

until 5pm in the summer, free) is said to be the same well that a Samaritan woman gave Jesus a drink of water from during a long journey 2,000 years ago. The well (also known as the Well of Sychar) is an object of pilgrimage, and is housed deep inside the caverns of a massive Eastern Orthodox Church on the grounds of Bir Ya'qub monastery that is built over and around a 4th-century church.

Beneath the high altar at the center of the church is the crypt that houses the well. You can descend into the cavernous crypt and draw a drink of cool, clear water from the same well Jesus drank from. The well has been measured

REFUGEE CAMPS THAT BECAME HOME

© GENEVIEVE BELMAKER

a street in Balata Refugee Camp

Since the establishment of the State of Israel, various regional wars and conflicts and disputes over land have forced displaced Arabs into refugee camps. In many cases, the refugee camps have perpetuated a situation of instability, poverty, and dependence for the people living there.

According to the United Nations, the West Bank is home to 771,000 registered refugees, and about a quarter of them live in refugee camps.

One of the largest, Balata Refugee Camp, is just outside of Nablus. It was established in 1950 and has continued to exist through today, with a current population of about 23,000 and an unemployment rate of 25 percent. Balata's civil society is extremely active and parts of its landscape are small, rough alleys between tightly packed stone buildings with piles of rubble instead of a simple playground or park. Balata's population is larger than most towns in the region.

Much of the support for residents of refugee camps comes from international bodies such as the United Nations, non-profits, and nongovernmental organizations.

as about 130 feet deep, adding to its reputation as one of the more authentic sites in the Holy Land because it would have been almost impossible to move.

Even though it is immediately off of a main road, the gate and high stone wall keep the area protected and give the very pretty grounds of the church the atmosphere of a calm oasis.

The church, grounds and well are closely guarded. You should call in advance of a visit to make sure it is open. Only call if you are certain you will visit, as they might open it especially for you and await your arrival.

Balata Refugee Camp

You won't notice it unless you ask around, but almost directly across the street from Jacob's Well is the **Balata Refugee Camp,** the largest refugee camp in the West Bank and home to about 23,000 people. If you're interested in seeing their community center, you can ask someone from the church for an introduction. The people running the community center are very friendly and willing

to chat about their living situation and the general conditions in the area. They also sell a number of very nice, handmade items that are small, lightweight, and easy to pack for a return trip. The profit from the sale of the handmade goods goes to support the community center and women artisans in the community.

ACCOMMODATIONS

There isn't much reason to stay overnight in Nablus, but if you do opt for a hotel, it would be advisable to gravitate toward an area where foreigners gather.

The **International Friends' Guest House** (Annajah Al Qadeem St., 09/238-1064, www.guesthouse.ps, US$50 d) can provide both an affordable place to stay and historical and current information about the political situation in the region. The guesthouse offers resources for researchers and those who want to make a trip to the Old City of Nablus and nearby refugee camps. There are also activities and seminars on a weekly basis. The building is a very sweet,

the community and information center in Balata Refugee Camp

© GENEVIEVE BELMAKER

older stone house with some nice gardens and is not far from the center of the city.

FOOD

For a wide variety of things to eat in Nablus, just head anywhere near the Old City. Here you will find everything from restaurants to snacks and sweets.

A very nice spot to sit for some light food and tea or coffee is **Zeit Ou Zaatar** (City Center downtown, inside the Al Yasmeen Hotel, 09/233-3555, 9am-9pm daily, NIS45). The furniture and appointments in the sitting area are mixed antiques and modern furniture, and the atmosphere is very Middle Eastern with old lamps and mirrors. It is the perfect spot for an intimate discussion, and the impeccable service is on par with a four-star hotel.

Part of the Saleem Afandi Group of restaurants, **Al Saraya** (Hiteen St. just east of the Nablus Mall, 09/233-5444, www.saleemafandi.ps/en/saraya.html, 11am-9pm daily, NIS55) serves up delightful Arabic dishes, such as *mansaf* (lamb in fermented dried yogurt) and *musakhan* (roasted chicken cooked with onions, sumac, allspice, and saffron), in the setting of a 140-year-old house. Old copper lights and oriental window frames add to the ambience of this favorite neighborhood spot. It is just on the outskirts of the old city of Nablus, making it an easy stop after an afternoon of sightseeing.

INFORMATION AND SERVICES

A very useful website about Nablus is www.nablusguide.com.

Most Israelis will not go to Nablus, nor do they want to, but it is a perfectly safe place for a foreign visitor. Keep in mind that it is a conservative, mostly Muslim town.

GETTING THERE AND AROUND

The two best ways to get to Nablus are by hired taxi or by share taxi. A hired taxi stops along the way to switch you to another car at a large taxi parking lot just outside of the city limits, so don't be surprised when this happens.

The easiest, cheapest, and safest way to get around Nablus is by hired taxi.

Checkpoints

The checkpoint situation surrounding Nablus has been changing in recent years, with some checkpoints closer to the city shutting down. You will go through at least one checkpoint, maybe more, to get here. Be prepared with a very clear, simple answer about the purpose of your visit and your passport in case you are stopped.

Jericho

About an hour northeast of Jerusalem is the ancient and low-lying city of Jericho. It sits at about 853 feet below sea level. There are some amazing archaeological and biblical sites here, reflecting its thousands of years of history as a continuously inhabited city.

It has been conquered repeatedly over the millennia, first by the Israelites after 40 years of desert wandering when, according to the Bible, Joshua made the walls come tumbling down. It was also conquered by the Babylonians, Romans, Byzantines, Crusaders, and Christians.

SIGHTS

◀ Mount of Temptation Monastery

Perched about 1,140 feet above Jericho and seemingly etched into the side of a cliff is the Greek Orthodox **Mount of Temptation Monastery** (8am-1pm and 3pm-4pm Mon.-Fri., one hour later in the summer, 8am-2pm Sat., free), also called Jabel Quruntul, which dates back to the 12th century. The Crusaders originally built one church in a cave part way up the cliff and another church on the summit.

The current monastery dates back to the 19th century. The mountain is believed to be

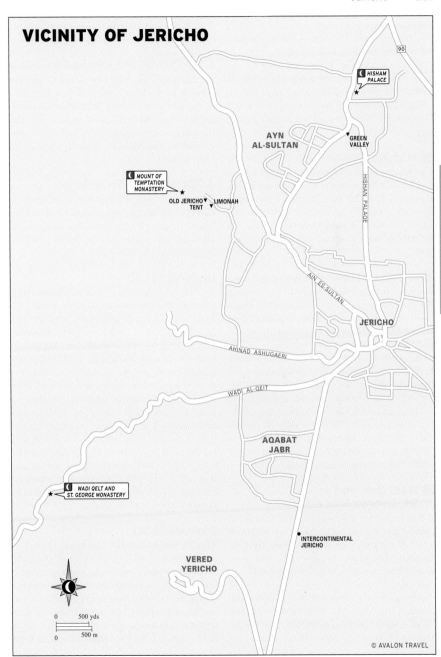

VICINITY OF JERICHO

90

🌙 HISHAM PALACE ★

AYN AL-SULTAN

▼ GREEN VALLEY

🌙 MOUNT OF TEMPTATION MONASTERY ★

OLD JERICHO ▼ TENT | ▼ LIMONAH

HISHAM PALACE

AIN ES-SULTAN

JERICHO

AHINAD ASHUGAERI

WADI AL-QEIT

AQABAT JABR

🌙 WADI QELT AND ST. GEORGE MONASTERY ★

● INTERCONTINENTAL JERICHO

VERED YERICHO

0   500 yds
0   500 m

© AVALON TRAVEL

the place where Jesus was tempted by Satan. If you take the cable car ride, you will pass over excavations of Biblical-era Jericho.

You can take the 30-minute hike up the mountainside or take the **cable car** (02/232-1590, 8:30am-6:30pm Mon.-Sat., adult NIS35, child NIS20) to reach the monastery in about five minutes, but the view from below can also satisfy.

◖ Hisham Palace

The gorgeous ruins of **Hisham Palace** (about 2 miles off Qasr Hisham St., follow guidepost signs, 09/232-2522, 8am-5pm daily, 8am-6pm Apr.-Sept., NIS10) are a major archaeological site in Jericho. The palace was built in the 8th century, possibly as a seasonal retreat of some kind.

It's just a mile north of Jericho proper, and the excavated site shows the remains that were destroyed in an earthquake in AD 747. Among the site's treasures are a mosque, water fountains, enormous mosaic floors, and decorative accents like the often-photographed carved six-pointed star window.

Restoration and preservation work on the site have been carried out with the cooperation and support of the Italian Government, UNESCO, the Palestinian Department of Antiquities, and the Franciscan Archaeological Institute. There is a small museum just to the right of the entrance that has a collection of pottery found on the site. You can see a short video about the site with a ticket at the visitor's center.

◖ Wadi Qelt and St. George Monastery

If you are up for a 90-minute hike through a canyon that has year-round flowing water fed by three streams, pass through **Wadi Qelt** (at Kosiba), where there are plenty of shady spots to stop and even play or swim in the water to cool off.

Along the way you will come upon the Greek Orthodox **St. George Monastery** (Wadi Qelt Rd. in Kosiba, 05/025-9949, 8am-11am and 3pm-5pm Mon.-Fri., 9am-noon

Sat., 9am-5pm Sun., but hours can change so call in advance, free), which you can also arrive at by car. While the original dates back to AD 420, the current structure is a restoration that was done by the Greek Orthodox Church in the 19th century. The upper floor of the monastery, which looks like it is clinging to the side of a cliff, is an ancient cave and there are three churches and a bell tower built around it. The building is about three miles from Jericho.

ACCOMMODATIONS

If you are passing through and want to stay a night in Jericho, the options are limited and the lower-end accommodations come and go. The safest bet is something on the higher end with international connections.

Under US$100

Not in Jericho proper, but reachable by a cab ride, the **Jericho Moon City Hotel** (Al-Furusieh St., outside of Jericho, 02/232-7292 and 02/232-6844, yusraswaity@yahoo.com and mooncityhotel@gmail.com, US$60 d) has friendly staff, an outdoor pool, and pretty grounds with fountains. The rooms are extremely basic with simple beds and very little furnishings or creature comforts, but they are clean and adequately equipped with private bathrooms. The hotel was created with the help of international support. But it is run by locals, so some customs might surprise foreign visitors. For example, if you are an unmarried couple traveling together, check in advance if they will allow you to stay in the same room.

Over US$200

The **Intercontinetal Jericho** (Jericho-Jerusalem Rd., 02/231-1200, www.ihg.com, US$200 d) offers every amenity typical of a luxury hotel, including a variety of options for dining, beautifully landscaped grounds, a Dead Sea Water pool, a full-service spa, and outdoor tennis courts. Set on the outskirts of Jericho, it is 30 minutes from the Dead Sea and an hour

St. George Monastery

from Jerusalem. It also has a full suite of business services. The 181 rooms are modern with nice furnishings, desks, TVs, and comfortable, large beds. Room service and free continental breakfast are also available.

FOOD

On a main road about a 15-minute walk to the cable car at the Mount of Temptation Monastery, **Limonah** (Muntazhat St., 02/231-2977, call for hours as they vary widely, NIS45) serves up a wide variety of food that ranges from hummus to pizza. The staff is helpful and friendly, and it's a remarkably clean establishment.

Just near the Mount of Temptation is **Old Jericho Tent** (Qarantal, 02/232-3820, 8am-midnight daily, NIS40), which is set up in Bedouin-tent style and serves up traditional Arab specialties. The interior of the tent is decorated with scenes of desert life.

An easy stop that is en route to Hisham Palace is **Green Valley** (Ein Al-Sultan St., 02/232-2349, noon-9pm daily, NIS60), an indoor-outdoor restaurant owned by a respected local family and partially supported by international charity. They serve up Middle Eastern dishes, mezze (appetizers), and meat grilled outdoors.

INFORMATION AND SERVICES

The **Municipality of Jericho** (www.jericho-city.org) has a nice, multi-lingual website with vital information, including some tourist maps.

GETTING THERE AND AROUND

As with everywhere else in the West Bank, keep your passport in case you need it at checkpoints. The easiest way to get to Jericho if you don't have a rental car is to go from Ramallah via buses that travel several times during the day. The schedules are fairly informal, so you might need to ask around once you are in Ramallah.

THE WEST BANK

Hebron

Known as the City of the Patriarchs, Hebron is thousands of years old and full of historical and religious significance and tension. Situated on four hills at an elevation of about 3,000 feet, it is holy to Muslims, Christians, and Jews alike because it is home to the tomb of Abraham and other patriarchs and matriarchs.

More than a dozen Jewish settlements surround the city, and several hundred Jewish settlers live in the city, which is under the jurisdiction of the Palestinian Authority. The settlers who live in the city are accompanied by armed Israeli military guards.

VISITING HEBRON

It is recommended that you visit Hebron with a tour guide or with a tour group, as it will take all of the guesswork out of where to go and what to do, and will give you smoother access to the sites because of the complicated security situation. A couple of good tour groups are **Green Olive Tours** (03/721-9540 in Israel, 612/276-2077 in the U.S., www.toursinenglish.com) and **Abraham Tours** (67 Hanevi'im St. in Jerusalem, 02/566-0045, http://abrahamtours.com).

SIGHTS
Old City

One of the oldest of its kind in the West Bank, Hebron's **Old City** includes a large *shuk* with gorgeous arched ceilings. Hebron is one of the only Islamic cities that has maintained its original urban layout, and is dominated by the Mamluk architectural style.

Cave of the Patriarchs (Cave of Machpelah) and Ibrahimi Mosque

The traditional burial site of Abraham and

© LEONID SPEKTOR/123RF.COM

Hebron

other patriarchs and matriarchs, the **Cave of the Patriarchs** (end of the street in the Old City, 052/429-5554 or 052/431-7055, http://machpela.com, 4am-8pm Sun.-Thurs., dress modestly, including head covering for women, free) is one of the most sacred sites in Judaism, Islam, and Christianity. The **Ibrahimi Mosque,** second only to Jerusalem's Al Aqsa Mosque in terms of regional significance to Muslims, is located here.

The existence of the mosque came about after the tombs were enclosed by Herod the Great, who built a huge wall around the burial sites and the cave. The structure was later turned into a church and then a mosque with four Mamluk minarets on the corners of the building (only two remain). The current structure includes prayer halls, inner and outer areas, and extremely steep stairs, which lead to the rooftop area where domes mark the burial sites.

In 1994, there was a shooting in the mosque of Muslims at prayer and the site is tightly guarded and controlled. The visiting hours of the cave and the mosque vary, especially during religious holidays, so it is best to call in advance. If you visit during a time when regional tensions are flaring, it might also be difficult to gain entrance; be sure to take your passport.

SHOPPING

Hebron is known for its grapes, leather work, glass blowing, colorful and attractive ceramics, and carpets. The *shuk* is unfortunately a bit of a touchy area because it is adjacent to a part of town that is tightly controlled, but you can find a great deal of local handiwork here. If you don't make it to the *shuk,* there are other options nearby.

Shuk

Boasting arched rooftops and vast alleys, Hebron's **shuk** (in the town center) is a site to explore for treats, souvenirs, or just for the fun of it. Things on sale include fresh and dried fruit, olive wood items, pottery, glass craftwork, and leather products.

THE WEST BANK

The Cave of the Patriarchs and Ibrahimi Mosque are sacred to Jews, Muslims, and Christians.

Glass Blowing

Hebron is famed throughout Israel and the West Bank for ceramics and glass blowing. The major glass blowing workshops of Hebron are near the northern entrance to the city in the direction of Bethlehem. One of these, the **Hebron Glass and Ceramics Factory** (Ras al Jora St., in the northern part of Hebron, 02/222-8502, hebronglass@yahoo.com, 10am-5pm Mon.-Fri.) sells beautiful, original pieces that range from multi-colored goblets to dishes and decorative boxes. You can take photographs, watch glass blowers using ancient techniques (probably imported to the area by Venetians), and buy products.

FOOD

The *shuk* is always a good place to pick up snacks and you can usually find things like falafel there. If that isn't enough to satisfy your appetite, Hebron has a few other options for something quick and inexpensive, particularly on and around Nimra Street.

Middle Eastern

The very popular **Abu Mazen** (Nimra St., 222-6168, 02/222-6168, 11am-9pm daily, NIS30) has a great reputation and is a good option for a delicious, affordable meal. It gets very crowded at lunchtime and serves up salads, fresh bread, Middle Eastern lamb dishes, and vegetarian choices, including soup. The atmosphere is a fairly typical home-style restaurant with simple furnishings and a lot of regulars.

INFORMATION AND SERVICES
Online Resources

There are only two websites with information about Hebron, the **Hebron Municipality** site (www.hebron-city.ps) and the site of the Jewish community of Hebron (www.hebron.com/english).

Safety and Security

Hebron's central Shuhada Street was closed years ago because of violence in the area. The street, which used to be a main thoroughfare and was full of shops, now has restricted access, despite the fact that it leads to the Tomb of the Patriarchs and Ibrahimi Mosque. International visitors should be able to walk down it, though be aware that there are sometimes clashes in this area.

GETTING THERE AND AROUND

From Jerusalem, take the bus from next to Damascus Gate at the Old City to Abu Dis, and make sure to tell the bus driver you are going to Khalil (Arabic for Hebron). From Beer Sheva's central bus station, there are several options for buses, but make sure you don't get a ride on the bus that's going to the nearby settlement of Kiryat Arba. From Ramallah and Bethlehem, take a *sherut* (share taxi) from the town centers.

Once you're in Hebron, you will need to choose different transportation routes for either the Palestinian Authority-controlled side or Israel-controlled side. For the Palestinian Authority-controlled side (which is most of the city), go from the bus station by Damascus Gate in Jerusalem on bus number 21 (NIS10). You will transfer at the Bethlehem bus station and switch to a *sherut* (NIS10). The Israeli-controlled side, including the Cave of the Patriarchs, requires bus number 160 from the Jerusalem Central Bus station (NIS9).

The simplest thing to do is take a *sherut* from Jerusalem to Bethlehem, and then ask your driver where to find another *sherut* to Hebron.

Ramallah and Al Bireh

Ramallah (and its twin city Al Bireh) is just a 15-minute drive from Jerusalem, and is known as an Arab cultural and arts hub, rather than a hotspot for archaeological or religious sightseeing. There are also a number of excellent restaurants in this area and some good hotels. Though Ramallah might seem like a good alternative place to stay if you are planning on sightseeing in Jerusalem, be aware that you will have to go back and forth through a checkpoint.

SIGHTS
Taybeh Brewery

A truly original stop on a trip to the Middle East is **Taybeh Brewery** (1 Taybeh Rd., Taybeh, just outside of Ramallah, 02/289-8868, www.taybehbeer.com, 8am-4pm Mon.-Sat., 30-minute tours 9am-2:30pm Mon.-Sat., free), the only Palestinian brewery in existence. Taybeh, a town of about 1,500 people, is the only majority-Christian Palestinian community in the Holy Land. The driving force

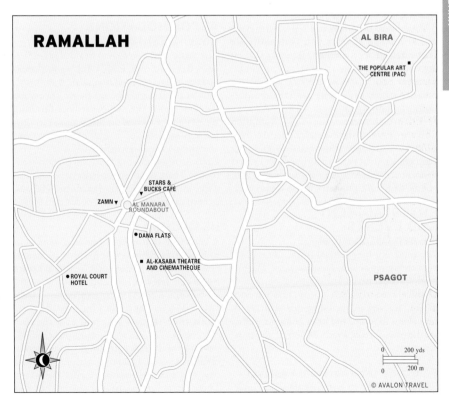

RAMALLAH

AL BIRA

THE POPULAR ART
CENTRE (PAC)

STARS &
BUCKS CAFÉ

ZAMN

AL MANARA
ROUNDABOUT

DANA FLATS

AL-KASABA THEATRE
AND CINEMATHEQUE

ROYAL COURT
HOTEL

PSAGOT

0   200 yds

0   200 m

© AVALON TRAVEL

behind the family-run brewery is a father-daughter team, and they are the main sponsors and advocates of Taybeh's annual Oktoberfest.

ARTS AND CULTURE CENTERS

Ramallah is home to several arts and culture centers that are NGOs and operate with international assistance. The centers put on all kinds of arts-related events throughout the year.

Most notable among these centers is **The Popular Art Centre (PAC)** (Al Bireh, 02/240-3891, www.popularartcentre.org), which is also home of the renowned Palestine International Festival. PAC runs a number of arts programs for children, has a cinemathéque, and promotes traditional music and dance.

Established originally in 1970 in Jerusalem, the **Al-Kasaba Theatre and Cinemathéque** (Hospital St. in Ramallah, 02/296-5292/3, www.alkasaba.org) works on a local and international level in arts promotion, including a past international film festival, theater productions, and hosting international artists.

Also worth mentioning is the **Ramallah Cultural Palace** (Industrial Zone, 02/298-4704, www.ramallahculturalpalace.org), which executes a similar mission as the other centers in the area in its promotion and support of arts, poetry, and music programs in the community.

ENTERTAINMENT AND EVENTS
Taybeh Oktoberfest

Yes, there is a beer festival in the West Bank even though it only has one brewery. The annual **Oktoberfest** (Taybeh, just outside of Ramallah, www.visitpalestine.ps, first Sat.-Sun. in Oct.) features an interesting mix of local folk musicians, hip-hop, and brass bands as well as local dishes for the food portion of the two-day event.

Palestine International Festival

Founded in 1993 to host and showcase international arts in the West Bank, the **Palestine**

International Festival (various locations, www.popularartcentre.org) includes a wide array of music, poetry, and performance events in surrounding Arab villages and refugee camps.

PalFest

The Palestine Festival of Literature, known as **PalFest** (http://palfest.org, free), showcases the Middle Eastern love for the written word with domestic and international writers, poets, and songwriters. They facilitate workshops and put on musical performances. Some events are in English and the festival is held in various locations throughout the West Bank and East Jerusalem.

ACCOMMODATIONS
Under US$100

The **Dana Flats** (Hospital St., 02/297-8882, www.danaflats.com, US$75 d) is a good lower-budget option in central Ramallah, near the Al-Kasaba Theatre and Cinemathéque. The white tile floors and white walls with black furniture accents give it a bit of an institutional feeling, but it is modern and has all of the necessary amenities, including satellite TV, free Wi-Fi, a kitchenette and dining area, and private bathrooms. There is a 24-hour front desk, and it is a five minutes to the Al Manara roundabout, a central transportation and pedestrian hub.

US$100-150

A very nice option that includes semi-luxury accommodations and rooms with balconies big enough to dine on, the **Royal Court Hotel** (24 Jaffa St., 02/296-4040, www.rcshotel.com, US$145 d) is a small hotel with only suites in Ramallah's business district, across from the city park and near the new city center. There is a roof restaurant, whirlpool tubs and kitchenettes in the comfortably furnished suites, balconies with views of the city, and a complimentary buffet breakfast. There are many restaurants nearby, but you can also dine at the hotel's bar with outdoor

© POLINITCHEN

Have a cup of coffee at the Stars & Bucks Café in Ramallah.

seating that is frequented by both locals and tourists.

FOOD
Cafés and Coffee Shops
ZAMN (off Al Teereh St. roundabout, 02/295-0600, 24 hours daily, NIS40) is one branch of a very successful local chain of upper-end coffee shops. It is a popular gathering place and serves up excellent coffee and sweets.

Just for the novelty and bizarre experience of it, try **Stars & Bucks Café** (City Center, 02/241-2502, www.starsandbuckscafe.com, 9am-10pm daily, NIS70) right in the center of Ramallah. You'll find yourself marveling at how they have managed to get away with such blatant brand infringement. Many tourists visit just to buy souvenir evidence to show people back home. It's a fairly large place (and a regional chain) that has mediocre coffee. It is on the second floor of a building at the center of the first major roundabout in town. They serve a wide variety of main dishes in addition to their coffee offerings, including noodle dishes, sandwiches, and Chinese food. It operates as both a coffee shop and a hookah lounge, so you can also smoke a water pipe while you're here.

Fine Dining
Locally-grown food and handmade pasta are the highlights of **Orjuwan Lounge** (Hope St. in central Ramallah, 02/297-6870, www.orjuwanlounge.com, 10:30am-midnight daily, NIS70), which has a classy, upscale atmosphere on par with something you'd find in Tel Aviv or Jerusalem. Serving a range of dishes that includes everything from arugula salad to lamb and chicken dishes, Orjuwan is decidedly Western food with an Asian flair. Their main offerings are soups and appetizers, salads, risottos, seafood, and favorite Italian dishes such as ravioli, prepared inventively with local flavors and ingredients, but they also have a surprising range of inventive main dishes. Try the halved

and baked pumpkin filled with chicken and couscous for a healthy option.

INFORMATION AND SERVICES
Online Resources

The **Municipality of Ramallah** (www.ramallah.ps) has a multi-lingual website, but the functions are a bit limited and it will basically provide you with some background information and a few pictures.

Safety and Security

Violence sometimes erupts in Ramallah, particularly near the Qalandia Checkpoint. It is always best to check with your embassy in advance of visiting.

GETTING THERE AND AROUND
Checkpoints

Ramallah's main drawback for visitors coming from Jerusalem is going through the infamous **Qalandia Checkpoint,** which involves a complex series of checks, especially in times of unrest. By far the easiest thing to do is get to the checkpoint, walk through, and take a taxi on the other side.

There are alternative routes that are longer and more circuitous, but unless you are riding in a *sherut* (share taxi) or a bus, just go through Qalandia.

Taxis and Share Taxis

Many taxis from Jerusalem won't go through the Qalandia Checkpoint because of the trouble in getting back through. No matter what you do, if you take a taxi insist that they set their meter. The driver might insist on a large sum of money on delivering you to Ramallah with the reasoning that they have to go to the trouble of driving back through the checkpoint.

Damascus Gate Buses

Ramallah is just 15 minutes from Jerusalem, so you can always find a bus at Damascus Gate that is going here, though the ride might be longer as they go around Qalandia to avoid the lines.

Information and Services

While tourism is being promoted more heavily in the West Bank in recent years, it is nowhere near the level of tourism in Israel. There are some good online resources and a governmental agency for information.

ONLINE RESOURCES

An excellent online guide for all things in the West Bank is **Visit Palestine** (www.visitpalestine.ps/en). The **Official Tourism Site** (travelpalestine.ps) for the region is less robust, but also has some good tips and information.

More of a West Bank version of Time Out than a tourism site, **This Week in Palestine** (www.thisweekinpalestine.com) is a great guide for events and happenings in the region.

TOUR GUIDE SERVICES

Offering a wide variety of tourism services, **BeinHarim Tourism Services Ltd.** (03/542-2000, www.beinharimtours.com) has an online chat service and offers tours to most areas in the West Bank.

NEWSPAPERS AND PRINT PUBLICATIONS

There are three major Arabic dailies in the region: *Al Quds, Al Ayyam* and *Al Hayyat* newspapers. Many shops and markets also sell foreign English newspapers and magazines. A popular English periodical, *This Week in Palestine,* has listings of major events, happenings, and tourism services.

BUSINESS HOURS

Keep in mind that the Muslim holy day of the week is Friday, so most businesses and services are shut down on that day.

LANGUAGE

The major languages spoken in the West Bank are Arabic and Hebrew; English is less common. It is advisable to learn a few key phrases in Arabic before traveling to the region, including common greetings and pleasantries. It will help break the ice and make it easier to communicate about more complicated topics.

SAFETY AND SECURITY

When traveling in the West Bank, the general rule of thumb is to always err on the side of being cautious and modest. Especially for women, conservative dress is a must, mainly because it will make you feel more comfortable in a region where women generally don't show much skin. Keep any electronics or camera equipment out of sight and close by.

THE WEST BANK

PETRA, JORDAN

Just across the border from Israel is the ancient Nabataean city
of Petra, a powerful civilization that worked the incense route
that supplied the Romans. Petra's remarkable architecture of
massive colonnade buildings is carved into the stone faces of
mountains. It is inexpressibly exquisite.

© GENEVIEVE BELMAKER

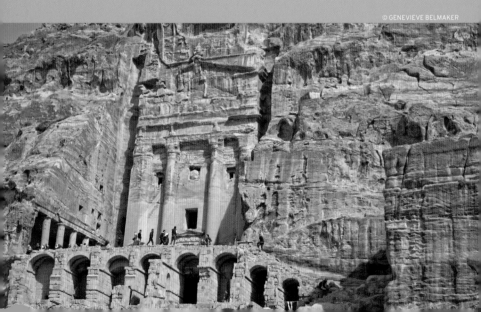

HIGHLIGHTS

LOOK FOR ⟨ TO FIND RECOMMENDED SIGHTS, ACTIVITIES, DINING, AND LODGING.

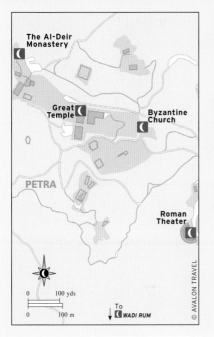

⟨ **Wadi Rum:** This expanse of desert in Jordan is full of unusual rock formations. Mountains of sandstone and granite rise as high as 5,500 feet (page 297).

⟨ **Roman Theater:** This Roman-style theater is a wonder of ancient architecture (page 300).

⟨ **Byzantine Church:** Built on top of other ruins, the Byzantine Church in Petra has 70 square meters of mosaic floors (page 301).

⟨ **Great Temple:** Petra's largest freestanding structure, the Great Temple underwent extensive excavation work by students from the Joukowsky Institute at Brown University (page 302).

⟨ **The Al-Deir Monastery:** Up 800 rock-cut steps above Petra's amphitheater is Al-Deir Monastery and its unique, massive urn (page 303).

PETRA, JORDAN

PLANNING YOUR TIME

Sometimes called the lost city, as outsiders were at one time banned from entering, Petra in its current state was rediscovered by Western society only about 200 years ago. In 1812 the Swiss traveler Johann Ludwig Burckhardt snuck into what was a closely guarded site by disguising himself as an Arab from India on his way to make a sacrifice at the tomb of the Prophet Aaron.

In 1985, UNESCO declared Petra a World Heritage Site, and in a global popular vote of more than 100 million people in 2007, it was honored as one of the New Seven Wonders of the World. Much of Petra's history has been lost in the sands of time, and much of what is believed to be known today about it is taken with a grain of salt instead of taken as fact.

Most people will tell you that you need several days to see Petra. If you have come over from Israel and are on a tight schedule, try to allow at least one overnight stay. It is possible to get the gist of and feel for Petra in one day. If you cross from the border at Aqaba, your time will be spent crossing the border, traveling to the site, walking in, walking around a bit, walking out, and then returning to the border. The whole process takes about 12 hours, and is the quickest possible version of a trip to Petra if you are coming directly from the border crossing at Eilat.

There are plenty of very affordable accommodations in the immediate area, within

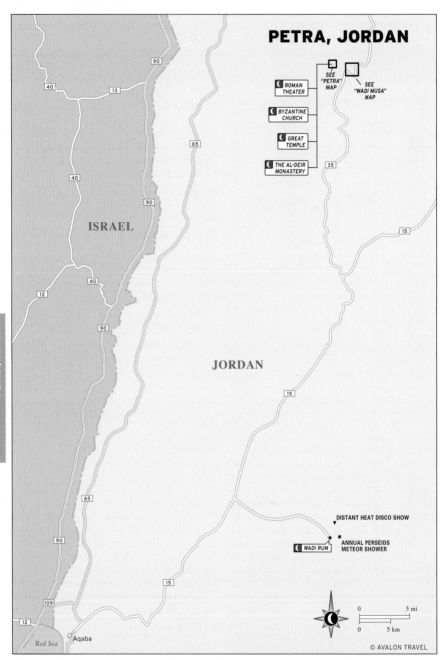

PETRA, JORDAN

SEE "PETRA" MAP

SEE "WADI MUSA" MAP

ROMAN THEATER

BYZANTINE CHURCH

GREAT TEMPLE

THE AL-DEIR MONASTERY

ISRAEL

JORDAN

DISTANT HEAT DISCO SHOW

WADI RUM

ANNUAL PERSEIDS METEOR SHOWER

Red Sea

Aqaba

0   5 mi

0   5 km

© AVALON TRAVEL

Jordan border crossing near Eilat

walking distance to Petra. In addition, a two-day entry ticket to Petra costs about US$5 more than the rather expensive single-entry ticket.

VISAS, PASSPORTS, AND ENTRANCE FEES

There are three land border crossings from Israel into Jordan in the north, center, and south of the country. The two most convenient and relevant for travelers to Petra are the Allenby/King Hussein Bridge Border Crossing and the border crossing at Eilat-Aqaba. Visas are issued on the spot at the Eilat crossing and you don't need to provide photographs.

If you cross at the Allenby/King Hussein Bridge border, you need to pay for your visa (about JD14) in advance at the Jordanian embassy in Tel Aviv. You will need two photographs and you'll get the visa within 24 hours.

If you enter Jordan by air, you will need to pay for a single-entry Jordanian visa (about JD20), which you can do at the airport, usually in the same place where you change money.

If you enter from Eilat to Aqaba by sea or land, through the port or at the crossing from Israel, your visa should be free for one month for most nationalities, including Americans and Canadians. The only fee you might be charged is an exit fee of JD5 for overland exits back into Israel. Aqaba is a Special Economic Zone Area (SEZA) set up for free trade, which is why the visa requirements are different.

When entering Aqaba, Do not pay tour guides on the Israeli side of the border who tell you to pay them cash for a visa, as they will simply pocket the money.

Make sure that your passport is valid for at least six months past the date you plan to leave Jordan.

CURRENCY AND CURRENCY EXCHANGE

The official currency of Jordan is the Jordanian Dinar (JD), and it is divided into 10 dirham, 100 qirsh (or piasters), or 1000 fils. Half dinar and 1 dinar coins are most common, and bills come in 1 dinar, 5 dinars, 10 dinars, 20 dinars, and 50 dinars denominations. JD1 is typically worth about US$1.40 or NIS5.20.

If you are coming from Israel, change your shekels to Jordanian Dinars before crossing the

© GENEVIEVE BELMAKER

Petra's structures are carved out of the rose-colored rocks.

border, or at one of the money-changing desks that are along the way as you pass through the many stops that you need to make it through the border (Wadi Araba Crossing/South Border). If you are trying to pay in shekels after entering Jordan, it will really put a damper on your trip, as most people will have no idea what to charge you.

You can also get by very easily in Wadi Musa

and Petra with U.S. currency, but don't expect change and keep the conversion rates in mind when getting prices.

HISTORY

Dating back to prehistoric times, Petra was at one time at a key crossroads point between Arabia, Egypt, and Syria-Phoenicia. It is widely believed to have been built and inhabited by the powerful Nabataean incense route traders, who used it as their capital city. The Byzantines, Romans, and Crusaders were also residents and contributed to the construction of different buildings and the city structure.

The structures of Petra are partially constructed and partially carved out of the rose-colored rock in the midst of a series of cavernous gorges and rocky mountain peaks. The color of the stone is where Petra gets its nickname of the "rose city."

One of the most famous archaeological sites in the world and an outstanding example of a blending of Hellenistic architecture and Eastern traditions, Petra is in a part of the world that suffered numerous earthquakes.

One of the most fascinating aspects of Petra's history is how much of it remains a question mark. On a guided trip through Petra, you may hear your guide refer to this uncertainty with the standard line that, "85 percent of Petra's history is unknown." Though the unknown is a bit frustrating as a visitor, the mystery makes it all the more enchanting and exciting. It's a

THE SHRINE OF AARON

At the very top of Mount Aaron (Jabal Haroun) in Petra is the modest, white-domed Shrine of Aaron. The shrine commemorates the death of Aaron, the elder brother of Moses, and was constructed by the Egyptian Mameluk Sultan in the 13th century.

The highest point in Petra, the shrine is perched on part of the Sharah mountain range. According to tradition, the location of the shrine is the place where Aaron died.

Since antiquity dating back to Byzantine times,

other religious structures have been built here. According to tradition, a 10-year-old Mohammed visited Aaron's shrine. The site was closely guarded by Bedouins to keep away non-Muslims for a long time, but now it is a site of pilgrimage for Jews, Christians, and Muslims. Aaron is considered a prophet in all three religions.

It is a long hike up a rugged mountain to the site. If you go, plan ahead, set out early in the morning, and take water and protection from the sun.

place where your imagination about the ancient world can run wild.

ORIENTATION

Petra is between the Dead Sea and the Red Sea in Jordan. If you set out from Petra from the southernmost border entry on the Israel side at Eilat (there are three border entries), you will find yourself in Aqaba, Jordan. From Aqaba, you can take a taxi, bus, or tour bus to Petra. It takes about two hours including one or two short stops.

About halfway along the way to Petra from the south, you will pass by **Wadi Rum,** a desert landscape that has been immortalized in Western films and is a popular destination for ecotourism.

In Wadi Rum and along the way to Petra you will see very unusual rock formations, including bright bands of colorful mineral deposits etched into the stone landscape in beautiful colors.

Once you arrive, you will find yourself in an Arab village called **Wadi Musa,** immediately adjacent to the archaeological site of Petra. Wadi Musa is home to about 99 percent of Petra's restaurants, accommodations, and services. The large Jordanian city of Amman is about 3.5 hours to the north.

Sights

The road from the border of Egypt at Aqaba, which most tour groups and guides use as a rally point for tours to Petra, is marked by the stark distinction of almost nothing but desert for about two hours, except for Wadi Rum. Once you get to Wadi Musa, the main site is Petra.

◖ WADI RUM

On the way to Petra is the incredible and unique landscape of the **Wadi Rum Protected Area** (Rte. 15 between Aqaba and Petra, www.wadirum.jo, JD2, under 12 free), the location where much of the 1962 classic by David Lean, *Lawrence of Arabia,* was filmed. *Transformers II*

© IMARLY/123RF.COM

a Bedouin tent in Wadi Rum

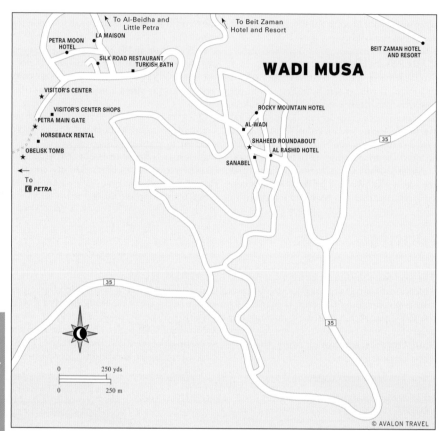

To Al-Beidha and
Little Petra

PETRA MOON
HOTEL
LA MAISON

SILK ROAD RESTAURANT
TURKISH BATH

VISITOR'S CENTER

VISITOR'S CENTER SHOPS
PETRA MAIN GATE

HORSEBACK RENTAL

OBELISK TOMB

To
PETRA

To Beit Zaman
Hotel and Resort

BEIT ZAMAN HOTEL
AND RESORT

WADI MUSA

ROCKY MOUNTAIN HOTEL
AL-WADI

SHAHEED ROUNDABOUT
AL RASHID HOTEL

SANABEL

35

35

35

0   250 yds

0   250 m

© AVALON TRAVEL

and part of one of the *Star Wars* movies were also filmed here.

Wadi Rum is a 720-square-kilometer expanse of desert that is full of unusual rock formations and mountains of sandstone and granite that rise to the heights of 5,500 feet in some areas and are often compared to the surface of the moon. Visiting Wadi Rum is strictly controlled. The safest and easiest thing to do is hire a travel guide through a hotel in Aqaba who can take you to Wadi Rum.

Another option is to go to Wadi Rum's **Visitors' Centre** (one hour northeast of Aqaba on Rte. 15, turn right at sign, 03/209-0600), which has posted prices for hiring a local Bedouin guide who can escort you by a

4x4 vehicle or camel. It's also possible to hire a guide for a camp-out in a Bedouin tent. Don't forget water, a hat with a brim, and sunscreen.

The Visitors' Centre is part of a complex of buildings that includes an interpretation center, crafts shops, a ticket office, and a restaurant.

PETRA

The ancient site of **Petra** (www.visitpetra.jo, 6am-6pm daily Apr.-Oct., 6am-4pm daily Nov.-Mar., 7am-4pm daily during the month of Ramadan, JD50 for one day, JD55 for two days) is next to the Arab village of Wadi Rum. The **Visitor Center** can sell you tickets, arrange for guides, and give you background information. It is located at the end of a row of small shops just before the entrance to Petra and downhill from the tourist bus parking lots.

Ticket prices differ based on whether you are a foreigner or local, the length of the stay, and the number of times you plan on entering. It is almost impossible to see the site adequately in one day. It is expensive to enter Petra, but quite affordable to add an extra day or two to the base ticket price for multiple entries.

Wear the most comfortable shoes you own, and be prepared for a mini-hike in and out of the site, which takes at least an hour each way. Once you are inside, you will have plenty of opportunities to climb up into buildings and explore different ruins.

Obelisk Tomb

Just between the siq (main passage) and the main entrance to Petra is the mysterious **Obelisk Tomb,** situated next to huge rocks with strange curves. The beautiful tomb is Egyptian with Nabataean and Egyptian inscriptions.

The Siq

The main passage into Petra is called the **siq,** which means cleft, and it is an almost 4,000-foot-long canyon cut through the mountains that leads to the breathtaking first view of Petra.

Along the way, there are all kinds of details worth stopping to take in, including notches for votives that might have been ceremonial,

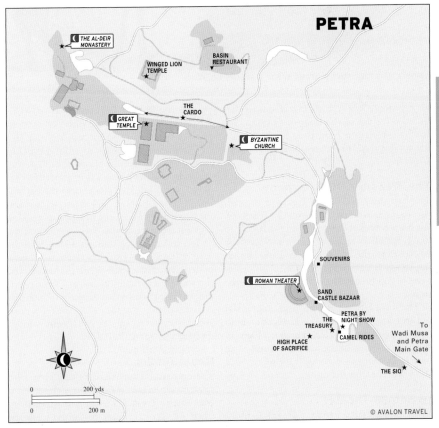

© AVALON TRAVEL

© GENEVIEVE BELMAKER

Camels wait for riders in front of the treasury building.

paving stones, and the waterway system that lines both sides of the floor of the siq. This is where Harrison Ford rode his horse in a memorable scene in *Indiana Jones and the Last Crusade.*

The Treasury (Al-Khazneh)

The first thing you see after passing through the siq is a breathtaking view of the **Treasury.** It's both impossible to miss and difficult to drag yourself away from. Known to locals as Al-Khazneh, the towering, colonnaded building facade is a towering 130 feet, with depictions of mythological figures carved into the stone.

The most famous and most photographed of Petra's many sites, the treasury is thought to house something valuable, money perhaps, in the urn at the top of the structure, and people have been trying to dislodge it for years to see if it really contains riches.

◖ Roman Theater

With an estimated capacity of 3,000-7,000 people, the **Roman Theater** is just past Al-Khazneh. There is only one direction you can go from the treasury, so you won't miss it.

The theater dates back to around 9 BC to AD 40 and was recently restored. Built during the reign of King Aretas IV, its capacity is believed to indicate that at one time the population of Petra was about 24,000 people, based on the Roman-style building practices of making one seat for every family.

You can climb up and get a view into the amphitheater from close up, where you'll get a better view of the semi-circular structure and the strange feature in the back of some previously existing tombs that were cut into during construction of the theater. It makes a great spot for a photograph, as you'll find yourself dwarfed by your surroundings.

Royal Tombs

There are several hundred elaborate tombs with intricate carvings in the rock throughout Petra. Many are empty and you can walk inside them (they are very cave-like). Just opposite of the

© GENEVIEVE BELMAKER

local residents on a high stone perch

amphitheater, you'll see the **Royal Tombs** above ground level with columns cut into the rock wall face. A Byzantine inscription states that one of the tombs was the final resting place of King Malichus II until it was converted into a church in AD 447.

In the immediate vicinity is the ceremonial Palace Tomb, likely used as a place to hold funerals or feasts, and the Tomb of Sextus Florentius, the Roman governor of Arabia who loved the desert region so much that he wanted to be buried here.

The Cardo

Though devastated by a major earthquake in AD 363, Petra's main street (originally Nabataean but reconstructed by the Romans around the time of early 1st century BC when it was a Roman outpost) still has some of its original marble stones and inscriptions. One inscription from AD 114 attests to the restoration of the cardo after Rome annexed the Nabataean Kingdom.

The Roman **cardo,** or main thoroughfare, a typical feature of cities conquered by Rome, served as the major street for commerce and ceremonial processions. As you walk, notice small patches of road underfoot that are easy to trip over if you're not careful.

◖ Byzantine Church

Probably built over the ruins of Petra is the **Byzantine Church,** just to the right of the cardo and notable for its remarkably-intact 70 square meters of mosaic floors. Pictures in the mosaics include depictions that include mythological figures and the four seasons. The church and the mosaics are still in the process of being excavated and preserved.

In 1993, the famed Petra Scrolls were discovered in the Byzantine Church. The collection of 152 papyrus scrolls date back to the 6th century AD (confounding because this was after Petra is believed to have already started to decline).

The scrolls represent the largest collection of written material from antiquity to have ever been found in Jordan. They are in the process of being deciphered and are believed to contain a great deal of information about the region in the Byzantine era.

◖ Great Temple

So much is unknown about the Nabataeans, and this includes who exactly they worshipped. The **Great Temple** is a perfect example of this. The largest freestanding structure in Petra, it recently underwent extensive excavation work by students from the Joukowsky Institute at Brown University. The Institute has a detailed, extensive, and interactive map of the excavation on their website (www.brown.edu/Departments/Joukowsky_Institute/Petra).

The temple is also known as the Temple of Dushara, after the god who some believe was worshipped here. It is generally agreed that it was probably the main place of worship in Nabataean Petra. Complete with its own

THE NABATAEAN CAPITAL

© GENEVIEVE BELMAKER

Petra is thought to be the capital city of the ancient Nabataeans.

Petra is believed to be the capital city of the Arab tribe of the Nabataeans, who made their first appearance around the time of the 6th century BC, just east of Jordan in the desert. Originating from the southeast of the Arabian Peninsula, they gradually expanded their terri-

tory and by the 2nd century BC had established a more organized society.

Highly independent and apt at dodging military conquest, the Nabataeans were influenced by Hellinistic culture, which can be seen in the remnants of their art and architecture. Herodotus, the Greek historian, refers to the Nabataeans in 312 BC and their capital city of Petra.

Petra has a long history of conquest. It was sacked in 312 BC by the army of King Antigonus. On their retreat, though, the army was destroyed in the desert after taking a massive haul of treasure from the city. Around 63 BC, King Aretas III somehow managed to prevent a Roman military conquest of Petra. After Julius Caesar's assassination and the ensuing chaos in 44 BC, Petra had to begin paying tribute to Rome. Failure to pay resulted in two invasions, one by Herod the Great, who gained control of part of their territory and lucrative trade routes.

After the death of the final Nabataean ruler, Rabbel II, Rome annexed Petra and redesigned parts of it in the Roman style. During Roman rule, it's believed that Petra's population grew to about 25,000. But over time and with shifts in trade routes, the Nabataeans profited less and less from trade and eventually abandoned Petra around the 4th century AD. Not much is known about the exact reasons Petra was abandoned, but very few possessions were left behind, suggesting a well-organized, planned departure.

the Al-Deir Monastery

theater, the entire site is 28 by 40 meters and features crafted limestone and a complex system of tunnels. Important to the Nabataeans during the 1st century BC, it was probably also used by the Byzantines.

The massive, complex structure sits on a slightly elevated position with stairs leading up to it and is rectangular in shape with major upper and lower sections. It is one of the most important archaeological and architectural structures in Petra. The detailed map of the site on Brown University's website gives a very complete picture of what used to exist here.

High Place of Sacrifice

A popular early-morning hike is the hike to the **High Place of Sacrifice** (take the steps to the left just near the amphitheater and go to the right at the top of the stairs), which takes about 90 minutes each way. The site is at the top of the ridge, where you can see where animals were sacrificed in two large depressions with drains for their blood. An altar, obelisks, and the ruins of a building that was probably used by priests is just before where the path leads down to a stone fountain. If you continue walking, you'll see a few more complexes and the ruins of tombs, halls, and an ancient garbage dump.

⟨ The Al-Deir Monastery

Another spot that requires a bit of a hike is the **Al-Deir Monastery** (up a flight of 800 rock-cut steps above the amphitheater), which takes about 90 minutes to reach one way. The path, though it has so many steps, is not too steep and is easy to follow. You'll know you're on the right track when you see a sign to the Lion Tomb.

The monastery stands at 164 feet wide and 147 feet tall and the inner walls are marked with the symbols of crosses.

The highlight of Al-Deir is the crowning urn, which you can walk around the top of

PETRA, JORDAN

THREE CUPS OF COFFEE:
THE BEDOUIN COFFEE CEREMONY

© PHILIP LANGE/123RF.COM

coffee, Bedouin style

If you get a chance to take part in a traditional Bedouin coffee ceremony while you're in Jordan, keep in mind that there will be three cups of (very strong) coffee. The Bedouin consider coffee to be a sacred beverage that is a symbol of wealth and hospitality.

The coffee ceremony is called a *jaha,* and can be extremely lengthy. Traditionally, the ceremony starts at dawn in a Bedouin tent, where water is boiled over coals, and the crushed Arabica beans and cardamom are added to the water and left to steep.

When you finally get down to drinking the coffee, there will be three cups. The first cup of coffee is for the soul, the second cup of coffee is for the sword, and the third cup of coffee is in honor of your status as a guest. Another interpretation is that the three cups symbolize hospitality, welcome, and cheer. Asking for a fourth cup of coffee could be considered greedy.

During the coffee ceremony, there is usually singing and the rattling of cups and thumping of a long wooden post. The singing was part of the Bedouin tradition in the past during long desert crossings.

by going up some steps. The view of the surrounding landscape from the rim of the urn is fantastic.

Petra Nabataean Museum

Opened in 1994, the **Petra Nabataean Museum** (03/215-6060, 9am-4pm daily, free with Petra entrance) has over 600 artifacts that have been discovered in Petra over the years. The three main exhibition halls include a depiction of Nabataean history, specific exhibitions in the area, and a collection of Neolithic artifacts, Nabataean pottery, bronze statues, jewelry, coins, and ornaments.

Petra Archaeological Museum

The older and smaller of two museums in Petra is the **Petra Archaeological Museum** (03/215-6060, 9am-4pm daily, free with Petra entrance) in an ancient Nabataean cave on the slope of Al-Habis. Opened in 1963, it has a main hall and two side rooms with finds from regional excavations that date to the Edomite, Nabataean, Roman, and Byzantine periods.

Entertainment and Events

Throughout the year Petra has some unusual entertainment offerings tailored around its sights. The modern-day village of neighboring Wadi Musa is a small Arab village that offers very little in the way of any kind of entertainment, other than eating out.

PETRA BY NIGHT SHOW

Petra shuts down early, but you can experience it by candlelight during the **Petra by Night Show** (8:30pm Mon., Wed.-Thurs., JD12, under 11 free). You can see the siq and the Treasury lit up with flickering light and listen to the ancient sounds of a Bedouin shepherd's flute for a soundtrack while local guides tell stories. On full moons, you can also get a guided night tour, but you must check with the visitor's center and reserve in advance.

DISTANT HEAT DISCO SHOW (WADI RUM)

About an hour from Petra in Wadi Rum, the **Distant Heat Disco Show** (Wadi Rum at the Seven Pillars of Wisdom, www.distantheat. com, late July) gets shaking to a soundtrack of pop music tunes and electronic dance music. The all night event has gotten more popular every year, and includes top DJs, dinner and breakfast, a light show, and tents to sleep in if you didn't come prepared to camp. It's a loud and all-out fun time in the midst of an ancient desert landscape and it typically continues the following night in Aqaba.

ANNUAL PERSEIDS METEOR SHOWER

The **Annual Perseids Meteor Shower** (Aug., peak nights are Aug. 12-13) is an incredible natural phenomena that is best seen from Wadi Rum because of the total lack of city lights and noise. At its peak, there are about 50-80 meteors per hour. Many tour companies have outings that you can join to see the showers.

PETRA, JORDAN

Shopping

Entering Petra is extremely cheap for Jordanians, which is part of the reason that you will see a huge number of locals, including young kids, selling all kinds of things from camel and donkey rides to carriage rides with horses, to cheap necklaces and postcards. Look closely at the animals before you buy a ride on one of them: Many are not well cared for and some even have repeated injuries from the makeshift gear they are wearing.

GIFTS AND SOUVENIRS

There are no shortage of places to buy cheap, low-end gifts and souvenirs in Petra and the surrounding area. There are many shops just before the entrance to the site that sell all kinds of items and even more vendors inside of Petra with makeshift stands selling everything from books about Petra to bottles of artistically arranged sand.

Feel free to bargain with vendors, as they will start with a high price, but don't try to go lower than a third of the original price.

Sand Castle Bazaar

Just by the Treasury inside Petra is the **Sand Castle Bazaar** (079/570-5064, http://petrasandcastle.com, 6:30am-5pm Sat.-Thurs.), which sells antiques, stone mosaic art panels, oil lamps, silver, ceramics, and sand bottles. The Bazaar has a second location near the Silk Road Hotel in Wadi Musa that ships items worldwide.

Ladies of the Queen Noor Foundation

Right along the road just outside of Wadi Musa is the silver workshop and large souvenir store with a small coffee stand of the **Ladies of the Queen Noor Foundation**

jewelry and souvenirs for sale

© GENEVIEVE BELMAKER

NABATAEAN POTTERY

Another enduring Nabataean treasure is their distinctive red clay pottery, which can be divided into two groups: coarser common wares and the more famous eggshell-thin wares embellished with black designs that ranged from very small saucers to trays about three feet across. Their pottery-making skills are believed to have been handed down to them from the Edomites.

The production source of Nabataean pottery was near Petra, and included oil lamps (thousands have been found throughout Petra), incense and perfume bottles (found throughout their former empire), and beautiful, thin serving dishes and platters.

Pottery kilns were discovered in the ash-Sharah Mountains northeast of Petra in 1979, and at least a dozen kilns and portions of numerous on-site workshops have been found since then. At least one kiln was discovered in Wadi Musa as well.

Excellent examples of fine Nabataean pottery can be seen in the museum at Masada and at museums in Petra and throughout Jordan. The kilns can be seen in the Petra Archaeological Museum.

(9am-6pm Mon.-Sat.), with a silver craft workshop and the option to have a necklace custom-made (which you need to wait a few days for).

Wadi Musa

The modern village adjacent to Petra has basic amenities, as well as several shops selling souvenirs. Another specialty of shops in Wadi Musa is heavy silver antique necklaces.

Local Crafts

Just next to the visitor's center at the entrance to Petra are two crafts shops that sell many locally handmade products that support local women's organizations. One shop is run for the benefit of the **Rural Women of Jordan** and the other is for the **Ladies' Working Circle of Wadi Musa** (both shop hours are generally the same as Petra). Beyond the more common embroidered items, both shops also sell jewelry boxes with inlaid mother-of-pearl, sand bottles, pottery, metal work, and woven pillows.

Sports and Recreation

Petra's options for recreation are mostly related to outdoor sports, and there are some great hikes. If you are confident on horseback you can take a ride through the siq to enter the main site. If you want to opt for something more luxurious, take in a spa or Turkish bath.

HIKING

There are several good hikes in Petra that range from 30 minutes to 90 minutes. One of the best trails is just at the entrance to Petra at the end of the siq, just **above the Treasury.** There are several stops along the trail that is about 90 minutes one way if you walk to the end.

You can also set out on the trail that starts out near the amphitheater, just to the left and leads to the lion tombs, the sacrificial altars, and Al-Deir Monastery.

If you are not an experienced hiker, it might be advisable to hire a guide in advance to lead you through this part of Petra, though getting lost is unlikely. Try to set out early in the morning, by at least 8am.

A couple of good choices are **Petra Moon Tours** (based in Wadi Musa, 03/215-6665,

PETRA, JORDAN

© GENEVIEVE BELMAKER

Ride a horse while in Petra.

www.petramoon.com) and **Bedouin Lifestyle** (Wadi Rum, 077/913-1803, www.bedouinlife-style.com).

HORSEBACK RIDING

At the entrance to Petra you will see several horses waiting to be taken for a **horseback ride** (included with price of the Petra entrance fee). If you are an animal lover, though, you might be turned off about using your money to support the apparent exploitation of the horses and other animals you'll see in Petra. Many of them are not well cared for and have injuries acquired from being made to work in the tourism trade.

If you find a horse that you are satisfied is well cared for, riding around the area could be a very enjoyable experience and add to the atmosphere of being in such an ancient location.

HORSE-DRAWN CARRIAGES

At first, the **horse-drawn carriages** (JD20) of Petra look charming and innocent. But they fly up and down the siq at breakneck speed, giving weary tourists a way to get out of the site more quickly; though, it is not a smooth ride. Most of the passengers look more terrified than enchanted when seen in passing. If you do take a carriage in or out of Petra, just remember that they will go at a fairly quick pace, and you won't be able to stop once you start.

CAMEL RIDES

At the entrance to Petra, in front of the Treasury, and throughout Petra, you will see camels being hired out for **camel rides** (JD15). It's more of a short stroll or a stand and pose for a picture than a ride, but the novelty of it is hard to resist, even if the price is a bit steep.

DONKEY RIDES

Also tempting, especially if you are getting a bit weary of walking around the loose, easy-to-stumble-over rocks, are **donkey rides** (JD10), which are usually rented out by young boys. If you act unsure about whether you want to buy a ride, you might get a little donkey shadow following you about until you cave in. Here again, look closely at the condition of the donkeys: Many of them have heavy chains across their noses for a harness, which cuts into the skin of the animal, causing multiple-layered injuries.

TURKISH BATHS

For some relaxation, try the **Salome Turkish Bath** (Wadi Musa, 03/215-7342, www.salometurkishbath.com), a family-owned and run operation that offers a steam room session, exfoliation, and massage. You can follow your massage with herbal tea. Ask for transportation to and from your hotel when calling to make a reservation, as it is included with their services.

© GENEVIEVE BELMAKER

a horse and buggy on a speedy ride to Petra

Accommodations

As a tourist destination, Petra's adjacent village of Wadi Musa offers a variety of accommodations from lower-end to luxury, but the large majority of the approximately three dozen hotels in the area cost under US$100.

UNDER US$100

Surprisingly upscale and modern for the price, the **Petra Moon Hotel** (Petra Visitor Center St., 03/215-6220, www.petramoonhotel.com, US$92 d) is a mere 100 yards from Petra. The rooms are spacious and have pretty, modern, art deco touches, such as purple walls next to black and white furnishings. The rooms have satellite TV, a DVD player, telephone, bathrobes and a bathtub, extra-long beds, a CD player, minibar, and tea service. The five-storey hotel also has a roof garden with an outdoor pool, buffet breakfast in the restaurant, and a small grocery store. You can set up a horseback ride through the concierge desk when you tire of hiking through Petra.

Near the Wadi Musa souk and its shopping opportunities, **Amra Palace Hotel** (just up from the Shaheed roundabout next to Cleopatra Hotel, 03/215-7070, www.amrapalace.com, US$82 d) is also in walking distance to Petra and has a warm, modern exterior and interior with huge beds and a small sitting area in the rooms. The hotel's high points include an indoor pool, a spa, flat-screen satellite TVs, and a terrace for drinks that overlooks the garden. The restaurant offerings in the hotel differ a bit by the season, but in the summer they include an outdoor Bedouin restaurant serving traditional barbecued meat.

A five-minute walk to Petra, the smaller **La Maison Hotel** (off Tourist St. behind Moevenpick Hotel, 03/215-6401, www.la-maisonhotel.com.jo, US$28 d) has recently renovated rooms with mountain views, free Wi-Fi, satellite TV, and minibars. The furnishings are very, very spare and include only the basics with white tile flooring, giving the general environment a slightly sterile feeling. But the recent renovation means everything that you do have in the rooms is top-notch and in very new condition. There is also a lobby lounge bar that serves food.

Known for its super-friendly staff, the **Al Rashid Hotel** (Main St. at the Shaheed roundabout, 03/215-6800, rashid@joinnet.com.jo, US$41 d) is right near Wadi Musa's main offerings for shopping. The recently renovated rooms have free Wi-Fi and are decorated very simply, but all include a private bathroom. The very small hotel (only 28 rooms) serves lunch and dinner in its restaurant and it is about half a mile from Petra.

For a completely different experience than what you could find in a hotel, **(The Rock Camp** (Beidha Little Petra, about 9 miles north of Petra, 06/567-9050, www.therockpetra.com, US$76 d) offers luxury Bedouin tent accommodations in the desert. While you're at the Rock Camp, you can try out henna tattoos or play dress up in Bedouin clothing. Meals are served in a large common tent and around a campfire. All of the tents are set up with beds and traditional fittings for bedding and flooring, and there are common bathrooms. The staff (available 24 hours) will also help you arrange outings in the area if you're interested.

A 10-minute walk to Wadi Musa's center, the **(Rocky Mountain Hotel** (Main St., 03/215-7393 and 03/215-5100, rockymountainhotel@yahoo.com, US$43 d) has some of the most fantastic views in town from its Bedouin tapestry-decorated dining room and is one of the more attractive budget hotels in town.

The small hotel is popular for its rooftop terrace where you can dine on request, private bathrooms, free Wi-Fi (as well as a lobby computer), and shuttle service to Petra. During the day, you can buy a lunch box or light snack and drink. The rooms are decorated with nice, comfy touches like fluffy, bright throw rugs and extra thick blankets for the cold desert nights.

US$100-150

Featuring the unique touch of 19th century-style furniture and housed in a stone building that evokes a bygone era, the **(Beit Zaman Hotel and Resort** (Al Nawafleh St., 03/215-7401, www.beitzaman.jordantourismresorts.com, US$100 d) is a medium-size hotel with both an indoor and outdoor pool.

The rooms succeed at combining local flavor with world-class luxury, including locally crafted tapestries on the walls and beds, some rooms with Arab-style architecture and arched doorways, minibar, safe, and private bathroom. The hotel's restaurant serves Arabic food, and you can arrange for outdoor excursions with the hotel staff. A small downside is that the hotel charges for their shuttle to Petra, which is two miles away.

US$150-200

About as close as you can get to the entrance of Petra, the **Moevenpick Resort Petra** (Tourism St., next to the Visitor's Center, 03/215-7111, www.moevenpick-hotels.com, US$155 d) is a five-star, large resort hotel (and part of a regional luxury chain) that features a ton of outdoor access without leaving the hotel grounds. There are balconies for every room and a rooftop terrace. The rooms themselves are pure luxury. Recently renovated, they all come with satellite TV, a desk, and every amenity you could need. The hotel also has a tea room, restaurant, lobby bar, and fitness center.

OVER US$200

Just a 10-minute drive from Wadi Musa, the **Marriott Petra** (Taybeh Rd., outside of Wadi Musa, 03/215-6407, www.marriott.com/hotels, $US 210 d) is one of the few high-end luxury accommodations in the area. Most of the hotel's rooms have views of Petra or Petra Valley. When you're not hiking in the hot and dust, you can stay in the hotel and luxuriate in the outdoor pool, sauna, or Turkish bath, or eat in the hotel restaurant. There's no need to hire a taxi to drive you to Petra: The hotel has free shuttles to take you. The rooms are nice and spacious; they include huge windows for the panoramic views and comfortable touches like couches.

Food

If you eliminate all of the three dozen hotels from the equation, Wadi Musa still has a nice range of at least 30 restaurants and eateries to choose from. Most of them are in the village center, and many are within easy walking distance of Petra.

ARABIC AND TRADITIONAL BEDOUIN

Of the many stops to eat near Petra's main gate, **Red Cave** (near Petra Main Gate, 03/215-7799 and 77/771-5223, 9am-11pm daily, JD10) is a slightly more expensive option among a field of tourist-centric choices. But they serve up very generous portions of Bedouin dishes, including *gallayah,* and have indoor and outdoor seating (in the shade). It is very easy to spot with its red sign that hangs over the sidewalk. They also have a wide selection of vegetarian dishes, including soups and stews.

Some of the most impeccable service and best coffee you will find in Wadi Musa are served up at the **❰ Silk Road Restaurant** (Silk Road Hotel, 03/215-7222, www.petrasilkroad.com, 8am-9pm daily, JD10 for buffet). The buffet here has a tasty, wide variety of salads and traditional, typical Arabic dishes. The hotel also has a traditional indoor-outdoor Bedouin-style

BEDOUIN CUISINE

© JASMIN MERDAN/123RF.COM

Bedouin *mansaf*

Traditionally cooked on an open fire, Bedouin food has a unique style that is worth sampling while you're in Petra. There are plenty of opportunities to try different Bedouin food, which is typically eaten with the hands, including dipping rolled-up rice balls into sauce.

There are a few styles of bread that come with Bedouin meals: the more standard pita; the thin, crepe-like **shraak** cooked on a domed pan over a fire; and **taboon,** usually thicker and made from darker flour.

Mansaf is a favorite dish usually reserved for special occasions or for special guests made of stewed lamb meat over rice with yogurt and pine nuts.

Maglubeh, which translates to "upside down," is a mixture of chicken, potatoes, peppers, vegetables, and rice stacked and layered in one pot and then flipped upside down onto a plate after it is cooked. It is usually eaten family style. Several restaurants in Petra serve *maglubeh.*

Fatteh, easy to find and simple, is a delicious dish made from bread and yogurt, which sometimes includes hummus, and is served with chopped raw onions and olive oil.

café that is very small but beautifully decorated with Bedouin tapestries, and makes a perfect spot for a quiet coffee or tea and a light snack.

It has a fairly typical setting (aside from the tables around the fountain) and fairly typical prices, but the **Al Arabi** restaurant (at the Shaheed roundabout, 03/215-7661, yhamadeen@link.net.jo, 6am-midnight daily, JD5) has some seriously delicious dishes and is very centrally located. For JD2 you can get a milk and fruit smoothie to go with the spicy Arabic food they serve.

BUFFET

One of the best buffets in town with the standard strong Turkish coffee, **Petra Zaman** (Main St., 079/553-6391, http://petrazamanrestaurant.weebly.com, 9am-11pm daily, JD3) serves a variety of salads and vegetarian dishes in their homey, central restaurant. They specialize in the regional favorite chicken and rice maklouba dish, which comes in a pot and is flipped onto your plate upside-down when served.

About one mile past the Treasury in Petra is **Basin Restaurant** (Petra near the monastery, 03/215-6266, 11:30am-3pm daily, JD17 for lunch buffet), run by the Crowne Plaza Hotel group. It is the most upscale option inside of the antiquities sites of Petra; you will see several other snack shops along the way. The restaurant serves a fairly large buffet, which includes several dessert options, and the typical offerings of hummus, salads, and some meat dishes. The patio seating is shaded and the restaurant has a great view of Petra, but they cater to groups and the prices are on the high end for Petra.

DESSERTS AND SWEETS

If you already had a meal somewhere else, consider stopping by **(€ Sanabel Bakery** (City Center near Rum Internet, 079/576-0605, yousef_tw2008@yahoo.com, 6am-midnight daily, JD2) for an alarmingly strong Turkish coffee and one of their little pastries. It's probably not the best bet for a breakfast croissant, but it's the perfect place for an after dinner visit.

INTERNATIONAL FUSION

Serving everything from pizza and pasta to hearty omelets and Bedouin food, **(€ Al-Wadi** (Shaheed roundabout, 77/633-1431 and 79/530-0135, mashalehl@yahoo.com, 7am-10:30pm daily, JD4) is a popular choice for people who are not sure what they are in the mood to eat. The atmosphere is quaint, though the interior is a bit dark, with Bedouin-style touches. Try the lamb casserole if you are in the mood for some local home cooking.

Information and Services

ONLINE RESOURCES AND TOURISM BOARDS

There are several very useful websites if you plan on doing any research about Petra and the surrounding area prior to or during your trip here.

For local information, try the **Petra Development and Tourism Regional Authority** website (28 Wadi Musa, 03/215-7093, www.visitpetra.jo), which has good general information about a wide range of things from currency rates to background information.

The website for the village of **Wadi Rum** (www.wadirum.jo) is also a good source for information about locals in the area and has a listing of tourism-related services.

For national information, the **Jordan Ministry of Tourism and Antiquities** (06/460-3360, www.tourism.jo/en) has tourism videos and statistics.

The official site of the **Jordan Tourism Board** (06/567-8294, www.visitjordan.com) is robust and has great photos, but doesn't always work on the first try.

Finally, the **Royal Society for the**

Conservation of Nature (www.rscn.org.jo) provides information about nature conservation and research, ecotourism, community projects, and handicrafts throughout Jordan.

For general background, **Nabatea.net** (nabataea.net) isn't the most modern website, but it has quite a few external links and more information about the Nabataeans than you will need.

The official website of the **Office of King Hussein I of Jordan** (www.kinghussein.gov.jo) also has quite a bit of background information about the history of Jordan, from ancient times through today.

PRIVATE TOUR COMPANIES

There are quite a few tour companies that operate in Petra. If you are coming from Israel and pay a company there for services, don't be surprised if you are passed off to a gauntlet of different companies and guides before you actually reach your destination.

To make arrangements directly with a company that works in Jordan, there are several good options. One of the most popular and experienced at working with English speakers is **Petra Moon Tours** (based in Wadi Musa, 03/215-6665, www.petramoon.com). They offer a very wide variety of tours, including archaeological, experiential, participatory, and alternative. They also host an annual two-week writing workshop in Petra in June.

Run by two Bedouin guides who are lifelong residents of Wadi Rum, **Bedouin Lifestyle** (077/913-1803, www.bedouinlifestyle.com) specializes in tours that expose visitors to Bedouin customs and traditions, including hiking, camel rides, camping under the stars, and jeep rides through the desert.

Run by a Jordanian family and in operation since 1994, **Jordan Travel** (07/436-3116, www.jordantoursandtravel.com) runs customized, private tours of sites all throughout Jordan.

The U.S.-based **Insider's Petra** (toll-free in the U.S. 855/928-2538, www.insiderspetra.com) is an alternative for making tour arrangements in advance without the guesswork of dealing with someone in another country. The company can arrange individual and group travel experiences, and the founder and president is an American based in the United States.

VISITOR'S CENTER

The Petra **Visitor's Center** (outside of Petra Main Gate, 03/215-6029, 6:30am-5pm Sat.-Thurs.) provides a variety of information about the site. Ask before entering if the price of a horse ride through the siq is still included in the admission fee (it was at time of publication).

Through the visitor's center, you can also arrange to hire a **Bedouin guide** (about JD50) for the entire day or for a half day. A **Jordanian guide** (JD9-57) can also be arranged.

Getting There and Around

Getting to Petra is relatively simple, but getting around is a bit harder. No vehicles are allowed inside the actual archaeological site and the village of Wadi Musa is a bit isolated.

ENTERING AND EXITING JORDAN

Transportation options to and from Wadi Musa are limited, as many people arrive and leave with large tour buses. The unofficial public transportation stop is the Shaheed roundabout; just ask anybody and they will be able to point you in the right direction.

By Air

Jordan has more than one airport, but the most common entry point is the Amman Airport, officially known as the **Queen Alia International Airport** (airport-authority.com/AMM). There are flights between Amman and Tel Aviv on a regular basis.

By Car

Aqaba is about a 10-minute drive from the Eilat border crossing and Wadi Musa is about two hours from Aqaba. If you are driving from Amman, it is about 3.5 hours.

After you cross into Aqaba, if you are driving yourself to Petra, you can visit one of the two **Hertz** locations (Alnahda St. and Aqaba Airport, 03/201-6206, www.hertz.com, 8am-1pm and 4pm-9pm daily, Aqaba airport closes at 7pm, US$84 d).

By Bus

If you are interested in getting to Amman, you can take the **JETT** bus (www.jett.com.jo), which is a big white vehicle that look just like a tourist bus (rather than a public bus). The bus leaves from Wadi Musa once a day at 5pm and costs JD9.5. There are several stops in Aqaba where buses depart about half a dozen times a day (8am-6:30pm).

Border Control

Don't be surprised by the incredibly complex, circuitous route that you will need to take through border control when you are coming from Eilat and crossing into Aqaba. You will have your passport checked and stamped several times. Just follow the general flow of traffic or ask any one of the guards standing about if you are unsure about which window to stop at next.

The border opens at 8am and it is best to be there before it opens to bypass the lines of people as much as possible.

GETTING AROUND

Once you are in Wadi Musa, if you need to drive anywhere it is easy and relatively cheap to take a taxi. If you do have a car, you won't be at much risk of getting lost. It is a fairly desolate area and Petra and Wadi Musa are the only attractions for miles around.

BACKGROUND

The Land

You will often hear Israelis say that theirs is a small country, and it's true. The total area of the State of Israel is 8,630 miles, comprised mostly of land mass. At its widest it is 85 miles across and from the northernmost point to the southernmost point it is 290 miles.

GEOGRAPHY

Israel's western coast runs along the Mediterranean Sea, and elsewhere Israel is bordered by several other countries, not all of which can be characterized as friendly. In the north, its neighbors are Lebanon and Syria; on the east is the Hashemite Kingdom of Jordan; and Egypt is in the south.

The West Bank, a land mass of about 2,270 square miles, sits between Israel and Jordan, and is also known as Judea and Samaria. To characterize the West Bank as part of Israel is a misnomer. The West Bank's three distinct divisions of area fall under the categories of A, B, and C: Palestinian Authority-controlled, joint Palestinian Authority and Israeli-controlled, and Israeli-controlled, respectively. About 60 percent of the West Bank is Area B or C, and there are 350,000 Israelis living there, including those who are residents of east Jerusalem.

© GENEVIEVE BELMAKER

© GIDON BELMAKER

Olive trees thrive in Israel's Mediterranean climate.

In the West Bank, a major feature of the landscape is the silvery-green olive trees. The terraced hillsides and fertile valleys have been farmed for generations. The landscape of the West Bank is gorgeous with its rocky, rolling hills.

Distances in Israel are strikingly small, but the changes in weather and landscape can be drastic. In one hour, you can go from the cool, breezy mountains of Jerusalem to the flat, humid seaside town of Tel Aviv.

The coastal plain of the north and its bordering rich farmland, with chalk and sandstone cliffs, is home to deep water ports and is where most of the country's population of 7.8 million lives.

A number of mountain ranges run from north to south through the landscape. In the perpetually green north, the volcanic eruption–created basalt Golan Heights tower over the Hula Valley. In the Galilee, where some elevations go as high as 4,000 feet above sea level, the hills are mostly dolomite and soft limestone.

Between Israel and the West Bank in the north is the Jezreel Valley, another fertile valley that is heavily cultivated.

The south of Israel is home to the Negev Desert, and although it makes up about half of the country's land mass, it is the least inhabited. The extremely arid south is made up of low sandstone hills and plains with a huge number of canyons amid the sandstone landscape that are prone to flash flooding in the winter.

A bit farther south, the Negev is characterized by barren stone peaks and plateaus littered with rocks. Here you will find three erosive craters that are so huge that they are tourist attractions. The largest, Mitzpe Ramon, is about 5 miles across at its widest, about 24 miles long, and about 1,600 feet deep.

At the very south of Israel is Eilat and the Red Sea, where gray and red granite and sandstone form the base of the landscape.

LAKES AND RIVERS

One of the most significant bodies of water in the region is the Sea of Galilee. At 695 feet

The Negev Desert is vast and barren.

below sea level and between the hills of the Galilee and the Golan Heights, it is the most important source of water in Israel and home to several significant historic and religious sites.

The Sea of Galilee feeds the Jordan River and has a circumference of only about 30 miles. On the southern shore of the Sea of Galilee, in the town of Tiberias, an electronic meter displays the Sea's water level, a number of national interest. In early 2013, following weeks of heavy rain, the sea level was higher than it had been in several years.

Coming from the southern mouth of the Sea of Galilee, the Jordan River runs for about 186 miles, descending 2,300 feet from north to south through the Syrian-African Rift that split the crust of the earth millions of years ago. The river is fed by tributaries from Mount Hermon and empties into the Dead Sea, the lowest point on Earth.

The Dead Sea sits at 1,300 feet below sea level on the southern end of the Jordan Valley. Its waters have the highest level of salinity and

density of any body of water in the world, and are famed for their rich mineral deposits (and mud), which include table and industrial salt, bromine, magnesium, and potash.

Since 1960, the water level of the Dead Sea has dropped by an incredible 35 feet, partially caused by massive water diversion projects conducted by Israel and Jordan. The water diversion projects have reduced the amount of incoming water to the Dead Sea by 75 percent.

Along the eastern side of Israel, part of the Syrian-African Rift that split the crust of the earth millions of years ago, are the Jordan Valley and the Arava. The land ranges from semi-arid in the south to fertile in the north.

South of the Dead Sea, which has separated into an upper section and a lower section over time, is the Arava, Israel's savannah region. The Arava continues to Israel's Red Sea outlet: the Gulf of Eilat, a sub-tropical region and home to some of the most remarkable coral reef and unusual marine life in the world.

© ELLA/123RF.COM

the Sea of Galilee

CLIMATE

The climate in Israel and the West Bank vary widely from temperate to tropical to alpine. There are two distinct seasons, though two additional very brief transitions are often evident in between those.

Between November to May is the rainy season, or winter. Though it does not rain constantly, rainfall and lower temperatures (about 31°F at the lowest in some areas) do predominate.

From June through October, there is little to no rainfall, and the temperature rises steadily to a daily low of 66°F in some areas before starting its decline in late September. The average high throughout the country during the dry season ranges from 84-104°F. The months of July and August are the most brutally punishing in terms of heat.

The variance in climate is marked by mild coastal winters, cooler summers in elevated regions (such as Jerusalem), and almost year-round semi-desert conditions in the Negev.

ENVIRONMENTAL ISSUES
Drought and Flash Floods

One of the major environmental issues in the region is drought. The mean annual rainfall is a mere 8 inches in the south and about 28 inches in the north.

In the winter months, the rainfall that does come can sometimes cause flash floods, particularly in the south with its canyons of bone-dry rock. On occasion, a person or an animal will get swept away by one of these flash floods that seem to come out of nowhere, though it is rare.

Heat Waves

The punishing heat of the summer months (particularly during July and August) becomes more pronounced during a prolonged heat wave when the temperature can reach 95-105°F and higher, even in typically temperate Jerusalem. The greatest risk during heat waves to humans is suffering from dehydration or heat stroke, of which some of the symptoms are dizziness, nausea, confusion, blurred vision, and vomiting.

the Jordan River

Left untreated, dehydration and heat stroke can lead to complications that can cause death. It is imperative to drink plenty of water while in the region and to protect yourself from the sun, even when there is no heat wave.

Sandstorms
On rare occasion the air in Tel Aviv and elsewhere will be filled with a very fine, yellow dust, typically at the end of a heat wave. It is not exactly a sandstorm, but it turns the air yellow and leaves a layer of dust on everything, including your skin. Sand in the air at the end of a heat wave typically indicates that the heat wave is about to break and is usually followed by a brief rainfall that turns things a bit muddy.

History

The histories of the regions of Israel, the West Bank, and Petra are long, winding, complex, and interconnected. In modern times, differing claims and versions of historical events are very much part of conversations and actions taken related to the land and political stances on important issues. In other words, the history of this region is very much alive and well and plays an active role in dictating the future.

ANCIENT CIVILIZATION
Canaan is the area generally defined as Palestine in historical and Biblical literature, and is known today as Israel and the West Bank (also called Judea and Samaria or Palestine). The name Canaan, and Canaanites, the name of its inhabitants, appear in Egyptian and Phoenician writings from approximately the 15th century BC and in the Old Testament of the Bible. The earliest human inhabitants

of coastal Canaan go back to Paleolithic and Mesolithic times. Evidence of human settlements have been found in Jericho dating back to 8,000 BC.

Israelites conquered Palestine around the late 2nd century BC or earlier, but there were others before them. The Egyptians, the Hyksos, and the Hurrians also invaded. During the Late Bronze Age, about 1550-1200 BC, the Egyptians were the main dominating power in the region, despite challenges from the Hittites, and the Hapiru, who some believe were the original Hebrews.

Most archaeological excavations of the area have been conducted since the 20th century, and the most significant literary texts on regional history are the Old Testament, the Ras Shamra texts, and the Amarna Letters, dispatches from the 14th century BC from Palestinian and Syrian governors to their Egyptian rulers.

The history and culture of the region has been influenced by a number of cultures, including Egyptian, Mycenaean, Cretan, Hurrian, Byzantine, Mesopotamian, Greek, Roman, and British. It is believed that the Canaanites were the first people to have used an alphabet, based on an archaeological discovery of a language that is widely recognized as a parent language to the Greek and Latin alphabets.

Around the time of the Early Iron Age, approximately 1250 BC, the Israelites came into Canaan after their exodus from Egypt and 40 years of wandering in the desert. In the next century, the Philistines invaded and established a strong hold over the region through a series of city-states, but were broken under King David's leadership. King David also managed to capture Jerusalem from the Canaanites. The 10th century marked the beginning of the land being known as Israel.

Around the time of King David (about 1000-960 BC), the various tribes of Israel were consolidated into a united kingdom. King David made the Canaanite city of Jerusalem his capital and according to tradition, moved the Ark of the Covenant there, which was believed to contain the living presence of God. Around the time of 960-920 BC, David's son, Solomon, carried out the wish of his deceased father to build a great temple to house the Ark. The period of Solomon's rule is associated with the peak of Israelite grandeur; King Solomon oversaw the building of the First Temple, which was later destroyed. He also managed to forge treaties with neighboring kingdoms, including Egypt and Sheba, and create other important building projects in addition to the Temple.

The Kingdom of Israel was guided by strong, spiritual, monotheistic beliefs in one all-powerful God (Yahweh), the Lord Creator of the Universe. That belief was often used by rulers to help unify the kingdom and its people.

Around 920 BC, Solomon died and the kingdom splintered into north and south halves. Israel was in the north with its capital Samaria, and the Kingdom of Judah was in the south with its capital Jerusalem. A period of frequent instability and lack of unity between the north and south followed, and by 721 BC, the Neo-Assyrian Empire became the new ruling force, expelling people to make room for their own settlements. In 587 BC, Jerusalem was sacked by the Babylonian King Nebuchadnezzar II. The Temple was destroyed, and the ruling class and skilled craftsmen were deported to Babylon.

The deportation by the Neo-Assyrians and Babylonians of the people of the Kingdom of Israel was the end of the existence of the nation of Israel until the modern state's creation in 1948. It also marked the beginning of the existence of the Jewish Diaspora and the beginning of the development of a religious framework in Judaism outside of the land of Israel. Connections between the ancient state and the modern state, including the name, remain an oft-debated and emotionally-charged issue.

EARLY HISTORY

After the destruction of the First Temple, between 538-142 BC, there were several waves of tens of thousands of Jews who were allowed to return to Israel. They had varying degrees of

pillars of an ancient Roman temple in Beit She'an

self-rule over a period of about four centuries under Persian and Hellenistic rule.

Construction of a Second Temple on the site of the first one began in 521 BC and was finished in 516, during a period when Jerusalem's city walls were refortified.

Around 37 BC, Herod the Great was appointed King of Judea by the Romans and he launched a massive construction campaign, the evidence of which can be seen today in Caesarea, Masada, Jerusalem, and Herodium. Herod remodeled and renewed the Temple to a state of grandeur, but his efforts to appease the subjects to his rule failed to win their loyalty.

After a relatively brief period rule by the Hasmonean dynasty of Seleucids, the Romans came into power around 40 BC and Israel became a Roman province. It was not long after this that Jesus appeared in Jerusalem and other areas in what is now Israel and the West Bank. According to tradition, he performed many miracles in Jerusalem, spread his teachings, and while standing atop the Mount of Olives, wept over the coming destruction of the holy city. Jerusalem is also where Jesus was crucified, buried, and said to have risen from the dead.

By AD 66, ongoing violence and anger against Roman rule and oppression erupted into full-scale revolt. By AD 70, Jerusalem, including the Second Temple, was razed to the ground by the Romans. The historic account of the well-known contemporary historian of the time, Josephus Flavius, recounts that hundreds of thousands of Jews died in the siege on Jerusalem and throughout Israel, including in the siege on the last stand of Jewish revolutionaries at Masada. Thousands more were sold into slavery.

Several hundred years later, after generations of Roman rule and the declaration of Christianity as the official religion of the Roman kingdom, around AD 325, Helena (mother of Constantine the Great) came to the Holy Land to begin construction of some of the world's first churches.

Under Helena's supervision, construction commenced on the Church of the Nativity (where Jesus is said to have been born), the

Chapel of the Apostles on the Mount of Olives (where Jesus is said to have ascended to heaven), the Church of the Holy Sepulchre (where Jesus is said to have been crucified, buried, and resurrected), and another structure near Hebron.

During the 7th century, Jerusalem was the object of military conquest multiple times. It was sacked and claimed first by the Persians, then taken back by the Byzantines, and finally by the Islamic Empire. Around 690 BC, under the rule of the Islamic Empire, the Dome of the Rock was built on the Temple Mount at the site of the First and Second Temples. According to Islamic tradition, the site is where Prophet Muhammed ascended to heaven. The region would remain under Islamic rule until about 1099.

Between the 8th and 9th centuries, the seventh of a series of historically massive and powerful earthquakes struck the region, destroying Tiberias, Beit She'an, Hippos, and Pella.

Between 1099 and 1291, the Crusaders and their multiple campaigns to reclaim the Holy Land dominated the region, until the ancient city of Akko fell to the Egyptians and the Crusader kingdom of Jerusalem was ended. The land was under Mamluk rule until 1516 when the Ottomans took over and ruled until 1917.

MODERN HISTORY

Near the end of the 400 years of Ottoman rule, in 1860, the first neighborhood was built outside the Old City walls of Jerusalem, and the First Aliya, or large-scale immigration of Jews, came to Israel. The Second Aliya came between 1904-1914, and both groups were mainly from Russia and Poland. By 1909, the first modern, all-Jewish city of Tel Aviv was founded, and by 1917, British conquest seized power from the Ottomans with the promise of a "Jewish national home in Palestine" by British Foreign Minister Balfour.

The years between 1918-1948 were marked by British rule, and more groups of Aliya from Europe. In 1922, the British granted the Mandate for Palestine, with 75 percent of

Jewish immigrants in 1947

PUBLIC DOMAIN / PIKIWIKI - FREE IMAGE COLLECTION OF ISRAEL

the area going to Transjordan (modern-day Jordan) and 25 percent designated for Jews. In this period, major universities were established in Haifa (Technion) and Jerusalem (Hebrew University).

During the British Mandate, prior to World War II, there were several instances of significant violence and fighting between Arabs and Jews. By 1947, the United Nations proposed the establishment of both Arab and Jewish states in the land of Israel.

MODERN WARS

Achieving the seemingly elusive peace between Arabs and Jews in the region has been an incredibly long and drawn-out process that started before Israel was ever officially a state. In May, 1948, the British Mandate ended and the State of Israel was established.

The day after the state was formally declared, five Arab states invaded Israel, marking the beginning of the War of Independence which lasted until 1949, when armistice agreements were signed with Egypt, Jordan, Syria, and Lebanon. Jerusalem was divided into east and west with east Jerusalem under Jordanian rule and west Jerusalem under Israeli rule. In 1948-1952, there were massive waves of immigration from European and Arab countries.

In 1967, the Six-Day War reunited Jerusalem's east and west sides of the city, though the east side is now technically part of the West Bank. The Six-Day War was followed by the Egyptian War of Attrition (1968-1970) and the Yom Kippur War (1973). Following the Camp David Accords, the Israel-Egypt Peace Treaty was signed, normalizing relations between the two countries.

After peace with Egypt and Jordan, internal domestic violence erupted in 1987 in Israel-administered areas with the First Intifada, followed by the Gulf War (1991). On the verge of a domestic peace agreement in 1995, then Prime Minister Yitzhak Rabin was assassinated in Tel Aviv. By 2000, the Second Intifada erupted, followed by years of violent internal regional instability.

In 2005, the highly controversial Gaza Disengagement Plan was carried out under the leadership of Prime Minister Ariel Sharon (who had a stroke and went into a coma almost immediately afterward), whereby Israel unilaterally withdrew all Jewish settlements in Gaza. Subsequently coming under the rule of the terrorist organization Hamas, Gaza has become a hotbed of violence and the center of destruction when fighting breaks out between Hamas and Israel.

Government

There are two governments in Israel and the West Bank: the government of the State of Israel and the Palestinian Authority. If and when there is an agreement made about a two-state solution for the region, it will be made between these two governmental bodies. However, the major power in the region, politically, economically, and militarily, is Israel.

SYMBOLISM

The flag of the State of Israel is designed based on the Jewish prayer shawl with the blue star of David in the center. Israel's official emblem is a menorah flanked by olive branches that represent Israel's desire for peace. The national anthem, *Hatikvah,* was penned by Jewish poet Naphtali Herz Imber in 1878, and the words express the hope of the Jewish people to live as a free and sovereign people in the land of Israel.

ISRAELI GOVERNMENT ORGANIZATION

The Israeli government is a parliamentary democracy, with free elections, a prime minister, and a president. The system is based on the concept of a division of powers between the legislative, executive, and judicial branches.

© FLIK47/123RF.COM

The Knesset is Israel's unicameral parliament.

Political Parties and Elections

Israel's unicameral parliament is called the Knesset, and functions in plenary sessions through 15 standing committees and 120 members. The Knesset generally runs for terms of four years, and its makeup is determined after general elections. Both Hebrew and Arabic are officially recognized languages of the Knesset, though debates on issues are conducted in Hebrew with simultaneous translation if a member wishes to speak Arabic.

The current parties that have the most power in the Knesset following the 2013 general election are Likud, Yisrael Beitenu, Kadima, Shas, Labour Party, and Hatnua. There are several others that have fewer than 9 members representing them in the Knesset.

Israeli citizens are eligible to vote from age 18, and they vote for a political party to represent them in the Knesset, not for individuals. There are a wide range of political parties that run for seats in the Knesset that represent a broad range of beliefs and positions on the issues.

Election day in Israel is a national holiday and if a voter is outside of their polling district, free transportation is provided to them. Polling stations are provided for military personnel, prisoners, hospital patients, merchant seamen and women, and Israelis on official work abroad.

Alliances and Enemies

Israel's political situation is characterized largely by a range of staunch advocates and lukewarm alliances. Immediately in Israel's neighborhood, Egypt and Jordan are border countries that have generally good relations with Israel. Relations with Turkey blow hot and cold (they recently re-normalized relations after a couple of years of political conflict), and they are not on good terms with Syria, Lebanon, and Iran.

The position of western countries vary, but the United States is Israel's single greatest ally in the world. Other countries like Australia and Canada are basically supportive, but

© GIDON BELMAKER

Military service is mandatory for Israeli men and women.

there is a great deal of political activism over the plight of Palestinians that originates in the west.

Judicial and Penal Systems

Israel's judiciary system is independent. Judges are appointed by the president after being recommended by a committee of Supreme Court judges, public figures, and members of the bar. Judicial appointments are permanent until mandatory retirement at age 70.

There are several types of courts, including special courts (including traffic, labor, juvenile), religious courts, magistrates' court, district court, and the Supreme Court.

Israeli Military

The Israeli Defense Force (IDF) has been tested in battle through several generations since the establishment of the State of Israel in 1948, and has fought in six major wars. The highest-level public officials and politicians were often individuals who distinguished themselves during military service and in war.

Service in the IDF is compulsory for all eligible men and women at the age of 18. The male term of service is three years, while women serve for two years, and deferments can be made for students or new immigrants. Reserve duty obligations continue for men until age 51, and every soldier serves in a reserve unit that they are called to work for at least once a year.

PALESTINIAN AUTHORITY GOVERNMENT ORGANIZATION

The Palestinian National Authority, also called the Palestinian Authority (PA), was established as an interim, self-governing authority following the Oslo accords in 2003. The PA governs parts of the West Bank. It used to also govern Gaza, but that area is now under the control of Hamas.

The PA embodies many of the characteristics of a state, including a legislative and executive body, and a semi-independent judiciary.

Leadership includes a president, cabinet, and a prime minister.

Palestinian Authority Military

The Palestinian Authority military patrols certain areas of the West Bank, including some parts of Bethlehem, Hebron, Ramallah, and some checkpoints. They are largely a peace-keeping force.

Economy

The Israeli economy was started virtually from scratch just 65 years ago (officially) and has weathered crises and deprivation of various kinds. The modern free-market economy is bolstered by R&D, high-tech industries, nano-technology, solar energy, irrigation innovation, agriculture, and start-ups.

EXPORTS AND IMPORTS

In the past 30 years, significant free trade agreements have been made with the United States, the European Union, and a number of countries in Latin America. Israel's export of goods and services is about $80 billion annually.

Israel has struggled to balance its hefty trade deficit, which has been the price for its rapid economic growth. The somewhat limited domestic market and small economy means that Israel must rely on expansion of exports, particularly industrial exports.

Most imports, about 85 percent, are

© GENEVIEVE BELMAKER

Apples roll through assembly at a packing plant in the Golan Heights.

production inputs and fuel, largely from Europe, followed by the Americas, then Asia, and other countries. Most exports of goods go to the United States, Europe, and Asia. Excluding the export of diamonds, Israel's exports to the United States exceed its imports, but its overall imports exceed its exports.

Almost two-thirds of Israel's annual trade deficits have been covered through unilateral transfers, including foreign pensions, money brought in by immigrants, and hefty donations from overseas Jewish fundraising organizations that have gone straight into the coffers of health, education, and social service organizations and institutions. Grants from generous foreign governments, particularly the United States, have also bolstered the economy.

AGRICULTURE

Scarce natural resources, particularly water and arable land, define Israel's production system in its agricultural sector. Aggressive innovation and ongoing cooperation between researchers, farmers, and agricultural industries drives the growth in agricultural production. The development and application of new methods across the board has fostered a sophisticated modern agricultural industry in a country that more than half of its land is desert.

The dogged innovation of the Israeli agricultural industry and its close cooperation with the R&D world have fostered a marketable international agri-business export sector with agro-technology solutions. Particularly valuable to the outside and developing world have been innovations in regards to water.

The wide variety of creative solutions developed in response to extremely limited water resources include desalinization plants and drip agriculture.

Most of the country's food and flowers are produced domestically and supplemented by imports that mainly include grain, oilseeds, meat, coffee, cocoa, and sugar. Israel exports

a vineyard in the Golan Heights

heavily to Europe during the winter, sending fruits, vegetables, and flowers.

INDUSTRY

Israel has overcome the small size of its country and its lack of raw materials and natural resources by focusing on its highly qualified workforce, R&D centers, and scientific institutes. The country's modern industry is centered around the manufacturing of products with added value. Today, over a quarter of the industrial workforce works in hi-tech manufacturing.

Much of Israel's modern manufacturing base was developed straight out of 19th-century workshops that manufactured farming implements and processed agricultural products. When entrepreneurs and engineers with years of experience immigrated to Israel in the 1930s, they were followed by an increased demand for industrial products during World War II.

Most of the industrial output from Israel centered around traditional products like food processing, furniture, chemicals, plastics, and other items, until the 1970s. This output was followed by a period marked by arms embargoes, which forced industrialization to focus on developing and manufacturing arms for self-defense. Massive investment in the arms industry and aviation gave life to new technologies that would later be the foundation of Israel's hi-tech industries. These include medical devices, telecommunications, computer software and hardware, and more.

Two waves of human resources in the 1980s and 1990s bolstered the fledgling hi-tech industries: first, the return of Israelis who had been working in Silicon Valley to open development centers for multinationals including Intel, Microsoft, and IBM; second, the huge wave of technicians, scientists, medical workers, and engineers who fled the former Soviet Union in the 1990s after its fall.

Another ace in the hole in Israel's industrial sector is their diamond industry. The country's reputation as a high-quality source for diamond manufacturing and trading has made it a leader in the industry. Tel Aviv's famed diamond district is just one of the ways that the country showcases its cutting-edge technologies, competitive prices, and high yield of polished diamonds from the rough. The Israel Diamond

tourists at Mount Zion's Room of the Last Supper in Jerusalem

© GENEVIEVE BELMAKER

Exchange is the largest diamond trading floor in the world, and diamond exports are in the neighborhood of about $10 billion a year. Most imports are sent to the United States, Hong Kong, Belgium, and Switzerland.

ENTREPRENEURSHIP AND INVENTION

Israel has earned a reputation for being a hotbed of entrepreneurship, innovation, and invention, bolstered in part by the recent publication of a book called *Start-up Nation: The Story of Israel's Economic Miracle,* which details the numerous ways in which the country has repeatedly innovated and invented its way into the 21st century.

The premise of the book is based on the fact that despite being a young country with a population of just over 7.8 million and surrounded by enemies, Israel is home to more start-up companies than Japan, China, India, Korea, Canada and the United Kingdom.

DISTRIBUTION OF WEALTH

In 2011, massive, long-term public protests over Israel's distribution of wealth broke out throughout the country, centered mostly in Tel Aviv. The protests evolved into weeks-long encampments, mostly of young people, who demanded a more equitable distribution of economic wealth and a more equitable distribution of economic burden in their society.

Between 2005-2007, Israel had a millionaire boom, producing more millionaires per capita than any country in the world. The current estimated net worth of Israel's 500 richest people is in the neighborhood of US$75 billion (the country's GDP is about US$195 billion).

One of the most serious issues in the debate about the distribution of wealth stems from the perceived affordability of housing among the middle and lower class. The purchase of second homes in Tel Aviv and Jerusalem by wealthy foreigners is seen as having a major impact on housing prices. In 2011, prime prices on Tel Aviv homes rose by 8 percent.

TOURISM

Israel's most frequently visited cities, Jerusalem and Tel Aviv, are working hard to become international tourist destinations. With the gradual stabilizing of the internal security of Israel has come a stabilized tourism base. Since 2010, the average number of visitors to the country has been about 2.8 million people per year. Most visitors come from Europe, and about a quarter are from the United States.

An average of about 30 percent of people visit Israel on a pilgrimage, while others come for leisure, to visit family, or on business. The vast majority of all tourists (about 80 percent), no matter why they are visiting the country, include Jerusalem as a destination. About 65 percent include Tel Aviv as a destination, about 45 percent go to the Dead Sea, and about 20 percent go to Tiberias and the Sea of Galilee.

People and Culture

DEMOGRAPHY

When the State of Israel was established, the country's population was about 806,000. Today it is more than 7.8 million. More than 75 percent of Israel's residents are Jewish, over 20 percent are Arab, and all other groups make up just over 4 percent of the population. Over 70 percent of the total Jewish population was born in Israel; a native-born Jewish Israeli is known as a *sabra*.

Israel has 14 cities with over 100,000 residents; the 6 cities of Jerusalem, Tel Aviv-Yafo, Haifa, Rishon LeTsiyon, Petah Tikva, and Ashdod all have over 200,000 residents.

Israel has had periods of massive, concentrated immigration tied to world events. In 1990 alone, after the fall of the Soviet Union, more than 199,000 immigrants came to Israel, and another 176,000 in 1991. In the past few years, however, there has been an average of 16,500 immigrants to the country per year.

Israel suffers from the image problem of religious and ethnic tensions between the Jewish majority and Arab minority, which impacts its ability to attract a larger number of tourists and immigrants. Though daily life in major cities such as Tel Aviv, Jerusalem, and elsewhere is largely peaceful and various ethnicities and

© ANDREY SAVELYEV/123RF.COM

women in traditional Arabic dress

Jewish orthodox men in typical black hats and coats

religions peacefully co-exist, violence does erupt on a fairly regular basis. With the rule of neighboring Gaza in the hands of Hamas, the greatest domestic threat comes from attacks that originate in Gaza, such as rocket attacks.

The West Bank, with its complex and multi-layered governance and distribution of security between the Palestinian Authority and Israel is also sometimes the source of religious and ethnic tension, protests, and violence.

Jews

As an ethnic group, Jews constitute about 76 percent of the population of Israel. Of those, about 67 percent are Israel-born and almost 23 percent are European or American-born. About 6 percent were born in Africa, and about 4 percent in Asia.

Arabs

The Arab population of Israel is about 23 percent of the population, and includes those who are Muslim, Christian, and Jewish. Bedouin and Druze peoples fall under the category of the Arab population.

RELIGION

Though Israel is officially a Jewish state, for all intents and purposes, residents of Israel enjoy religious freedom to practice whatever faith they choose.

Those who are registered with the government as practicing Jews comprise almost 80 percent of the population, non-Arab Christians are about half a percent, and those not classified by religion are almost 5 percent. 84 percent of Israel's Arabs (about 20 percent of the population) are practicing Muslims, and almost 8 percent are Arab Christians. Another 8 percent are Druze.

Judaism

More than 75 percent of the people of Israel practice the religion of Judaism, an ancient monotheistic faith with varying degrees of orthodoxy. The degree of orthodoxy of the Diaspora of people who practice Judaism around the world varies. The same is true in Israel, with pockets of people practicing orthodox, ultra-orthodox, and reform Judaism.

The Jerusalem Great Synagogue can hold 2,000 people.

a depiction of Christ in the Church of the Multiplication in Tagbha near the Sea of Galilee

Particularly in Jerusalem but also throughout Israel and the West Bank, religious individuals can be identified by their dress. The men wear long, black coats and large black hats, and the women dress in long skirts and dresses with their arms and legs covered, and their heads covered with a hat, scarf, or wig.

On the day of worship on Friday, religious services are performed in synagogues. The more religious synagogues separate men and women into different worship areas. The holiest site in the holiest city to Jews is the Western Wall in Jerusalem (also known as the Kotel). It is the last remaining piece of the great temple that was twice built and destroyed on that spot in history.

Christianity

The Christian community in Israel, which is about 2 percent of the population, represents a wide variety of different sects of the Christianity from all over the world. There are Greek Orthodox, Russian Orthodox, Catholic, and others. Though they are only a small part of the population overall in the country, the Roman Catholic Church owns a large portion of land in Jerusalem.

Islam

About 17 percent of Israel's population practices the religion of Islam; they are known as Muslims. The Muslim religion, in general, is fairly strict and generally forbids drinking alcohol. Friday is the day of prayer for Muslims, which makes it a difficult day to visit the Old City, as Al Aqsa Mosque (the third holiest site in Islam) becomes very crowded.

Religious services are performed in mosques, which can often be distinguished by the nearby minaret (tower) from which the call to prayer is broadcast five times a day. In terms of dress, Muslim women (especially in more conservative areas like Nablus) dress in a very covered-up manner with headscarves, long sleeves, and covered legs.

sign in Hebrew, Arabic, and English

LANGUAGE

Israel has two official languages: Hebrew and Arabic. But English is a compulsory second language taught throughout much of the secondary level education system, so the majority of Hebrew speakers and many Arabic speakers also speak and understand English at least at a conversational level.

Almost all signs, menus, transportation tables, and tourist information are written in English.

The Arts

The arts in Israel are a well-developed and robust part of society. In addition to the many skills and traditions that generations of immigrants have brought with them from their original countries, the indigenous arts, crafts, and culture play a significant role.

LITERATURE

Israel's literary culture is dominated by Hebrew-speaking authors, but in recent years the Arab-speaking community has also made significant breakthroughs and contributions.

An ongoing issue in Israel's literary community is the slow death that independent book sellers are suffering due to the existence of a couple of major national chains. These chains are often accused of selling books at much less than their value, angering both authors and independent book sellers, who cannot compete with the prices. In recent years, many independent book sellers have been forced into closing.

Despite the challenges to independent sellers, you can still find a variety of different types of bookstores in major cities that sell material in a variety of languages, including Hebrew, Arabic, French, and English. Major periodicals in English, Arabic, French, and sometimes Russian are also sold at national chain stores and smaller shops.

Jerusalem hosts a renowned international

literature conference every year, but it is sometimes overshadowed by authors who choose to publicly boycott attending on the grounds of concerns over Israel's presence in the West Bank and its position on issues related to the Arab population.

VISUAL ARTS

The thriving visual arts scene in Israel is supported by the large number of museums, from the Israel Museum in Jerusalem to the Tel Aviv Museum of Art, to scores of venues of all sizes. Modern visual art in Israel shows international influences and the meeting of East and West, and reflects the influences of the land, traditions, and cultures.

Visual artists in Israel are engaged in a wide range of disciplines, including painting, photography, and sculpture. Part of what makes Israeli visual art unique is its emphasis and reflections on the local landscape, domestic social issues, and politics.

MUSIC AND DANCE

The thriving dance scene in Israel has developed mainly in the Jewish folk dance genre and artistic dance centered around stage productions. The major influence of European dance began in the 1920s, and has developed to a highly professional level through a number of companies and ensembles. Dance in Israel is influenced by the region's various social, cultural, and religious backgrounds.

There are currently over a dozen major professional dance companies in Israel, mostly in Tel Aviv, that perform domestically and internationally.

The annual Israel Festival is the country's major multidisciplinary arts festival, held over a period of a few weeks in Jerusalem.

The music scene in Israel is just as vibrant, if not more. The country's offerings range from the world-class classical music of the Israeli Philharmonic Orchestra and the New Israeli Opera. The country's music scene has been enhanced by waves of European immigrants who brought traditions, skills, and influences from the best traditions in the world. The variations of music genres range from Arabic and Hebrew pop to Middle Eastern jazz, rock, and mainstream American music.

© ISRAELI MINISTRY OF TOURISM/WWW.GOISRAEL.COM

Tel Aviv Opera House

ESSENTIALS

Getting There

There are a variety of ways to arrive in Israel, though most visitors arrive by air through the international airport in Tel Aviv.

BY AIR

Tel Aviv's **Ben Gurion International Airport** (03/975-2386, www.iaa.gov.il) is a massive, modern airport with flights to and from almost everywhere in the world. It is about a 15-minute drive from Tel Aviv's center and about one hour from Jerusalem's center. Once at the airport, you can easily get to your destination by hotel shuttle, train, taxi, *sherut* (share) taxi, or bus.

During the Jewish Sabbath—late Friday afternoon until Saturday night—things slow down considerably. The airport is still open, but certain airlines might not operate (such as Israel's El Al) and public transportation to and from the airport doesn't operate. Yom Kippur, when almost nobody drives and all public transportation shuts down, would present a challenge getting to or from the airport.

BY BOAT

Some people traveling by boat end up visiting Israel while on their way to somewhere else, such as cruise ship passengers who stay for 1-2 days and liner or ferry passengers who are

© KUNA GEORGE/123RF.COM

traveling with cars. Both types of passengers go through the international **Port of Haifa** (www.haifaport.co.il). The port includes a large terminal with a wide variety of passenger facilities, including a waiting area, a duty-free shop, a souvenir shop, a cafeteria, a VAT (Value Added Tax) reimbursement counter and currency exchange, a Ministry of Interior services office, and other travel-related services.

Typical customs and immigrations procedures apply for passengers who want to exit from the port and enter Israel. There is long- and short-term parking next to the passenger terminal. People on foot can walk about 10 minutes to the port's exit and take a taxi cab to wherever they are going in Haifa.

BY LAND

From Jordan (www.visitjordan.com) there are three land border crossings into Israel from the north, center, and south. The center and southern border crossings are the most convenient and frequently used, while the northernmost crossing is isolated from major cities and attractions.

The **Wadi Araba Crossing/South Border** (6:30am-8pm Sun.-Thurs., 8am-8pm Fri.-Sat.) connects the resort towns of Eilat in Israel and Aqaba in Jordan. Visas are issued on the spot at the Eilat crossing and you don't need to provide photographs.

The **Allenby/King Hussein Bridge** is in the southern Jordan Valley (8am-8pm for entering Jordan, 8am-2pm for leaving Jordan Sun.-Thurs., 8am-1pm Fri.-Sat.). Private cars and tour buses are not allowed to cross, so you have to change vehicles when crossing the border. If coming from Israel, pay for your visa in advance (about JD14) at the Jordanian embassy in Tel Aviv, and you will need two photographs and you will receive a visa within 24 hours.

Americans and Canadians coming from Jordan into Israel do not need to apply for a visa in advance. They will be issued a visa at the crossing. There will usually be an exit fee of JD5 when coming from Jordan into Israel. Always travel with a passport that is valid for at least six months beyond your dates of travel.

Getting Around

It is fairly easy to get around Israel because of the superior bus systems that exist nationally and within the large cities. You can basically get almost anywhere you want by bus, including areas in the West bank near Jewish settlements. The various train systems are less convenient because of their somewhat limited routes, but they do offer a good option for transportation.

BY TRAIN

The national train system, the **Israel Railways** (www.rail.co.il/EN), is a fairly convenient way to get around many parts of Israel, particularly useful for north to south routes. Just be aware that the railway system is also plagued by ongoing issues that include labor strikes and problems with keeping to the timetable. Daily and multi-journey tickets are available, and kids under the age of 5 travel for free.

The station stops in Jerusalem are quite far off the beaten path, on the outskirts of town near the zoo and the Malha Mall. Just to get to and from the Jerusalem train station to the city center, you will need to take a taxi, bus, or car. The station stops in Tel Aviv are numerous, convenient, and centrally located.

If you go by train from the airport, you can be in Tel Aviv's city center in about 10 minutes and in Jerusalem in about 2.5 hours (the route from the airport to Jerusalem is abnormally long). There are several train lines that leave every 20-30 minutes from the airport.

Train etiquette at crowded stops when passengers are boarding and disembarking is somewhat of a free for all. Basically, be prepared to shove your way on or off the train or risk getting stuck.

© WAJAN/123RF.COM

There are numerous transportation options in Israel.

BY LIGHT RAIL (JERUSALEM ONLY)

Though as of 2013, Haifa was in the process of constructing a light rail train, currently the only city that has a functioning **light rail** is Jerusalem (073/210-0601 or *3686 from any local phone, www.citypass.co.il, 5:30am-midnight Sun.-Thurs., 8:30pm-10pm Sat., 5:30am-11:30am Fri. and holiday eves, and ceasing at about 2pm, NIS6.60 for a single ride). Tourists get a discounted public transportation ticket, but there is not an extensive network of stops throughout the city. All tickets are valid for continued use for 90 minutes from the time they were purchased.

The route of Jerusalem's light rail is fairly limited but there are plans to expand it. Its route is roughly along the old border between east and west Jerusalem, and it is convenient if you want to get somewhere in east Jerusalem. It has stops next to the *shuk,* city center, Mount Herzl, and Yad Vashem.

BY SUBWAY (HAIFA ONLY)

The only subway in Israel is the six-station Haifa subway, the **Carmelit** (http://carmelithaifa.com, 6am-midnight Sun.-Thurs., 6am-3pm Fri., after sunset-midnight Sat., single ticket about NIS7). It is most useful for going between the lower city, Wadi Nisnas, and straight up the mountain until Hanassi Boulevard. You can buy a single, daily, or 10-ride ticket.

BY BUS

The main bus company that essentially comprises the national bus system in Israel is the green and white **Egged** (www.egged.co.il/Eng) buses. They can get you almost anywhere you want to go, including to some areas in the West Bank.

You can pay cash for your bus ticket (about NIS7 within the city) while boarding the bus and do not need to wait at the ticket window if you are traveling from the central bus station.

If you know you'll be making a return trip (say between Jerusalem and Tel Aviv), buy your ticket on the bus and you will get a small discount. Central bus stations in major cities such as Tel Aviv, Jerusalem, and Beer Sheva display route information in English and Hebrew on monitors in the station.

Once on the bus, depending on where you are going, there are a few things to be aware of. First of all, the safety rules are fairly loose and when seats are sold out, you can sit or stand in the aisle or the stairwell at the back of the bus. Eating and drinking are allowed, but if traveling with Jewish orthodox passengers (distinguishable by their black hats, black coats, beards, and white shirts), it is advisable to avoid sitting next to them if you are a woman as it might be offensive to their religious practices of keeping physical distance from the opposite gender. It depends on how religious they are. If you are traveling into the West Bank or on a route to or from Jerusalem, you might encounter ultra-orthodox Jews.

The public transportation depot at the Tel Aviv airport is on the second floor near Gates 21 and 23. Busses go from there to the Egged station at nearby Airport City, and then you can transfer to regular Egged bus lines. The busses from Airport City to the airport are free. The Egged buses will get you into south Tel Aviv's Central Bus Station.

You can also go between Jerusalem's Central Bus Station and the airport by Egged bus. It takes about one hour in normal traffic. Try to avoid making the trip on a Friday afternoon, as traffic will typically be the worst at that time.

The Tel Aviv, Jerusalem, and Beer Sheva central bus stations have tons of taxis available for hire, as do many of the smaller city bus stations. Once in Tel Aviv, the city bus line, **Dan** (03/639-4444, www.dan.co.il/english) operates a series of very convenient lines throughout the city, and they have detailed information on their English language website. They shut down for Shabbat.

Once in Jerusalem, the bus system is extremely convenient and the buses are frequent. There is a discounted public transportation ticket for tourists for public buses, operated by Egged. There is also a double-decker city tour bus that you can hop on and off all day long at major sights after buying a 24- or 48-hour ticket. The one-stop shop for Jerusalem transportation information, including the buses, is **Jerusalem Transportation** (www.jet.org.il). A one-way ticket for about NIS7 can be used for transfers and return trips for up to 90 minutes from the time the ticket was purchased.

Though there have been efforts in recent years to have some buses operate during the weekend in Tel Aviv, at the time of publication the only city in the entire country of Israel with buses that operate on the weekend (with partial service) is in Haifa. The closest thing to public transportation that is available on the weekend is the *sherut* (share taxis), which are more expensive and less convenient.

Other bus operators work throughout the country. In the center of the country, bus operators include **Superbus** (www.superbus.co.il), as well as **Kavim** (www.kavim-t.co.il) and **Connex** (www.connex.co.il). Kavim and Connex also operate in the north. Other operators in the north include **Nazareth Buses** (www.ntt-buses.com) and **Golan Bus** (www.golanbus.co.il). In the south, the major bus operator is **Metropoline** (www.metropoline.com). Many bus operators do not have English websites available.

BY TAXI AND SHARE TAXI

Throughout Israel, taxi cabs are everywhere, but most cost 25 percent more on weekends and between 9pm-5am. One good option if you want to order a cab to come and pick you up (which will cost about NIS5 extra) is to ask any hotel front desk for the name of a taxi company. A company that operates nationally and is recommended by the Municipality of Jerusalem is **Rehavya Taxi** (Taxi Stand at 3 Agron St. in Jerusalem, 02/625-4444 or 02/622-2444).

Sherut (share taxis) are an option in most parts of the country, and especially for travel between Tel Aviv and Jerusalem. On the weekend, they are your best (and almost only) option. A *sherut* from Jerusalem to Tel Aviv is about NIS30 or less, and leaves from the base of Zion Square seven days a week. The *sherut* from Tel Aviv leaves from the Central Bus Station (106 Levinski St.), just east of Neve Tzedek and Florentin. Keep in mind that a *sherut* will only depart when all of the seats are full. Depending on how you time it, you might be waiting for 20-30 minutes for the taxi to fill up. While you're riding in the *sherut,* if you need to get out somewhere, it's perfectly acceptable to ask the driver to let you out as soon as possible; drivers stop upon request at the first chance they have to pull over.

BY CAR

Americans in Israel are allowed to drive with their foreign license for up to one year after arriving in the country. There are quite a number of rental car companies that operate throughout Israel, the most prevalent of which are **Hertz** (19 King David St. in Jerusalem, 02/623-1351, www.hertz.co.il) and **Budget** (23 King David St. in Jerusalem, 03/935-0015), offering a wide variety of options; car rentals run about US$40 day. The largest domestic car rental company in Israel is **Eldan** (114 HaYarkon St. in Tel Aviv, 03/527-1166, www.eldan.co.il); **Shlomo Sixt** (122 HaYarkon St. in Tel Aviv, 03/524-4935, www.shlomo.co.il) is another good option. The central area for car rental offices in Jerusalem is on King David Street, just across from the King David Hotel, near Mamilla shopping center. In Tel Aviv, there is a stretch of car rental companies right on the promenade to the beach around 114 HaYarkon Street.

The parking system throughout Israel is uniform and has strict rules, but there are many unspoken exceptions, especially during the weekend when parking rules are suspended. For instance, you might see cars parked on the

a taxi in Tel Aviv

© ELDAD CARIN/123RF.COM

sidewalk, or facing the wrong direction when parked along the street.

Red and white stripes mean no parking; blue and white stripes signify paid parking by a street meter (a machine that sometimes only takes cash); and gray means free. Other paid parking in certain neighborhoods or small lots will have a yellow and black sign with hours of paid parking where you must buy a ticket and leave it in your car dash with the date stamp showing. Paid parking costs approximately NIS10 for 90 minutes.

If you are going to be driving on a daily basis for an extended period of time, Yellow gas stations sell an automatic pay in advance meter that you leave on the side of your vehicle. The meter costs NIS100 and you can pay for time on it as you go.

Driving yourself is fairly straightforward, as 99 percent of the road signs are posted in English, Hebrew, and Arabic. Don't panic if you think you're on the right road but don't see signs, or see signs for something with a different spelling. It is not uncommon to have no signage to a certain place until the last minute, or for signage names to change in their spelling of the place. The best thing to do is stop and ask for directions. But be prepared to stop more than once because when people give directions in Israel they typically tell you to go to a certain point and then ask someone.

If you drive into Tel Aviv, take Highway 1 coming from the direction of Jerusalem, and Highway 2 when coming from the direction of Haifa. You will merge onto Highway 20, also known as Ayalon Highway, which runs through the center of Tel Aviv; about half a dozen exits on the Ayalon get you into different parts of the city.

If you drive into Jerusalem, take Highway 1 and just follow the signs. There are several exits to Jerusalem, some of which will take you far into the outskirts and hills of town. Try to keep as close to City Center as possible, as that is where most hotels are, and where you will have the best luck getting your bearings. Driving within the city of Jerusalem can be extremely complicated and confusing, so take your time and if you think you are lost, don't hesitate to stop.

Tips for Driving

The key to driving while you're in the Middle East is to stay calm and focused, which will help you navigate the tricky road rules. The general guidelines are to keep moving, don't be afraid to improvise (especially in Jerusalem), and don't be afraid to honk your horn. Particularly for Americans, honking can be taken as rude, but it is an important mode of communication in the Middle East, where the roads are often older and narrower.

Some roads were built during times when they were used by donkey carts and horses, so they aren't quite wide enough for cars. Other roads were built up the side of mountains as cities grew over hundreds of years and are extremely steep. Take your time and have a GPS with you wherever you go.

There is no right turn on red, and you probably won't get a ticket if you park on the side of the street facing the wrong way.

Checkpoints

There are checkpoints posted in various locations between Israel and the West Bank, inside the West Bank at the edge of Israel-controlled territory, at the Tel Aviv airport, and at Gaza. Sometimes officers at a checkpoint will ask you to open your trunk, so know where that is located and be ready to open it. If you are stopped at the airport, you might be asked a series of questions. Don't panic if you are questioned. It is typically related to whatever the current security situation is, and not you personally.

Gas Conversion

The price of 95 octane gas in the government-regulated system at gas stations throughout Israel is NIS7.95 per liter. At full-service gas stations, it costs 0.18 more per liter. The price of gas is updated by the government once a month and published in all daily newspapers.

BY AIR

At Israel's domestic airport, **Dov Hoz** (www.iaa.gov.il), you can catch flights to the popular southern tourist city of Eilat and the **Eilat Domestic Airport** (08/636-3800, www.iaa.gov.il), which takes flights from Arkia, El Al, Israir, and Sun Dor airlines. It is small and convenient, and a good option if you plan to also take in a trip to Petra, Jordan, while you're in the area. Most tour companies will pick you up directly from the airport.

HITCHHIKING

Hitchhiking for a ride in Israel and the West Bank is fairly common, but carries the same risks as hitchhiking anywhere else. The regional signal for someone seeking a ride is to point their index finger at the ground in front of them. Especially on the weekend or on Friday afternoons, you will see more hitchhikers than usual.

If you are driving and see a soldier hitchhiking, understand that it is against military regulations for soldiers to hitchhike and they could face time in the brig if they are caught taking a ride.

Visas and Officialdom

Israeli bureaucracy is infamous, but getting into Israel from one of the many countries that they have a visa waiver program with is fairly easy.

VISAS AND PASSPORTS

If you have a passport that is valid for a minimum of six months after your date of exit from the country and you are coming from a visa waiver country, you do not have to arrange for a visa in advance to enter Israel. You will be automatically granted a three-month tourist visa upon entering Israel and there is no fee. The countries that have a visa waiver program with Israel include the United States, the United Kingdom, Australia, Canada, New Zealand, South Africa, and others.

The same six-month rule for passports applies to entering Jordan. If you plan to visit Arab countries (aside from Jordan) for the duration of your passport, ask for your visa stamp to Israel to be put on a separate piece of paper. It is not an uncommon request, as a passport with a stamp from Israel might make it very difficult or impossible to gain entry into many Arab countries.

Visas to Jordan are usually good for one month and can be obtained from the Jordanian

embassy in Tel Aviv (14 Abba Hillel St., in the Tel Aviv suburb of Ramat Gan, 03/751-7752), in your home country, or at the Wadi Araba Crossing/South Border. Aqaba is a special economic zone and there should be no visa fee for Americans.

ISRAELI EMBASSIES AND CONSULATES ABROAD

Israel maintains embassies and consulates all over the world. In the United States, there are Consulate General offices of Israel in New York, Atlanta, Boston, Houston, Chicago, Miami, Philadelphia, San Francisco, and Los Angeles, as well as the Israeli Embassy in Washington, D.C.

FOREIGN EMBASSIES AND CONSULATES IN ISRAEL

Though Jerusalem is Israel's capital city and the seat of its federal government, countries with diplomatic relations with Israel maintain their embassies in Tel Aviv. The reason for this is related to Jerusalem's complicated international legal status. If a foreign government established their embassy in Jerusalem (instead of the consulates they have), it might be seen as an indication of the recognition of Jerusalem as the capital city of Israel. It would also seriously complicate matters in the event that an independent Palestinian state was established. For that reason, embassies of foreign governments, including the United States, are located in Tel Aviv.

The **Consulate of the United States in Jerusalem** (near the intersection of Hebron Rd. and Yehuda St., 02/630-4000 and 02/622-7230 for emergencies and during non-business hours, http://jerusalem.usconsulate.gov), is located essentially on the border between east and west Jerusalem, and is very tricky to find. Appointments are mandatory for all visits to the consulate.

The **U.S. Embassy in Tel Aviv** (71 HaYarkon St., 03/519-7475 and 03/519-7575 for emergencies and during non-business hours, http://israel.usembassy.gov) has a useful email alert system that tells American citizens of serious security threats and advises areas not to travel in during times of violence and unrest in the region. Before traveling to Israel, you can register with the consulate or embassy for alerts.

TAXES

The Israeli taxing system uses what they call a Value Added Tax (VAT) of more than 16 percent for the purchase of goods and services. VAT is included in the price of many items (such as restaurants). However, if you purchase a more expensive item as a gift or souvenir while in the country (minimum NIS400), ask for tax refund forms. You will be eligible to get the VAT back when going through customs. Note that non-Israeli citizens or people who are not residents of Israel are not required to pay VAT for items like hotels and car rentals.

CUSTOMS

The standard fare of items are prohibited for import by Israeli customs, including weapons and drugs. They also restrict the import of games of chance, pornographic material, plants and soil, and pets. You can bring up to US$200 worth of tax-free gifts into Israel, 250 grams of cigarettes, and one bottle of liquor. You can convert up to US$3,000 in cash at the airport when you leave.

Be particularly careful about buying any kind of antiquities or archaeological artifacts and then transporting them out of the country; you must have a certificate that identifies the object in question. If you buy from a licensed antiquities dealer, they will provide you with such a certificate.

MEDICAL REQUIREMENTS

Inoculations and vaccinations are not required for entry to Israel and Jordan.

POLITICAL AFFILIATIONS AND AGENDAS

If you enter Israel with a specific, intended action that relates to a political agenda (particularly one that would be seen as anti-Israel), you might be prevented from entering the country. This usually applies to large groups with a high profile, but you might be questioned by customs about the purpose of your trip to Israel.

POLICE

In some areas of Israel, there are **Tourist Police** (03/516-5382) who specifically work to serve tourists with any criminal matter (such as theft) or an emergency. There are tourist police offices in Tel Aviv near the beach, on the corner of Herbert Samuel and Geula Streets. You can also call the tourist police if you have an emergency.

Recreation

Though it is a small country, the options for outdoor recreation in Israel are staggering. In addition to a wide variety of archaeological sites that have national parks around them and serve the dual purpose of hiking spots and sightseeing locations, there are nature reserves and options for hiking, biking, diving, camping, swimming, and many other sports.

The recreation opportunities in the West Bank are much less developed, but if you're an experienced hiker you can find your way to some really nice spots and walk among groves of olive and lemon trees.

Petra and Jordan in general are home to vast expanses of desert that offer the unique experiences that can only be found in the desert, and within a fairly well-developed tourism industry.

NATIONAL PARKS AND NATURE RESERVES

The **Israel Nature and Parks Authority** (3 Am Ve'Olamo St., Jerusalem, 02/500-5444 or dial *3639 in-country, www.parks.org.il, for information and tour reservations email moked@npa.org.il) maintains parks and nature reserves all over the country that vary widely in price. Many of these include archaeological sites. The least expensive are about NIS5 and the most expensive are about NIS40.

Jordan also has a nice national parks system, though it is recommended to travel with a tour guide or go on a guided outing. The most highly recommended of Jordan's national park experiences is **Wadi Rum** (Rte. 15 between Aqaba and Petra, www.wadirum.jo), which is on the way to Petra from the border crossing at Eilat-Aqaba.

HIKING

Hiking in Israel, the West Bank, and Jordan is a very popular pastime and favorite family outing, particularly in the warmer dry season. Depending on the area you go hiking in, there are a few things to be aware of. Always bring water, sunscreen, and a hat, even if you are accustomed to being in a warm climate. If you get dehydrated or get sun stroke, the symptoms might not appear until you are in a dangerous condition. Experienced hikers will tell you that if you are drinking enough water, you should be looking for a restroom about every 90 minutes or so.

Along many hiking routes, there are places to swim that include streams, waterfalls, springs, and ancient cisterns (artificially-constructed cave-like structures that were once used to gather water from the rainfall). It is culturally acceptable to swim in these areas, though you will always want to have some kind of swimwear or clothes you don't mind getting wet.

If you go for a hike in an area where you think there might be swimming, take some kind of shoes that you can wear while in the water, as the bottom of water springs is often very rocky.

The biggest and most well-marked hike is Israel's **National Trail** (www.israelnationaltrail.com), a 620-mile route that stretches from the Red Sea to Israel's border with Lebanon. The National Trail passes through many cities, including Tel Aviv, Haifa, and Netanya. It is possible to follow the trail for any portion you want.

BICYCLING

One of the best and least-advertised features of the boutique hotel industry is that they often offer **free bicycle rentals** to guests. The phrase bicycle rental is a misnomer that you might see on hotel websites; there is typically no fee involved. You can just borrow a bike for free for the day. This custom is particularly common among the boutique hotels in Israel's north coast, in the south, and in Eilat. Ask your hotel when booking if they let guests borrow bikes for free.

In Tel Aviv, the green bicycles of the **Tel-o-Fun** (www.tel-o-fun.co.il/en, NIS17 for one

There are sometimes restrictions on swimming with separated male and female times and areas when the pools are visited by orthodox Jews. If a pool has designated hours for male and female swimming, it will be listed on their schedule, but it is always best to ask. Some beaches, particularly along the Mediterranean, have designated male and female hours, or designated male and female beaches.

DIVING

The hottest diving spots in the region are in the **Red Sea,** with its world-renowned coral reef, year-round warm temperatures, and well-developed tourism industry that is able to cater to the needs of visitors.

COOKING OUT

In general, as with many other things in this region, the rules about cooking out are much looser than in the United States. Basically, you can cook out almost anywhere you want to (within reason).

If you happen to be in Israel during the **Yom Ha'atzmaut** holiday (National Independence Day, around May 14, corresponding to the Jewish calendar), you will see cooking out like you have probably never witnessed. Most businesses shut down and people go out in droves to find any piece of ground they can to cook out on. Even the pristine grass on the grounds of the national rose garden next to the Israeli Knesset is fair game for setting up a small grill and starting a fire. If you pass by one of the large (or small) parks in any city, you will see a cloud of smoke hovering above it from the cookout frenzy.

If you want to take part, it is easy to buy a small grill (NIS20) prior to the holiday at most grocery stores and small convenience stores.

© KUNA GEORGE/123RF.COM

a bicycle lane in Tel Aviv

day) bike rental system can be found throughout the city, and you can pick up and drop off a bike at any Tel-o-Fun location. The first half-hour of usage is free, and there is no law in Tel Aviv that requires bicyclists to wear a helmet.

SWIMMING

There are many, many places throughout Israel to swim that include the Mediterranean Sea, public pools, hotel pools (sometimes even if you are not staying there you can use them for a fee), springs and related streams, cisterns, the Sea of Galilee, the Dead Sea, and the Red Sea. In the hot summer month of August in Jerusalem, you might even see fully clothed ultra-orthodox families swimming in the public fountains in the parks.

Accommodations

There are several different types of accommodation options when traveling throughout Israel, the West Bank, and Jordan. Options range from five-star resorts to extremely casual accommodations, such as renting a room in someone's home.

GUESTHOUSES *(ZIMMERS)*

The fairly ubiquitous and lovely option of a **zimmer** (also spelled *tsimmer*) is one of the best ways to experience regional hospitality, food, and culture. A *zimmer* is typically family owned and operated and set up as a series of private cabins or bungalows spread across the *zimmer* grounds and centered around a main building where meals and sometimes recreation can be found.

There are two main categories of *zimmers:* luxury and luxury-rustic. The luxury-level *zimmers* include amenities such as a large, flat-screen TV and a whirlpool hot tub. The rustic *zimmers* usually won't include any kind of a TV, and will emphasize a more natural, country experience. *Zimmer* cabins often have private porches, but ask in advance about bathing accommodations, because the bathtub (and sometimes the toilet) are sometimes placed in a prominent place in your room and not inside a closed-off bathroom.

While the north of Israel, in the Galilee and Golan Heights, is full of *zimmers,* they can be found throughout Israel. The website for **Rural Tourism in Israel** (www.zimmeril.com) is an invaluable resource, as many *zimmers* don't maintain their own website, social media pages, or even have an email address.

Some *zimmers* are located in moshavs, which are basically cooperative neighborhoods that are sometimes located a bit off the beaten path.

GUEST ROOMS

Arranging for a guest room is a tricky matter, and you probably need to be in the country already or have a trusted go-between like a tour guide to make arrangements. Particularly in the West Bank, you can inquire at the shops that cater to tourists (especially in Bethlehem) if they know of any houses in town that rent rooms out.

BUDGET, MIDRANGE, BOUTIQUE, AND HIGH-END HOTELS

The range of hotels in Israel, the West Bank, and Jordan is just as broad as any other region that caters to tourists, but the main thing to be aware of is the size of rooms, even in higher-end hotels, are often on the smaller side, more in accordance with European standards. Budget hotels and midrange hotels will often be a bit sparse in the furnishings and will have tile floors (not carpeting), but they usually have free Wi-Fi. High-end and luxury hotels, in turn, will usually charge for Wi-Fi, but have every amenity you can imagine, down to the smallest detail.

There are a couple of common features for the majority of hotels in the region. One is that breakfast is included with the rate of your room. In some cases, you can upgrade your room rate to have all meals included. Once in a blue moon, the standard breakfast-included practice is not kept at a hotel, so it is always best to ask in advance.

The included breakfast is typically served around 7am-9am, but always ask in advance. It includes hot and cold drinks, salads, eggs, toast, and more. If you try to take food out of the breakfast area, hotel staff will charge you extra.

The general practice for room service in midrange hotels and up is that you can often get at least hot and cold drinks delivered to your room.

HOSTELS

The hostel system in Israel is surprisingly well-developed and the best of the hostels book extremely far in advance, sometimes as far as six months. Hostel options in Jerusalem include places to stay in the Old City as well as near City Center. The **Israel Youth Hostel Association (IYHA)** (059/951-0511, www.iyha.org.il/eng) has English-speaking hotline representatives and a very easy-to-use booking website for hostels throughout the region. Though the hostel listing is not comprehensive, it includes hostels that are sanctioned members of the IYHA.

FIELD SCHOOLS

The **Society for Protection of Nature in Israel** (03/638-8688, www.teva.org.il/english) is more than just a resource for nature activities in Israel. They also maintain a group of affordable, hostel-like accommodations throughout Israel that are called field schools. Many field schools are located near major tourist destinations and offer an excellent alternative to a more expensive hotel. The organization's emphasis on nature preservation also means that field school staff are knowledgeable about outdoor activities in the region where they are located.

KIBBUTZIM

There are a number of kibbutzim in Israel that generate part of their economy from operating luxury, resort-like hotels or more midrange accommodations. When you stay at one of these kibbutz hotels (Ramat Rachel on the outskirts of Jerusalem is a good example), you will typically have access to certain kibbutz amenities, including a swimming pool, playgrounds, and the like.

CAMPING

You will be hard-pressed to find a clearinghouse of published information in English about camping in Israel, the West Bank, and Jordan. Though there are many, many excellent camping sites throughout the area, and particularly in Israel, information about campsites, costs, and regulations is generally only published in Hebrew.

The two best resources to check for camping information are the Israel **National Parks** (02/500-5444 or dial *3639 in-country, www.parks.org.il) and the **Society for Protection of Nature in Israel** (03/638-8688, www.teva.org.il/english).

ARAB AND BEDOUIN GUEST ENCAMPMENTS

Throughout the south of Israel, the Negev, in the Golan Heights, and in Petra, you can experience Arab and Bedouin culture by visiting a **Bedouin tent.** The easiest areas to find these are in the Negev at Sefinat Hamidbar, Khan Hashayarot, and Khan Beerotayim, as well as at the Mashabei Sadeh junction, near the ancient city of Avdat and the village of Ezuz. Surrounding Petra and near Petra are also excellent places to find Bedouin tent encampments, in which you can stay overnight.

Food

The food in Israel and Jordan is basically a combination of a Mediterranean and Middle Eastern diet that emphasizes fruits, vegetables, whole grains, and non-processed foods, with a few common threads that can be found almost everywhere you go.

HUMMUS AND FALAFEL

Two of the most famous and favorite food dishes are hummus and falafel. Hummus is a sort of paste that is generally made from chickpeas, olive oil, and tahini. Hummus can be used as a dip on pita or on the side of your plate with main dishes, or as a sort of dressing on top of dishes like salad. It is also commonly used in shwarma sandwiches.

Falafel are deep fried balls of mashed chickpeas that have been blended with onions and herbs. They can be bought from street vendors, in the *shuk,* and from small shops that

© GENEVIEVE BELMAKER

cured olives, a staple food of the Mediterranean

specialize in falafel. Falafel is commonly served stuffed inside of a pita sandwich with lettuce, tomatoes, pickles, and tahini (a commonly served paste of sesame seeds and olive oil). It makes a filling and sometimes very cheap meal if you are not buying it in a tourist area.

SHWARMA

The many shops that sell shwarma are distinguishable by the large chunk of lamb meat cooking on a spit in a prominent location. The meat is cut directly off of the spit and typically served in a pita sandwich. You can usually tell if a shwarma shop is good by how juicy the meat is. If customers are not coming to eat frequently, the meat might look a bit dried out.

BEDOUIN

Bedouin food, which can be found throughout the region but particularly in the south of Israel and in Jordan, is traditionally cooked on an open fire and eaten with the hands. Common Bedouin meals include the more standard pita; the thin, crepe-like *shraak* pita that is cooked on a domed pan over a fire; and *taboon,* which is usually thicker and made from darker flour. Other typical Bedouin ingredients and dishes focus on lamb meat, rice, and yogurt.

DRUZE

Arab people of Syrian descent, the Druze are known for their delicious dishes that include many typical facets of Middle Eastern food, such as pita, hummus, vegetables, and lamb and chicken dishes. Druze stew, a delicious combination of meat, potatoes, and vegetables, is worth trying when you're in the region.

KOSHER AND NON-KOSHER

Some areas of Israel have a multi-layered system of following the religious dietary laws of being kosher. The level to which the restaurant follows kosher regulations determines the type of certificate they display. Kosher certifications are always posted in public view and are often advertised on websites.

Particularly in Jerusalem, most restaurants are kosher, so they will either serve milk or meat, but not both. At a kosher restaurant that serves meat, for example, you will not be able to get a latte or ice cream for dessert. They might serve milk-substitute dishes, though, so it is always worth asking.

The production of kosher food is overseen by a rabbi who certifies the food as being kosher according to Jewish law. The level of supervision and adherence to religious dietary law determines the differing types of kosher certification. The three levels from least restricted to most restricted are kosher, glatt kosher, and mehadrin kosher.

Some hotels cater to religious Jewish customers and adhere to kosher religious laws. These establishments will basically not serve a hot meal on Friday night (unless it was cooked hours earlier and kept warm somehow) or on Saturday until nighttime. Restaurants that keep kosher close on Friday in the late afternoon (depending on the time of the year, around 3 or 4pm). Some will not open again until Sunday morning, but many open later in the evening on Saturday night after the Sabbath has ended, generally around 9pm, and then stay open later than usual.

Conduct and Customs

The general rule with conduct and customs in Israel, the West Bank, and Jordan balances on two ends of the spectrum: live and let live or extremely strict. In general, the more religious the area you are in (Jewish, Muslim, or Christian), the more strictly the conservative conduct and religious customs are adhered to. This includes everything from clothing to food, and it particularly applies to women.

ETIQUETTE

There are a few things to keep in mind when navigating the general regional etiquette of the Middle East. One is that you will likely encounter at least one person who is unwilling to shake your hand for religious reasons, again, particularly if you are a woman.

Also in a general sense, people are more direct, less prone to effected pleasantries, and often more willing to get involved in other people's personal affairs (including giving unwelcome advice or directions). This directness and familiar approach to communicating takes some getting used to.

CONVERSATION

When talking with people, it is advisable to be as loud, direct, and decisive as possible. If you know what you want or what you are after in a conversation or interaction, you're likely to get better results than if you hesitate or are timid about what you're saying. Don't be alarmed or intimidated if someone speaks to you in a loud voice that sounds like yelling. It is just conversation.

In Israel, the common greeting is "shalom," which means peace. In Arabic, it is "as-salaam alaikum," which means peace be upon you. If you say nothing else in the native languages, try these two phrases out.

CLOTHING

Before you travel to any area, check in advance what the customs regarding clothing (especially for women) are. In some towns in the West Bank, women don't show their bare arms and legs. In these places, even a man in shorts might stick out. In the ultra-orthodox areas of certain towns in Israel, people also dress extremely conservatively. If you walk through these areas in shorts and a tank top on a hot

© VADIM BERESTETSKY

Dress appropriately for your surroundings.

summer day, don't expect to get a warm reception. There have been cases of women being accosted and even physically attacked for dressing in a manner that is considered immodest by the religious.

Jerusalem is more conservative, while Tel Aviv is a bit more wild, but if you are in any area with a predominately religious population, toning down your appearance is highly recommended.

Religious Sites

Most religious sites have signage to explain the site's expectations. Depending on the site, this can include covering your head, taking off your hat, covering your shoulders (if you're a woman), having covered legs, keeping your cell phone off, refraining from flash photography, refraining from photography completely, keeping your speaking voice low, no public displays of affection, and on and on.

DINING

When you go out to eat, you can stay as long as you want. It is the rare waiter who will approach you in any eating establishment to ask if you want the check, unless the restaurant is extremely busy. The custom, particularly in Israel, is to let customers sit as long as they want until they are ready to leave. The waiter might continue to come back and ask if you want more of something, but they will not prompt you to leave.

The one exception to this is the preemptive measure some places will take during Shabbat (particularly in Jerusalem) if you come in without a reservation. The customary approach is to explain that you don't have a reservation, to which the host or hostess might say they have a table for you but it is reserved for a group that is arriving in a certain amount of time. That is your cue to understand that you can sit and eat, but you must leave within the allotted time.

SHABBAT (SABBATH)

The Jewish Shabbat (or Sabbath) starts on Friday at sundown and ends on Saturday night after three stars are out in the sky (when it is fully dark). Depending on how religious

A sign in Capernaum asks visitors to adhere to certain rules.

public transportation shutdowns is in Haifa, where some public buses run on a limited schedule throughout Shabbat.

In Israel, Shabbat is the weekend for everyone (except Muslims and most Arabs) whether they are religious or not. All government offices and services stop, including public transportation. One exception to a major shutdown is east Jerusalem, which is predominately Arab, and where everything continues to hum along as normal. Arab areas shut down on Friday afternoon, which is their major prayer time during the week. Also, any restaurant that is kosher is closed. In Jerusalem, that means that all but about 15 restaurants shut down for almost two days.

RAMADAN

The holy month of Ramadan is generally from early July to early August; the exact dates vary slightly every year. Ramadan involves fasting from morning until evening, when a large meal is eaten. It is the one time of the year during which it would be quite inconvenient to visit a predominately Arab area, as many things close or operate on a special schedule.

someone is, Shabbat can involve restrictions on using motorized transport, electricity, and working. Taxi cabs still operate, but their fees are higher than normal. The one exception to

Tips for Travelers

WHEN TO GO

You will generally want to avoid traveling to Israel, Jordan, and the West Bank during major religious holidays. Jewish, Muslim, and Christian calendars are available online, but the biggest holidays are Passover and Easter, Hanukkah, Sukkot, Ramadan, and Christmas. Hotel rates will be higher during these times and many venues will be closed in certain areas.

The month of August in Jerusalem is not an advisable time to visit. It is a time of year when many children are not in camp, daycare, or school, and it is also a major holiday for the ultra-orthodox community. Jerusalem becomes extraordinarily crowded (including

the museums, roads, and restaurants) during this time.

SHOPPING AND BARGAINING

There are a few unique aspects to shopping in the region. One is that if you are in Tel Aviv or Jerusalem, there are numerous Israeli designers who design and make wonderful clothes, shoes, bags, and other accessories. These are unique, domestically-produced items that are largely sold only in Israel. They are typically extremely well made, durable, and attractive. Made in Israel products are sold everywhere from large shopping malls to small boutique stores on the street.

One of the worst types of places to shop is

© GENEVIEVE BELMAKER

relaxing at an outdoor café in Rehavia

in tourist areas. The prices, quality, and selection are often worse than elsewhere, and vendors will often try to convince you that something is antique or much more valuable than what they are selling it for. The upside, however, is that if you have the stamina, you can drive a pretty hard bargain with shopkeepers, particularly in Jerusalem's Old City shops. Shop owners might chase you after you start walking away in refusal of a price they offered, shouting out an even lower price. The general rule of thumb is not to expect to negotiate the price down by more than a third.

When buying antiquities of any kind, always get the certificate of authenticity from the seller, as grave robbers and antiquities thieves are a major regional problem. If an antique item you bought is discovered by customs, you will not be able to leave the country without a certificate from the seller.

If someone bought you a present while you are in the country, don't leave it wrapped; be prepared to have it scanned for bombing materials by the Israeli security personnel at the airport if you mention you are carrying a gift someone gave you.

TIPPING

It is customary to tip about 15 precent to service personnel, including waiters and bellhops, but it is not customary to tip taxi drivers. In restaurants, you will often see a note on your receipt which says Service is Not Included, indicating that you are in a place where it is customary to tip.

OPPORTUNITIES FOR STUDY AND EMPLOYMENT

There are many work and study opportunities in Israel, but unless you plan on staying long-term, most of the work opportunities are voluntary and unpaid. There are several types of programs that you can participate in, including, internships and fellowships, touring and experiential activities, volunteering programs, Hebrew language programs, Arabic language programs, academic programs, Jewish studies

© YAIRA YASMIN

shopping for *kippas* in Old Jaffa

programs, and activist-based travel (similar to voluntary experiences).

ACCESS FOR TRAVELERS WITH DISABILITIES

Israel is pretty well-equipped for travelers with disabilities, but the older sections of cities, such as Jerusalem's Old City, are less so.

The West Bank and Jordan are not really set up to serve travelers with disabilities, though some of the nicer hotels do make certain accommodations.

TRAVELING WITH CHILDREN

Though it might seem like a tricky area to travel with children, nothing could be further from the truth. As long as adequate preparations are made for sun protection and hydration, it is very easy to travel in the region with a child. The general culture in this part of the world is centered around family life (including extended families) and people are accustomed to families that have 3-7 children. More religious families are generally larger.

© SERGEY KARPOV/123RF.COM

A family trip to Israel will be an unforgettable experience for a child.

For this reason, it is easy to be accommodated for your needs with children in hotels, restaurants, and in tourist destinations. One caveat to this is that the public safety standards are not as strict as North Americans are accustomed to, so it's best to be a bit more alert about what's going on around you. Most hotels will have very nice cribs (some charge a bit extra, but not all) that you can use in your hotel room. Ask for the crib in advance and it will be set up in your room on arrival.

The general regional atmosphere in regards to children is accepting also in restaurants, where something like a crying baby likely won't cause any of the customers to even bat an eye. The typical sounds and actions of babies and children are so familiar in the culture that you can usually expect a very understanding and helpful reaction when traveling with children.

WOMEN TRAVELING ALONE

It can be a bit tricky for a woman to travel solo in certain parts of Israel (such as the more religious areas), and in the West Bank and Jordan. The best way to keep a low profile is to dress conservatively. There aren't any real dangers for a woman traveling alone in this region, but it is also not that common, and it is a male-dominated society with widely varying expectations about the role women play.

SENIOR TRAVELERS

The most important thing for senior travelers to keep in mind while traveling in the region is to be cautious about the potential dangers of the Middle East sun. In the hottest summer months, it's advisable to conduct outdoor activities before 10:30am and after 3pm. When it's hottest, always drink plenty of water and wear a hat and sunscreen.

GAY AND LESBIAN TRAVELERS

The main place in the region where gay and lesbian people are openly accepted is Tel Aviv and its immediate suburbs. The city caters to gay and lesbian travelers so openly that its municipal website has a special section for gay and lesbian travel.

In much more conservative Jerusalem, there are some gay bars and clubs, but in day-to-day life, gays and lesbians are very much under the radar. Jerusalem is a city where you will seldom see anybody, gay or straight, making public displays of affection.

Health and Safety

MEDICAL CARE IN ISRAEL

Israel's healthcare facilities are modern, world-class operations and if you need medical service you can go to one of its many hospitals. Dial 101 from any phone at any time if you have an emergency (most people speak English). Some cities also have pharmacies and drugstores that operate 24 hours a day.

VACCINATIONS

You do not need vaccinations to enter Israel or Jordan, but it is best to travel with valid health insurance. You can get travel insurance for your trip, which will protect you in the case of any major mishaps.

You will see signs posted from the Israeli Ministry of Health reminding people to drink water and to carry it with you and drink it regularly (even if you're not thirsty) to avoid dehydration and heatstroke. Tap water is perfectly safe to drink in all parts of Israel.

BOMB SHELTERS AND ALARMS

Many houses, buildings, and hotels have bomb shelters. If you don't know where a bomb shelter is, the next safest place is in a stairwell as far from windows as possible.

The sound of a wailing bomb alarm is unmistakable and could go off at any time of day

© GENEVIEVE BELMAKER

Don't be tempted to pet or feed the stray cats.

or night. From the time you hear the sound of the alarm, you will have about two minutes to get to a bomb shelter or safety before impact.

Israel's highly sophisticated Iron Dome system (partly funded by the U.S. government) has been sorely tested as recently as 2013, and it is very effective at intercepting and detonating incoming rockets while they are still in the air, and most of them never hit the ground.

CONTACT LENSES AND GLASSES

If you wear contacts lenses or glasses, note your prescription level in advance, as you will be able to easily buy contacts or glasses in any drug store, optometrist shop, or glasses store once you are in the country. There is no doctor's prescription required.

STRAY CATS

You might notice a large number of stray cats wandering around different cities, particularly in areas where there are more people. Most of these cats are not only strays, they were born on the streets and might carry disease. Don't pet stray cats or try to feed them.

Information and Services

MONEY
Israel

The Israeli currency is the New Israeli Shekel (NIS or shekel) and it is divided into 100 Agorot. The most current exchange rates are available from the **Bank of Israel** (02/655-2211, www.bankisrael.gov.il). The U.S. dollar generally hovers around an exchange rate US$1 to NIS4. Major tourist areas have currency exchange services.

Israeli banks are open Sunday-Thursday from about 9am-noon, then close for a few hours and open again from about 2pm-5pm. Cash can be withdrawn from ATMs 24 hours a day.

Non-Israeli citizens can get a VAT (Value Added Tax) refund if they don't have an Israeli passport and are visiting Israel as a tourist. The goods should have been bought in a store included in the VAT refund program and the purchase amount in one tax invoice including VAT must exceed NIS400.

The West Bank

You can pay for goods and services in the West Bank using U.S. dollars or Israeli shekels, though it is best to use shekels.

Jordan

The official currency of Jordan is the Jordanian Dinar (JD), and it is divided into 10 dirham, 100 qirsh (or piasters), or 1,000 fils. Half dinar and 1 dinar coins are most common, and bills come in 1 dinar, 5 dinars, 10 dinars, 20 dinars, and 50 dinars denominations. JD1 is typically worth about US$1.40 or NIS5.20.

If you are coming from Israel, change your shekels to Jordanian Dinars before crossing the border, or at one of the money-changing desks that are along the way as you pass through the

The Israeli currency is the New Israeli Shekel (NIS).

many stops that you need to make it through the border (Eilat-Aqaba border crossing). If you are trying to pay in shekels after entering Jordan, it will really put a damper on your trip, as most people will have no idea what to charge you.

Traveler's Checks and Credit Cards

It's possible to pay for goods and services with traveler's checks in Israel, but it might be a bit inconvenient. A good bet is to change traveler's checks to cash as needed. Major credit cards are accepted almost everywhere.

CONSULATES

Israel's designation of Jerusalem as its national capital is a matter of some dispute in the international arena. In diplomatic terms, this translates to foreign embassies being located in Tel Aviv and some foreign consulates being located in Jerusalem. Only some countries with an embassy in Tel Aviv also have a consulate in Jerusalem.

The **U.S. Consulate General** (14 David Flusser Rd., 02/622-7230, http://jerusalem.usconsulate.gov, jerusalemvisa@state.gov for non-immigrant visa questions) recently relocated and is almost impossible to find on Google maps or by searching the Internet. It is located between the neighborhoods of German Colony and Bak'a and the Sherover-Haas Promenade. To reach the consulate, go south on Derech Hevron Street and left onto Daniel Yonovsky Street (the road to the Sherover-Haas Promenade). Turn right at the first light to Betar Street and continue on Betar until you make a left on Moshe Aryeh Kurtz Street. Go right at the bottom of the hill to David Flusser Street and go uphill to the building. At the roundabout, go right and then turn left into the parking garage (with permission), where you'll get directions to the entrance.

The **U.K. Consulate General** (19 Nashashibi St. in Sheikh Jarrah, 02/541-4100, http://ukinjerusalem.fco.gov.uk, britain.jerusalem@fco.gov.uk) is located in east Jerusalem.

The **Embassy of Canada** (3/5 Nirim St., Tel Aviv, 03/636-3300, www.canadainternational.gc.ca/israel, taviv@international.gc.ca) is located in Tel Aviv. Canada does not maintain a consulate in Jerusalem.

The **Embassy of Australia** (Discount Bank Tower, Level 28, 23 Yehuda Halevi St., Tel Aviv, 03/693-5000, www.israel.embassy.gov.au) is located in Tel Aviv. Australia does not maintain a consulate in Jerusalem.

COMMUNICATIONS AND MEDIA
Internet Access

One of the best features of Israel is the fact that you get free Wi-Fi almost everywhere you go. Most restaurants, cafés, and coffee shops have free Wi-Fi, so as long as you have a computer you can get Internet access. Internet cafés are much less common, but most large luxury hotels with business centers will agree to let you use their business center computers for a small fee.

Printed and Online News

There are several major newspapers in English, Arabic, Hebrew, and Russian that are distributed throughout Israel and the West Bank. Those published in English and Hebrew include the *Jerusalem Post, Ha'aretz,* and *Yedioth Ahronoth* (known online as Ynet). The *International Herald Tribune* (*New York Times* international edition) is published only in English and the *Jerusalem Report* is an English-only magazine sold in bookstores and on newsstands.

Arabic publications include *al-Sennara* and *al-Ittihad,* among others.

MAPS AND TOURIST INFORMATION
Maps

Israel's **Ministry of Tourism** (goisrael.com) has online maps of major cities and pilgrimage sites as PDF files that can be easily printed. **Eye on Israel** (www.eyeonisrael.com) has interactive maps of Israel and major cities, including tourist sites, hotels, geographical information, and a historical atlas. Hard copy maps, including city maps, road maps, touring maps, and hiking maps are available for online purchase on the Ministry of Housing and Construction's website (www.gov.il).

Tourism Offices

There are tourist offices located throughout Israel in major cities, including in **Tel Aviv** (Ben-Gurion International Airport, 03/975-4260, doritk@tourism.gov.il, open 24 hours a day); **Jerusalem** (Jaffa Gate, 02/628-0403, orenm@tourism.gov.il, 8:30am-5pm Sat.-Thurs., 8:30am-1pm Fri.); **Nazareth** (58 Casanova St., 04/675-0555, ronnye@tourism.gov.il, 8:30am-5pm Mon.-Fri., 9am-1pm Sat.); **Eilat** (8 Beit Hagesher St., 08/630-9111, eilatinfo@tourism.gov.il, 8:30am-5pm Sun.-Thurs., 8am-1pm Sat.); and **Haifa** (48 Ben-Gurion St., www.tour-haifa.co.il/eng, 9am-5pm Sun.-Thurs., 9am-1pm Fri., 10am-3pm Sat.).

WEIGHTS AND MEASURES

The Israeli system of weights and measures is based on the metric system. The most common conversions include 1 kilogram (2.2 pounds), 1 meter (1.1 yards), 1 liter (1 quart), 1 dunnam (0.22 acres), and 1 kilometer (about 0.6 miles).

ELECTRICITY

Similar to most European systems, Asia, and the Middle East in general, Israel uses a 220V system (220V-240V) at 50 Hz. European visitors shouldn't have any trouble, except for a possible converter for the unique Israeli outlet system of a type H plug that has two flat prongs that form a V, and one vertical grounding prong on the bottom. You can buy a converter for an American plug at any electronics store for about NIS4.

Visitors from the United States will need to make a few adjustments because they use 110V appliances, and also visitors need to be aware that Israel's 50 Hz system might cause some problems with appliances (such as analog clocks), even with a transformer. Don't plug your 110V directly into an Israeli outlet, and be careful with bringing a hair dryer from America.

TIME ZONES

Israel, the West Bank, and Jordan all operate three hours ahead of Greenwich Mean Time (GMT+3), but only Israel and the West Bank also operate on daylight saving time. They switch to daylight saving time on the last Friday before April 2 and switch back on the last Sunday before Yom Kippur (about late Sept.-Oct.) every year.

RESOURCES

Hebrew Phrasebook

PRONUNCIATION
Hebrew is, for the most part, a straightforward language that is logical and doesn't have very many exceptions.

Consonants

Aleph	Ah-lehf
Bet	BEHT
Gimel	GEE-mel
Dalet	DAH-let
Hey	Hay
Vav	Vahv
Zayin	ZAIN
Khet	het
Tet	TEHT
Yud	YOOD
Kaf	KAHF
Lamed	LAH-med
Mem	Mehm
Nun	NOON
Samech	Sah-Mekh
Ayin	Ah-yeen
Pe	PEH
Tsadi	SAH-di
Quf	KOOF
Resh	Rehsh
Shin	SHEEN
Tav	TAHV

Accent
Through the ages, as the Jewish population spread throughout the world, different accents developed. Most people who speak Hebrew today speak what is known as modern Hebrew, which is the Hebrew that is spoken in Israel. The variance in pronunciations is seen primarily during religious ceremonies, especially when reading from the Torah.

COMMON PHRASES
Hello, good-bye, or peace *Shalom*
Good morning *Boker tov*
Good evening *Erev tov*
See you soon *L'hitra'ot*
What's up? *Ma nishma?*
Yes *Ken*
No *Lo*
Thank you *Toda*
Excuse me/I'm sorry *Slicha*
Please/You're welcome *Bevakasha*
What is your name? (male/female) *Eich korim lecha/lach?*
My name is... *Shmi...*
How are you? (male/female) *Ma shlomcha/ shlomech?*
Fine, OK *B'seder*
Not good *Lo tov*
Excellent *Metzuyan*
I'm tired (male/female) *Ani ayef/ayefa*

BASIC, COURTEOUS, AND RELIGIOUS EXPRESSIONS
Please excuse me *Slee-KHA Beh-va-ka-SHA*
Just a minute *Shneeyah*
Just hold on a minute *Shneeyah Rega*
No thank you *Lo Toda*
Thanks to God *Toda le-El*
Happy holiday *Hag Sahmeah*

EATING AND SHOPPING

Do you have…(male/female) *Yesh lecha/ lach…?*
How much? *Kama zeh oleh?*
I want…(male/female) *Ani rotzeh/rotzah*
I don't want…(male/female) *Ani lo rotzeh/ rotzah…*
Money *Kesef*
Change (literally, "leftovers") *Odef*
Waiter/waitress *Meltzar/meltzarit* (though you will always just say *Slicha*)
Water *Mayim*
Coffee *Kafeh*
Latte *Kafeh Afuh*
Tea *Tay*

GETTING AROUND

I'm going to…(male/female) *Ani nose'a l'…/ Ani nosa'at l'…*
There is… *Yesh…*
There is no… *Ain…*
Do you know where…is (female/male) *Ata yodea eifoh nimtza…/aht yoda'at eifoh nimtza…*
Wait/Just a moment *Rega*
Restaurant *Mis'adah*
Bathroom (services) *Sherutim*
Post office (mail) *Do'ar*
Street *Rechov*
Boulevard *Sderot*
Market *Shuk*
Museum *Muzion*
Synagogue *Beit knesset*
Church *Knaissia*
Central bus station *Tachana merkazit*
Taxi (regular) *Monit*
Shared taxi *Sherut*
Automobile *Mechonit*
Train *Rakevet*
Bus *Otoboos*
Hotel *Malon*
Hostel *Akhsaniya*
Room *Cheder*
Beach *Chof*
Grocery store *Makolet*
What is this/What is the reason for this? *Ma zeh?*
Food *Okhel*

Right *Yemina*
Left *Smola*
Straight *Yashar*

AT THE BORDER AND AT CHECKPOINTS

Passport *Darkon*
Open (your trunk) *Leef to ach*
Are you American? *Ahtah Amerikai?*

EMERGENCIES

Do you speak English? (female/male) *Aaht medaberet Anglit?/Ata medaber Anglit?*
I don't speak Hebrew (female/male) *Ani lo medaberet Ivrit/Ani lo medaber Ivrit*
Police *Mishtara*
Doctor *Rofe*
Hospital *Beit cholim*
Passport *Darkon*

USEFUL QUESTIONS

Who *Mi*
What *Mah*
When *Matai*
Where *Eh-fo*
Why *Lama*
What is this? *Mah zeh*
How *Eich*
How much does it cost? *Kamah zeh oleh?*
Where are the restrooms? *Eifo Hasherutim?*
What time is it? *Mah hasha'ah?*
What happened? *Mah karah?*

NUMBERS

One *Achat*
Two *Shtayim*
Three *Shalosh*
Four *Arba*
Five *Chamesh*
Six *Shesh*
Seven *Sheva*
Eight *Shmone*
Nine *Tesha*
Ten *Eser*
Eleven *Achat esrey*
Twelve *Shtem esrey*
Thirteen *Shlosh esrey*

Fourteen *Arba esrey*
Fifteen *Chamesh esrey*
Sixteen *Shesh esrey*
Seventeen *Shva esrey*
Eighteen *Shmoneh esrey*
Nineteen *Tsha esrey*
Twenty *Esrim*
Thirty *Shloshim*
Forty *Arbaim*
Fifty *Chamishim*
Sixty *Shishim*
Seventy *Shivim*
Eighty *Shmonim*
Ninety *Tishim*
One hundred *Mea*
Two hundred *Mataim*
Three hundred *Shlosh meot*
Four hundred *Arba meot*
Five hundred *Chamesh meot*
Six hundred *Shesh meot*
Seven hundred *Shva meot*
Eight hundred *Shmone meot*
Nine hundred *Tsha meot*

One thousand *Elef*
Two thousand *Alpayeem*
Three thousand *Shloshet alafim*

DAYS OF THE WEEK
Sunday *Yom rishon*
Monday *Yom shenee*
Tuesday *Yom shlishi*
Wednesday *Yom revi'i*
Thursday *Yom chamishi*
Friday *Yom shishi*
Saturday (Sabbath) *Shabbat*

TIMES
Hour, time *Sha'a*
Day *Yom*
Week *Shavua*
Month *Chodesh*
Year *Shana*
Today *Ha'yom*
Yesterday *Etmol*
Tomorrow *Machar*

Arabic Phrasebook

BASIC PHRASES
Hello, nice to meet you *Marhaba ana saeed b-mareftak*
Do you speak English? *Hal tatakallam al ingliyziyya?*
Do you understand English? *Hal tafham al ingliyziyya?*
Yes *Na-am*
No *Laa*
I understand *Fahamt*
I do not understand *Laa afham*
Please repeat *Aiyd law samaht*
Good morning *Sabaah il-khair*
Good evening *Masa il-khair*
Good night *Tisibh ala khair*

Hello *Marhaba*
Hello (response) *Ahlan*
Goodbye *Ma-a is-salaama*
How are you? *Kayf haalak?* (male); *kayf haalik?* (female)
Fine *Bikhair*

ASKING FOR HELP
I don't speak Arabic *Ana laa atahadith al-arabiya*
Please speak more slowly *Laww samaht tahadith ala mahil*
Where is the bathroom? *Ayn il-hammaam?*
I'm sorry *Ana aasiff*

Suggested Reading

MODERN HISTORY AND CURRENT AFFAIRS

There are numerous books about the current affairs and modern history of Israel and the region, but a few stand out. Also, once you are in Israel, look for the fairly robust selections in the English sections of bookstores that have titles by regional authors.

Carter, Jimmy. *Palestine: Peace Not Apartheid.* Simon and Schuster, 2006. A controversial look by former President Carter on how to bring peace to Israel and justice to Palestine.

Cohen, Rich. *Israel is Real: An Obsessive Quest to Understand the Jewish Nation and Its History.* Picador, 2009. An entertaining yet scholarly look at the history of the Jewish people from the time of the destruction of the Second Temple through modern times.

Oz, Amos. *How to Cure a Fanatic.* Princeton University Press, 2010. Amos Oz is a beloved Israeli author and also internationally acclaimed. His pair of essays about how to settle the question of real estate will bring peace to the Israeli-Palestinian relationship.

Senor, Dan and Saul Singer. *Start-up Nation: The Story of Israel's Economic Miracle.* Twelve, 2009. A comprehensive and illuminating look at how Israel, a country of just over 7 million people and limited resources, manages to produce more start-ups than more stable and well-developed countries like Japan, Canada, and the United Kingdom.

Zertal, Idith and Akiva Eldar. *Lords of the Land: The War for Israel's Settlements in the Occupied Territories, 1967-2007.* Nation Books, 2009. The tragic yet gripping story of Jewish settlement in the West Bank and Gaza Strip and how it has impacted every facet of modern Israeli life, as told by a professor (Zertal) and a leading journalist (Eldar).

HISTORICAL CHRONICLES

Among the mountains of historical chronicles that have been published, there are several that are must-reads.

Collins, Larry and Dominique LaPierre. *O Jerusalem!* Simon and Schuster, 1972. The extremely thick book is an account of the bitter 1948 dispute between the Arabs and Jews over Jerusalem, and emphasizes prominent individuals and the British in the process.

Flavius, Josephus and William Whiston (translation). *The Wars of the Jews.* Digireads.com, 2010. One of the most frequently referenced historians of his time, Flavius Josephus was a Jewish historian and Roman citizen who wrote detailed (and some say questionable) accounts of the events of his time in AD 75.

Oren, Michael. *Six Days of War: June 1967 and the Making of the Modern Middle East.* Presidio Press/Random House, 2002. This international best-seller by the U.S. Ambassador to Israel details six days of the definitive Arab-Israeli battle in June, 1967 and its lingering impact on the peace process and the world.

Suha, Sabbagh. *Palestinian Women of Gaza and the West Bank.* Indiana University Press, 1998. A collection of insider perspective essays on the roles of women in Gaza and the West Bank and their approach to dealing with issues of gender, feminism, and politics.

LITERATURE

The literary scene in Israel and the West Bank is robust, but there are a few voices who dominate the industry.

Grossman, David. *Someone to Run With.* Farrar, Straus and Giroux, 2000. The fictional story of life and love on the streets of Jerusalem, told from the perspective of a 16-year-old boy.

FOOD

A great selection of books on food in the region can be found at local bookstores.

El-Haddad, Laila and Maggie Schmitt. *The Gaza Kitchen: A Palestinian Culinary Journey.* Just World Books, 2013. Full of rich illustrations, this book explores the culinary heritage of people living in Gaza and the West Bank, using recipes from their kitchens.

Ottolenghi, Yotam and Sami Tamimi. *Jerusalem: A Cookbook.* Ten Speed Press, 2012. Jerusalem locals Ottolenghi and Tamimi explore the cuisine of their home city with its varied cultural and religious influences.

TRAVEL AND EXPLORATION

Insider guides to the region are largely published in Hebrew, and there are a few specialized guides to specific regional travel experiences.

Saar, Jacob. *Israel National Trail and the Jerusalem Trail (Hike the Land of Israel).* Gefen, 2011. A full guide to the Israel National Trail and the Jerusalem Trail and the hiking experiences they present, including maps and tips for the trail.

Szepsi, Stefan. *Walking Palestine: 25 Journeys into the West Bank.* Interlink Books, 2012. An alternative look at how to skip the politics of the West Bank and just experience its natural beauty through beginner walks and more advanced hikes, including information for local guides, restaurants, and accommodations.

POLITICAL

The plethora of political books related to Israel and the West Bank is astounding, but you can start with some classics, old and new.

Said, Edward. *Orientalism.* Vintage Books, 1979. From one of the region's most noted critics and authors comes an examination of how the West observes Arabs.

Yousef, Mosab Hassan and Brackin, Ron. *Son of Hamas: A Gripping Account of Terror, Betrayal, Political Intrigue, and Unthinkable Choices.* Tyndale, 2010. A controversial, real-life account from the eldest son of a founding member of Hamas.

THE HOLOCAUST

The number of books written on the Holocaust is almost countless, but it is possible to examine it through an alternative viewpoint.

Safdie, Moshe. *Yad Vashem: Moshe Safdie—The Architecture of Memory.* Lars Mueller Publishers, 2006. Israel's most famous and prolific architect examines his painstakingly designed project: the Yad Vashem Holocaust memorial in Jerusalem.

Internet Resources

There is a surprisingly limited number of websites with really solid information about Israel, the West Bank, and Jordan. Some websites lack good usability or are missing information. The following is a selection of the best, most relevant, and most useful.

JERUSALEM

GoJerusalem.com
www.gojerusalem.com
A private venture dubbed simply GoJerusalem. com contains helpful, descriptive, and fairly up-to-date listings on hotels, tours, and sightseeing, though much of the information has been republished on iTravelJerusalem.

iTravelJerusalem
www.itraveljerusalem.com
The official tourism website of the city of Jerusalem was launched in 2012 and has current information on food, accommodations, sightseeing, and events.

The Municipality of the City of Jerusalem
www.jerusalem-oldcity.org.il
The Municipality of the City of Jerusalem website has basic information about the city and some resources for visitors.

GOVERNMENT

Israeli Government
www.gov.il
The Israeli government portal is a good jumping-off point for any branch of the Israeli government online.

Israeli Ministry of Foreign Affairs
www.mfa.gov.il
The official site for the Israeli Ministry of Foreign Affairs has domestic facts, issues, statistics, and foreign government relations information.

TOURISM AND CITIES

City of Haifa
www.tour-haifa.co.il/eng
The City of Haifa's official tourism website is a good resource for navigating the city.

City of Tel Aviv
www.tel-aviv.gov.il
The City of Tel Aviv's official website also has useful information, maps, and tips.

Eye on Israel
www.eyeonisrael.com
The private enterprise Eye on Israel offers interactive maps of Israel and its major cities, including tourist sites, hotels, geographical information, and a historical atlas.

Israeli Ministry of Tourism
www.goisrael.com
The official Israeli Ministry of Tourism website has online maps of major cities and pilgrimage sites as PDF files that can be easily printed.

Tel Aviv Tourism Board
www.visit-tlv.com
The Tel Aviv Tourism Board's official website has every kind of information you could possibly need to enjoy the city by day or night.

PARKS AND RECREATION

Israel Nature and Parks Authority
www.parks.org.il
The official website of the Israel Nature and Parks Authority contains a comprehensive listing of the names, locations, admission fees, descriptions, and contact information for national parks and nature reserves throughout Israel (if you can get the spelling of the park right).

Israel's National Trail
www.israelnationaltrail.com
A useful guide to Israel's National Trail, with maps, information, and guidelines to taking the hike.

FOOD
Tel Aviv Food
http://telavivfood.wordpress.com
An extremely useful guide to dining in Tel Aviv's many restaurants, this blog is run by a team of local Tel Aviv foodies with a distinctive fork-rating system and tons of photographs.

ACCOMMODATIONS
Israel Youth Hostel Association (IYHA)
www.iyha.org.il/eng
The official website of the Israel Youth Hostel Association (IYHA) is easy to use and allows you to check the availability of youth hostels in Israel by region.

Zimmeril.com
www.zimmeril.com
Though not an official site for *zimmers,* this site has a fairly comprehensive listing of Israel's *zimmers* (guesthouses) throughout the country, including their contact information, which can be very hard to find otherwise.

TRANSPORTATION
Dan Buses
www.dan.co.il/english
The official website of the Tel Aviv city bus line Dan has route and ticketing information.

Egged
www.egged.co.il/Eng
The official website of Israel's national bus company Egged, which also operates throughout Jerusalem, has route and ticket information, but you need to dig a bit to get the right bus number.

Israel Railways
www.rail.co.il/EN
The official website of Israel's national train system has convenient and easy to use listings of times and prices for rail tickets.

Light Rail
www.citypass.co.il
Jerusalem's official Light Rail website has schedule, ticketing, a route map, and news updates for passengers.

Tel-o-Fun Bikes
www.tel-o-fun.co.il/en
Tel Aviv's citywide bicycle rental website for the green Tel-o-Fun Bikes has detailed instructions and payment and usage information for bike rentals.

WEST BANK
This Week in Palestine
www.thisweekinpalestine.com
The website of the weekly publication *This Week in Palestine* is a useful guide for events and things happening in the West Bank.

Travel Palestine
http://travelpalestine.ps
The official tourism website for the West Bank is not as robust or user-friendly as it could be, but it is one of the few online resources of its kind available in English.

Visit Palestine
www.visitpalestine.ps/en
Another tourism website called Visit Palestine is more detailed and comprehensive than Travel Palestine site, and it's very easy to use.

JORDAN
Jordan Ministry of Tourism and Antiquities
www.tourism.jo/en
The official website of the Jordan Ministry of Tourism and Antiquities is particularly useful for background and historical information.

Jordan Tourism Board
www.visitjordan.com
The official tourism website of Jordan has the basic information you might need before visiting.

Petra Development and Tourism Regional Authority
www.visitpetra.jo
The official website of the Petra Development and Tourism Regional Authority has good general information about a wide range of things from currency rates to background information.

Wadi Rum
www.wadirum.jo
Petra's neighboring village Wadi Rum has a website that is a good resource for local information on restaurants, hotels, and resources.

Index

List of Maps

www.moon.com

DESTINATIONS | ACTIVITIES | BLOGS | MAPS | BOOKS

MOON.COM is ready to help plan your next trip! Filled with fresh trip ideas and strategies, author interviews, informative travel blogs, a detailed map library, and descriptions of all the Moon guidebooks, Moon.com is all you need to get out and explore the world—or even places in your own backyard. While at Moon.com, sign up for our monthly e-newsletter for updates on new releases, travel tips, and expert advice from our on-the-go Moon authors. As always, when you travel with Moon, expect an experience that is uncommon and truly unique.

KEEP UP WITH MOON:

MAP SYMBOLS

═══════	Expressway	**〖**	Highlight	✈	Airport	⚲	Golf Course
═══════	Primary Road	○	City/Town	✈	Airfield	**P**	Parking Area
═══════	Secondary Road	◉	State Capital	▲	Mountain	≜	Archaeological Site
┈┈┈┈┈	Unpaved Road	✪	National Capital	✛	Unique Natural Feature	⌖	Church
┅┅┅┅┅	Trail	★	Point of Interest			⛽	Gas Station
┄┄┄┄┄	Ferry	•	Accommodation	🗑	Waterfall	🐢	Dive Site
┅┉┅┉┅	Railroad	▼	Restaurant/Bar	▲	Park		Mangrove
═══════	Pedestrian Walkway	■	Other Location	**D**	Trailhead		Reef
▮▮▮▮▮▮	Stairs	**Λ**	Campground	🗼	Lighthouse		Swamp

CONVERSION TABLES

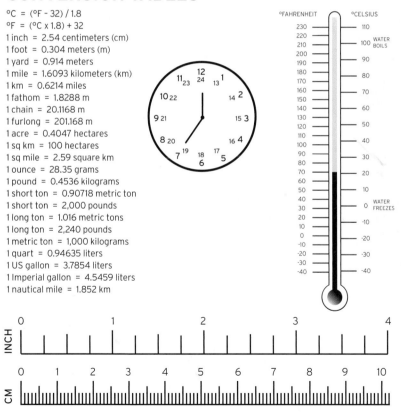

°C = (°F - 32) / 1.8
°F = (°C x 1.8) + 32
1 inch = 2.54 centimeters (cm)
1 foot = 0.304 meters (m)
1 yard = 0.914 meters
1 mile = 1.6093 kilometers (km)
1 km = 0.6214 miles
1 fathom = 1.8288 m
1 chain = 20.1168 m
1 furlong = 201.168 m
1 acre = 0.4047 hectares
1 sq km = 100 hectares
1 sq mile = 2.59 square km
1 ounce = 28.35 grams
1 pound = 0.4536 kilograms
1 short ton = 0.90718 metric ton
1 short ton = 2,000 pounds
1 long ton = 1.016 metric tons
1 long ton = 2,240 pounds
1 metric ton = 1,000 kilograms
1 quart = 0.94635 liters
1 US gallon = 3.7854 liters
1 Imperial gallon = 4.5459 liters
1 nautical mile = 1.852 km

MOON JERUSALEM & THE HOLY LAND
Avalon Travel
a member of the Perseus Books Group
1700 Fourth Street
Berkeley, CA 94710, USA
www.moon.com

Editors: Elizabeth Hollis Hansen, Nikki Ioakimedes
Series Manager: Kathryn Ettinger
Copy Editor: Naomi Adler Dancis
Graphics Coordinator: Elizabeth Jang
Production Coordinator: Elizabeth Jang
Cover Designer: Domini Dragoone
Map Editor: Albert Angulo
Cartographers: Stephanie Poulain, Brian Shotwell,
   Albert Angulo, Chris Henrick
Indexer: Rachel Kuhn

ISBN-13: 978-1-61238-623-2
ISSN: 2331-6101

Printing History
1st Edition – January 2014
5 4 3 2 1

Text © 2013 by Genevieve Belmaker.
Maps © 2013 by Avalon Travel.

Some photos and illustrations are used by permission
and are the property of the original copyright owners.

Front cover photo: Dome of the Rock and Jerusalem's
skyline © Sean Pavone/123rf.com

Title Page: interior of Monastery of the Twelve
Apostles © Genevieve Belmaker

Front Matter Photos: p. 4 mosaic tiles on the Dome
of the Rock © jvdwolf/123rf.com; p. 5 the Church of
the Holy Sepulchre © Gidon Belmaker; p. 6 (upper
left) young boy running through a West Bank village
© Genevieve Belmaker; (upper right) incense vendor
in Jerusalem's Old City © Gidon Belmaker; (bottom)
praying at Jerusalem's Western Wall © Roman
Sigaev/123rf.com; p. 7 (upper right) the golden Dome
of the Rock © Oleksandr Lysenko/123rf.com; (lower
left) the Treasury in Petra © Genevieve Belmaker
(lower right) walking through Jerusalem's Old City
© Genevieve Belmaker; p. 8 the Church of the
Annunciation © Rostislav Ageev/123rf.com; p. 9 (top) a
candy shop in East Jerusalem © Genevieve Belmaker;
(lower left) beach in Netanya © Genevieve Belmaker;
(lower right) fruit for sale at Jerusalem's shuk ©
Genevieve Belmaker; p. 10 © Genevieve Belmaker; p. 11
© Julius Fekete/123rf.com; p. 12 © Genevieve Belmaker;
p. 13 (left) © Genevieve Belmaker; (right) © Borya
Galperin/123rf.com; p. 14 © silverjohn/123rf.com; p. 15 ©
Genevieve Belmaker; p. 16 © Vadim Berestetsky; p. 17-20
© Genevieve Belmaker; p. 21 © karammiri/123rf.com; p.
22 © Mikhail Markovskiy/123rf.com; p. 23 © Vladimir
Liverts/123rf.com; p. 24 © Genevieve Belmaker; p. 25
© flik47/123rf.com; p. 26 © Genevieve Belmaker; p. 27
© kavram/123rf.com; p. 28 © Gidon Belmaker; p. 29 ©
Valery Voennyy/123rf.com; p. 30 © Genevieve Belmaker;
p. 31 © Yaira Yasmin; p. 32 (top) © Vadim Berestetsky;
(bottom) © Vladimir Blinov/123rf.com

Printed in China by RR Donnelley

All recommendations, including those for sights,
activities, hotels, restaurants, and shops, are based
on each author's individual judgment. We do not
accept payment for inclusion in our travel guides, and
our authors don't accept free goods or services in
exchange for positive coverage.

Although every effort was made to ensure that
the information was correct at the time of going to
press, the author and publisher do not assume and
hereby disclaim any liability to any party for any
loss or damage caused by errors, omissions, or any
potential travel disruption due to labor or financial
difficulty, whether such errors or omissions result
from negligence, accident, or any other cause.

KEEPING CURRENT

If you have a favorite gem you'd like to see included in the next edition, or see anything
that needs updating, clarification, or correction, please drop us a line. Send your com-
ments via email to feedback@moon.com, or use the address above.